LOMBARDI DIES, ORR FLIES, MARSHALL CRIES

LOMBARDI DIES, ORR FLIES, MARSHALL CRIES

The Sports Legacy of 1970

Brad Schultz

ROWMAN & LITTLEFIELD
Lanham • Boulder • New York • London

Published by Rowman & Littlefield
A wholly owned subsidary of The Rowman & Littlefield Publishing Group, Inc.
4501 Forbes Boulevard, Suite 200, Lanham, Maryland 20706
www.rowman.com

Unit A, Whitacre Mews, 26-34 Stannary Street, London SE11 4AB

British Library Cataloguing in Publication Information Available

Library of Congress Cataloging-in-Publication Data

Schultz, Brad.
Lombardi dies, Orr flies, Marshall cries : the sports legacy of 1970 / Brad Schultz.
pages cm
Includes bibliographical references and index.
ISBN 978-1-4422-5629-3 (hardback : alk. paper) — ISBN 978-1-4422-5630-9 (ebook) 1. Sports—
United States—History. 2. Sports—Social aspects—United States—History. I. Title.
GV583.S38 2016
796.0973—dc23
2015019480

Printed in the United States of America

For Darlene,
who loves to read but never has enough time to do so.
I know it's not antebellum, but I hope 1970 will do.

CONTENTS

TIMELINE

January 1: The University of Texas becomes the last all-white team to win a national championship, defeating Notre Dame 21–17 in a dramatic Cotton Bowl.

January 11: The Kansas City Chiefs defeat the Minnesota Vikings in Super Bowl IV, the last time the champions of the AFL and NFL would meet. The battle was also symbolic of the cultural war being fought over hair.

January 16: Curt Flood files suit against baseball commissioner Bowie Kuhn, the presidents of the American and National Leagues, and all 24 teams in Major League Baseball, challenging baseball's reserve clause.

January 20: As part of a promotional stunt, two of the greatest heavyweight fighters in boxing history—Muhammad Ali and Rocky Marciano—fight a staged match on film with the winner determined by computer.

January 28–29: The annual NFL Draft takes place in New York City. Tiny Grambling College has nine players drafted—more than Texas and Notre Dame combined.

February 7–21: "Pistol" Pete Maravich of LSU torches the college basketball landscape to become the all-time NCAA scoring leader.

February 16: "Smokin'" Joe Frazier unifies the heavyweight boxing titles with an impressive win over Jimmy Ellis. The victory sets up three dramatic confrontations with Muhammad Ali.

February 19: Commissioner Bowie Kuhn suspends star pitcher Denny McLain in what will become the start of McLain's descent into prison.

February 24: Marquette University becomes the last big-college team to turn down an invitation to the NCAA Basketball Tournament.

March 12–15: Escorted by armed sheriff's deputies, Gary Player competes in the PGA's Pensacola Open. Player had been targeted by protestors for his alleged support of South Africa's apartheid policies.

March 21: Paul Haber wins his fourth U.S. National Handball Championship, defeating Lou Russo in the finals. Despite his unorthodox training and dissolute lifestyle, Haber will eventually win nine national titles and rank as one of the greatest handball players of all time.

March 21: Yugoslav Vinko Bogataj crashes at the World Ski Jumping Championships; his pratfall will endure for years on ABC's *Wide World of Sports*.

March 29: Unbeaten Dan Gable of Iowa State is upset in the finals of the NCAA Wrestling Championships, his first loss in eight years and 182 matches.

April 4: Bobby Fischer leads a U.S. team to a near upset of the powerful Soviet squad in a chess showdown in Belgrade, Yugoslavia. Despite the defeat, the enigmatic and troubled Fischer sparks a chess revival in the United States and around the world.

April 6: Former NBA star Maurice Stokes dies. While a debilitating illness cut him down in the prime of his career, he forged a short but memorable friendship with rival player turned teammate Jack Twyman.

April 6: The career of Morganna "The Kissing Bandit" Roberts takes off when she runs onto the field to kiss Frank Howard of the Washington Senators. Morganna turns it into a career and becomes the most famous gate-crasher in professional sports.

April 13: Billy Casper wins the Masters golf title and momentarily escapes the shadow of the "Big Three" of Jack Nicklaus, Arnold Palmer, and Gary Player.

April 16: Oscar Robertson, head of the NBA Players Association, ends possible merger talks with the ABA by filing a lawsuit against the NBA.

April 25: UCLA defeats Long Beach State to win the first-ever NCAA Men's Volleyball Championship. It is the first of 19 NCAA crowns for head coach Al Scates.

May 2: Diane Crump becomes the first woman jockey in the Kentucky Derby, finishing next to last in a field of 17 aboard Fathom.

May 4–21: The shooting deaths of four student protesters at Kent State lead to campus unrest across the nation. With the situation at Ohio State near the boiling point, football coach Woody Hayes appeals to students to keep the peace.

May 8: Willis Reed makes a dramatic return from injury to lead the New York Knicks to their first NBA title with a Game 7 win over the Los Angeles Lakers.

May 10: Bobby Orr scores the winning goal in overtime to give the Boston Bruins the Stanley Cup over the St. Louis Blues. The picture of Orr celebrating the score becomes one of the most iconic images in the NHL.

May 13: The International Olympic Committee awards the 1976 Winter Olympics to Denver, but city voters will later stunningly reject the Olympics in a referendum.

June 12: Dock Ellis of the Pittsburgh Pirates no-hits San Diego while allegedly high on LSD.

June 16: Brian Piccolo of the Chicago Bears succumbs to cancer, ending one of the most poignant stories in the NFL.

June 21: The great Pelé leads Brazil to the World Cup soccer title with a 4–1 win over Italy in the final. The performance of Pelé and the Brazilians is considered the greatest in World Cup history.

June 24: *Ball Four* is released and becomes an immediate sensation. Lurid, provocative, and scandalous, the book by pitcher Jim Bouton revolutionizes the practice of sports journalism.

June 24–30: Two old ballparks, Crosley Field in Cincinnati and Forbes Field in Pittsburgh, give way to new multipurpose stadiums, signaling the end of a baseball era.

June 27: Lubbock, Texas, hosts the AFCA All-America Game, less than two months after a deadly tornado nearly destroyed the city.

July 11: Golfer Doug Sanders agonizingly misses a 30-inch putt that would have won him the British Open title. Sanders loses a playoff the next day to Jack Nicklaus.

July 14: At the All-Star baseball game in Cincinnati, hometown hero Pete Rose barrels over Ray Fosse at the plate to win the game for the National League, 5–4. Fosse is injured on the play and never recovers his All-Star form.

July 18: Daredevil Karl Wallenda calmly crosses over Tallulah Gorge in Georgia on a high wire. There is no net to protect him from a potential drop of 750 feet into a rocky abyss.

July 30: All-Pro linebacker Mike Curtis of the Colts is the most notable NFL veteran to report to training camp in the midst of a players' strike. The strike is the first tangible sign of growing power for NFL players and their union.

August 1: Fall football practice begins at Syracuse University without seven black players who protested during the spring. The resulting racial controversy ruins Syracuse's season and hastens the exit of longtime coach Ben Schwartzwalder.

August 2: Cliff Richey wins the U.S. Clay Court Championships, but it's the boorish, angry behavior of the players that signals a drastic change in how tennis is played.

August 8: Triple Crown racehorse Citation dies at age 25. Just four months earlier, Secretariat is born, and will go on to become the first Thoroughbred to win the Triple Crown since Citation in 1948.

August–September: Bill Ficker skippers *Intrepid* to a successful defense of the America's Cup yacht race, an event Americans had won every year since 1851.

September 3: Legendary football coach Vince Lombardi dies from cancer in a Washington, DC, hospital. Millions mourn the loss of a man considered one of the greatest coaches in any sport.

September 5: Killed in a practice run in Italy, Jochen Rindt becomes the latest casualty on the Grand Prix driving circuit. His death leads to a drivers' revolt and paves the way for more safety improvements.

September 12: Tennis star Margaret Court wins the U.S. Open to capture the women's Grand Slam. Her success prompts a challenge from tennis huckster Bobby Riggs, which eventually leads to his historic showdown with Billie Jean King.

September 21: *Monday Night Football* debuts as the Browns beat the Jets 31–21, and the show becomes an immediate cultural sensation.

October: Heisman front-runner and Mississippi favorite son Archie Manning leads the Ole Miss Rebels to impressive wins over Alabama and Georgia before a broken arm ruins his season. It is the beginning of a series of difficult turns in Manning's star-crossed career.

October 15: Brooks Robinson caps off an incredible World Series and playoff run, leading the Baltimore Orioles to the baseball title in five games over the Cincinnati Reds.

October 23: Gary Gabelich becomes the "Fastest Man on Wheels," breaking the land speed record on the Bonneville Salt Flats at 622 miles per hour.

October 25: Ted Green scores a goal to help the Boston Bruins beat the Philadelphia Flyers 4–3. It's the first goal in more than a year for Green, who was nearly killed in a violent stick-swinging accident with Wayne Maki.

November 3: Former Bills' quarterback Jack Kemp begins his long political career by winning a congressional seat in Buffalo.

November 8: Tom Dempsey, born with deformities of his right hand and foot, sets an NFL record by kicking a 63-yard field goal. The kick comes on the last play of the game and enables the New Orleans Saints to beat the Detroit Lions 19–17.

November 14: A plane carrying the Marshall University football team crashes, killing all 75 people on board. Just six weeks earlier, a plane crash devastated the football program at Wichita State.

December 12: Brian "Spinner" Spencer is interviewed during intermission of a game on *Hockey Night in Canada*. Because his father cannot get the telecast in British Columbia, he takes a gun to the local television station and threatens station personnel. When police respond, Spencer's father is shot and killed.

December 13: Now quarterbacking the Boston Patriots, Joe Kapp loses to Minnesota 35–14. Kapp will sue the NFL, and the lawsuit will eventually pave the way for free agency.

December 20: The St. Louis Cardinals blow a potential playoff berth in an upset loss to the Washington Redskins on the final day of the regular season. One of the Washington stars is tight end Jerry Smith, who kept his homosexuality secret for his entire career. Some speculate that Smith's homosexuality and his eventual death from AIDS is keeping him out of the Hall of Fame.

December 30 (or so): The exact date is unknown, but former heavy-weight champ Sonny Liston dies under mysterious circumstances in Las Vegas, ending one of the most controversial chapters in boxing history.

INTRODUCTION

WHY 1970?

The athletes who made headlines that year have long since left the scene and their records are mostly forgotten—buried deep within the recesses of dusty books or hidden Internet files. By any measure, those records seem miniscule by today's standards. In August 1970, the great Mark Spitz set a world record of 51.94 in the 100-meter swimming freestyle. Today, that time wouldn't even get you in the pool, as the record is 46.91 seconds, held by César Cielo of Brazil.

The year itself was grim. The seeming never-ending morass in Vietnam, continuing civil and political division, and a fear of growing lawlessness all pointed to a bleak future. Former Soviet leader Nikita Khrushchev had once boasted that by 1970 America would "be compared to a worn-out runner. He had the prize, but others have been born, trained and are now running. The United States is running on its past reputation, but at the finish line the young, fresh, strong runner will break the tape."[1]

Traditional boundaries were being challenged; everything from the color of skin to the length of hair. As the country divided into young and old, hawk and dove, hip and square, there was a sense that the outdated was passing away, if not by natural forces then by force itself—part evolution and part revolution.

Nowhere was that more evident than in college football, where the University of Texas became the last all-white national champion, even as a freshman still ineligible to play was standing by to bring about integration. Texas and Alabama, representing the last of the exclusive, segregated programs, finally came to embrace change for the basest of reasons—they wanted to keep winning. It was change, not at the point of a gun, but at the end of a touchdown pass.

Change came more forcefully at the University of Wyoming, where a group of black players demanded their rights and paid the price for not getting them. It was a revolution played out on football fields, baseball diamonds, and tennis courts all across the nation. Sometimes, such as at Wyoming, the divide was racial. But whether it was over race, gender, or simply money, more and more athletes were refusing to accept the status quo. In many areas, not only was change bringing things crashing down, it was turning them inside out.

Any new decade brings with it a sense of freshness and possibility, and 1970 seemed to offer the dazzle of a new penny. The National Football League (NFL) and American Football League (AFL) would have a common schedule for the first time, creating new rivalries that would play out in gleaming new stadiums on synthetic surfaces. Baseball also moved into suburbia, turning its back on more than a half century of play in the city neighborhoods. For every old relic that came crashing down, a gleaming new palace took its place.

The same thing was happening to the athletes. Johnny Unitas gave way to Joe Namath, and Muhammad Ali replaced Rocky Marciano. Ali and Namath became the poster boys for the new breed of athlete: one unafraid of expressing his love for sports, women, and having a good time. Novelist and sports fan Norman Mailer wrote that "ego is the great word of the 20th century, which gives us authority to declare we are sure of ourselves when we are not. Ali begins with the most unsettling ego of all."[2] Unsettling, perhaps, but also pioneering. Ali and Namath were Thomas Wolfe's *homo novus*, the new man, the liberated man, and helped launch his "me" decade of the 1970s.

Solomon (the Israelite king, not the 49ers' receiver Freddie) wisely noted in Ecclesiastes 1, "What has been will be again, what has been done will be done again; there is nothing new under the sun."[3] Perhaps what happened in 1970, at least in a sports sense, was just part of an ongoing cycle—as Vince Lombardi painfully leaves the scene and takes with him the admiration of millions, a young Bobby Orr reaches the pinnacle and those same millions find a new reason to hope. As tragedy engulfs the football programs at Marshall University and Wichita State, triumph can be found in the heroic Willis Reed or the stoic Billy Casper. Their stories are still worth telling more than 40 years after they took place.

Maverick baseball owner Bill Veeck once said, "If you dust off old junk sometimes, you come up with a gem."[4] That's what this book is about—digging deep into the dirt of a long-forgotten sports year to look for buried treasure. It is hoped that you find some little gems here worth polishing and retelling.

I

JANUARY

THE LAST GASP

January 1, 1970, dawned bright and chilly in Dallas, the site of the annual Cotton Bowl game. The event usually didn't attract as much attention as the Rose Bowl, which would take place later that afternoon in California, but on this day all eyes focused on Dallas. In the Cotton Bowl, the University of Texas would put a 19-game winning streak and possible national championship on the line against Notre Dame, a team that had not played in a bowl game since Grantland Rice described the exploits of the Four Horsemen in the 1925 Rose Bowl. It was a dream matchup that everyone guessed would be the main attraction of the New Year's bowl games.

As the Cotton Bowl parade wound its way downtown, with three of the surviving Horsemen riding as grand marshals, few could guess that Texas would try to make history as the last all-white team to win a national title.

An integrated Penn State team, led by future pros Franco Harris and Lydell Mitchell, was also unbeaten and hoped to claim at least part of a national championship. "I don't know if we're No. 1," said Penn State coach Joe Paterno. "But we have as much right as anybody else to be No. 1."[1] Paterno and Penn State, riding the nation's longest winning streak at 21 games, would meet Missouri in the Orange Bowl, while Arkansas and Ole Miss played in the Sugar Bowl. The Rose Bowl featured underdog Stanford and Heisman Trophy winner Jim Plunkett against Michigan.

The drama would unfold over the course of about 12 hours, from kickoff in Dallas to the final gun in Miami. Part of the millions sitting at home and watching the action included those college teams that went uninvited in the bowl season. That group included Ohio State, a team that in late November was ranked number one, had won 22 straight games, and was being called the greatest team of all time. Sportswriters said that only the NFL's Minnesota Vikings could give them a game, unless Ohio State's first-team offense played against its first-team defense.

Ohio State could not go back to the Rose Bowl because the Big Ten Conference had a no-repeat rule and the Buckeyes had gone the previous year in beating USC (University of Southern California) for the national championship. But it all became a moot point in the last game of the year when Michigan beat Ohio State 24–12 in a victory "that will forever be etched in the record books as one of the collegiate game's most stunning."[2] Ohio State stayed home for the bowl season and Texas took over the top spot in the rankings. "All good things must come to an end," said a crestfallen Ohio State coach Woody Hayes after the game, "and that's what happened today. We just got outplayed, outpunched and outcoached."[3]

But of all the frustrated college teams that would have to watch the action on television, perhaps none was more agonized than the University of Wyoming.

Wyoming was a talented team that just two years earlier had been ranked fifth in the nation and played in the Sugar Bowl. Unbeaten midway through the 1969 season, the Cowboys seemed a lock to earn some kind of bowl bid, but that unraveled on the Friday before an October game with Brigham Young University (BYU) when 14 black players went to see coach Lloyd Eaton. They were wearing black armbands and asked if they could wear the armbands during the game as a form of silent protest. The year before, Wyoming players complained of several racial epithets from the all-white BYU players. Several were also critical of Mormon church policies, which they believed restricted blacks. "We knew how Lloyd Eaton would respond, but we certainly didn't know he'd say what he did," said receiver John Griffin, "and that he would eventually ruin a football program for over 10 years."[4]

Declaring that he could not tolerate open defiance of the coaching staff, Eaton immediately suspended the players for the rest of the season.[5] "It was simply a matter of discipline," said Eaton. "Black or white, it didn't matter to me. They broke the rule and I told them they were no longer members of the team."[6] Joe Williams said they knew about the rule prohibiting protest, but went to Eaton only to see if a compromise could be worked out. "We just wanted to talk to him," said Williams. "We wanted to see if we could wear black armbands in the game, or black socks, or black X's on our helmets. And if he had said no we had already agreed that we would be willing to protest with nothing but our black skins."[7] Williams and the other suspended players soon became known as the "Black 14."

Even though Wyoming routed BYU the next day, the dispirited Cowboys lost the last four games of the season, and won only one game in 1970, costing Eaton his job. Griffin was right—a team that had won three straight conference championships would endure three straight losing seasons. The Black 14 filed a lawsuit against the university seeking reinstatement and more than a million dollars in damages, but a federal judge dismissed the case. "We were young and a bit naive, and there were some things we all wish hadn't happened," said Tony McGee, a Wyoming defensive lineman who went on to a successful pro career. "But I am glad it did happen. Perhaps that was our mission."[8]

McGee and his teammates watched a Sugar Bowl that New Year's Day that featured two all-white teams in Ole Miss and Arkansas, while all-white Texas played in the Cotton Bowl.

The integration of college football in the South was much more volatile than it was in Wyoming or in other parts of the nation. Schools in the West, East, and Midwest had been integrated for years, in part because of restrictive Jim Crow laws down south. Talented black players from the area who wanted to play major college football often headed elsewhere in search of opportunity. In 1965 and again in 1966, Michigan State claimed a share of the national championship with eight blacks starting on defense, including stars Bubba Smith from Texas, Charlie Thornhill from Virginia, and George Webster from South Carolina. Both of Michigan State's captains were black. "I was not recruited," said Gene Washington, a receiver from Baytown, Texas, who went on to play at Michigan State and then seven years in the NFL. "I was denied admission at the University of Texas. All of the Texas schools were completely closed to us—not just athletes, but students."[9]

Black players were also no doubt aware of the situation at places like Ole Miss, where the admission of James Meredith in 1962 sparked a campus riot that killed two people, and at the University of Alabama, where in 1963 Governor George Wallace stood in the door of the school's administration building to try and prevent integration. Yet the introduction of black players in the South finally happened for a very simple reason—teams wanted to win. The University of Houston, a school that didn't open until 1927 and didn't field a football team until 1945, broke a color barrier with the recruitment of Warren McVea in 1964. Houston was unaffiliated with any conference and looked to McVea and other black players as a means of gaining recognition and respectability. McVea fumbled four times in his 1965 varsity debut, but after that rocky beginning went on to earn All-America honors for two seasons. With McVea at receiver and running back, Houston led the nation in total offense and in 1968 scored an astounding 100 points in a game against Tulsa. In his sophomore year McVea personally taught all-white Ole Miss a lesson in integration by catching six passes for 201 yards and scoring touchdowns of 84 and 80 yards. Rebel coach Johnny Vaught said after the game that Ole Miss needed its own black player, but immediately added he was kidding and asked reporters to keep the comment off the record. "We have not found one good enough yet," he said. "None have been invited to campus. By the time we find one good enough, I'll be gone."[10]

The situation at Ole Miss was indicative of almost the entire South. Traditional beliefs and institutions—and there was no more traditional belief than football—suddenly found themselves swimming against changing cultural tides that threatened to overwhelm the sport. Since Vaught represented an older generation unlikely to embrace change, what was needed were younger coaches willing to take a chance.

The glory days of Southern Methodist football had long passed when 33-year-old Hayden Fry took over as coach in 1962, and Fry's first three seasons also failed to produce winning records. But Fry had promised to recruit black athletes, and in 1966 Jerry LeVias of Beaumont, Texas, helped to integrate the Southwest Conference in spectacular fashion.[11] "We screened black athletes for three years before deciding on Jerry," said Fry. "The first one we would take had to be a winner three ways—in character, academically and athletically. We had the complete student-athlete in Jerry."[12]

In his very first conference game against Rice University, with time running out and Southern Methodist (SMU) trailing, LeVias, who stood all of five seven and 150 pounds, grabbed a high pass with one hand and landed in the end zone with the winning score. LeVias went on to win All-Conference honors as well as All-America academic honors three times, and in his senior year he was named to the All-America team. Yet he was virtually alone on the SMU campus, often taunted by other students and even his own teammates. LeVias received hate mail and death threats; a teammate once spit in his face and his first roommate left him.

Not even a private meeting with Dr. Martin Luther King Jr. offered much solace. In April 1966 King came to SMU to make a speech, and for ten minutes he and LeVias met privately. King complimented LeVias on how he was handling the situation and reminded him to always keep his emotions under control. But both King and LeVias knew there was little more that could be done to help. "If they thought Dr. King was coming across the country, making the university sign black players," LeVias said, "I think he'd caught much more hell than he caught, and I would have, definitely."[13]

He caught enough hell as it was. "We always went on quick snaps," LeVias said of SMU's offense, "so if there was a sniper in the stands, he couldn't get a good shot. If you counted the players in the huddle you only counted ten, because I was in the middle of it."[14] But his effect on the football field was undeniable, and in 1966 he helped SMU win the conference championship and a trip to the Cotton Bowl. "The true mark of a champion is one who overcomes all these things and Jerry did," said Fry. "He could never appreciate us as much as we appreciate him."[15]

LeVias and McVea helped open the door a bit for blacks in Texas, but it would never be completely wide open until a black played at the mighty University of Texas; the same University of Texas that on January 1, 1970, still had no black players on its varsity football roster as it stood on the threshold of a national title.

The focal point of the Texas program was Darrell Royal, a highly successful coach who became extremely powerful within the program and the state. When Houston recruited McVea in 1963, Royal was in the process of leading Texas to an unbeaten season and a national championship, and the feeling among the Longhorn power brokers was that the team didn't need blacks to be successful. In October of that year, the marching band admitted its first black member, Edwin Guinn, calling him the first of his race who had "qualified."[16] A month later, the university opened the door for black athletes, announcing that any student who met athletic and academic requirements was eligible to try out for any sport.

Texas was trying to straddle a very difficult line that placated both segregationists and integrationists. Caught in the middle was Royal, a genuinely decent man who wanted to do the right thing. While McVea and LeVias starred at other Texas schools, Royal and the Longhorns maintained that they were waiting for the right kind of athlete. Like Fry at SMU, Royal said he was looking for someone who could meet the school's high academic standards, succeed on the football field, and handle the segregationist backlash that was sure to follow. Critics claimed Texas was simply looking for excuses not to integrate. According to those on the Texas faculty at the time, "Powerful forces on the Athletic Council and the Board of Regents impressed upon Royal that there was no need to hurry integration, but no less significant was the huge number of UT alumni, most of whom wanted to keep the school like it was in the old days."[17]

The tipping point for Royal and the program came when the juggernaut he had created stopped winning. After a national championship in 1963 and an Orange Bowl win in 1964, Texas lost four games each of the next three seasons. That included back-to-back losses to SMU, which came to Austin in 1966 with LeVias and beat the Longhorns 13–12. "The reason all this is so hard to take is because we could have been a good team this year," Royal lamented after the game. "But there's nothing wrong we can't fix."[18]

Fixing it apparently included reaching out to blacks. In 1967 Texas made overtures to local schoolboy star Don Baylor, who played three sports at Austin High. When Royal insisted Baylor play only football, Baylor instead launched a pro baseball career that lasted 19 seasons. He always felt Texas was never really serious about his recruitment nor ready to break the color barrier.

Royal would not give up. In 1967 a student named E. A. Curry walked on and made the freshman team, but eventually quit because of academic issues. A year later, the team's first black scholarship player, Leon Neal, lasted only one season and had no significant role. Finally, Royal found someone he believed had the right combination of talent and intangibles—linebacker Julius Whittier, an all-city selection from San Antonio Highlands. "Coach Royal was a second daddy, and I say that sincerely,"

Whittier said. "He knew that he was stepping out on a limb by recruiting me, and I think he was fairly courageous in taking that step."[19]

Whittier knew it would not be easy. He never saw any overt racism but heard the whispers behind his back. Other teammates did not include him in drinking or parties, and for a while it was difficult just to find someone who would room with him. Finally, white running back Billy Dale offered. "I lost all my friends," said Dale, "[but] I chose to live with Julius because I believed it would add that much more dimension to me as a person."[20]

Julius Whittier would play no part in the dramatic Cotton Bowl against Notre Dame. As a member of the freshman team when freshmen were still ineligible to play, he could only watch, as he had done with all the varsity games throughout the season. But whether he knew it or not, Whittier was watching a piece of history.

The game itself offered several story lines. It would culminate the 100th year of college football, and less than a month earlier President Nixon had already awarded Texas a trophy for its 15–14 win over Arkansas in a battle of unbeaten teams that came to be known as "The Big Shootout." In that game, Texas defensive back Freddie Steinmark seemed a step slower than usual and gave up several big plays. It turned out that what Steinmark thought was a deep bruise on his left leg was actually bone sarcoma, and the leg had to be amputated at the hip. Steinmark would watch this game from the sidelines on crutches.

Texas and Notre Dame kicked off in less than ideal playing conditions. It had rained all week in Dallas, and the previous Sunday the Dallas Cowboys and Cleveland Browns tore up the field during an NFL playoff game played in a constant downpour. Despite sunny skies and chilly temperatures the Cotton Bowl grass had not dried out, prompting stadium officials to cover it with dirt in several places.

Just as Jerry LeVias had done, a black Notre Dame player named Tom Gatewood helped teach the Longhorns a lesson on the value of integration. Gatewood would play a key role in the rematch between the two teams in next year's Cotton Bowl; this time around he burned the Texas secondary for a 54-yard touchdown pass from Joe Theismann that gave Notre Dame a 10–0 lead. Texas rallied for a 14–10 lead in the fourth quarter, but another Theismann touchdown pass, this time to Jim Yoder, put the Irish ahead with just six minutes to play. Texas stayed with its ground-oriented wishbone attack, slowly moving downfield a few yards at a time. Finally, the drive reached the Irish ten-yard line, leaving Texas with a fourth-and-two with just over two minutes to play.

Faced with a similar situation in the "Big Shootout" against Arkansas, Royal took a drastic gamble, calling a deep pass instead of using the favored triple option run. Randy Peschel, the only receiver on the play, caught a long pass from quarterback James Street, and moments later Texas scored the winning touchdown. Clearly, the Longhorns were in field goal range, and a kick would tie the game and likely give them at least a piece of some version of the championship, but Royal would have none of that. "When you're No. 1," he said, "you've got to try and stay that way or get carried out feet first."[21] Just as in Arkansas, Royal bypassed the running game again for a pass, this time to Cotton Speyrer. Notre Dame put a hard rush on Street, who made a low throw, but Speyrer stopped, curved his body back, and made the catch just before the ball hit the ground.

Just seconds later Texas was at the two-yard line with a minute to play, and this time Royal did go with his triple option. Reserve Billy Dale—the same Billy Dale who would room with Julius Whittier—carried the ball in for the touchdown that won it for Texas, 21–17. That made the bowls that followed anticlimactic, at least in terms of the national championship: Stanford upset Michigan, Archie Manning and Ole Miss knocked off Arkansas, and after beating Missouri in the Orange Bowl, unbeaten Penn State howled for some sort of recognition. But the Nittany Lions had little cause for complaint after passing up a chance to play Texas in the Cotton Bowl.

That Dale scored seemed like a fitting transition; the last gasp of all-white football before the coming wave of integration. Any doubts about the role of blacks in Southern football were laid to rest nine months later in Birmingham, Alabama. Paul "Bear" Bryant had built a dynasty at the University of Alabama, winning three national titles in the 1960s, but he did it in a heavily segregated state with white players only. Los Angeles sportswriter Jim Murray mockingly referred to Bryant's teams as "champions of the white leagues."[22]

Bryant was in an even more difficult position than Royal. While his own governor, George Wallace, famously proclaimed that he would protect segregation now, tomorrow, and forever, Birmingham public safety commissioner Bull Connor turned fire hoses on protesting blacks. To a nation of onlookers, Alabama became the face of Southern resistance to integration.

Like Royal, Bryant saw his teams begin to slip in the late 1960s. Alabama won eight games in both 1967 and 1968, and then fell to a disastrous 6–5 in 1969. That year, Bryant flew out to Los Angeles to meet with USC coach John McKay. Facing much less resistance to integration on the West Coast, McKay had built a powerhouse in Los Angeles that would go unbeaten in 1969.[23] The two met briefly at the airport where Bryant offered McKay $150,000 to bring his team to Birmingham and play Alabama in 1970. When McKay agreed, Bryant adjusted his famous houndstooth hat, got back on the plane, and returned home. The game was set for September 13.

Alabama often played games in Birmingham because it had a bigger stadium than its home field in Tuscaloosa, but as a symbolic act the location was of great importance. Here was an integrated USC team playing against an all-white Alabama team before an all-white crowd in Bull Connor's backyard. If those in Alabama were shocked, the players at USC, especially the blacks, were concerned. "All of this is running through your mind," said USC player Charles Young, "and you're only nineteen years old. You're going down there into the lion's den, so to speak."[24]

Several of the USC players clandestinely brought guns with them to the game, but there were no incidents, especially on the field. No doubt that many in the crowd found the presence of blacks on the field unsettling, but for the majority of Alabama fans the most disturbing sight was the way USC manhandled the Tide. Before a stunned crowd of more than 72,000, USC ran over Alabama, 42–21. The Trojans got two touchdowns from Birmingham native Clarence Davis, but the real star was black sophomore Sam Cunningham, who ran for 135 yards and two more touchdowns. Alabama assistant coach Jerry Claiborne remarked, "Sam Cunningham did more to integrate Alabama in 60 minutes than Martin Luther King did in 20 years."[25]

There is a persistent story that Bryant brought Cunningham to the Alabama locker room after the game and introduced him to his players by saying, "Gentlemen, this is what a football player looks like."[26] Cunningham admitted that the meeting was not that dramatic, but there can be no doubt that the game was earth-shattering for Southern football. The humiliation for Alabama fans made it easier for them to accept an integrated team, just as Bryant seemed to know that it would. After the game, Bryant found McKay and told him, "John, thank you for what you did for me and the University of Alabama."[27] Within three years, a third of the Alabama football team was black, and Bryant went on to win two more national championships.

Bryant and Royal, coaching in the segregated South, had both made their own personal statements about the value of integration. After the win over Notre Dame, Royal took a congratulatory phone call from President Nixon, saying he was glad Texas did not embarrass the president's choice of the Longhorns as the nation's top team. Then, Royal handed the game ball to Freddie Steinmark, who wept unashamedly.

Whittier, who earned three degrees from Texas and became a criminal defense attorney, came to care deeply for Royal. When Royal passed away in 2012, Whittier was among the many who eulogized his former coach:

> He made a difference in black athletes having access to play football at a top-notch university. There were alumni and regents who did not want black kids on this campus. Coach Royal bucked that. That's one of the things I admired about him, he was a man who had his own independent image about what was right and wrong. He had a big view of the world, and I was glad to be a part of his program. I love him.[28]

Even before he could finish, Julius Whittier broke down and cried.

The repercussions for Wyoming and BYU, especially BYU, took a long time to die down. A week after the Cotton Bowl, nine black students protested a basketball game between BYU and Arizona in Tucson. They poured lighter fluid on the court and set it on fire, prompting Arizona students to demand severing athletic relations with BYU. The Cougars faced incidents at their basketball games throughout the winter, and one protest at Colorado State involving hundreds of students and security personnel turned violent. "How far will it go?" asked BYU basketball coach Stan Watts. "One of these days, you know, somebody might pull a gun or something."[29]

Ten of the Black 14 went on to get their college degrees and two, Tony McGee and Joe Williams, went on to play in the NFL. The final postscript to the episode may have been written by Mel Hamilton, a Black 14 member who eventually became a school principal. Around 1999,

Hamilton's son Malik was attending Utah State and had some news for him.

Malik Hamilton, son of a Wyoming football player who had been dismissed from the team for protesting against BYU, had met a woman and wanted to become a Mormon.

"He agonized about this for months," Hamilton said. "I said, 'Malik, what did I fight for? I fought for you to be able to do that and feel like you'd be accepted in this religion totally.'"[30]

A HAIR-RAISING PROBLEM

On January 11, 1970, the Kansas City Chiefs decisively beat the Minnesota Vikings 23–7 in Super Bowl IV, marking the last time that champions of the American and National Football Leagues would meet. As part of the merger between the leagues the AFL would cease operations and its teams would become part of an enlarged NFL in the fall of 1970. Once ridiculed by NFL players and fans as a Mickey Mouse league, the AFL had won the last two Super Bowls.

Super Bowl IV was not only a battle for pro football supremacy, it was also symbolic of the cultural war being fought over hair. The Vikings had several players, including star defensive linemen Carl Eller and Jim Marshall, who wore long sideburns or sported mustaches. By contrast, the Chiefs were mainly clean-cut, with no mustaches or beards, thanks to coach Hank Stram, who enforced a $500 fine for any facial hair or excessive hair length. "I use my own sideburns as a gauge," said Stram, whose hair went down only to mid-ear. "If anybody's hair gets any longer, he's in trouble."[31]

Like any cultural trend, facial hair had changed throughout the years, and athletes had changed right along with it. The 1890s, of course, were known for facial growth, and an account of the 1891 football game between the University of Kansas and the University of Missouri noted that "at center for Missouri was A. P. Rummans . . . he weighed more than 240 pounds, was more than six feet tall and sported a handle-bar mustache."[32] In 1913, Nelson Norgren, a halfback at the University of Chicago and a member of the All-America team, "was declared the most successful cultivator of a mustache in the university. He was presented with a handsome set of shaving 'tools' by the girls of the senior class."[33]

The conservative 1950s brought a temporary end to facial hair, which was overturned by the youthful rebellion of the 1960s. In the counterculture hippie and drug movements, long hair, beards, and mustaches became a statement against the establishment, and even kids who weren't into drugs or overthrowing society saw long hair as a harmless symbol of empowerment. The Broadway musical *Hair*, which opened in 1967 and soon became a smash hit, celebrated the movement as a "tribal love rock musical" that highlighted America's cultural divide.[34] While England's Princess Anne jumped into the communal dance that ended one performance, astronauts James Lovell and Jack Swigert walked out on the play when it appeared in New York. "This is the age of polarization—no middle ground. The decals on automobiles are peace symbols or the flag. You wear your hair long, your lapels wide and your trousers flared, or you wear a thin tie, tie clip and three-button jacket."[35]

The same disgust that caused Apollo astronauts to walk out on *Hair* was now simmering in college and professional coaches across the country. Some of it was well intentioned. "When I recruit 'em, I tell them I want them to be clean-cut college men," said Florida A&M coach Jake Gaithers. "To look like college men, to act like college men, that I want to be proud of them. I tell them, 'Boys, you come to me when you're in trouble. Now I have a favor to ask. I don't want to see long, wild-looking hair and I don't want to see any whiskers.'"[36]

Stram was not some fossilized leftover from the crew cut 1950s, but rather an egalitarian who had helped the Chiefs become one of the most successfully integrated teams in the NFL. Kansas City had a full-time scout, Lloyd Wells, combing the small black colleges for talent, and when Wells found linebacker Willie Lanier of Morgan State, Stram made him the first black middle linebacker in pro football, beating out favorite Jim Lynch. "I wondered if there was going to be an open competition," said Lanier. "One day Hank called us in and said he wanted the best guys on the field, and I was going to be the middle linebacker and Jim was going to play outside."[37]

But while skin color made no difference to Stram, length of hair did, and he truly believed that unruly hair would set a bad example for America's youth. There were similar arguments going in ballparks, in living rooms, and across the nation. When major league pitcher Jim Bouton appeared at a father-son banquet, he defended the kids' rights and told the parents that they should not expel otherwise good students simply because they had long hair. "I got a big cheer from the kids," Bouton said. "The parents sat there with clenched teeth resolving never to invite Jim Bouton again."[38]

For some coaches, the issue spoke more to control and discipline, and for them, letting the players grow their hair long was just another name for anarchy. John Pont convened spring football practice at Indiana University by asking his players to keep their hair above their collars. When fullback John Isenbarger pointedly asked if shorter hair would make him run faster, Pont replied, "No, John, it won't make you any faster, but it'll make us a better team because it'll be a sign to me that you accept discipline."[39] UCLA basketball center Bill Walton similarly challenged coach John Wooden's rule about short hair, to which Wooden answered, "That's good, Bill. I admire people who have strong beliefs and stick by them. We're going to miss you." Walton got on his bike, raced to the barber, and made it back in time for practice.[40]

Most of it was resolved just as easily, but by far the most serious incident took place at Oregon State. Head football coach Dee Andros, a mountain of a man nicknamed "The Great Pumpkin" for how his girth squeezed into an orange Oregon State coaching shirt, didn't have many rules, but he was a fanatic about no facial hair. Linebacker Fred Milton figured the rule didn't apply during the off-season and grew a stylish mustache and Vandyke beard. Andros found out and asked Milton to shave, but Milton refused, citing racial and cultural reasons. Soon, representatives of the Black Student Union appealed to President James Jensen to intervene, and when he refused, the group called for a boycott of classes and athletic events. The campus, overwhelmingly white, seemed split right down the middle.

A committee of the faculty senate voted in support of Milton, but Andros said privately that "the faculty senate could write resolutions until its fingers fell off; he wasn't going to have any one-sided committee overseeing his program."[41] He got strong support from athletic director Jim Barratt, who was fearful of any compromise that created two sets of rules—one black and the other white.

Andros won the battle but lost the war. Milton transferred to Utah State, and others followed in his wake, so by the fall of 1970 the Beavers had only two black players on the roster. A team that went 7–3 and came within one game of the Rose Bowl in 1968 sank to consecutive 2–9 seasons starting in 1972, and won just one game in 1975 when Andros was forced out. "Did it all stem from the black athlete revolt and the decision by Dee Andros that Fred Milton had to shave his goatee?" asked one Oregon sportswriter. "It isn't that simple, but it's a start."[42]

The problem is that Andros and all the other establishment types were on the wrong side of a war they couldn't win. The kids heard the messages—such as the one from AFL president Milt Woodard, who wrote to the New York Jets and told them that their beards and mustaches were bad for pro football's image—but they paid more attention to the reality: quarterback Joe Namath looked really cool in his Fu Manchu mustache, he won a Super Bowl title, and he earned ten grand from an advertising company to shave it off. "I didn't like what the league said about the mustaches and sideburns," said Namath, who admitted that he only got rid of the hair for the money. "And I wonder why, all of a sudden, hair became bad. The most perfect guy in the world had long hair and a beard."[43]

Namath was the poster boy for the rebellious athletes of 1970, and when Namath's Jets beat the crew cuts out of Johnny Unitas and Earl Morrall in Super Bowl III, it killed the idea that athletes with short hair were somehow more disciplined and would win more championships. After that, the hair got longer and the Afros more outrageous, and even while some teams like the Cincinnati Reds tried to hold the line, soon facial hair was the norm rather than the exception. In 1972, Oakland Athletics' owner Charlie Finley, long considered a maverick by the baseball establishment, paid his players to grow mustaches as a publicity stunt, and the players liked the look so much they kept it. When reliever Rollie Fingers, widely known for his Snidely Whiplash handlebar mustache, signed a new contract in 1973, Finley included a year's supply of mustache wax as part of the deal.

Today, facial hair is not only accepted, it is often embraced. After the Boston Red Sox finished last in the American League East in 2012, they started 2013 with a new attitude and new beards. Outfielder Johnny Gomes led a group of Red Sox players who grew beards all during the summer, and credited the facial hair with helping them win a World Series title. In 2014, defensive lineman Brett Keisel of the Pittsburgh Steelers grew a mountain-man beard that had its own Facebook page with nearly 50,000 likes. Keisel eventually shaved off the beard for charity.

Cultures and styles change, but one thing in sports never changes—winning. Keisel's shave made no difference to the Steelers, who in March

2015 cut ties with him after 13 seasons. That's the message kids are hearing today, and it probably hasn't changed all that much since Hank Stram and Dee Andros.

THE FLOODGATES CRACK

The NFL was not the 24/7 league that it is today and after the Chiefs' win over the Vikings, sports attention shifted to basketball and hockey. It also shifted to baseball, which was in the middle of its hot stove league—that part of the year between the World Series and spring training in which fans discussed trade possibilities and how their teams were faring in the off-season. The annual baseball amateur draft took place on January 17, with the Cleveland Indians selecting Chris Chambliss as the overall number-one pick. Chambliss would go on to have a solid 17-year career highlighted by two world titles with the Yankees and his dramatic home run that won the 1976 American League Championship against Kansas City.

But the real drama began January 16, 1970. That's when Curt Flood filed suit in federal court against baseball commissioner Bowie Kuhn, the presidents of the American and National Leagues, and all 24 teams in Major League Baseball. Flood was a highly successful outfielder known for his defensive prowess who had helped the St. Louis Cardinals win two World Series titles. After the 1969 season St. Louis traded Flood to Philadelphia, but he refused to report. Nothing personal, Flood said, and it had nothing to do with money. He just didn't want to go without his permission.

Flood legally challenged baseball's reserve clause, a contractual agreement that bound a player to one team for as long as that team wished. Thus, teams owned players like property, having the right to trade, sell, or release them at will. Flood contended that such an arrangement was a form of slavery that violated the 13th Amendment to the U.S. Constitution. "I do not feel I am a piece of property to be bought or sold irrespective of my wishes," he said.[44]

Tension between baseball players and owners was as old as the game itself. As early as 1885, players sought to protect themselves against ownership by forming the Brotherhood of Professional Base-Ball Players. The union gained considerable strength, but was eventually crushed by ownership. The formation of the competing Federal League in 1914 helped the players' position (and their salaries), but when the league folded after two seasons the players lost all that leverage. It is widely believed that the penuriousness of White Sox owner Charles Comiskey is what led eight players on the team to accept bribes to throw the 1919 World Series. "A monetary frustration hung over them all," wrote Eliot Asinof. "If the public looked up to them, admired them, chased after them, this very prominence served to exacerbate their sense of helplessness."[45]

A formal challenge to baseball's power came in 1922. The owner of the defunct Baltimore Federal League team had filed a lawsuit claiming that the established major leagues had conspired to destroy the Federal League and effectively formed a monopoly in violation of the Sherman Anti-Trust Act. The case eventually wound its way to the Supreme Court, which in 1922 sided with the established National and American Leagues. In its decision, the court argued that baseball games were an "amusement" that did not constitute interstate commerce as defined by the Sherman Act.[46] The court reaffirmed that opinion in 1953, although by that time Justice Harold Burton noted in his dissent, "It is a contradiction in terms to say that the defendants in the cases before us are not now engaged in interstate trade or commerce as those terms are used in the Constitution of the United States and in the Sherman Act."[47]

The players lost even more power in 1965 when baseball instituted a draft of all first-year players to prevent teams from getting in costly bidding wars over young players. Previously, high school and college players could sign with any team they wished, which made them de facto free agents. With the draft, players could no longer choose the team they played for, which severely limited their earning potential. "I think possibly the draft may result in some of the players not fortunate enough to be drafted in the first round getting less to sign than they would have otherwise," said Rick Monday, an outfielder taken first overall in the initial 1965 draft.[48]

Frustrated by the courts and now restricted by the draft, professional baseball players seemingly had nowhere to turn. That's when Marvin Miller appeared on the scene.

Miller, a tough-talking Brooklyn native, spent his entire adult life as a union representative and negotiator, working his way up to represent the 1.2 million members of the United Steelworkers. In 1966, he took over as head of the Major League Baseball Players Association (MLBPA), a largely ceremonial and ineffectual unit that had no collective bargaining, no grievance committee, and around $5,000 in assets.

Miller immediately set out to improve player salaries and increase owner contributions to the player pension fund, both of which he accomplished. He was extremely successful at creating a sense of solidarity among the players and instilling in them the need for collective action. An early test came in the winter of 1969 when Miller and the MLBPA threatened a boycott of spring training unless pension benefits were increased. "It's the principle of the thing," said Atlanta Braves' star Hank Aaron. "I can't sign until it's settled. These are the people I play with."[49]

Yet, the players' solidarity apparently had limits, and Miller had trouble finding someone willing to take on the reserve clause. "I'm going to fight it," said Carl Yastrzemski of Miller's plans. "I am against [it] because it would ruin the game."[50] Yastrzemski wanted Miller to poll MLBPA players to see if they really were in favor of pursuing legal action.

Baseball owners moved to exploit the players' concerns and essentially parroted Yastrzemski's arguments. The National and American Leagues, which usually found it hard to agree on anything, issued a joint statement that said Flood's lawsuit would lower baseball into anarchy. The statement asserted that a challenge to the reserve clause threatened the integrity of the game, would destroy the minor leagues, and make it impossible to conduct business. In dire tones, the leagues concluded that if Flood was successful, professional baseball would simply cease to exist.

Thus, Miller's problems in finding a player to test the reserve clause were multiple. Owners and many players were firmly lined up against him. Even more ominously, public opinion seemed to favor the owners' position. Fans still tended to think of the players as privileged and looked upon them as overpaid, citing the large contracts of stars such as Willie Mays. The Phillies had offered Flood a $100,000 contract, but his response was that "a peon remains a peon no matter how much money you pay him."[51] In truth, the majority of player salaries were much more pedestrian; at the time of Flood's suit the minimum salary was $10,000 and the average salary was just under $25,000.[52] "If we see the athlete as a mere clockpuncher and then compare his pay scale with ours," noted longtime baseball writer Roger Angell, "we feel envy and rage. By God, he is being paid for having fun!"[53]

Despite his salary, Flood would prove the ideal candidate to help Miller challenge baseball's ultimate power. In St. Louis, he was considered a star on one of baseball's best teams, winning seven consecutive Gold Gloves for defensive play and six times hitting better than .300. Flood's success on the field gave his case a legitimacy that a lesser player would not have had. He was also an outspoken supporter of the civil rights movement and accustomed to fighting for unpopular causes. Finally, challenging the power structure of Major League Baseball would certainly threaten Flood's career, but at 32 he didn't figure to play much longer anyway. "I told him that given the courts' history of bias towards the owners and their monopoly, he didn't have a chance in hell of winning," said Miller. "Even if he won, he would never get anything out of it; he'd never get a job in baseball again."[54]

Despite Miller's warning Flood pressed ahead. He flew to New York to meet with Miller. "I want to give the courts a chance to outlaw the reserve system," Flood told him. "I want to go out like a man instead of disappearing like a bottle cap."[55] When Kuhn refused to intervene, citing the reserve clause, Flood filed his lawsuit on January 16. The $3.1 million suit was unique in that unlike the previous two cases it directly challenged baseball's authority to enforce the reserve clause. Flood had some powerful legal talent on his side, including former U.S. Supreme Court justice Arthur Goldberg, but baseball officials insisted there would be no compromise and vowed to fight to the end.

The case wound its way through the court system through the spring and summer of 1970. When Kuhn was called to testify he again argued that overturning the reserve clause would result in the wealthy clubs getting all the top players. He also rebuffed assertions by Flood's lawyers that if professional football could exist without monopoly protection, so could baseball. Kuhn said the differences between the sports made comparisons impractical.

"If you took Joe Namath away from the New York Jets how would the Jets do?" asked one of Flood's attorneys, Jay Topkis.

"Very well," countered Kuhn.

"You're not a betting man, are you commissioner?" Topkis replied.[56]

A few retired players such as Jackie Robinson and Hank Greenberg testified for Flood, but otherwise he had little help. Even though the

MLBPA executive committee voted to support the lawsuit, no active players testified on Flood's behalf for fear of reprisal. "Was I behind Curt?" asked pitcher Bob Gibson, his roommate on the Cardinals. "Absolutely. But I was about ten steps back just in case there was some fallout."[57]

Interestingly, one person who did testify for Flood was former baseball owner Bill Veeck. While owner of the Cleveland Indians, St. Louis Browns, and Chicago White Sox, Veeck had alienated his fellow owners through such actions as breaking the American League's color barrier and sending up a little person to pinch-hit as a publicity stunt. Even though he had hopes of returning to ownership (which he eventually did), Veeck was unafraid of crossing baseball's power structure. "The argument that a change in the reserve clause will destroy baseball is absurd," he testified on June 10. "It would certainly help the players and the game itself to no longer be one of the few places where there is human bondage."[58]

Despite Veeck's testimony, the federal court upheld the reserve clause, as did a court of appeals. The legal losses took their toll on Flood, as did a worsening financial situation complicated by failing business interests, alimony, and child support for five children. "Like everyone else I've had some business reverses and I need the money," admitted Flood, who also said he was just a "hop and jump from bankruptcy. That's enough to drive any man back into the game."[59] Having sat out an entire season and feeling he could no longer be considered a sellout, Flood accepted a trade to the Senators toward the end of 1970, but played only 13 games for Washington in 1971 before retiring for good.

By that point the U.S. Supreme Court agreed to hear the case. The decision came down on June 19, 1972, and by a five-to-three margin the high court denied Flood's claim and upheld the reserve clause. While considered a victory for baseball owners, the court also noted that baseball's antitrust exemption was an "aberration" that could be corrected by legislation. Chief Justice Warren Burger went along with the opinion with "grave reservations," noting that the "courts are not the forum in which this tangled web ought to be unsnarled."[60]

The door had been opened just a crack, which soon erupted into a massive fissure. Even before the decision Miller and the MLBPA brazenly voted to strike during spring training in 1972. At first baseball owners did not take the work stoppage seriously, but when it reached nine days President Nixon stepped in to try to restore peace. The strike finally ended after two weeks, prompting Kuhn to wishfully hope that all parties had learned a lesson.

The lesson learned was that the players were gaining more power, a point that was brought home with stunning clarity in December 1975. A three-person arbitration panel met to discuss the fates of pitchers Andy Messersmith and Dave McNally, both of whom had played the previous season without signing a contract. The panel included Miller, who voted for the players, and owners' representative John Gaherin, who obviously supported the reserve clause. That left the tie-breaking vote to arbitrator Peter Seitz, who ruled that both players had fulfilled their contractual obligations and thus were no longer legally bound to their teams. Kuhn was quick to understand the impact of the decision. "If this interpretation prevails, baseball's reserve system will be eliminated by the stroke of a pen. It would be a disaster for the great majority of the players, clubs, and most of all, the fans."[61]

Seitz obviously disagreed, and no sooner had his signature on the order dried than baseball owners fired him for his intransigence. But the damage was indeed done. The ruling neutered the reserve clause and created true free agency in baseball, paving the way for a dramatic escalation in player power and salaries. The average player salary, which had stood at around $25,000 when Flood filed his lawsuit, more than doubled after Seitz's decision and by 2008 rocketed to more than $2.9 million. Perhaps more importantly, it forever changed the way ballplayers thought about themselves and their relationship to baseball ownership. "For me to say 'my owner' is the most ridiculous thing in the world," Mets pitcher Tom Seaver said not long after the decision was announced. "Does somebody own you? Does anybody *own* anybody else in this country?"[62]

By the time of the Seitz decision Curt Flood was long gone from organized baseball. He briefly lived overseas in the wake of bankruptcy before returning to do broadcasting work for the Oakland A's. Following Flood's death from cancer in 1997, Congress passed legislation in his name, giving federal antitrust protection for professional baseball players similar to that enjoyed by players in other sports. His impact on the modern game of baseball, born with his federal lawsuit in January 1970, is undeniable. "Flood's legacy to baseball lives on, every day," sportscaster Howard Cosell once wrote. "What he did when he challenged the reserve clause changed baseball forever, for the betterment of every single player in the major leagues."[63]

THE GREATEST VERSUS THE ROCK

As Curt Flood began his odyssey through the U.S. judicial system, boxer Muhammad Ali was preparing for a different kind of fight. The former heavyweight champion had not fought in three years, the result of his refusal to accept induction into the U.S. Army and possibly serve in Vietnam. But on January 20, 1970, through the magic of film and with the help of a computer, Ali returned to the ring to face one of the greatest heavyweight champions in history.

Ali had already become a lightning rod for controversy in the supercharged civil rights era of the 1960s. Born as Cassius Clay Jr., he had won an Olympic gold medal and dethroned heavyweight champion Sonny Liston in two controversial fights. In the second of those fights in 1965, Ali knocked out Liston in less than two minutes of the first round in Lewiston, Maine. The punch was so quick that many in the sparse crowd of 4,200 never saw it and called it a "phantom punch."

As Liston lay on the canvas, Ali did not head to his neutral corner but pranced around the ring, pointing to Liston and mugging for fans in the audience. Unable to contain Ali, referee Jersey Joe Walcott was also unable to begin his count on Liston. When order was finally restored, Liston had gotten back on his feet and the two men had resumed fighting. But timekeeper Francis McDonough informed Walcott that Liston had been on the deck for more than 12 seconds, so Walcott stopped the fight and awarded it to Ali by knockout. "It was really a 12-count," said McDonough. "When it got to 12 I clicked the stopwatch. Walcott was supposed to pick up the count when I did. There is no doubt in my mind that Liston was knocked out."[64]

Ali was not a popular champion, at least among white Americans. In an age when athletes were still supposed to carry themselves with an air of humility as represented by men such as Johnny Unitas, Ali was outspoken and brash, often predicting in which round he would knock out opponents. He had also embraced the Nation of Islam, a militant black organization that many whites saw as dangerous. It was the Nation of Islam that had Ali drop his given name of Cassius Clay. "That's an Uncle Tom name," Ali said of his birth name. "That's a slave name, a white man's name."[65] It took years for newspapers and sportswriters to acknowledge the new name in their stories, and when Ali met Ernie Terrell in a 1966 bout, Terrell also refused to address him by his new name. En route to a fifteen-round unanimous-decision victory, Ali taunted Terrell throughout, after each stinging jab asking him, "What's my name?"[66]

Less than a month after he knocked out Zora Folley in a title defense in March 1967, Ali appeared at an army induction center in Houston and refused induction on religious grounds. Ali met with reporters afterward but refused to talk on camera. Instead, he passed out copies of a fairly terse statement that said answering the call would violate his religious beliefs. It was a bit more eloquent than Ali's earlier response when the army classified him A-1 and eligible for the draft: "I ain't got nothing against those Vietcong," he said. "Why should I fight them fellows?"[67]

White America turned on Ali with vehemence, calling him a faker, a hustler, and even a traitor. "It's difficult to find another character like this heavyweight champ who does a better job of talking out of both sides of his mouth," opined sportswriter Ray Grody, who still refused to call Ali by his new name. Mocking Ali for his claim that he wanted to be the busiest heavyweight champ in history, Grody wrote, "That doesn't seem to leave much time for pulpit work, now does it Cass?"[68]

In the long run, Ali faced the possibility of a felony conviction, five years in prison, and a $10,000 fine. Ali went free on bond and the penalties were eventually negated through a protracted series of legal appeals, but he was immediately stripped of his world heavyweight boxing title and of his license to fight in every state. In effect, Ali had lost his ability to earn a living and would not get it back until July 1970, when a federal court ruling forced the state of New York to reinstated his license to box.

The Supreme Court reversal of his conviction would not come until 1971, but here it was January of 1970 and Muhammad Ali was finally stepping back into the ring. But this was not to be a typical fight.

Around the time of Ali's refusal to accept his army induction, a radio producer and boxing promoter named Murray Woroner came up with an interesting idea. Woroner wanted to determine the greatest heavyweight champion of all time by staging a series of fantasy fights involving such greats as Joe Louis, Jack Dempsey, and of course, Muhammad Ali. Obviously, the men would not actually fight, but their bouts would be simulated by feeding detailed information into an NCR 315 computer. Each boxer's strengths, weaknesses, and fighting styles were fed into the computer, and the bouts were announced on radio as if they were happening live. After a series of bouts, Rocky Marciano was declared the winner by knocking out Jack Dempsey in the final, for which Woroner awarded

Marciano a championship belt and $10,000. The series was a surprise hit, carried by 400 radio stations around the country and earning $3.5 million in advertising. Woroner announced plans for a similar middleweight series and wanted the computer to crown an all-time college football champion. Everyone, it seems, was delighted.

Everyone except Muhammad Ali.

Ali, who had lost a second-round computerized bout against Jim Jeffries, sued Woroner for $1 million claiming defamation of character. "We did everything humanly possible," responded Woroner, "everything logic, statistics and raw research could do, to make those fights authentic and accurate. I don't mind the criticism and jokes about us in the press. But when the writers imply that we did this thing superficially—that makes me mad."[69]

Ali's lawsuit did not make Woroner mad; it just gave him his next big idea. In exchange for dropping the suit, he proposed a simulated fight between Ali and Marciano, this time on film, to determine the greatest heavyweight of all time. Woroner agreed to pay Ali $10,000 for the fight, with the NCR 315 to determine the ultimate winner.

So in 1969 Ali and Rocky Marciano stepped into a ring in Miami to begin filming sequences for what would become known as the "Super Fight." Marciano was 45 years old at the time and had not fought for 13 years, but the only heavyweight to retire unbeaten got his body back into shape by losing 50 pounds. He also wore a toupee to approximate how he looked during his prime.

The two boxers sparred with each other for 72 rounds to simulate every possible outcome of the computer. As the filming progressed the blows became more intense, each champion determined to prove that he was the better fighter. "If I could corner him maybe I could knock him out," Marciano said during filming, alluding to the fact that he was giving away 14 inches in reach to the younger fighter.[70] "Marciano and I actually fought," Ali said, "and believe me it is the greatest fight of the century. Nobody but me could have fought that man in a fight like that."[71] At the time Ali made those statements he had no idea how the fight would turn out. Filming was done in total secrecy, and the computer analyzed about a dozen different outcomes.

Finally, the edited bout was ready for its premiere on January 20. Fans in 1,500 closed-circuit theaters in the United States, Canada, and Europe paid $5 each for the viewing, resulting in a gross of $5 million and another successful venture for Woroner. Whether it was artistically successful is another question. "Nothing could cover [Marciano's] stiff limbs, his slow reflexes and his drifting waistline," wrote one particularly harsh critic. "He looked a lumbering clown for 12 rounds only to produce a cream puff left swing in the 13th that knocked out Ali."[72] This time, there would be no threat of legal action from Ali, who seemed to take the result in good humor. "That computer must have been made in Alabama," he joked, referencing the fact that Marciano was white.[73]

Ali would get the last laugh on his detractors, returning to boxing in 1971 and eventually winning the heavyweight title three times. His computer loss to Marciano notwithstanding, he is arguably the greatest fighter of all time in any weight class.

Sadly, Marciano never saw the outcome of the fight. Three weeks after filming for the Super Fight ended, Marciano died in a plane crash on the eve of his 46th birthday. He had won respect as one of boxing's greatest fighters from everyone in the sport, including the man he had just beaten on film. If the two had met for real during their primes, wrote Norman Mailer, it would have been like two Mack trucks hitting head-on, then backing up and hitting again until the wheels were off the axles. "I'd wear him on the end of my glove for 10 rounds," said Ali, "but he'd still be coming. The man's tough. He'd be hell to fight."[74]

CAUGHT IN THE DRAFT

Just as Curt Flood was beginning his quixotic battle with Major League Baseball, the lesser-known James "Yazoo" Smith was formulating a similar plan. Named for his hometown of Yazoo City, Mississippi, Smith was a defensive back from the University of Oregon drafted in the first round of the 1968 NFL Draft by the Washington Redskins. Smith played in all 14 games for Washington that season, but a neck fracture suffered in the season finale against Detroit made it his one and only year in the NFL.

Now, two years into retirement, Smith sued the NFL, arguing that "had it not been for the draft he would have been able to negotiate a more lucrative contract for his one year as a professional. And he demanded that the NFL make up the difference."[75] Smith, who drifted for a while and then became a singer and guitarist for a Tacoma, Washington, rock band called Happiness, said, "If I hadn't done it [the lawsuit], I think someone else would have. I think it's a good thing for the players."[76]

Smith's lawsuit would take years to work its way through the courts and would not affect the 1970 NFL Draft, scheduled for January 28–29 in New York. The event itself was still years away from ESPN, Wonderlic scores, and Mel Kiper Jr., and was in many ways as quaint as the very first draft in 1936. It began that year as the brainchild of NFL commissioner Bert Bell as a way of evenly distributing college talent and helping the weaker teams compete with the established Bears and Giants. In that first draft the owners selected players over drinks in Bell's hotel room. Such was the modesty of the affair that the number-one overall pick, Heisman winner Jay Berwanger of the University of Chicago, turned down the Bears' offer and decided instead to go into private business.

Things were only slightly more sophisticated in 1970 as the names of selected players were written on a chalkboard in a makeshift press room at draft headquarters at the Roosevelt Hotel. Steelers' owner Art Rooney stayed only for the first round, barely enough time for him to smoke through one of his ubiquitous cigars. "After the first choice, the other choices are like the races they run after the [Kentucky] Derby," he said. "Everybody goes home."[77] Rooney lit a fresh cigar and promptly left.

Perhaps Rooney was feeling smug because his Steelers, 1–13 the previous season, had won a coin flip with Chicago for the first overall pick and selected Louisiana Tech quarterback Terry Bradshaw. Draft guru Gil Brandt of the Dallas Cowboys called Bradshaw the best college quarterback since Joe Namath, while Kansas City scout Lloyd Wells gave him the highest grade of any prospect he had ever scouted. Bradshaw would eventually justify his selection, winning four Super Bowls and a spot in the Hall of Fame.

Beyond Bradshaw, Wells's fingerprints were all over the draft. He was the first full-time black scout in professional football and was primarily in charge of mining the country's historically black colleges and universities (HBCUs). His work over the years, including the scouting of Willie Lanier, Otis Taylor, and Ted Washington, had turned Kansas City into an American Football League power and Super Bowl champion. His pursuit of Taylor, a future All-Pro from Prairie View A&M, was indicative of the fight for talent between the NFL and AFL, and Wells ended up sneaking Taylor out a the hotel room window to get him away from the Cowboys.

The success of Wells and the Chiefs opened the eyes of teams around the league, and the 1970 draft was a gold mine of HBCU talent. Texas and Notre Dame, the schools that played for the national championship on New Year's Day, had a combined total of eight players taken in the 17 rounds of the draft. Yet that was still not as much as tiny Grambling, which had nine players drafted, tied with USC for most in the country. HBCUs had 60 players drafted in the two days, which accounted for nearly 14 percent of the 442 players taken.

Some of them came at the very top of the draft. Ken Burrough of Texas Southern went tenth overall to New Orleans, and although he would not stay with the Saints, Burrough went on to a productive 12-year career. Also taken in the first round was Raymond Chester of Morgan State, who had a long career with Oakland and Baltimore. Morgan State also contributed defensive back Mark Washington, who played a pivotal role for two Super Bowl championships in Dallas. Another defensive back, Mel Blount of Southern University, led the Steelers to four Super Bowls, while college teammate and Saints draftee Willie Davenport preferred to stick with the hurdles, where he won gold and bronze medals in two separate Olympics.

Others came later in the draft, and in the case of linebacker Rayford Jenkins of Alcorn State, at the very bottom. Jenkins was 1970's "Mr. Irrelevant," the very last of all the draft picks, taken by Kansas City. "Mentally, it doesn't bother me at all," he said, "but it's the principle of the thing. I don't claim to be the best football player in the world, but I think I'm a pretty good one."[78] Pretty good, but not good enough to make it out of training camp, and Jenkins never played in the NFL.

The heyday for the HBCUs was 1975, when four players—Walter Payton and Robert Brazile of Jackson State, Gary "Big Hands" Johnson of Grambling, and Thomas "Hollywood" Henderson of Langston—were taken in the first round. The previous year, Ed "Too Tall" Jones of Tennessee State was the first overall pick, and with five overall picks the school dominated the draft that season. But soon the drafting of HBCU players slowed to a stream and then a weak trickle. There were notable exceptions, such as Doug Williams of Grambling and Jerry Rice of Mississippi Valley State, but every year since 1995, the NFL has drafted only one HBCU player or none at all.

There were high hopes for HBCU players in the 2013 draft, with ESPN's Jay Walker saying, "For the first time in a number of years, this is a deep draft for HBCUs."[79] But only one player was selected through seven rounds. In 2014, only two players, both of Tennessee State, were taken in the entire draft. Kadeem Edwards went in the fifth round, while Demetrius Rhaney was picked just six spots from the bottom of all 256 selections. "It's always good to see those schools get players," Brandt said, "but the odds are dwindling."[80]

A lot of factors have played a role in this, including fewer rounds in the draft. The *Journal of Blacks in Higher Education* also cited "a lack of national television and media exposure for HBCU players, low regard for HBCU football by NFL scouts, and the unproven ability of HBCU athletes to perform on 'the big stage.'"[81] Keith Pough, a conference player of the year his senior year at Howard in 2013, was a top pro prospect who went undrafted. "I'm from a small black college," he said. "That's synonymous with lack of competition."[82] Pough received a free agent invitation from the Buffalo Bills, but did not make the team.

But the biggest reason may be the integration of major college football in the South, which many have called the death knell of black college football. Much like the integration of Major League Baseball killed the Negro Leagues, the opening of bigger football schools in the South hurt HBCUs. "These guys that used to go to those types of schools are now all at the LSUs and Texases and so forth," Brandt said. "Walter Payton wouldn't be at Jackson State today."[83] Richard Dent, a Super Bowl MVP with the Bears who played at Tennessee State, said, "The black schools don't have the funds, the facilities or the TV deals to compete with the huge colleges and universities for these kids."[84]

On the subject of facilities, Thomas Henderson recalled that during his time at Langston University in the 1970s "our rickety old bus seated thirty-three and we would have sixty people on there. We would be hanging out of the luggage rack, little bitty school chairs in the aisle, it was pitiful. And that's the way we traveled."[85] Certainly, the situation has improved since those days, but consider what happened at Grambling in 2013. Citing substandard facilities, unhealthy conditions, and long bus rides, players refused to play or practice, causing the school to forfeit a game to Jackson State. "It was tough, but we had to take a stand to get our point across," said defensive back Naquan Smith. "If we didn't take a stand, things would have been the same."[86]

Few believe that HBCU schools can recapture their dominance that flowered in the 1970 draft, but suggestions include:

- More consistent media coverage
- Attracting young and connected coaching talent
- Developing relationships with high school programs
- Consistent conference membership requirements
- College presidents making athletics a top priority[87]

Of course, all of that takes money, which is in short supply at a lot of universities, especially HBCUs. Even as Grambling officials helped end the 2013 boycott and get the players back on the field, school president Frank Pogue admitted, "We've had a chance to tell the world that we are broke. Grambling has insufficient funds to do what Grambling needs to do."[88]

Yazoo Smith made a little bit of money for his trouble. It took six years for his case to wind its way through the courts, but in 1976 U.S. District Court judge William B. Bryant ruled in Smith's favor and awarded him $276,000 in damages. "The current system is absolutely the most restrictive one imaginable," wrote Bryant. "It utterly strips [the players] of control over the marketing of their talents."[89] When the U.S. Court of Appeals for the DC Circuit upheld the decision, saying that the draft robbed the players of any bargaining power, the NFL Draft, along with drafts in other sports, was in real trouble.

But in March 1977, NFL lawyers, including future commissioner Paul Tagliabue, sought a backroom deal with the NFL Players Association that would explicitly approve a draft of college players. "The NFL is a private government of the owners, by the owners and for the owners," warned Yazoo Smith's lawyer Stuart H. Johnson Jr. before players voted on the deal. "NFL players [should] stop, look, and listen before voting on the proposed agreement."[90] The players union ignored Johnson, and in a staggering repudiation of its newfound rights, especially in light of the financial gains made by baseball players in free agency, approved the measure in a new collective bargaining agreement.

The NFL Draft, now a prime-time television event that is discussed, debated, and dissected for months before it actually takes place, was saved. And the name of James "Yazoo" Smith, which could have been as paramount in sports history as that of Flood or Joe Kapp (see chapter 12), was soon forgotten. Smith said he does not begrudge modern players all the financial success they now enjoy, and even enjoys the small part he played in it. "I think a player has the right to pick where he wants to play, raise a family and things like that," said Smith. "A lot of things enter into it."[91]

2

FEBRUARY

THE CHAMP IS SMOKIN'

While Ali and Marciano punched it out on a movie screen, Joe Frazier was making plans to take Ali's vacated heavyweight title. Frazier was part of a jumbled mess in a heavyweight division in which there was no clear champion. While Frazier had been declared champion by six different state boxing organizations, Jimmy Ellis laid claim to the World Boxing Association (WBA) title. As Frazier destroyed Jerry Quarry in a 1969 title defense, Ellis looked on from ringside. "You're no champ," Frazier yelled at Ellis after the bout. "You won't fight anybody. A champ's got to fight everybody." Ellis shot back, "I told him I would beat him and shut his mouth. I want that man."[1]

Frazier was almost the polar opposite of Ali—a quiet, diminutive boxer who succeeded through power and determination rather than Ali's combination of fanfare and finesse. While Ali seemed constantly surrounded by attention and controversy, Frazier worked in the shadows, content to let his devastating left hook speak to his abilities. Their disparate styles, personalities, and unblemished records ensured that Frazier and Ali would meet in a titanic struggle down the road. But before that could happen Ali would have to regain his license to fight and Frazier would have to unify the disputed heavyweight titles.

Frazier believed Ellis had ducked him for months, charges that Ellis vehemently denied. But when an Ellis bout in Argentina against Gregorio Peralta had to be canceled for lack of interest in December 1969, the

WBA champ finally relented. He would meet Frazier at Madison Square Garden in New York on February 16, 1970.

In the weeks leading up to the fight, experts continued to underestimate Frazier, including former heavyweight champ James Braddock, who predicted an Ellis win. "I'm tired of talking about the fight," Ellis said just days before the bout. "It's here. He [Frazier] is talking. He better save his wind."[2] Perhaps Ellis should have taken a cue from Eddie Futch, one of Frazier's handlers. "I've seen it before," he said, "and when an opponent's mouth gets to Joe, they are in trouble. They had better run—run like thieves."[3] If Frazier was concerned about the fight, he didn't show it. The night before the bout he appeared in a tuxedo on Ed Sullivan's popular television show to sing "Knock on Wood."[4]

When the fight began the evening of February 16, it was Ellis's wind that was more of an issue. Ellis had not fought in 17 months and it showed. After a respectable first round, he began to weaken under the steady pounding of Frazier's advancing blows. By the third round Frazier had taken control of the fight, and in the fourth he put Ellis down with a trademark left. Ellis managed to get up before the ten count, but Frazier flattened him with another left hook and this time Ellis's corner stopped the fight, refusing to let Ellis come out for the fifth round.

The final bell of the fight had barely sounded when boxing experts and writers began pointing to a potential Frazier-Ali match. "Regardless of how you feel about Clay's reluctance to do his part with the military," wrote one, "you have to agree that a Frazier-Clay fight would have folks hanging from the rafters. The prospect of such a payday is going to cause promoters to get the pot boiling for such a match."[5]

When his license to box in New York was reinstated in 1970, he was free to meet his destiny with Frazier. Their fights were a bloody trilogy that polarized fans along racial lines, even though both fighters were black. The fast-talking, outspoken Ali symbolized the oppression of the black man in white America, and he became a hero to those struggling to identify the emerging black consciousness of the 1970s. To his fans, Ali was a misunderstood, unappreciated artist who was being marginalized by society because he had the courage to speak out.

To his detractors, Ali was an agitator and a showboat, someone who would rather talk about his greatness than prove it in the ring. He was disdained by what President Nixon called the "silent majority"—those who were not out burning their draft cards or their bras, but simply did their jobs every day without complaint or fanfare. Joe Frazier, with his stolid approach and unassuming style, appealed greatly to the majority, most of whom wanted Frazier to put his left hook in Ali's mouth and close it for good. "Fans in most cases are not for or against Frazier, they are for or against Ali," wrote Ira Berkow. "For Ali represents, depending on your background and perspectives, a knave or a knight, an Army slacker or a hero, a racist or a rational man."[6]

That first match, March 8, 1971, at Madison Square Garden, was rightly called "The Fight of the Century" for the level of interest it held across the country and the world. Frazier emerged victorious that night, using his left hook to floor Ali in the final round and handing him the first loss of his career with a unanimous decision. "If he really wants to come back for more, it's alright for me," said the champ. "But I doubt if he ever comes back. I hit him hard a lot of times, and that beating had to take everything out of him."[7]

But Ali did come back, and got his revenge in two subsequent rematches, the most famous coming in their "Thrilla in Manila" held in the Philippines in September 1975. That third act seemed to crystallize the tortured nature of the Ali-Frazier relationship—Ali calling Frazier a "gorilla" and an Uncle Tom, his invective becoming so personal that Frazier could barely keep from fighting Ali before the actual bout began. Frazier never came to understand or accept why Ali tortured him with so much verbal abuse, especially in light of the fact that Frazier had publicly and privately supported Ali during his suspension.

Frazier's simmering hatred fueled him through 14 brutal rounds in Manila. The combination of the violence and the muggy, steamy atmosphere emptied both men to the point that each wanted to quit. Ali would later say that the fight was like "being close to death,"[8] but it was Frazier, his eyes barely open and his body in agony, who finally capitulated before the 15th. "It is a dramatic exhibition of genius in the ring," went one account, "an exhibition which places the men far beyond the likes of Joe Louis and Rocky Marciano."[9]

The love-hate relationship between Ali and Frazier lasted for decades after that, and even though the two publicly made up, Frazier carried both the physical and emotional scars from the three fights. He passed away from liver cancer in November 2011.

"Not only was he a great fighter but also a great man," said boxing promoter Don King. "He lived as he fought with courage and commitment at a time when African-Americans in all spheres of life were engaged in a struggle for emancipation and respect. Smokin' Joe brought honor, dignity and pride for his people, and brought the nation together as only sports can."[10]

A PISTOL GOES OFF

Starting on February 7, college basketball would see some high drama courtesy of a white kid with moppish hair and droopy socks. He looked like he belonged backstage at a Beatles concert, not backcourt for one of the nation's best basketball teams, but for two weeks he set records that still haven't been broken.

If any sport needed a shot of excitement in the winter of 1970, it was college basketball. UCLA was in the midst of one of the great dynasties in all of sports, as the Bruins would eventually win ten national titles for coach John Wooden. But there was actually hope in 1970 that some other school could supplant UCLA, as Lew Alcindor had left for the NBA after leading the Bruins to three straight championships.

A Cinderella soon emerged in Jacksonville University, a relatively unknown school that had played major college basketball for only four years. Jacksonville did it with size—more specifically, two junior college transfers, seven-foot-two Artis Gilmore and seven-foot Pembrook Burrows III. In a typical game against the University of Richmond, Gilmore scored 38 points, pulled in 25 rebounds, and blocked 11 shots, while Burrows added 15 points. The Dolphins averaged 101 points per game, the highest scoring average in big school basketball history, and beat opponents by nearly 40 points a game to advance to the NCAA Championship. "If there's a better team in America, I don't want to play them," said Morehead State coach Bill Harrell, whose team fell to the Dolphins by 54.[11]

Midnight struck for Cinderella in March when UCLA held Gilmore to nine-of-29 shooting and beat Jacksonville 80–69 for its fourth straight title and sixth in seven years. "Every time somebody mentions the three in a row they say Lew did it," Wooden mused. "Now we just proved that four other men from that team could play basketball with the best of them."[12] Jacksonville, still the smallest school ever to play for a national title, has not returned to the NCAA Tournament since 1986, and has not made it out of the first round since 1973.

While Wooden and UCLA silenced critics who said the Bruins couldn't win without Alcindor, in February a true one-man team was making headlines at Louisiana State University. LSU almost matched Jacksonville's scoring output, as the Tigers hit 100 points nine times during the year compared to 18 for the Dolphins. While Jacksonville did it with size, LSU did it with flair, thanks mainly to a slick-handling guard who stood nearly half a foot shorter than either of Jacksonville's twin towers: "Pistol" Pete Maravich was on his way to breaking almost every scoring record in history.

The six-five senior guard ended January by burning Ole Miss for 53 points in a 109–86 win. The big basket came with 4:43 left in the game when Maravich hit a jumper that pushed him past Oscar Robertson as college basketball's all-time leading scorer. "Look, we've still got to finish the game," he told admiring fans who mobbed him and hoisted him on their shoulders after the shot.[13] "Some of these young kids will come along and score the points to beat Pete's record," said his coach and father, Press Maravich, "but Pete's name will be in the record books for the next 30 to 40 years."[14]

In the next game a few days later against Mississippi State, Pete cooled off only slightly, hitting for 49 points, but still managed to become the first NCAA player to eclipse the 3,000-point mark as the Tigers won 100–91. Heading into the game at Alabama, Maravich had now broken two NCAA records within the span of a single week. What could he possibly do for an encore?

On February 7, a record crowd of 15,043 jammed Coleman Coliseum in Tuscaloosa to find out. "From the plane we saw a double line of people, a quarter mile long waiting for tickets to see Pete," said his tutor at the time, Donald Kennard. "Waiting in line at three o'clock in the afternoon for a chance to see the Pistol."[15] Many of those fans chanted "Hot dog!" every time Maravich touched the ball, and the intensity of the game was such that LSU's Doug Hester was ejected after getting into an altercation, and Maravich was given a technical foul for arguing the call. The tension was muted somewhat when Alabama president Dr. David Matthews presented Maravich a ball at halftime, citing his unique contributions to the game.

Playing with two pulled muscles and then a sore ankle, Maravich finally got going in the second half. His 47 points in the half, most of them on jumpers or on twisting drives to the basket, gave him 69 for the game, a new single-game scoring record against a Division I opponent. Yet it wasn't enough as somehow Alabama held on for a 106–104 win. Adding to Pete's frustration was an Alabama fan who allegedly hit Maravich in the back after the game. Maravich chased down the offender before being restrained by LSU officials.

LSU then reeled off five straight victories, Pete hitting for 49 against Tulane and 46 against Auburn. That set up a showdown with perennial conference power Kentucky, a team Maravich had never beaten. The scene in Baton Rouge on February 21 was electric—two highly regarded teams playing on national television and jockeying for conference supremacy in Maravich's final college home game. And both teams, including Maravich, rose to the occasion.

Pete showed the Wildcats his full repertoire—the behind-the-back passes, the stop-and-go dribbling, the long-range shooting—and he finished with 64 points. But Kentucky's Dan Issel, himself averaging 32 points a game coming in, seemed inspired by the Maravich performance and he retaliated with 51. The Wildcats balance and depth overwhelmed Pete's one-man show, 121–105, and they essentially ruined LSU's conference title hopes. Kentucky coach Adolph Rupp, who had admitted that there was no real way to stop Maravich, used what had become a standard strategy for LSU opponents—let Maravich have his points and stop everyone else.

Maravich finished his senior season with a slew of NCAA records, including most points in a career and in a single season, and highest scoring average for a season and a career. And he accomplished it at a time when freshmen were still ineligible to play and when there was no three-point shot. Pete's records are generally considered untouchable, but they would be stratospheric had he played four full seasons. Charting the shots he did take, a three-point line could have conceivably increased his final scoring average from 44.2 to an incredible 57 points per game.

Yet, for all his accomplishments Maravich's college career was considered incomplete. He never beat Kentucky and as a result LSU never won a conference championship or advanced to the NCAA Tournament. In the three years Maravich played, only once did LSU have a winning conference record or win 20 games. Even the glorious senior season in which LSU reached the semifinals of the National Invitational Tournament in New York was tarnished when Pete seemed disinterested in a semifinal loss to Marquette. He later admitted that his off-court drinking played a major role in the defeat.

As a result, Maravich got the reputation as a selfish player, one interested only in his own statistics who got to fire away so often only because his father was the coach. While Pete bristled at such suggestions, he also admitted his father's tremendous influence. "If he had put a football in my hand I would have wanted to be a football player," he said, "or if he had been a plumber, maybe I would have been tough with a wrench."[16]

It was a complicated father-son relationship and a family torn by mother Helen's suicide. The only place Pete could find peace was on the basketball court. Away from it he seemed lost, almost like a trembling fawn, an image that was perpetuated by his youthful looks and mop of hair. He continued to take solace in drink, especially after he joined the NBA's Atlanta Hawks and his flashy style and huge contract didn't sit well with established players. "I've been the worldly way. I know what it can do," he said. "Success buys more liquor, more drugs, more ladies. By being successful, we can destroy ourselves."[17]

If drink didn't destroy Maravich, losing almost surely did, as he had the misfortune of playing for some of the worst teams in the league during a ten-year pro career. Just like at LSU, Pete kept scoring—enough to be named as one of the top 50 players in NBA history— but it never got him close enough to the one thing he really wanted: a championship.

Pete's restlessness eventually led him to born-again Christianity, a later-in-life conversion he shared with his father. Press did not quite live long enough to see Pete enshrined in the Hall of Fame, and before his death from cancer in April 1987 Pete reportedly told him, "I'll see you soon." If true, it was an eerily prescient statement, as less than nine months later Pete collapsed and died of a congenital heart defect. He had given his life to the game and it was somehow fitting, even at the young age of 40, that he should die on the court during a pickup game.

The untimely death seemed to freeze Maravich in popular opinion as the perpetual youth; the shaggy teenager with the moppish hair and sagging socks, somehow eluding defenders to pull off another impossible pass or long-distance shot with defenders draped all over him, as he so often had in his career.

"I'm going to go out shooting and passing in my own way," he said during those shaggy-haired, floppy-socked days at LSU. "I can't change now. It's the only style I have, even if it is one long show. After all, everybody loves a show."[18]

DENNY'S DOWNFALL

Back in January, Curt Flood's lawsuit tried to persuade the legal system that baseball was indeed a business. A month later, on February 19, 1970, the unsavory downfall of pitcher Denny McLain convinced everyone that the game could be a very *bad* business. Better said, there were some very bad people in baseball.

In 1968, McLain was riding high as perhaps the premier pitcher in baseball. In "The Year of the Pitcher"—a season that saw Don Drysdale of the Dodgers throw 58 consecutive scoreless innings and starter Bob Gibson of the Cardinals go through the entire year with an ERA of 1.12— McLain may have topped them both. He pitched the Tigers to a World Series championship with a 31–6 record, 28 complete games, and an ERA of 1.96. He became the first pitcher since Dizzy Dean to win 30 games in a season, a feat no pitcher since has matched. "Without the pennant it would be meaningless," McLain said. "But I think about my career, too. I'm a mercenary. I love to play this game, but anyone who can't see the dollar potential is nuts."[19]

It was a telling comment from someone who loved to play it fast and loose. In the midst of his final win of the year, he allegedly grooved a pitch so his idol, Mickey Mantle, could hit a home run. With Mantle at bat in the eighth inning and Detroit ahead comfortably 6–1, McLain met with catcher Jim Price in front of the plate and said in a loud voice that they should let Mantle hit one. "It was the right situation," McLain said later. "We had clinched the pennant and were up 6–1 in the game. It wasn't like he was going to hit a six-run homer."[20] It was home run number 535, the next-to-last of his career for Mantle, who gave McLain a playful wink as he rounded the bases. On his way to 24 wins and another Cy Young Award in 1969, McLain skipped the All-Star Game because of a dental appointment, only to fly in at the last minute on his private plane and pitch an inning. All the time his salary, and his social circles in darker parts of Detroit, kept growing.

McLain was well known among his teammates as a heavy sports bettor and typically a big loser. Perhaps as a way of trying to recoup his losses he went in with Detroit soft drink executive Edwin Schober and started a bookmaking operation. Thousands of dollars in loans were taken out to stake their operation, but both men were in way over their heads. There were rumors of mob ties, and specifically a run-in with Detroit mobster Tony Giacalone, who allegedly dislocated toes on McLain's foot, an injury that may have cost the Tigers the pennant in 1967. McLain's excuse at the time was that the foot had simply fallen asleep.

Baseball has always had its share of shady characters. Even before the 1919 Black Sox scandal and the fixing of the World Series, early twentieth-century first baseman Hal Chase was often called a "malignant genius" in reference to his outstanding play and his penchant for throwing games and corrupting other players to help him do so.[21] Immortals Ty Cobb and Tris Speaker were tainted by allegations of fixing games, and in modern times Pete Rose's lifetime ban from the game is a testament to the dangers of betting on baseball.

But the mob? This was somehow more sinister, more evil than what had gone before. Even *Sports Illustrated*, which helped break the story, seemed almost apologetic for publishing the details. Its February 23, 1970, edition opined, "The unhappy revelation that pitcher Denny McLain was a partner in a bookie operation dominated by mobsters is not a story we take pleasure in printing. Professional sport lives on the confidence of its audience, and exposing ugly facts may momentarily shake that confidence; but trying to hide them would destroy it."[22]

Given baseball's modern zero-tolerance policy for gambling, McLain could have had the book thrown at him by Commissioner Bowie Kuhn, but he got off with a relatively light sentence. The same week the *Sports Illustrated* story came out (along with similar allegations in *Penthouse*) Kuhn met twice with McLain before suspending him indefinitely on February 19. Kuhn said that he thought that many charges in the *Sports Illustrated* article would turn out to be false and that McLain was not involved in betting on any baseball games.

McLain, who had already testified to a federal grand jury in Detroit and was careening toward bankruptcy with debts of nearly half a million dollars, had once again seemingly charmed his way out of danger. "I think a few people tried and hanged me. It [the suspension] was unfortunate, but it was all the Commissioner could do under the circumstances. As far as the allegations are concerned, very few are true."[23]

He returned from suspension in July, a season-high crowd of 53,863 greeting McLain in his first start in nine months. "Everybody is waiting," said catcher Jim Price. "They're waiting to see if he has learned to live with others, to be one of the team from now on."[24] They did not have to wait very long. McLain struggled right from that first game, a no-decision against the Yankees in which he gave up five runs in as many innings, and he would go on to win only three games in his shortened season. The frustration built to the point that in September, McLain earned another suspension, this one a week and handed down by the Tigers, for dousing with water sportswriters Jim Hawkins and Watson Spoelstra.[25] When McLain's abysmal season ended the team shipped him off in a trade to Washington. He was out of baseball for good by 1972 at the age of 28.

By then, Denny McLain's charm had run out. The Tiger who had the world by the tail, the life of the party who often entertained Detroit bar patrons with his mastery of the organ, had finally reached closing time. "No wave of sympathy swept the baseball fraternity at Denny's downfall," wrote Arthur Daley. "The men who knew him best like him least. Although his roughshod ride over the sensibilities of other people may have been slowed, such is his monumental selfishness that it is unlikely to have been stopped completely."[26]

That was absolutely true. He served time for conspiracy, extortion, and racketeering in the mid-1980s, the judge giving him the maximum sentence and admonishing McLain for his "failure to admit to yourself your own guilt." "I'll pay for my conviction the rest of my life," he said at sentencing. "The lessons I've learned have prepared me for the rest of my life."[27] A decade later he was back to prison on charges of embezzling and laundering money from a private pension fund. "He was a daring, swashbuckling gambler," said a friend, Eli Zaret, a sportscaster who at one time worked with McLain. "'Maybe things got too good and he had to find an edge.'"[28]

Maybe all those months in prison made Denny McLain reflect on his life and career. Maybe at some point he thought about the 31-win season, or the World Series championship in 1968, or the two Cy Young Awards.

Maybe he also thought about the last game he ever pitched in the majors, a nondescript appearance in 1972 against Cincinnati. Maybe he thought about the last batter he ever faced as his life and career careened downhill.

Pete Rose.

"SURLY, OBNOXIOUS AND ARROGANT"

One by one, the challengers to UCLA's basketball dominance fell by the wayside. Jacksonville went down in the finals, and Kentucky was beaten by Jacksonville. Kentucky had knocked off Notre Dame, which earlier had beaten Ohio University behind an NCAA Tournament record 61 points from junior guard Austin Carr. Four different players had unsuccessfully tried to cover Carr, who torched the Bobcats by hitting 25 of 44 shots, many of them from long range. The outburst is an NCAA record that still stands today.

The one team that might have given UCLA a run for its money was Al McGuire's Marquette Warriors. Marquette finished the season at 22–3 and was ranked eighth in the final Associated Press poll and tenth by United Press International. As an independent, Marquette could not win a conference championship to claim a spot in the tournament, but instead counted on getting one of the ten at-large bids the NCAA extended for the field of 25 teams. On February 24, 1970, the NCAA did invite Marquette as one of its at-large teams, with the Warriors slated to begin play in the Midwest Regional in Ft. Worth, Texas.

Marquette said no thanks, and instead accepted an invitation to the National Invitation Tournament (NIT).

"I'm deeply disappointed," said a shaken coach Al McGuire after the team and the university announced the rejection on the afternoon the bids came out.[29]

The reasons for the decision were as complex as they were varied. Much of it stemmed from McGuire, a tough, streetwise Brooklyn kid who wore his heart on his sleeve, and coached more on emotion than strategy. "I want my teams to have my personality," he once said, "surly, obnoxious and arrogant."[30] McGuire was brash and outspoken and had a massive ego that was easily bruised. His stated reason for skipping the NCAA was that going to the Midwest Regional in Texas was an insult because the team deserved to play closer to home at the Mideast Regional in Dayton, Ohio. "I can't believe it," he said. "We belong in Dayton. That's all there is to it. I tried to reach certain men on the committee and get to the bottom of it."[31]

The five men on the Mideast Regional selection committee included Kentucky coach Adolph Rupp, a man every bit as stubborn, irascible, and egotistical as McGuire. The two had faced each other in the NCAA Tournament the previous two seasons, splitting the games, and a genuine dislike had escalated into a feud. When they met in the 1968 NCAA Tournament in Rupp's backyard of Lexington, he invited McGuire to be on his television show, but McGuire didn't want to do it for free and turned him down. When the show came on and viewers were invited to call in questions, one caller asked why Kentucky should get a home game in the NCAA Tournament. "Rupp was not fooled. Leaning forward, he angrily peered out into the television cameras and made a face. 'I know you're out there somewhere, McGuire,' he said bitterly."[32]

Now, his team forced to travel to Texas instead of nearby Ohio where it could expect a friendly crowd, McGuire again smelled a rat named Rupp. "All our fans had already bought tickets to the Mideast," said Marquette captain Joe Thomas. "Al was incensed. He kept saying, 'I know Adolph Rupp is behind this.'"[33] Rupp tweaked McGuire after the decision by saying that his Kentucky team would have played anywhere, but publicly denied any responsibility for the decision. To that, McGuire responded, "Well, of course, he's apt to say anything. It sounds like a lot of hogwash."[34]

Instead of staying home, Marquette opted for the NIT, which was a logical move for several reasons. For one, McGuire would be returning home to New York and Madison Square Garden, which at the time still held a magical place in college basketball. Ever since sportswriter and promoter Ned Irish conceived the first college basketball doubleheader at the Garden in 1934, the place had become a mecca for the game. "The Garden became the proving ground of college basketball. Ignatz Glutz could average 60 points a game in Peoria or Laramie, but until he did something of note in the cigar-smoke haze of the Garden, he was just another unproven hotshot from the sticks."[35] Dean Meminger, a slick ball-handling guard for Marquette, starred at Rice High School in Harlem and on the playgrounds at West 135th Street. "I remember the doubleheaders, the tripleheaders at the Garden," he later said. "College basketball was more important than pro ball."[36]

In addition, even while the NCAA Tournament was growing in public perception, the NIT was still a tournament of importance in 1970. In fact, at one time the NIT was *the* dominant postseason tournament, and teams would often prefer to play there instead of the NCAAs. When DePaul University and George Mikan dominated the college game in the 1940s, the team decided to play the NIT in New York. In 1943, DePaul beat Bowling Green in the finals, and the games in the Garden attracted a four-night total of 72,622 to set an attendance record. Oklahoma A&M (now Oklahoma State) won the NCAA that year, and in a special matchup of tournament winners to benefit the Red Cross, Bob Kurland led A&M to a 52–44 win over Mikan's Blue Demons.

So McGuire went back to New York and played the role of martyr to perfection. First came LSU and Pete Maravich, who was averaging more than 40 points a game. The day before the game, LSU coach Press Maravich told the media that watching the Marquette offense was like watching grass grow. "When he said that, we decided we'd be the lawnmowers," said Thomas. "We scored 100 points once all year. You know who that was against? LSU. Maravich scored 20. He kept saying all week that he was sick, the flu or something. That night he was sick of seeing our defense."[37]

After the easy 101–79 win over LSU, Marquette faced local favorite St. John's in the final before a sold-out Garden. Meminger scored 16 points and won tournament MVP honors in leading the Warriors to an easy 65–53 win, giving McGuire his first championship of any kind. McGuire, whose penchant for hyperbole and colorful language would later make him one of college basketball's most popular television analysts, called Meminger "the finest ball handler who ever lived, and I'm not kidding. I include the great ones, and I've seen a lot of them in my time."[38]

McGuire had his measure of satisfaction, at least on a much smaller scale. Even then, the NIT was dwarfed by the NCAA in terms of money. Winning the NIT was worth about $21,000 for Marquette, while Jacksonville, after finishing runner-up to UCLA in the NCAA, earned nearly $50,000. Those figures seem laughable considering that in 2015 a team made $1.67 million just for making the tournament.

Marquette and St. John's, loaded with New York players and coaches, may have played the last relevant final in the NIT. Incensed that a school would turn down its invitation, and locked in a battle with the NIT and

Amateur Athletic Union for control of college basketball, the NCAA made sure it would never be spurned again. In 1971, it passed a bylaw that came to be known as the "McGuire Rule," which forbids a member school to turn down an NCAA invitation in favor of another postseason tournament. CBS soon dropped its coverage and the NIT shrank from the national spotlight. The process has further been accelerated by the ever-expanding size of the NCAA Tournament, and the once-proud NIT, now derided as the "Nobody Interested Tournament," has been relegated to taking NCAA leftovers.

In a strange bit of karma, the NCAA became McGuire's great white whale, the one championship he couldn't seem to get. His continual sniping at the NCAA—at one point he accused the committee of jealousy and a guilt complex—did him no favors in 1972 when the Warriors were removed from the tournament for allegedly using an ineligible player. That situation was quickly resolved and Marquette reinstated, but the succeeding years brought mostly frustration. Except for a loss in the 1974 title game to North Carolina State, the Warriors never could get out of their own regional.

Finally, in 1977, with an underdog team that had seven losses and was lucky even to make the tournament, McGuire got his final revenge. Having already announced his retirement, he guided Marquette into the NCAA Championship against North Carolina, and wept on the bench as the Warriors prevailed, 67–59. Even before the game ended, with eight seconds remaining, McGuire walked off the court and headed to the locker room with a towel covering his face. "It just doesn't seem real," he said. "When you've always been an alley fighter, you think you'll never get into the silk lace areas."[39]

Quite possibly, McGuire could have gotten there seven years earlier, if only he would have given his team a chance.

"I haven't seen UCLA, but we're quicker than Jacksonville," he said when someone asked him how his NIT champs would have fared in the NCAAs. "Aw, let's drop it. I'm not looking for comparisons. I have enough trouble without taking on the world."[40]

3

MARCH

A PLAYER'S AWAKENING

By the middle of March the professional golf tour, already in full swing since January, made a stop in Pensacola, Florida, for the Monsanto Open. The first three months of the season focused on places such as California, Arizona, and Florida as pros waited for the weather to warm up. The first two tournament winners in March were relative journeymen—Mike Hill at Doral in Miami, and Bob Lunn at the Florida Citrus Open outside Orlando.

On March 15, another relative unknown, Dick Lotz of California, would shoot a nine-under 275 to win the Monsanto for one of his three career PGA tournament wins. But it was not Lotz who was the focus during the week in Pensacola, but rather a man described as the "cocky, jazz-loving bantam from South Africa," Gary Player. [1]

By the spring of 1970 Player was already being mentioned with Jack Nicklaus and Arnold Palmer as part of the "Big Three" of professional golf. He more than held his own against both players with wins in the U.S. and British Opens, the Masters, and the PGA Championship, as well as tournaments all over the world.

Player hardly seemed the type to dominate international golf, growing to reach only five six and 150 pounds. Perhaps as a result of his lack of size he took up physical fitness and weight training at an early age, which he believed helped him maintain a competitive edge. "Arnie Palmer's not in good shape," said fellow pro Bob Goalby. "Bob Murphy sits on a walking cane between shots. Julius Boros could be one hell of a player, but he's 20 pounds overweight and he doesn't want to fight it. Gary Player is an athlete. He works at it."[2]

As if needing to prove himself, Player was willing to go anywhere and play anyone to be the best. Relatively isolated in his native South Africa, Player knew he would need to travel to find the competition, and by the end of his career had racked up some 15 million air miles. "When we traveled from South Africa to America for example, it took us over 40 hours and four stops," Player admitted. "We used to stop at a place called Cocos Island and I remember the captain saying 'Folks we're going to be here for two hours—lie on the beach, you can have some coconut juice, there's some sun screen, have a drink and when you hear TO WOOOO, come and get back on the plane.'"[3]

By the time he had reached Pensacola, Player had earned the respect of almost everyone in the world of golf. It was the people *outside* of golf who were starting to notice him in something less than a favorable light.

It began at the PGA Championship in Ohio the previous year when some fans gave Player a jostling during a round and threw a cup of water in his face. Player's description of his treatment seems more like a scene from *Caddyshack* than a major golf tournament: people throwing ice in his eyes and throwing balls and screaming as he tried to putt.

Hardly the way to treat one of the greatest players in the sport, but these spectators could not care less about Player's game. They were there to protest his role, or alleged role, in apartheid. "The opposition to apartheid was vicious in the USA," he said, "and being a South African, I was immediately considered to be a racist white man who supported apartheid."[4]

Apartheid was the official policy of the ruling party in South Africa, and by it the minority Afrikaners subjugated the majority black population in the country. It was considered an odious policy seemingly everywhere outside of South Africa, and in 1962 a United Nations resolution effectively banned the country from participating in the Olympic Games. Even as the country was trying to make accommodations in order to participate in the Olympics, such as fielding an integrated squad, such compromises were only for traveling athletes and would not be observed at home. South Africa made further headlines by refusing to let black tennis star Arthur Ashe compete in the country. "Inside South Africa, it is pointed out, racial separation and discrimination in sport, as in other things, are tighter than ever."[5] In a sporting sense, South Africa was now effectively cut off from the rest of the world.

Except for Gary Player.

Player became the walking, golfing embodiment of his country's racial policies, in great part due to a statement he made in 1965: "I am of the South Africa of Verwoerd and apartheid."[6]

Hendrik Frensch Verwoerd was the prime minister of South Africa at the time and the main architect of apartheid. Player could not have made a more damning statement about his beliefs unless he had burned a cross on Dr. Martin Luther King's front yard.

Whether it was because he realized his position was unpopular or whether he went through a true moral epiphany, Player eventually backtracked. "My views began to change, particularly as I travelled around the world," he said later. "The injustice was so obvious and the implications quite chilling."[7]

Others were not so willing to forgive and forget, which is why in March 1970 in Pensacola, Player was followed during his rounds by Sergeant Bill Lynch and four deputies from the Escambia County Sheriff's Office. Even before Player arrived in Pensacola he had prepared a paper to explain his position, in which he rejected the Ashe decision and offered to play a series of matches against the leading black golfers of the day. Some took it as an honest attempt to correct past wrongs, while others were not so sure. Charlie Sifford countered that if Player really wanted to do something he should support the invitation of a black player to the Masters.

Tension, like the armed guards trailing Player, seemed to be everywhere. Just to lighten the mood, playing partner Steve Reid told Player during a rain delay, "Don't let this weather bother you, Gary. The water will get in the gun sights and make it harder to aim."[8]

The pressure was unrelenting, even for a man of Player's remarkable concentration. He finished eighth at Pensacola and then the following week missed the cut in Jacksonville. Everywhere he went all anyone wanted to talk about was apartheid. "I think we have a greater love for and understanding of the non-white people in [South Africa] than they have in America for their Negroes," he said.[9] It was a comment almost guaranteed to cause him more trouble in the galleries, but it was food for thought considering the recent U.S. history with race riots, Jim Crow laws, and forced desegregation efforts.

Plainclothes policemen were now following him in every tournament, but so were the hecklers. Somehow, two weeks after Jacksonville, Player managed to pull himself together by winning the Greater Greensboro Open. It was a remarkable performance from a man whose greatest acts were to take place off the golf course.

It started with a call for the Masters to open up to blacks. Technically, it didn't mean much because the only way for a black to play in the invitation-only tournament would be to win a PGA event, which none had done so far. The only role for blacks at the Masters had been as caddies. "I don't want to create a controversy," Player said understandably, "and I am aware rules are rules, but with the number of good black players increasing on the tour I think it is a shame none has enjoyed the experience. It will be a better tournament when there are better chances for black men to make it."[10]

The most promising black golfer with the best chance of qualifying for the Masters seemed to be Lee Elder, who was quickly taken under Player's wing. A couple of years before Elder finally qualified for Augusta in 1975, Player not only brought him to play on the South African Tour but also invited him to stay as his houseguest. About the same time, Player hired a black caddy, Rabbit Dyer, to work with him in the United States, and also brought Dyer over to carry his clubs at the British Open, integrating that tournament for the first time. His actions were speaking much louder than his words, but his words also indicated a change of heart. "I am opposed to apartheid in sports," he said firmly. "Every sportsman I know of in my country is just as against it as I am."[11]

Even as Player continued his crusade, the controversy would not die out. The protests continued through 1970, and at the 1971 U.S. Open two black men heckled Player on the course. He then pulled out of the Cleveland Open citing family reasons, but most observers felt he just wanted to escape an issue that now followed him across the years and around the world. In 1974, he played the final two rounds of the Wills Masters in Sydney, Australia, under constant heckling that fellow golfers called the worst they had ever seen. Twenty protestors had been evicted after clashes with police, while others tried to deface course property. A week later he met with students at a local Australian college to try to derail possible protests at another tournament in Perth.

Times and attitudes finally changed, much along the lines of what was happening in the United States. Violence was a part of it; Verwoerd was assassinated in 1966, and the country went through a series of mass protests and uprisings similar to the 1960s Jim Crow South. South Africa also faced sanctions like the Olympic boycott, which led the government to very slowly enact reforms. Finally, in 1990, the last of the apartheid laws was repealed and by 1994 Nelson Mandela, a black African National Congress candidate who had spent 27 years in prison for challenging the system, was elected the country's president.

But for some reason, the ghosts of political controversy would simply not let go of Gary Player. In 2007, by now a respected elder statesman of the game all over the world, Player was criticized by South African bishop Desmond Tutu for conducting business in Burma. A golf course that Player's company designed in Burma was allegedly used by the country's brutal ruling junta. That then led to the postponing of the Nelson Mandela Invitational, a charity event Player had created in South Africa.

He had been down this road and back many times before, and he had outlasted everyone who had stood against him.

Perhaps the detractors could take a lesson from what happened at the Australian Masters in 1974. Protestors went beyond their normal heckling to vandalizing the course. On Friday night of the tournament several people poured chemicals on the greens, hoping to make them unplayable. It turned out they had used garden lime stolen from the groundkeeper's shed. Instead of killing the grass, the lime only made it grow faster.

Gary Player could have told them that sometimes things can grow from the worst of intentions.

"EVIL IS GOING TO WIN"

The end of the 1960s and the beginning of the 1970s marked a transition in the public persona of athletes. For years, athletes had been idealized as the epitome of hard work, fair play, and humility. In part because of the efforts of the media, they were mythologized as larger-than-life figures fighting heroic battles. This goes all the way back to the late 1800s, when the athlete was seen as representing the amateur ideal—someone who played the game for love of honor and country, not just for financial gain. No one expressed this ideal better than the fictional Frank Merriwell, who in a series of magazine serials in the early 1900s played football at Yale with style, supreme ability, and above all, character.

Merriwell had to be fictional, of course, because no such person could or did exist. And the press and public maintained the fantasy even in the face of such sporting rogues as Ty Cobb, Babe Ruth, and Hal Chase, all of whom were later exposed in less than flattering terms. Cobb was an unflinching racist, Ruth a womanizer, and Chase so often threw or fixed baseball games as a player that he came to be known as an "evil genius, the master of baseball corruption."[12]

The new morality of the 1960s that continued into 1970 turned sports mythology on its head. Men such as Johnny Unitas, whose crew cut hair and high-top shoes defined him as the standard of athletic greatness in the 1950s, came to be viewed as old and outdated. They were replaced by Joe Namath and Muhammad Ali, both young and outspoken, especially when it came to defying the accepted conventions. "Namath was the first white athlete to rise above the long-standing hallucination that public humility was the appropriate repayment for the opportunity to succeed in sports. Namath reveled in his self-indulgence . . . why, [he said], can't an athlete admit publicly to drinking alcohol, smoking tobacco and making love to beautiful women—if, indeed, he does?"[13] When Namath led the New York Jets to victory over the Colts and Unitas in Super Bowl III in 1969, it was viewed as a cultural turning point—the young dragon had slain the old knight, and things would somehow never be the same.

In March 1970, a man named Paul Haber believed in everything Namath stood for, and even more. And just like the famous quarterback, he embodied the new morality. The 33-year- old native of Milwaukee was the best handball player in the world, but hardly the best role model. He drank beer, smoked cigarettes, and enjoyed the nightlife as much as his idol. With no trace of shame, he said, "I guess you could call me the Joe Namath of handball."[14]

Haber grew up around the game, which takes place in an enclosed 20-foot-by-40-foot area and involves the strategy of hitting the ball with the hand so that an opponent cannot successfully return it. His father, Sam Haber, won the national title eight times, and by 1970 Paul had won four U.S. titles and a world championship. The fourth title came on March 21 when he defeated Lou Russo in Los Angeles.

One would think such dominance of a sport, even one as relatively unknown as handball, would make Haber a popular champion, if not an outright star, but his lifestyle led many to recoil in horror. The face of handball, a sport desperate for any recognition it could get, was a self-described playboy who said, "I'm a great ad for booze and smoking. If I win, I'll set handball back 20 years."[15] So, just as many in the establishment hoped Unitas would shut Namath's mouth, and Joe Frazier would put a permanent left hook into Muhammad Ali, those in handball openly rooted against Paul Haber. "If Haber were to retire, I'm sure many of us would be very happy," said Robert Kendler, president of the U.S. Handball Association. "We'd be happier if someone could knock him off; that would be even better. But he has proven he can beat them all."[16]

Haber's final totals were nine national championships—five in four-wall competition, and the others in three-wall. His lifestyle obscured the fact that Haber was a true genius at the sport, able to play a variety of shots with either hand. In its profile of Haber, the U.S. Handball Association noted, "He could drop the ball into the left rear corner from any place on the court, with any stroke: overhand, underhand, or sidearm. Paul was the first player to use the ceiling as an offensive weapon; his patience and determination with it were legendary."[17]

Just how he did it was a mystery to most people, considering Haber's nightlife. He smoked three packs of cigarettes a day. At one event in Birmingham, Alabama, Haber polished off 28 cans of beer on his way to another trophy. "In a tournament in New Orleans we really tore things up," he said. "Drunk all night, handball all day. I got about an hour's sleep each night. I lost the first game in every match. I was still trying to find out if I was alive or not. But I won the tournament."[18] Haber worked himself into shape during the season by playing as many as 20 games a day and four hours at a time. During the summer months, he worked as a golf pro in California, but mostly he made money on the side by hustling handball matches. In 1973, Haber won $30,000 in a special exhibition match with racquetball champion Bud Muehleisen, who used his racquet while Haber used only his hands.

Haber played seriously into his forties, even trying out a fledgling professional handball circuit that never caught on. All his detractors, who were frustrated in their attempts to see Haber lose during his career, may have felt a tinge of satisfaction as to how the story turned out. Haber's slight, five-ten, 175-pound body simply couldn't take the punishment over all those years. Worse yet, he continued to make as many bad choices off the handball court. He married, the ceremony taking place inside a court at the Jewish Community Center in Milwaukee, but later divorced. And as he got older, there was no way to keep up the high-rolling lifestyle he so loved. "He was no good at keeping a job because he would skip out of work to play handball," said his former wife. "That was the love of his life."[19] He fathered four children he barely knew and spent time in jail for forgery and failure to pay child support. Haber's sister blamed abuse he suffered when he was a child. When she learned that a filmmaker was trying to gather information for a documentary on Haber's life, she asked, "What would be the point? What would be the message or the saving grace at the end of the story?"[20] Haber died penniless in 2003.

Part of the mythology of athletics includes the idea of redemption; the belief that somehow the true hero can find a way to overcome obstacles and triumph in the end. Ali rehabilitated his image and became a revered figure in his old age, and Namath became more sympathetic after a highly publicized bout with alcohol.

But there does not seem to be any lesson with Paul Haber. He was who he was, with no apologies and no redemption.

During his heyday, Haber once stayed up until four in the morning partying, then had to get up to face the clean-cut Claude Benham in a tournament final. "Here goes evil against good," he said, grinning. "And I guarantee you evil is going to win."[21]

Evil did win the match, 21–18. It also seemed to win in the end.

"THE AGONY OF DEFEAT"

With the exception of the Winter Olympics, Americans usually pay little attention to ski jumping, and the event that took place on March 21 in Oberstdorf, West Germany, received almost no coverage in the United States. It would, however, ultimately resonate for the next two decades on American television.

A 22-year-old Yugoslavian factory worker named Vinko Bogataj was competing in the World Ski Jumping Championship. On his first attempt in the 120-meter event, Bogataj accelerated down the ramp through the swirling snow. After landing, he put too much weight on the front of his skis. He ended up on his back, then his belly, like an airborne snow angel, before settling in a snowbank. Bogataj was carried off on a stretcher and taken to a hospital, but incredibly he had only a broken ankle, bruises, and a slight concussion. He even asked doctors permission to return to the competition.

It was like dozens of other ski jumping accidents, and in fact, there was an even more serious fall that day when an East German named Horst Queck crashed and lost consciousness for several hours. He too was taken to the hospital and eventually recovered. Bogataj quickly forgot about his accident and went on with his life, which included driving a forklift at a factory during the day. Even by his own admission, Bogataj quickly slipped back into a relatively anonymous life in Yugoslavia. There was absolutely no reason to believe that he would soon become an iconic sports figure in the United States.

Except for "the thrill of victory . . . and the agony of defeat."

Bogataj's dramatic fall was captured by ABC, which was covering the event for its *Wide World of Sports* series. The crash seemed so compelling, so visceral, that ABC producers decided to incorporate it into the opening for the program. For the next 30 years, whenever viewers tuned into *Wide World*, they would see Bogataj's dramatic spill over and over as they heard about "the agony of defeat." He became as famous to U.S. television audiences as Walter Cronkite, although no one knew his name or anything else about him. "I knew right away that this was going to be something extraordinary on the air," said ABC producer Doug Wilson. "Vinko was taken into the hearts of the nation, and it became part of our culture. We're inundated with great wins in sports, but people also love a glorious loser."[22]

"Spanning the globe to bring you the constant variety of sport . . . the thrill of victory . . . the agony of defeat . . . the human drama of athletic competition, this is ABC's Wide World of Sports !"

And this was Vinko Bogataj, a factory worker from Yugoslavia whose life at home remained unchanged despite his fame halfway across the world. "Here, my fellow countrymen don't know who I am," he said. "It is just as well." [23]

What fascinated America about a man whom they knew for only eight seconds each week?

Maybe there is something in the underdog, the athlete who gives it his best, comes up short, but picks himself up and tries again—"the glorious loser," as Wilson had said. Americans loved *Peanuts* character Charlie Brown, despite the fact that every time he tried to kick the football Lucy pulled it away from him. Charlie's sad-sack baseball team could not win a

Little League baseball game for 42 years, but there he was on the mound every week, hopeful as ever.

"I look at it this way," said the man who never finished higher than 57th. "I would prefer it to be a shot of me being a champion. But if it can't be, well, why not?" [24]

In 1981, ABC held a 20th anniversary program for Wide World and decided to fly in Bogataj for the event. "We had the greatest athletes of the last 20 years together in one room, but the biggest ovation of the night, by far, was for Vinko Bogataj," said Dennis Lewin of ABC. [25] Among the many athletes who asked for Bogataj's autograph that night was Muhammad Ali.

It could be argued that unlike Charlie Brown, Vinko Bogataj had but a single moment of failure that followed him the rest of his life. But consider a story from ABC commentator Terry Gannon, who met Bogataj during a ski jumping competition in Slovenia.

"On his way to the meeting with us," recalled Gannon in 2002, "he had a fender-bender with four old ladies in a compact car, who chased him furiously to the parking lot of our hotel.

"Vinko was quick-witted enough to say upon arrival, 'Every time I'm on ABC, I crash.'" [26]

ALMOST PERFECT

John Wooden knew about the pressure of unbeaten seasons. In 1964, his UCLA basketball team was 26–0 heading into the NCAA Tournament. "Our kids were pressing to complete the regular season undefeated," he said. "They made it. And that took the pressure off. Now we feel we're starting all over again." [27] Four wins later, Wooden had a perfect 30–0 season and his first national championship. At one point later in his tenure, Wooden guided the Bruins to 88 consecutive wins, the longest streak in men's history. [28]

But even Wooden lost every once in a while. In 29 seasons he finished with a winning percentage of .804 and "only" had four unbeaten teams. Vince Lombardi often told his great Green Bay Packer teams, "We are going to relentlessly chase perfection, knowing full well we will not catch it, because perfection is not attainable. But we are going to relentlessly chase it because in the process we will catch excellence." [29]

No one chased perfection harder than a 21-year-old college senior who in March 1970 was preparing for the NCAA wrestling tournament. Dan Gable of Iowa State University headed to the NCAA meet having won 118 matches with no defeats. Before that, he was a three-time, unbeaten high school wrestler in Waterloo, Iowa, with a record of 64–0. That's 182 wins without a loss going back almost eight years.

Gable grew up in wrestling-mad Iowa, where "teenagers pound their bodies until they scream, and sweat out boxes of salt; they push their muscles somewhere beyond whatever they may have imagined as the snapping point."[30] Even in that culture, Gable took fanaticism to a whole new level. He trained seven days a week, and as part of his regimen mowed the lawn by running while wearing a rubber suit and body weights. On another occasion, he ignored torn cartilage in his knee so he could keep wrestling. At the NCAA meet his junior year in 1969, competing in the 137-pound weight class, Gable pinned all five opponents he faced, and was named the meet's outstanding wrestler. As he led the Cyclones to the team title, Gable was carried off on the shoulders of teammates to a standing ovation.

Part of what fueled Gable was the 1964 rape and stabbing death of his 19-year-old sister, Diane. Gable funneled the pain of her death into wrestling, almost as if he were wrestling for Diane and his parents instead of himself. He compared himself to a horse with blinders on, looking only for the moment when his hand was raised in triumph, so he "wrestled with a fury his opponents did not understand."[31]

In March 1970, Gable prepared to unleash that fury one more time in the NCAA Tournament. No one, certainly not Gable himself, expected him to do anything but sweep through the meet and win his third straight national championship. Everything went to plan, this time in the 142-pound weight class, as Gable pinned his first five opponents in an average of less than four minutes. That set up a meeting in the finals against unheralded Larry Owings from the University of Washington, who had dropped 31 pounds so he could move down in weight class and face the champion. When Gable's father Mack admitted he was worried about Owings, Dan told him, "Don't. I know I can beat him."[32]

The final took place on March 29. Owings proved much more difficult than expected and after two rounds he had an 8–6 lead, working the crowd into a frenzy. Gable had rallied for a 10–9 lead with time running out in the third and final period, but Owings got a takedown and put

Gable's shoulders on the mat, which gave him four quick points. "I looked down and saw his feet, and I knew I had to go for them," said Owings.[33] There was simply not enough time to rally and a few seconds later the match ended, 13–11.

Dan Gable had lost. The man who had spent most of his life in the obsessive pursuit of perfection had it within his grasp, only to lose it in the last 30 seconds.

"When it was over," said Owings, "I looked at Dan and he looked like he didn't know what had happened."[34] As he stood on the second-place podium during the awards ceremony, Gable bit his lip to keep from crying and put his head in his hands. "I made too many mistakes," he admitted. "I can't remember anything that happened in the last 40 seconds. . . . I couldn't believe it."[35] He also found it difficult to face his parents, fearing that he had let them down.

Gable had turned to wrestling after the loss of his sister, and now he turned to wrestling again. This time the goal was the 1972 Olympic Games in Munich, an event for which he was working out about seven hours a day. "I feel I should win the gold medal," he said before the Olympics began. "I'm the best. If I lose it will be my fault."[36] First came a satisfying win over Owings at the Olympic Trials. Then in Munich, Gable rolled through the 149.5-pound weight class, pinning three of his six opponents and beating Soviet Ruslan Ashuraliyev in the finals, 3–0. Calling it the greatest moment of his life, Gable had not allowed a single point in the entire tournament. Maybe perfection was possible after all.

Gable's competitive career ended the following year, but he could not let go of wrestling. He now turned to coaching and in 1976 became head coach at the University of Iowa. Instilling in his players the same kind of dedication and work ethic he had shown in college, and combining it with the work of a master motivator, Gable launched the Hawkeyes on one of the greatest championship runs in sports history. "All that stuff that Gable preaches," said one of his Hawkeye wrestlers, Bill Zadick, "all the hard work and pain and tears that go into the preparation, they all pay off."[37]

The records include nine straight national championships and 15 overall, 152 All-Americans, 45 individual NCAA champions, 106 Big Ten champions, and a coaching record of 355–21–5. And don't forget to throw in the seven gold medals and two silvers his wrestlers earned while Gable coached the 1984 Olympic Games. "It's not a profession where I work at it eight hours a day," he said at the height of his coaching career.

"It's a profession where I work at it all day long and all night long, basically."[38]

Gable's record at Iowa State was eventually beaten by another Cyclone, Cael Sanderson, who went 159–0 during his college career. Sanderson also won Olympic gold and coached Penn State to an NCAA title. But no matter. The records may fall, and others may come to claim his place, but almost without question, no figure in the history of American sports ever had such success as both player and coach. "If a scientist set out to build an invincible robot coach," one newspaper said, "his prototype would have to be Dan Gable."[39]

He retired as coach in 1997, came back for a while, and then retired again, although he is still deeply connected to the Iowa program. So deeply, in fact, that the university built a statue of him outside the arena on campus. In everything, he continues to look for ways to fill a void that only wrestling can fill.

Dan Gable is now in his mid-60s and in pain from a lifetime of takedowns, reversals, and escapes. The physical pain he deals with, working out every day on a schedule that would fatigue much younger men. The emotional pain is a little more difficult. The pain of losing a sister. The pain of his one and only college defeat coming in an NCAA final.

Gable admits to thinking about that loss to Owings in March 1970 about once a day.

"It was like a death in the family."[40]

4

APRIL

L'ENFANT TERRIBLE

April was a difficult month from any vantage point. The Beatles official-ly split on April 10, ending one of the greatest musical collaborations in history. On April 30, U.S. troops invaded Cambodia, a sign that peace in Southeast Asia was still a long way off.

On April 13, newspapers reported that the latest manned space mis-sion, *Apollo 13*, was headed quietly on its way to a Tuesday rendezvous with the moon. By the following day, media around the world were reporting on a serious explosion on the ship that threatened the lives of all three astronauts aboard—Commander Jim Lovell, Fred Haise, and Jack Swigert. Lovell's terse "Houston, we've had a problem"[1] signaled the start of a weeklong drama to get the crew back to Earth. Millions of viewers around the world watched breathlessly as the crew successfully splashed down April 17 in the southern Pacific Ocean.

The near disaster of the *Apollo 13* flight was partially a result of a Cold War space race between the United States and the Soviet Union. From the time the Soviets launched the Sputnik satellite in 1957, the two powers were desperate to beat each other in the new frontier. The United States pulled ahead and seemingly won the race by landing men on the moon with *Apollo 11*, but the furious pace cost both sides. Dozens of Soviet cosmonauts, scientists, and technicians had died in failed rocket missions, including cosmonaut Vladimir Komarov, who in 1967 crashed piloting the *Soyuz I* craft when his parachute lines twisted on reentry. The most tragic American failure came that same year when a cabin fire during a test launch of *Apollo 1* killed astronauts Gus Grissom, Ed White, and Roger Chaffee.

Space, military weapons, and geopolitics were the most common Cold War battlegrounds, but the conflict spread quickly into the sports arena. The Soviet Union's entry in the Olympics in 1952 turned the Cold War into the major story line of the games for the next two generations. The most dramatic confrontation came in the gold medal basketball game of the 1972 Games in Munich, West Germany, an event already stained by an attack that resulted in the deaths of 11 Israeli athletes at the hands of Palestinian terrorists. The United States seemingly had the game and the gold medal won on two different occasions, but both times the final three seconds were replayed due to scoreboard malfunctions and confusion over time-outs. Finally, on the third try, the Soviets scored the winning basket as time expired to hand the United States its first-ever Olympic loss, 51–50. The Americans officially protested the game, and when that failed refused to attend the medal ceremony or pick up their silver medals.[2] "They've been trying to rook the Americans in the Olympics," said U.S. player Kevin Joyce, "and they've finally done it."[3]

There were no Olympic Games in 1970, so the Cold War simply moved to the next available battlefield—the chessboard.

Starting on March 29 and running through April 4 in Belgrade, Yugoslavia, the best ten players from the Soviet Union took on the ten best players from the rest of the world in a classic Cold War confrontation. The 2,000-seat Dom Sindikata Theater was filled to capacity for every match and those who could not get a seat could follow the moves on a large electronic chessboard in the city square. The final round was broadcast live in its entirety for an hour and a half.

The interest in the matches was somewhat surprising since the Soviets were heavily favored to win. Their lineup featured four former world champions and the current title holder, Boris Spassky, who could best be described as a conflicted champion. He enjoyed the game, but not necessarily the pressure to win, and certainly not the idea that he was representing the Soviet ideology. "With Spassky you feel he is treating it like a job. He comes over as a genuinely impressive figure who just happens to have turned his talents to chess. Spassky [does] not enjoy being world champion."[4] Spassky himself admitted, "I am lazy. I don't take months to prepare for a tournament the way the old chess masters did. But I make up for it by working much harder while the game is in progress." [5]

But conflicted does not even begin to describe the most intriguing performer on the challenging team, U.S champion Robert James Fischer.

Easily America's greatest chess prodigy, Fischer began playing at six and by 13 won the first of eight straight U.S. championships. He also became the youngest grand master at the age of 15, and such were his accomplishments that he was profiled in *Life* magazine. At one point he won 20 consecutive matches against some of the toughest competition in the world.

Chess consumed Fischer to the point that he had virtually no outside interests other than an occasional pinball game—no dates, no drinking, and no smoking. He quit high school because it interfered with his playing and learned Russian so he could read Russian chess magazines and understand their game better. Those who looked upon him favorably called it the effects of genius; others were less kind. *Sports Illustrated* called him "the most individualistic, intransigent, uncommunicative, uncooperative, solitary, self-contained and independent chess master of all time."[6]

Fisher argued with judges, walked out during tournaments, and generally enraged the entire chess community with his unpredictable behavior. The Soviets in particular called him a "sore loser, a spoilsport, a loudmouth, and a conceited braggart."[7] When things didn't suit him he tended to withdraw into his own world, and coming into the 1970 matches in Belgrade he had essentially been in self-exile—he had not played an international tournament in two years. As the competition got under way, the chess community, not to mention the 63 foreign correspondents covering the event, had a great deal of interest in the petulant U.S. prodigy.

The tournament would consist of four rounds with ten matches in each round, the winner of a match getting a single point while both players would receive a half point in the event of a draw. Fischer opened against former world champion Tigran Petrosian, the match taking place on a green-and-white marble table donated as a gift by Cuban leader Fidel Castro. Showing no ill effects from his layoff, Fischer trounced Petrosian, who fell into a hopeless situation after only 15 moves and resigned after 39. Spassky managed a draw with Denmark's Bent Larsen, and after the first round the Soviets held a slim lead, five and a half points to four and a half.

Maybe the Soviets could be beaten.

Actually, the bottom half of the Soviet team was doing well; it was the top half, headlined by Spassky and Petrosian, that was having difficulty. Even as the Soviets increased their lead to three points after two rounds, Spassky lost to Larsen. The world team won the third round by a score of 6–4, cutting the Soviets' lead to a single point with but ten matches remaining.

Fischer had not lost his touch for chess or the peculiar. In his match with Petrosian he demanded that the board not be too shiny, and at all his games, along with several sandwiches and bottles of apple juice, he drank a special cocktail of milk and mineral water that was to be neither warm, nor cold, but tepid. At one point, Soviet team member Lev Abramov approached the director of the tournament and asked, "May I, in the name of the Soviet Union, ask just one question, to Fischer's one thousand questions?"[8]

But for the most part Fischer kept his idiosyncrasies in check and played brilliantly, winning two matches and pulling draws in the other two, as the Soviets barely won, 20.5 points to 19.5. After the event, several of the chess masters moved on to a tournament in Zagreb and Fischer cleaned up again, winning ten matches and 13 of 17 possible points. Observers called his play "elegant, forceful, and exciting, and of a quality that placed him in a class by himself."[9]

Fischer had become a celebrity, and his reemergence on the world scene rekindled interest in chess, especially in terms of East versus West. Fischer and Spassky played in September 1970 at the World Chess Olympiad in Siegen, West Germany, with Spassky winning before 4,000 spectators. Fischer, who resigned after 39 moves, said that "Spassky was lucky. Wait till next time."[10] Despite winning seven games and losing five at the Olympiad, Fischer could not help the United States break the Soviet stranglehold on the championship, as the Americans finished fourth. "They don't look on me as a chess player trying to win the championship," Fisher said. "They act as if I were a thief trying to steal something that belonged to them."[11]

Fischer's obsessive odyssey led him through a series of qualifying tournaments and finally to Reykjavik, Iceland, and the 1972 World Championship Chess Match against Spassky. Actually, it was a series of 24 matches that would end when either Fischer or Spassky reached 12.5 points. Fischer was his usual self before the matches began, demanding a bigger cut of the box office receipts and failing to show up in Iceland on time for the opening ceremony on July 1. Things were finally squared away after Fischer offered a written apology for his actions and asked Spassky to accept his apology.

Fischer, who had never beaten Spassky in five previous meetings, blundered badly in the opening match and resigned. He then made further demands of event organizers, asking cameras to be removed, and when they were not, he refused to appear. That gave the second game to Spassky as a forfeit and once again left chess observers wondering what the American enfant terrible was up to.

One might guess chess warfare of the highest order. The written apology, the incessant demands, and now the inexplicable walkout all had a "costly psychological effect on Spassky,"[12] who somehow agreed to play the third game in a small back room with no cameras. Fischer won the game easily and went on to win or draw the next eight games. The American was now playing a bold, confident style, while Spassky sought delays and postponements. When the end finally came after two months and 21 matches, Spassky was not even there to see it. After the match was delayed he left Iceland with his family and resigned by telephone.

Bobby Fischer, age 29, was now the best chess player in the world, a position he gladly accepted. He was also an international celebrity, a position he accepted not at all.

Even before the tournament was over, dozens of women were sending him letters to his hotel room requesting dates or marriage. Interest in chess boomed, and Fischer's smiling face appeared on a Bob Hope television special and the cover of *Sports Illustrated*, a new American Cold War hero in the likes of John Glenn or Mark Spitz.

Bobby Fischer would not be smiling for long.

He never considered himself a representative of the American way of life, and in fact often criticized his home country. He spoke out against U.S. nuclear weapons buildups, pollution, war, and just about everything else that defined the American Cold War position. Fischer's personality also made it difficult for Americans to warm to him as they had with the humble Glenn or the handsome Spitz. In the America of 1970, a sporting public that "wanted its athletes dished up on celibate platters with no side orders of humanity,"[13] Fischer was seemingly a man without a country.

So, first figuratively and then literally, he left.

After the 1972 matches with Spassky, Fischer virtually retired from chess and did not play a competitive game in public for nearly 20 years. A rematch with Spassky in 1992 in Yugoslavia violated a U.S. presidential order forbidding activities in the country. Fischer responded by calling a press conference and spitting on a copy of the order. After he defeated Spassky, he remained wanted by the U.S. government and never returned to the country. He reportedly lived in Hungary, the Philippines, and Japan, all the while railing against the United States and its policies, becoming seemingly more erratic and embittered with each passing year. In 2005, facing arrest in Japan by U.S. authorities, Fischer renounced his U.S. citizenship and received asylum in Iceland, the scene of his great triumph over Spassky in 1972.

Bobby Fischer died a virtual recluse in 2008, his name all but forgotten to American sports audiences. But for a brief period that began in Belgrade in April 1970, he was the toast of the sporting world. "A child who is a genius at chess can look at a board and see a universe that is invisible to the wisest adult. This is both a blessing and a curse. There is a beauty to the gift, but it does not necessarily lead to greater happiness in life as a whole."[14] Fischer found the beauty, but not the happiness. Years after their Cold War chess struggle, Boris Spassky said of his former rival, "I love him and feel for him. As a person he is tragic because he was born to play chess and now he doesn't. In life we all have to find compromises, but Bobby could not adapt himself."[15]

FRIENDS FOR LIFE

Maurice Stokes never saw the drama of *Apollo 13*—neither the near catastrophe nor the heroic return, as he had passed away on April 6, 1970, from a heart attack. His death ended one of the NBA's most tragic stories, and also its greatest friendship.

At six foot six, 220 pounds, Stokes had come out of St. Francis College in Pennsylvania, where he had led the tiny school to the semifinals of the 1955 National Invitation Tournament. Despite a 79–73 loss, "all the guy did was take on Dayton single-handed and he almost pulled it off," read one game report. "Stokes had Dayton on the ropes throughout, totaling 43 points and playing like a man and a half under the boards and on defense. If he doesn't get the nod as the most valuable player in the tournament it's time for another investigation of college basketball."[16]

His NBA career began later that year with the Rochester Royals, and immediately Stokes showed his ruggedness, especially on the boards. Stokes collected 38 rebounds in one game, averaged 16.3 for the season, and won Rookie of the Year honors. The next year he did even better, setting a league record for rebounds and making the All-Star team for a second time, while also showing he could score. After three seasons, Stokes had compiled averages of 16 points and 17 rebounds a game, and seemed headed to a Hall of Fame career.

But on March 15, 1958, Stokes complained of headaches after a game in Detroit and collapsed on the team plane, where only the quick work of flight attendant Jeanne Phillips administering oxygen saved his life. Rushed to the hospital, he fell into a coma and was listed in critical condition with what was determined to be encephalitis, or brain inflammation. Doctors further said that the illness appeared to be a form of sleeping sickness caused by an insect bite, and that Stokes appeared to be in a deep sleep.

Stokes eventually awoke and became alert but months later was still unable to move or speak. He had to communicate by nodding his head when someone pointed to the correct word or letter on a piece of paper. After agonizing months of rehabilitation, Stokes patiently learned all over again how to eat, talk, and move. Still only 26 years old, he told the *Saturday Evening Post* that he would also play basketball again.

But as the weeks stretched into months and then years, it became apparent that Stokes was simply lucky to be alive. Although it was hoped he would eventually be able to feed and clothe himself, he still needed some ten hours of hospital therapy every day. The medical costs were estimated at $400,000—a staggering sum that would be around $3 million today. So the immediate concerns were twofold: how to pay the bills and finding a full-time caretaker.

The bills were addressed through a series of benefit games staged across the country. One such game matched a collection of college stars from Stokes's hometown of Pittsburgh and raised $5,000. A much bigger event began in 1959 when NBA players staged a charity game that netted more than $10,000. The Maurice Stokes Benefit Game would become an annual event at Kutsher's Hotel in the Catskill Mountains in upstate New York where it became the must-see basketball game of the summer.

Players never received any money or expenses but still came from all across the country. Wilt Chamberlain, who bellhopped at Kutsher's during his teenage years, once chartered a plane from London to New York, helicoptered to the game from the airport, and then repeated the process to return overseas after the game ended.

The major benefactor of the game was Milton Kutsher, an entrepreneur whose family owned a country club in Monticello, New York. Not only did Kutsher offer his rooms free to players and families, he spent more than $100,000 of his own money to keep the game going.[17] "Some of the players who played with and against Stokes felt they were helping out a companion," Kutsher said. "They deem it a privilege to be invited to give back to one of the game's all-time greats."[18] Kutscher made it to Stokes's deathbed in time to hear him say, "Thanks for everything, Milt."[19]

The other question about Stokes's caretaker was solved quickly and poignantly by his former Royals' teammate, Jack Twyman. Twyman was every bit the player Stokes was and perhaps a better scorer. In the 1959–1960 season he scored 59 points in a single game and became the first player in NBA history to average more than 30 points (31.2) for an entire year. Like Stokes, he grew up in Pittsburgh, but played his college ball in Cincinnati.

Shortly after Stokes fell ill in 1958, Twyman became his legal guardian. Part of the story is that Stokes was black and Twyman white. The bigger part of the story is that neither man cared. "Maurice was on his own, something had to be done, and somebody had to do it," said Twyman. "I was the only one that was there, so I became that someone."[20]

Friendship was one thing; guardianship was another. Twyman became fully involved in every aspect of Stokes's life, from organizing the charity games to working with him during his painful rehabilitation. "It's so damn slow," Twyman said a year into the rehab process. "He has licked his mental problem and now he has to beat the physical illness."[21] At first, communication was blinking and nodding. More years passed before Stokes was able to use his fingers and type. One of the first things he typed was, "Dear Jack, how can I ever thank you?"[22]

Twyman's devotion to Stokes was almost total. It was a physically and emotionally draining experience, not only when he was with Stokes, but also off the court, where Twyman worried about neglecting his own family and tried to keep his NBA career going. He drew his strength from a man who could only occasionally get out of a hospital bed. "I get renewed from him," Twyman said. "When I need to be picked up I go see him. He doesn't feel sorry for himself. He's going to beat this thing. I really believe that."[23]

Sadly, he could not. For the rest of his life Stokes lived in a Cincinnati hospital, traveling outside only occasionally, such as to go to the games named in his honor or to Sunday dinner at the Twyman household. While it was a brain illness that changed his life, it was a heart attack that ended it on April 6, 1970, at the age of 36. Twyman was faithful to the end and beyond. He handled Stokes's estate, half of which went to his alma mater St. Francis where Stokes is buried, and ceaselessly pushed for his friend's induction into the Hall of Fame. When Stokes was finally inducted in 2004 it was Twyman who accepted on his behalf. Twyman had been inducted into the Hall in 1983 and died from cancer in 2012 at the age of 78.

While both Maurice Stokes and Jack Twyman have passed on, the NBA is determined to keep their story alive. In 2013, the league created the Twyman-Stokes Teammate of the Year Award to honor the same spirit of humanitarianism. Chauncey Billups was named the first recipient.

"Never, ever in the 12 years did I ever see him depressed or angry or 'Why me?' or 'How did this happen?'" Twyman said in his speech when the NBA inducted Stokes into the Hall of Fame. "He looked forward to the new day every day. He was an amazing person, and it was an unbelievable opportunity for me to be exposed to this man and to see what he was made of. He inspired everybody who came in contact with him."[24]

When a movie came out in 1973 about Twyman and Stokes called *Maurie*, producers originally had the movie ending with Stokes's death but changed it because they felt audiences would not like a sad ending. Perhaps it's better to remember the brief time of Stokes's playing career, either with the Royals or with St. Francis. Maybe we should remember those incredible NIT games in New York in 1955 where despite losing two games, Stokes won tournament MVP honors for "the greatest one man show in NIT history."[25]

After the loss to Dayton, Stokes and St. Francis fell in the consolation game to the University of Cincinnati. Maurice Stokes led all scorers in that game with 31 points, but it wasn't enough.

Cincinnati pulled out a 96–91 win in overtime behind 29 points from Jack Twyman.

THE BANDIT BEGINS

April was not all rain and gloom. The same day that Maurice Stokes died, April 6, Mickey Lolich of the Detroit Tigers shut out the Washington Senators 5–0. Lolich allowed only seven hits, three of them by Washington's Frank Howard. "Personally," Howard lamented after the game, "I wish it had never happened."[26]

He was not talking about the shutout.

During the game Howard had been at bat when a well-endowed woman in a short skirt climbed over the railing, rushed onto the field, and planted a platonic kiss on Howard's cheek. It was not the first time that Morganna Roberts had kissed a ballplayer during a game and it would not be the last. "I just pick a team I like and then pick the best player," she said.[27]

A burlesque dancer then working at the Gaiety Theater in Washington, Roberts claimed to wear an I-cup bra and have monumental measurements of 60–23–39, although other published reports put them closer to 44–22–37. She had a difficult childhood in her hometown of Louisville, Kentucky, and at age 13 turned to dancing in clubs around the country. One night at the Gaiety she came onstage wearing only perfume and a ring on her left hand; that resulted in a $5,000 fine and ten days in jail, which she never served.

Roberts was also a huge baseball fan and began going to Reds games during the day before her performances at night. Given that she was somewhat hard to miss, players would whistle at her in the stands. Only outfielder Pete Rose seemed to ignore her, which Roberts and spectators around her could not understand. When one of the spectators dared her to do something about it, "I leaped over the wall and ran on the field and kissed him. He used terrible language and I was kind of hurt, [but] the next night he tracked me down where I was appearing and apologized with a bunch of roses."[28]

Also endowed with a keen sense of publicity, Roberts had hit on a new way to drum up business. Soon, Clete Boyer and Wes Parker were victimized, as was Howard, who was kissed with Vice President Spiro Agnew in attendance. Even though two policemen grabbed her when she tried to crash the 1970 All-Star Game in Cincinnati, the few seconds of publicity before a national television audience were more than worth it. Morganna the Kissing Bandit was born.

Morganna hit the American sports scene at the perfect time. In the 1960s, television had given athletes an international stage and turned them into celebrities as familiar as any movie stars or politicians. Spectators soon learned that while it might last only a few seconds, they too could enjoy the spotlight. In the early 1970s a man named Rollen Stewart donned a rainbow Afro wig and began showing up at sporting events as "Rockin' Rollen Stewart." Pretty soon, Stewart and his ubiquitous "John 3:16" sign were as famous as the athletes themselves. [29]

And when you add sex appeal it's an irresistible combination.

In the late 1960s a stripper named Bubbles Cash began appearing at Dallas Cowboy games and she made quite an impression at the Cotton Bowl. Cash claimed she never intended to cause a stir, which seems unlikely considering "she tiptoed down the steps atop white high heels, wearing a leopard mini-skirt that revealed all the legs there were to see."[30] Cash, who signed her autograph by making a breast with nipples out of the *B* in Bubbles, was featured in both Dallas newspapers and appeared on a few seconds of NFL Films. She worked in a few low-budget movies and even ran for governor of Texas as a write-in candidate, but her 15 minutes of fame were relatively brief.

Morganna's career, launched with a kiss in April 1970, would last more than 25 years.

It would not always be easy. She was arrested for trespassing more than 20 times and during one court appearance her lawyer successfully argued what he called a "gravity defense," claiming that Morganna was simply leaning over a railing and her ample physique did the rest, depositing her on the field. She had been tackled, trampled, and taken down, cracking her spine when she attempted to kiss Reds' catcher Johnny Bench.

But persistence paid off. The players, with the possible exception of Frank Howard and Wes Parker, who made a run for it when he saw Morganna coming, didn't seem to mind and the crowd always got a kick out of it. Eventually, major and minor league teams began to invite Morganna as a publicity stunt, and she kissed the likes of Nolan Ryan, George Brett, and Cal Ripken Jr. Brett responded by catching her act the next night and jumping onstage to give her a kiss. As her celebrity grew, she expanded her list of victims to include NBA players, hockey players, and coaches. "It was like hugging a mattress," said Kelly Tripucka of the Detroit Pistons. "When I saw her coming at me I thought it was a Mack truck. I had two options—either get hit or get out of the way. I decided to get hit."[31]

Roberts kept her regular job as a dancer but was now making a better living as a paid gate-crasher. "She's the highest-paid stripper in the country," boasted her agent. "She's booked a year ahead."[32] Morganna endorsed products, posed nude for *Playboy*, and appeared late night with Johnny Carson. She made enough money to become part owner of a minor league team, the Utica Blue Sox, and a picture of her kissing Frank Howard—with Morganna having to stand on tiptoe to reach the six-seven giant nicknamed "The Capitol Punisher"—made its way to the Baseball Hall of Fame in Cooperstown. "The poor thing," she said of Howard. "He almost fainted."[33]

Then, suddenly, it stopped. Just as players get old and past their prime, Morganna got into her late 40s and decided to retire the Bandit. "I just got sick of talking about myself and always being the center of attention," she said in one of her last public statements in 1999. "Morganna has left the building."[34] Said her manager Jon Terry, "I have no information on why it was so abrupt, as she was someone who obviously loved attention. I don't know if she thought she was too old or it if was a health problem. But she was as vivacious as ever."[35]

With the announcement, Morganna essentially disappeared from the public eye, choosing instead a quiet retirement life in Columbus, Ohio. A woman who had spent the better part of 30 years revealing a great deal of herself was now revealing nothing. But it sure was fun while it lasted.

"When somebody says that I'm a sex symbol, I almost get a little embarrassed," she said a few years before her retirement. "I'm a comedian. I make folks smile; I make them laugh and that makes my day. What are we here for, if not that?"[36]

A SOLDIER SHINES

For many in sports, April opens only as do the azaleas and dogwoods at the Augusta National Golf Club in Georgia. Augusta National hosts the

Masters, an event that in recent years had been dominated by the "Big Three" of Arnold Palmer, Jack Nicklaus, and Gary Player. Between them, the three had already won the event eight times, including seven years in a row between 1960 and 1966. As golfers gathered in Augusta for the opening round on April 9, 1970, very few people were paying much attention to the defending champion, George Archer, or the man who finished runner-up, Billy Casper.

Casper was often the Unknown Soldier golfer of the decade and a man who always seemed to be playing in the shadow of the Big Three. But between 1964 and 1970 Casper won 27 PGA tournaments—two more than Nicklaus and six more than Player and Palmer combined. He was the leading money winner on tour in both 1966 and 1968 and won the scoring title five times in the 1960s. When Casper won the opening event of the 1970 PGA season, the Los Angeles Open, he joined Palmer as the only golfers to win a million dollars on tour.

Casper had also beaten Palmer head to head at the U.S. Open in 1966. That year at the Olympic Club in San Francisco, Palmer had an astounding seven-shot lead on the back nine in the final round, forcing Casper to set his sights on second place. Playing with house money, Palmer decided to see if he could break Ben Hogan's U.S. Open scoring record and pushed all his chips to the center of the table. Never abandoning his pants-on-fire, shoot-for-the-flagstick style, Palmer started to make mistakes and come back to the field. And as the hare finally slowed down, the tortoise just kept plugging away. "Arnold was the most aggressive player ever and he was concerned with beating Hogan's record," said Casper. "I just continued to play my game, and I played so well."[37]

That is an understatement. While Palmer ballooned to a 39 on the back side, Casper caught him by shooting a 32, creating a tie after 72 holes. When Casper won the playoff by four shots the following day he got the trophy, but it was Palmer who got all the headlines. The 1966 Open is always remembered as the tournament Arnold gave away, except that the principals knew differently. "I didn't just lose the Open," Palmer said. "Billy Casper's brilliant play won it."[38]

It was Casper's second Open title, but the recognition was somehow fleeting, which speaks more to his quiet, unassuming nature than to his golf ability. His fellow pros considered him serious and drab, while one magazine article called him "phlegmatic to the point of dullness. Casper is so austere in his personal life that by contrast a Franciscan monk looks like a swinger."[39] In that regard he was much like his idol Ben Hogan, another steely, quiet type after whom a young Casper patterned his game. Casper lived at home in Utah running an orchard with his wife and 11 children, and credited his conversion to Mormonism in 1966 for giving him a calming presence on the course.

Maybe that was the problem. Determined, methodical Billy Casper just did not grab the headlines like flashy dresser Jimmy Demaret, talkative Lee Trevino, or tempestuous Tommy Bolt, a player known as much for throwing clubs as swinging them. In each case, even for Bolt, the player was creating a persona calculated to attract fans and attention. "They love to see golf get the better of someone," Bolt once said of the fans. "That's why I threw the clubs so often. It thrills the crowds to see a guy suffer."[40]

Casper had certainly suffered, no more so than at the 1969 Masters. He opened with a 66 and started the final round one shot ahead of George Archer, who warned, "Casper has to be the hardest in the world to catch. You know he'll be steady."[41] But Casper was not, bogeying five of the first ten holes and generally looking like a man who had just wandered over from a nearby concession stand and started hitting shots. "I never was so discombobulated," he said after the round. "I played like a 14-handicapper out there for 10 holes. I'm sure there were a lot of people in galleries who were thinking they could have been doing as well as me."[42] Archer won by a single shot over Casper, Tom Weiskopf, and George Knudson.

So, the second weekend in April 1970, the soldier returned to Augusta, a little wobbly from his misadventure the previous year, but certainly not discouraged. As they had for the past ten years, the Big Three would stand in Casper's way. Palmer left the chase early, shooting all four rounds over par "as if his intent were to show the world how badly he could really putt if he put his mind to it."[43] Nicklaus closed better than anyone on the course, firing a pair of 69s over the weekend, but a 75 on Friday doomed his chances. That left Player, who came to 18 on Sunday in a three-way tie with Casper and Gene Littler, but missed a tortuous six-foot par putt and finished one out of the money. Clicking cameras had disturbed Player as he lined up for the putt, but he later said he had no excuses.

The survivors were Casper and Littler, who each barely missed birdie putts on the final hole and headed for a playoff.[44] The two were natives of

San Diego, where Casper had started caddying at age 11, and had played together since the Korean War, so the playoff hardly felt like a life-and-death matter. "I'll tee it high and let it fly," Casper joked before the Monday playoff. "He'll tee it low and let it go."[45]

The playoff was anticlimactic as Billy birdied three of the first seven, while Littler bumped along with bogeys and shot himself out of the tournament with a double bogey on ten. Casper's 69 was five better than Littler and gave him the Masters' green jacket. As he walked off 18, Casper was met by tournament chairman Cliff Roberts. "I expected him to say congratulations, but he didn't," said Casper. "He said, 'Thank you, Billy, thank you.' He'd been rooting for me to win and finally I had."[46]

The 1970 Masters would be the third and last major championship of Billy Casper's career, who after winning PGA Player of the Year honors, left the stage to Nicklaus, Player, and Tom Watson for the rest of the decade. If it's possible for someone to fly under the radar with 51 career victories, nine Ryder Cup wins (one as captain), and election to the World Golf Hall of Fame, Billy Casper did. In the introduction to Casper's autobiography, which he appropriately titled *The Big Three and Me*, Nicklaus, Palmer, and Player honored their former competitor. "Why our friend Billy Casper was so successful yet received so relatively little attention has many possible answers. Whatever it was, his stature as one of golf's all-time greats, whether heralded or not, is beyond doubt."[47]

In retirement, Casper maintained a similar low profile. He did not become a commercial pitchman like Palmer, a golf course designer like Nicklaus, or a jet-setter like Player. He stayed close to home and family, especially his wife of 62 years. When he died at the age of 83 in 2015, Nicklaus paid him one final, fitting tribute.

"You want to talk about someone who could perform under pressure, if you wanted someone to get up and down for you, Billy Casper was your man," said Nicklaus. "I think it is fair to say that Billy was probably under-rated by those who didn't play against him. Those who did compete against him knew how special he was."[48]

THEY OWE THE BIG O

By April, the NFL and AFL were preparing to play a common schedule as a single league after nearly a decade of acrimonious warfare. The fight between the two organizations had been a costly one, creating a bidding war for college talent that dramatically escalated the cost of doing business for owners on both sides. The leagues had formally merged in 1966 but played separate schedules until 1970. From now on, there would be just one league under the command of Commissioner Pete Rozelle.

Only three years old in 1970, the fledgling American Basketball Association was already going through many of the same growing pains as its older AFL cousin. Begun in 1967, the ABA was looked upon as a poor stepchild to the established NBA, and its first few years were spent trying to attract fans just to stay alive. That was a tall order, as the Houston Mavericks reportedly drew just 89 fans for one home game, while a game in Jackson, Mississippi, featuring the Memphis Tams had an announced crowd of fewer than 500 fans. In its first two months of operation, the Memphis franchise lost $200,000.

The league became a three-ring circus, offering a little something for everyone. The most visible, and enduring, innovations included a long-distance three-point shot and the league's distinctive red, white, and blue ball. Both were derided by critics, especially the ball "which would only look good on the nose of a seal."[49] In Miami, the Floridians introduced ball girls in bikini tops and hot pants, while the Kentucky Colonels went even further. In 1968, the Colonels put Penny Ann Early into a game, making her the first woman to play in a men's professional basketball league. Her appearance against the Los Angeles Stars lasted all of one second—just long enough for her to pass the ball inbounds before returning to the bench.

The ABA might have disappeared altogether if it had not followed the lead of the AFL in chasing top college talent. The ABA approach was twofold: pay big money for college seniors and entice current NBA stars such as Rick Barry to jump leagues. Actually, there was a third method as well, as the ABA began pursuing underclass college players, a practice forbidden in the NBA.[50] When the Denver Rockets signed Spencer Haywood before his college class graduated, citing his financial hardship, and Haywood went on to lead the league in scoring and rebounding, the NBA considered it an act of open warfare.

NBA hard-liners wanted no compromises with the ABA, especially after the younger league filed an antitrust lawsuit against the NBA in 1969. "We'll fight them directly to the finish now," said one NBA owner.[51] When asked if there was any possibility of a compromise that might lead to a merger, Boston Celtics' executive Red Auerbach tersely replied, "I would rather see the ABA go bankrupt."[52]

By the spring of 1970, such a hard line was becoming more costly to hold, as the price of doing business in pro basketball was escalating dramatically. The NBA and ABA bid against each other for the top college talent, and soon graduating seniors like Pete Maravich, Bob Lanier, and Dan Issel became instant millionaires. Even as those players were negotiating their contracts, merger talks between the leagues had begun and it appeared that a settlement was imminent. The commissioners of both leagues approached Congress with the idea of getting legislation that would allow the merger to take place and end the financial bloodletting of a competitive draft.

Then, it all came to a halt on April 16.

On that day, Cincinnati Royals' star Oscar Robertson, in his role as president of the NBA Players Association, filed a class-action lawsuit against the NBA in U.S. District Court, the Southern District of New York. The suit specifically asked to block any merger agreement or even merger discussions until larger issues could be decided. It wasn't necessarily that Robertson was against a merger, but he and other NBA players felt that if the leagues combined it would create a monopoly that would severely restrict what little freedom they had.

In many ways, Robertson was waging the same fight as Curt Flood. NBA rules were very similar to those of baseball in that there was a reserve clause that bound one player to one team in perpetuity. Robertson sought the same kind of player freedom as did Flood, and his suit argued for unrestricted free agency for NBA players. He was also similar to Flood in temperament, refusing a trade that would have sent him to Baltimore, and becoming extremely active in union activities. "You're playing a game of basketball, all of a sudden someone gets hurt, they kick him out of the league, they're not worried about him at all," said Robertson. "Or if an owner doesn't like the car you drive, he has perpetual rights to you forever whereby you can never play for anybody else." [53]

But Robertson also had advantages Flood did not. Considered to be the best non-center in the history of the game, Robertson rang up numbers that are still eye-popping today, including the 1961–1962 season when he *averaged* a triple-double for the entire season. His status as a superstar gave him a credibility and cachet that Flood did not have. And while most baseball players refused to publicly support Flood for fear of recrimination, Robertson had the backing of the player representatives from the remaining 13 NBA teams, all of whom signed on to the suit as coplaintiffs.

While Flood's career ended shortly after his challenge, Robertson won one NBA title and played for another as his case wound its way through the courts. NBA owners tried to circumvent the process by going to Congress for help, but when they were rebuffed the handwriting was on the wall. It finally ended in 1976 when NBA owners settled, some might say capitulated, a day before the case went to trial. The league agreed to scrap the option year and compensation as well as compensate the players to the tune of $5 million. In short, NBA players got almost everything they wanted, and eventually complete free agency, thanks in great part to what became known as "The Robertson Case."

The settlement cleared the way for a merger, and shortly afterward the NBA agreed to absorb four ABA franchises into a newly expanded league. From a league that was once ridiculed as unable to compete with the NBA, the ABA had now reached at least some level of parity and respect. In the five years that the leagues played a series of exhibition games prior to the merger, the ABA won 79 games to the NBA's 76.

In a very real sense, it might not have happened without the "Big O," Oscar Robertson. Yet Robertson is hardly mentioned as a pioneer in the same vein as Flood or Joe Kapp (see chapter 12). During his playing career it was noted that "unlike most of the dynamic stars of the sport—people like Elgin Baylor, Rick Barry, Bill Russell and Elvin Hayes—Oscar manages to be superior in an unobtrusive, almost quiet way."[54] The Robertson Case proved the same thing—Oscar showing his superiority while others got the headlines. After his career ended, he observed with a trace of sadness but not bitterness, "People don't seem to realize what I accomplished."[55]

Today's generation of multimillionaire players should know, and be thankful.

THE TWO WIZARDS OF WESTWOOD

On the last weekend of April in Los Angeles, UCLA wrapped up an easy national championship. The Bruins' victory was not considered a surprise, and it would be just another in a long line of titles for the team's head coach.

Most surprisingly, that head coach was not John Wooden.

Wooden had already wrapped up his fourth straight NCAA basketball title back in March, and by this time many had begun to consider him perhaps the greatest coach of all time in any sport. Wooden would go on to win seven straight championships and ten overall, putting him in some rarified air, even considering the other sports dynasties of the 1960s and '70s. Vince Lombardi was often acknowledged as the gold standard by winning three straight NFL titles and the first two Super Bowls, but at the same time Red Auerbach was in the process of winning eight straight NBA championships. In 2015, Geno Auriemma tied Wooden by winning his tenth NCAA women's basketball title, all at the University of Connecticut.

Each man succeeded in his own way: Lombardi the martinet pushed his players beyond their limits and then asked for more, and usually got it. Auerbach was the theoretician, the man who reinvented the game with his unmatched knowledge of strategy and psychology, and his thousand little tricks to throw opponents off balance. Wooden looked every bit the grandfatherly Presbyterian Sunday school teacher and spoke in homespun homilies that earned him the nickname "St. John." He was often deluged with requests for his "Pyramid of Success," which included such building blocks as "industriousness," "loyalty," and "self-control."[56]

But right down the hall from Wooden, and in later years right next door, was another quiet, scholarly coach who ranks with any of those legendary figures. In fact, if you go by winning percentage and number of championships, he ranks above any coach from any era.

When Al Scates came to UCLA as a freshman volleyball player in 1959, he certainly didn't expect to stay for the next 53 years. But when Scates finished his All-American career in 1963, UCLA head coach Glen Egstrom left on sabbatical for Japan and encouraged Scates to apply for the job. Scates did, and got an audience with athletic director Wilbur Johns. "So I'm standing there giving my spiel that I'd like to be the head coach, that I was the team captain last year and ran things from time to time," said Scates. "Then I told him I couldn't receive any salary because I was going to try out for the Olympic volleyball team, and he jumped up and said, 'Congratulations, son, you're hired. Your budget is 100 dollars.'"[57]

Scates spent the hundred dollars on volleyballs and used hand-me-down jerseys from Wooden, grateful for every time the basketball team got new uniforms because he got the old ones. Any pictures of those 1960s UCLA volleyball teams show players who look like they just wandered over from the basketball court. In fact, a couple of players did just that, including John Vallely and Keith Erickson, the latter of whom Scates said could walk over after basketball season ended and play volleyball as if he had never missed a minute of practice.

Like Wooden, Scates also believed in conditioning and preparation. Practice started with the circle drill, in which for 45 minutes players would run and dive, followed by hundreds of push-ups and sit-ups. The mental preparation may have been even more exhausting, and in later years his assistant coaches would frequently get e-mails sent by Scates at 4:30 in the morning. "He seemed to study and pick apart and prepare for opponents at a level that people were not familiar with," said Karch Kiraly, one of the dozens of All-Americans who played for Scates. "I was often astounded at the level of detail and study. He was the best-prepared coach and had the best prepared teams."[58]

When Scates started at UCLA there was no NCAA Tournament, at least for men's volleyball, so the Bruins contented themselves with winning the U.S. Volleyball Association National Championship in 1965 and 1967. All the while, Scates also taught physical education in the Santa Monica schools and continued to play international volleyball. It was an international match against the Japanese in 1965 in UCLA's Pauley Pavilion, arranged by Scates, which attracted 5,000 fans and ultimately led to NCAA sanctioning. UCLA athletic director J. D. Morgan was so impressed that he told Scates he would make volleyball an NCAA sport. Five years later the Bruins were playing for an NCAA championship at Pauley.

That NCAA event took place the last weekend in April 1970, and UCLA came in as heavy favorites over Long Beach, Cal Santa Barbara, and Ball State. Ball State was the best team in the Midwest, but "in California they were like a bunch of Irishmen trying to beat Italians at boccie."[59] The three California schools had a wealth of year-round beach talent to recruit from, including players such as Kirk Kilgour, who became a three-time All-American. Scates found him at a beach volleyball tournament and offered him a scholarship on the spot. "He was so quick and jumped so high out of the sand," said Scates. "He had an arm like a whip [and] could hit from anywhere."[60]

As the NCAA Tournament started on Friday, April 24, the teams played a round-robin to establish seeding, and UCLA won all three matches, although Long Beach did take a game off the Bruins. The same teams met in the finals on Saturday, which may have caused some concern for UCLA, as Long Beach handed the Bruins their only loss of the regular season. But preparation and training paid off handsomely as UCLA easily swept aside the 49ers in three straight games. The all-tournament team included Kilgour, Ed Becker, and Most Outstanding Player Dane Holtzman. They were among the UCLA players who threw Scates into the shower after the awards presentation.

If the Bruins had kept that tradition going in succeeding years, Scates may never have dried out. His teams won the next two titles, six in seven years, and four in a row during the 1980s. By the time he finally stepped down in 2012, Scates had won 1,239 matches and lost only 290, a winning percentage of .812. He also had had 19 NCAA titles—the same total as Wooden, Adolph Rupp, and Mike Krzyzewski *combined*—won over the course of four different decades.[61] It got to the point that when he needed a gift and didn't feel like shopping, Scates would hand out a championship ring. "I wasn't worried," he admitted, "because I knew I'd keep winning more of them."[62]

It sounds like boasting, but even more than Wooden symbolized basketball and Lombardi football, Scates *was* volleyball. "Trying to [separate] Coach Scates from volleyball is like trying to imagine 'The Godfather' without Marlon Brando. It can't be done," said former UCLA standout Jeff Nygaard. "His tenure and influence has shaped the game in ways that are innumerable."[63] He was sometimes referred to as the "John Wooden of Volleyball," but such was his success that many suggested that Wooden should be called the "Al Scates of Basketball."

Actually, the two became good friends, especially in Wooden's retirement years when he kept an office at UCLA next to Scates. In 2006, the volleyball team got off to a mediocre start, winning only half of its first 24 matches. Somehow, the team pulled it together and surprisingly won the last of Scates's 19 championships. When Scates returned from the NCAA Tournament he found a phone message waiting for him. "This is a disgruntled alumnus," the message said. "I'm just glad you finally got down to work and did something right at the end of the year. How could that team lose 12 games like that?"[64]

"I knew it was him," Scates said of Wooden, who later called back to make sure Scates got the joke. "Did you get my message, coach?" asked Wooden.[65]

The John Wooden of Volleyball laughed and told the Al Scates of Basketball, yes, indeed, he did.

5

MAY

THE TRAIL IS BLAZED

Not everyone was on board with Morganna's kissing banditry. Some objected to the sexual connotation, but that was becoming a harder argument to make in a culture where morals seemed to loosen by the minute. When the Minnesota Vikings and Kansas City Chiefs met in Super Bowl IV back in January, the host city of New Orleans published the *Special New Orleans Super Bowl Guide*, which advised visitors, "If your thing is striptease, try catching Linda Brigette at the 500 Club. Depending on her mood, she either sheds in front of the cash customers or comes on stage 'au naturel.' Should you prefer your sex packaged in lovely costume leaving a little to the imagination, then your place is the 809 Club where Chris Owens has been packing them in for a dozen years."[1]

Instead, much of the criticism came from the growing feminist movement, which saw Morganna's antics as just more sexual objectification of women. Betty Freidan's 1963 book *The Feminine Mystique* is credited with reigniting the movement in the United States, and in August of 1970 she would organize the nationwide Women's Strike for Equality. The march in New York City attracted more than 50,000 people. That same month, a newspaper editorial commented on a judge fining Morganna for her latest escapade, "Even in the bad old days when we kept our women chained to the cookstove and the washtub, this, we think, was an area where few men would have undertaken to challenge women's rights.

Now that women's lib is with us, such a pronouncement from a mere man sounds downright foolhardy."[2]

Old attitudes die hard, especially in the boys' club mentality of sports, which is a lesson that by May 1970 Diane Crump had already learned.

Born in Connecticut in 1948, Crump soon moved to Florida and began working at a Thoroughbred horse farm. She started by breaking yearlings, and almost from the first time she learned to gallop she fell in love with riding and harbored the dream of one day becoming a jockey. Crump trained at Sunshine Park in Oldsmar. She recalled, "I was the only kid there. A couple of the old guys around there who were trainers, they'd let me sit in the back seat and they'd throw orange blankets over me and smuggle me into the track."[3]

It was obviously a difficult time breaking in and even finding a place to ride, especially in the United States where male jockeys often refused to race against her, so Crump raced in places like Venezuela and Puerto Rico:

> The first time I was asked to ride in Puerto Rico I was in a match race with the leading rider. My horse pulled ahead and the Puerto Rican was holding on to my saddle cloth and let my horse carry him. Then he came back head and head and pulled my stirrup leather and knocked my foot out of the iron, then jerked on my rein as he got close to my horse's head. Through the stretch I cracked him with my stick but he wound up beating me by a length. When we pulled up and came back to unsaddle, the women in the crowd were throwing tomatoes at him and cussing him out.[4]

To get her license in the United States, Crump would need to ride in two pari-mutuel races, which she did in February 1969. Crump needed a police escort to get through the crowd at Hialeah Park in Florida, running a gauntlet of swarming, jeering fans. "They were crazy, up in arms," she said. "The hecklers were yelling, 'Go back to the kitchen and cook dinner.' That was the mentality of the time. They thought I was going to be the downfall of the whole sport."[5] Six jockeys, including Ron Turcotte who would later ride Secretariat to fame, still refused to race against her. Crump had to change into her silks in a small office as the track didn't have a women's locker room.

But despite all the obstacles, Crump accomplished her mission, bringing home a 48-to-1 long shot named Bridle 'N Bit to tenth place in a field of 12. By doing so, she had officially broken the gender barrier in Thoroughbred racing.[6] "She looked good out there," said Turcotte, who was curious enough to stay and watch the race. "You could see she was getting tired at the end, but heck, I get tired myself sometimes."[7] Just a few weeks later, Crump, who some newspapers referred to as a "jock-ette," won her first race at Louisville's Churchill Downs aboard four-to-one shot Tou Ritzi, and immediately speculation began as to whether she would attempt to ride in the upcoming Kentucky Derby.

Crump continued to ride and get that experience, but a year later still did not expect to be in the derby. She was riding Fathom, a horse like Tou Ritzi trained by Don Divine, who was struggling in the spring of 1970. When Fathom had a disappointing run and finished seventh at the Derby Trial, Divine wanted to skip the derby itself, but he was overruled by the horse's owner, W. L. Brown. Whether Brown knew it or not, his decision made history. Diane Crump would become the first female jockey to ride in the Kentucky Derby.

Derby Day, May 2, dawned bright and sunny after an all-night rain. In fact, it had rained most of the week in Louisville, but the sudden sunshine dried the track to the point that it was listed as "good." Crump won the opening race on the card, rallying Right Sean to win by a nose, and also finished fourth on Tanzanite in the two-year-old filly Debutante Stakes. "Just the thrill of being there," she marveled. "The excitement of it all. The thing about Louisville in the spring, it's the essence of the Derby. People talk about it all over the world."[8]

Crump didn't expect Fathom to challenge for the derby. The horse was not really bred for the mile-and-a-quarter distance and was still recover-ing from a leg operation the previous year. The favorites were Terlago and My Dad George, both of whom went off at about four-to-one, while Fathom was a 15-to-1 long shot. "Going to post and warming up, them playing 'My Old Kentucky Home,' just all the thoughts and feelings that go through your head at that time," she said. "At that point, you're think-ing, 'Hey, there's always a chance.' That's what life gives us every single day. It was a chance."[9]

In her turquoise-and-white silks, Crump had Fathom in the 11th posi-tion among 17 horses, making it one of the largest Derby fields in the past 20 years. At the start, Rancho Lejos set the pace but soon faded badly. As she had feared, Fathom just didn't have the legs to compete, and Crump watched as the field began to pull away from her. Silent Screen took the lead coming around the last turn, but from out of nowhere another 15-to-1 shot, Dust Commander, shot to the lead and held on for a five-length win over My Dad George, with High Echelon another length back. The winning time was 2:03 and 2/5.

Aside from his derby win, Dust Commander has generally been lost to horse racing history. He finished a disappointing ninth in the Preakness, nearly ten lengths behind winner Personality, and didn't even race in the Belmont because of a gimpy ankle.[10] He did win seven other races in his Thoroughbred career and sired 1975 Preakness winner Master Derby.

The real story of the 1970 Kentucky Derby was the horse that finished next to last in the field, beating only Rancho Lejos. Rather, the story is the woman who rode that horse into derby history and opened the door for all female jockeys to follow. Six other women have now ridden in the derby, with Rosie Napravnik finishing as high as fifth in 2013, and dozens of other women are now riding in races all across the world. In 1993, Julie Krone became the first woman to ride a Triple Crown winner when she guided Colonial Affair to victory in the Belmont. Krone was inducted into the Thoroughbred Racing Hall of Fame in 2000.

"Somebody had to open the door," said Crump, who has been in the horse training and sales business since she stopped riding. "It wasn't all down to me but I think I was a big part of that. The women's rights movement was happening, but to be honest all I cared about was horses. I just wanted to ride. I marched to the beat of my own drum." But, she added with a slight smile, "I like to think I was a little footprint on the path to equality."[11]

THE UNLIKELY PEACEKEEPER

The first week of May began with Dust Commander's win in the derby. It would end with the shooting of four college students, a massive peace demonstration on the National Mall, and a sleepless President Nixon wandering among protestors in the predawn hours at the Lincoln Memorial. By the end of the month, just as it seemed that the country would come apart at the seams, a hard-nosed college football coach waded into the controversy and tried to calm the waters.

All weekend those first days of May, antiwar demonstrations on the campus of Kent State University had threatened to get out of control.

Ohio governor James Rhodes had called in the National Guard after some 1,000 students demonstrated on Saturday and burned the Army ROTC building. Tensions were even higher when classes resumed on Monday, May 4.

Around one o'clock in the afternoon, as students continued to harass Guardsmen, several shots rang out. The Guard first claimed that it had spotted a sniper on a nearby building, and then said it was responding to small-arms fire from the crowd. But students refuted those claims and said the supposed sniper was only a photographer from the campus newspaper. That photographer, Jerry Stoklas, had a rooftop view of the confrontation between the Guard and about 400 students. From his vantage point, the Guardsmen appeared to open fire first.

No matter how it started, four students now lay dead, leading to the evacuation and closing of the campus. Virtually deserted, Kent State was placed under heavy guard. A further tragedy was that after years of investigation it was never determined exactly what prompted the shootings or who was responsible. [12]

The shootings at Kent State further fanned the flames of campus demonstrations across the country, and more than 400 colleges and high schools would eventually take part in a national student strike. Governor Warren Knowles of Wisconsin also called out the Guardsmen after a night of student protests at the University of Wisconsin in Madison. At the University of Tennessee, the Students for a Democratic Society burned the ROTC building and wanted to burn the administration building. Across the country, students wore black armbands, carried flower-draped crosses, and held candlelight vigils. Some administrators tried to help by canceling classes, while others, like Florida governor Claude Kirk, denounced campus protestors for their "disheveled filth and long hair." [13]

The Vietnam War polarized the country into for and against—hawks and doves—and with a military draft still in place, both professional and college athletes obviously had a passionate interest. Historically, there had always been a curious relationship between athletes and military service. In World War I, the government ruled baseball "nonessential" to the war effort, and baseball players either served in the military or got off-season jobs in defense industries. Pitching great Christy Mathewson was among many who served in France, and accidental poisoning by gas during a training exercise was a contributing factor to his early death.

The government was a little more tolerant during World War II and Korea, allowing many athletes to serve as roving goodwill ambassadors during their military service. Joe DiMaggio enlisted in the army, but spent most of his time entertaining troops in baseball exhibition games. But again, several athletes saw extensive combat, including Bob Feller, who earned eight battle stars and six campaign ribbons in the navy, and Ted Williams, who flew bombing missions for the Marines in both wars.

But by 1970 the Vietnam War had become increasingly unpopular and athletes were not as willing to serve. Some "hid" from the draft by enlisting in the National Guard, while others sought draft deferments, using personal and political connections to have their draft status reclassified. [14] When receiver Pete Gent was playing for the Dallas Cowboys in 1966 and faced induction, his lawyer (also a former army inspector general) wrote letters to Congress on Gent's behalf. Texas senator Lloyd Bentsen stopped the induction by getting Gent a medical deferral.

Then there was the unthinkable—dodge the draft by heading to Canada. That meant the possibility of a permanent life in exile, and always looking over one's shoulder to stay ahead of U.S. authorities. While at the University of Tennessee, star linebacker Steve Kiner briefly considered the possibility. "I said, 'Dad, there's a war going on.' He said, 'You need to stay the hell away from that place. If you have to go to Canada, you go to Canada.' That was pretty clear thinking to me." [15] Kiner opted to take his chances and stay in school, and by May 1970 was preparing for his rookie season with the Dallas Cowboys.

Such thinking was going on all across the country, and it was further complicated for athletes. All their lives they had been trained to respect the authority of their coach, the program, and the school. A lot of coaches at the time were old-school authoritarians, such as UCLA's John Wooden, who enforced rules and discipline to the point that players were instructed on the correct way to tie shoelaces. The players knew Wooden was serious and didn't try to cross him, but many, like All-American Bill Walton, were radicals at heart. On one occasion, Wooden had to bail Walton out of jail after he was arrested with around 50 other students in an antiwar demonstration. "Being arrested is nothing compared to what the [Nixon] administration is trying to do," Walton said. "It's very important that the administration know how I feel about their actions in Vietnam." [16]

A smaller, less vocal group believed in the war and their responsibility to take part. Bohdan "Bud" Neswiacheny captained the 1967 Army football team and won the National Football Foundation's Scholar-Athlete Award. After his graduation in 1968, he served in West Germany while his older brother Myron was in Vietnam. Just two weeks before Kent State, Myron was killed in combat jumping out of a helicopter. "Myron believed it was worth his life, what he was fighting for," Bud said at his brother's funeral. "He didn't die in vain."[17]

Bud had a wife and young daughter to take care of, as well as immigrant Ukrainian parents who did not want him to go. As the oldest surviving son he could have received a war zone exemption, "but now it's a real personal challenge with me," said Bud. "I have to live my own life. I guess I appreciate this country a little more than most people because my parents can remember a time when they literally had nothing. This is my country and I have a duty to it."[18]

Perhaps no place was as conflicted about the war as the University of Michigan. Ann Arbor had long been a hotbed of campus radicalism, and even before Kent State, students there had gone on a two-week strike instigated by the school's Black Action Movement. Coach Bo Schembechler was another hard-liner who was not happy when more than half his team signed a petition in support of an antiwar protest staged during halftime of the homecoming game. As black balloons were released to commemorate the war dead, the PA announcer asked for a withdrawal of American troops from Vietnam.

Watching with interest was a freshman kicker still ineligible to play. Mike Lantry had joined the army after his high school graduation and spent 1969 in Vietnam. "For a full year, my parents agonized, hoping they wouldn't get the call that so many other parents received," he said, describing himself as a "proud Vietnam veteran."[19] Lantry had come to Michigan to run track but also decided to try out for the football team. Initially wary of how others would react, Lantry became a popular teammate.[20]

No one ever called Columbus, Ohio, a hotbed of controversy, and in fact the city had often been described as having the most middle of middle-American values. But Ohio State University stood only about a two-hour drive from Kent, and after the shootings there OSU officials decided to close the school until further notice, a suspension that lasted nearly two weeks. When the school finally reopened on May 19, thousands of students were still upset and demonstrating on campus, and the potential for a tragic incident was very real.

Enter Ohio State football coach Wayne Woodrow Hayes.

In an era when protesting, demonstrating, and criticizing the establishment was becoming increasingly common, Woody Hayes bragged unapologetically, "Hell, we *are* the establishment."[21] A former navy captain, Hayes believed in the flag, apple pie, and John Wayne, not to mention U.S. intervention in Vietnam. He made several tours of Vietnam with his players, visiting troops and bringing game films of the Buckeyes. After Ohio State beat USC to win the Rose Bowl and the national championship in 1969, Hayes immediately left for a 12-day tour of Vietnam. "I promised that I'd bring the pictures back if we won the title," he said, "and I couldn't get here any sooner."[22]

Hayes was not narrow-minded. He was a student of military history who often taught classes on the subject at Ohio State. But he was also fanatical, disciplined, and stubborn. When the award-winning movie *Patton* came out in the spring of 1970, Hayes embraced it wholeheartedly, and it would be screened for years to come to his players on the Friday nights before a game. In fact, many of his players would swear that Hayes *was* Patton, at least in his approach to game preparation and tactics. When Hayes wanted to run the ball, which was almost every play, the fullback would go off tackle as "Patton left" or "Patton right."

Hayes loved Ohio State and saw himself as more than just the school's football coach. When the 1961 Buckeyes finished the season unbeaten, the team was denied a trip to the Rose Bowl by OSU's faculty council. University administrators had felt the football program had become too big and was threatening to overwhelm the school's academic mission. When the council voted 28–25 not to allow the team to go to Pasadena, the campus erupted in protest, as some 5,000 students marched and hung in effigy campus officials. A former Ohio State Heisman winner, Les Horvath, stoked the fire by calling the faculty hypocrites, but Hayes refused to join the protest. "I would not want football to drive a line of cleavage in our university," he said. "Football is not worth that."[23]

Now, with his campus and his university once again on the brink of chaos, the unlikely peacemaker stepped in.

Hayes waded into the protest, which saw some 5,000 students smash dozens of store windows and block entrances to several buildings. Just two days after the school reopened, about 1,000 Ohio National Guardsmen were called to Columbus, making a repeat of Kent State a real possibility. Woody appeared with several of his players at the demonstrations, claiming only that he was there as a citizen and an interested observer, but anyone who knew Woody Hayes knew he could not leave it at that. Standing on a battered garbage can, Hayes addressed the crowd and asked for peace, if not peace in Vietnam at least peace on campus. Using football terminology, he said the students should work within the system so that everyone could "win together," and that sometimes "you can't get a touchdown; you go for a field goal."[24]

Did Woody's appearance make any difference? Some students mocked his football analogies, chanting, "First and ten, do it again," as if they were at one of the Ohio State games.[25] But the fact remains that Kent State did not happen again, even on a campus of nearly 50,000 angry students. Eventually the protests dimmed and students resumed their classes. And it is important to remember that very few other coaches would take the stand that Hayes did. Many were of the mind of Schembechler, who told his own players that while they had a right to their own opinion about the war it should not interfere with football.

Five months after the demonstrations, Richard Nixon went to Columbus for a midterm election rally and became the first sitting president to visit the campus. This time, there were no protests and the few dissenting voices were shouted down. Standing right by the president was his close personal friend Woody Hayes, who urged those in attendance to win the election for the Republicans.

Both men would end their public careers in disgrace, with Nixon forced to resign after Watergate and Hayes fired after he hit a Clemson player during the 1978 Gator Bowl. For a time, Nixon and Hayes were reviled as pathetic figures, with Hayes especially criticized as an old man who was "grouchy and self-righteous."[26] The years healed their reputations, and at the time of his death in 1987 Hayes was fondly remembered as the educator who loved to read Emerson and who called his speech to the 1986 graduating class of OSU the greatest day of his life. "Pay forward," he told the graduates that day. "So seldom can we pay back because those whom you owe, your parents and those people, will be gone."[27]

Hayes also used his speech to say that wars always produce bigger problems than they settle. It was a message that college students in May 1970 would have loved to hear.

"I THINK WE SEE WILLIS COMING OUT!"

The long NBA season was finally winding down by May, and it had featured some fresh, new faces. The freshest was Lew Alcindor, the rookie from UCLA who became a dominant player from the time he entered the league.[28] As expected, Alcindor made the Milwaukee Bucks instantly competitive, leading a team that went 27–55 the previous year to a record of 56–26 and a playoff berth. "Nobody of his age has comparable talent," said the Knicks' Willis Reed. "He has the speed and he's agile."[29] Alcindor led the league in points scored, finished second with 28.8 points per game, and was third in rebounding at 14.5. After a name change to Kareem Abdul-Jabbar, he would go on to win six NBA titles with Milwaukee and Los Angeles, six league Most Valuable Player Awards, 19 All-Star Game appearances, and become the leading scorer in league history.

In the 1970 playoffs, the Bucks knocked off Philadelphia in the first round and then ran into Reed and the Knicks. In the Eastern Division Finals, Alcindor outscored Reed, but his inexperience showed and he didn't get as much help from his teammates, as the Knicks won four games to one. "You can't build a championship team in two years," Bucks' coach Larry Costello lamented after the Bucks were eliminated.[30]

An original league member, the Knicks had never before won a championship but now had shrewdly assembled one of the best teams in NBA history. The headliner was Reed, not the biggest center at six ten, but "muscular as a blacksmith" who would win MVP honors with 21.7 points and 13.9 rebounds per game.[31] Bill Bradley, a Rhodes Scholar and future U.S. senator, was almost like a coach on the floor with his clever passes and deadly outside shooting. A fanatic about practice and conditioning, he took a dormant Princeton program to the Final Four in 1965, scoring a record 58 points in the consolation game.[32]

Guard Walt Frazier earned the nickname "Clyde," as in Clyde Barrow, for his flashy dressing and cool demeanor on the court. Frazier loved the pressure moment with the game on the line and the crowd at Madison Square Garden chanting for a big play. At such times he often made the key steal or basket, and he became known for his ball handling and defensive ability. "I get a lot of attention from my public," he said. "I dig the adulation."[33] Adulation never was a problem for forward Dave De-Busschere, who nonetheless may have had the most important role on the team. He was the Knicks' muscle, the man not afraid to go after the crucial rebound or trade elbows underneath the basket.

Coach Red Holzman masterfully integrated the pieces together and brought some much-needed discipline. A former league Rookie of the Year as a player, Holzman scouted for the Knicks for ten years before taking over as coach in 1967. "It's not rocket science," he used to tell his players. "See the ball on defense and hit the open man on offense."[34] By the end of the regular season, New York had rolled up a league-best record of 60–22. More importantly, the Knicks led the league in defense, giving up at least six points per game fewer than any other team. New York beat Baltimore in seven games and then Milwaukee in five to reach the finals.

The regular season winner in the Western Division was the Atlanta Hawks, but with a record of just 48–34 no one expected them to threaten the Knicks. Instead, the team everyone looked at as the most serious challenger was a team that had struggled most of the year and as late as February was in danger of missing the playoffs.

At the start of the season, the Los Angeles Lakers had assembled a "dream team" while Magic Johnson and Larry Bird were still in grade school. The bedrocks were Elgin Baylor, an 11-time All-Star who once scored 71 points in a game, and Jerry West, the NBA's "Mr. Clutch," whose quick release and deadly accuracy made him almost impossible to stop. The biggest member of the Lakers was perhaps the greatest physical specimen ever to play the game and maybe the greatest to play in any sport ever. Wilt Chamberlain stood seven foot two and weighed close to 300 pounds, but he had the agility and speed of a much smaller man.

Many of Chamberlain's superhuman records still stand today, including the 55 rebounds he pulled down in a game in 1960 and the 50.4 points per game he *averaged* in 1962. That season, Chamberlain set a record that will likely never be broken, scoring 100 points against the Knicks in a game held in Hershey, Pennsylvania. Chamberlain set league records for field goals (36), points in a quarter (31), and points in a half (59) as the Philadelphia Warriors beat the Knicks 169–147. Wilt's battles with Boston's Bill Russell were legendary, and although Russell's Celtics usually got the better of it in the playoffs, Chamberlain did lead the Philadelphia 76ers to an NBA title in 1967 on a team that ranks with the greatest in league history.[35]

Chamberlain sat out much of the 1969–1970 season after injuring his knee in November, and Los Angeles struggled in his absence. The Lakers were still under .500 in late January, and although they soon went on a nine-game winning streak that vaulted them into the playoffs, at times they played as if they were just trying to hold on until their star center could return. Wilt did return March 18, ironically in a loss to Boston, and he used the final three regular season games to get himself ready for the playoffs. The Lakers got a scare from Phoenix in the opening round, but Chamberlain showed little rust, scoring 30 points in the clinching win. It was much easier in the Western Division Finals as Los Angeles swept Atlanta in four straight.

The 1970 finals opened in New York with the teams splitting the first two games. Reed's 37 points offset West's 33 in a Game 1 Knicks victory, but West came right back with 34 in a Game 2 win. Frazier was having trouble guarding West, so Holzman gave the assignment to Dick Barnett.

Now in Los Angeles, the Knicks looked to have Game 3 in hand until West hit a desperation 60-foot heave as the buzzer sounded to tie the game 102–102. Frazier admitted he was on his way to the locker room as the shot was in the air, but he returned to help the Knicks win it in overtime, 111–108. The Lakers shrugged off the loss and won Game 4 to tie the series 121–115 as West continued his dominance with 37 points.

Aside from West, the most dominant player in the finals had been Willis Reed. Giving away four inches to Chamberlain, he simply maneuvered around the less mobile Wilt or shot over him with his fadeaway jumper. Reed had led the Knicks in scoring in three of the first four games, including a 38-point effort in Game 3. As the series returned to New York, he got off to a similar good start in Game 5, scoring seven early points. But with 3:46 left in the first quarter, Reed made a quick move to the basket and then collapsed on the floor. As the crowd at Madison Square Garden looked on in horror, Reed limped off the court with strained muscles in his hip. As Reed retired to the locker room for treatment, the prospect of containing West, Baylor, and especially Chamberlain seemed remote.

Yet, as they had done all season, the Knicks pulled together and simply found other heroes. This time it was Dave Stallworth and Cazzie Russell, who helped New York overcome a 13-point halftime deficit. Stallworth scored 12 points off the bench and helped defend against

Chamberlain, who sat out much of the game with foul trouble. New York pulled away to win, 107–100, as Willis listened from the locker room. "I couldn't hear the crowd through the door," he said, "but every time we did something right they must have gone wild."[36] The Knick dressing room was bedlam after the game, with players coming to the injured Reed offering their support. "All of us wanted to win it for Willis," said Bradley. "We all pulled together. It was a terrific effort at both ends. It had to be; I don't believe in miracles."[37]

Reed was in no shape to play in Game 6 in Los Angeles, and Chamberlain ran wild—45 points and 27 rebounds in a 135–113 rout—as Knick reserves Nate Bowman and Bill Hosket were completely unable to slow him down. "Before the game doctors told me he couldn't be of any use to us and if he played he would hurt himself," said Holzman. "Naturally, we didn't want to take the risk."[38]

So as the teams flew back across country for the climactic Game 7 in New York there was only one question on everyone's mind: *Would Willis play?* The Knicks had prided themselves on team play throughout the year, but it now seemed the entire season and a potential championship rested on just one person. "If Reed can't play Friday night I'm going to the movies," joked Holzman.[39]

"The Garden will be pandemonium," Frazier predicted, and he was right.[40] On May 8, a standing room crowd of 19,500 packed Madison Square Garden, with all of them watching for Reed. "When Willis comes out they're going to pull the roof down," thought Stallworth.[41] The Knicks came out in pregame warm-ups without Reed, who was still in the locker room receiving last-minute shots of cortisone. "I'll play if I can crawl," he had said. "I said to myself 'You must do the job; your team needs you.'"[42] Finally, just a few minutes before tip-off, Reed emerged onto the floor to a standing ovation that rocked the building—and the Lakers. "The Lakers, including Wilt, turned and saw this," said *New York Daily News* sportswriter Phil Pepe, "and they lost the game right there."[43]

When he hit his first few practice shots, the crowd went crazy again. "It's like getting your left arm sewed back on," said Russell.[44] When the game began Reed hit his first two shots, sending the crowd into chaos. He was limping noticeably at both ends of the floor and played only 27 minutes, scoring just the four points, but it didn't matter. "He hits the second shot," said Bill Bradley, "and at that point, it's over."[45]

Reed's brief appearance inspired the other Knicks, especially Frazier, who finished with 36 points and 19 assists. Barnett added 21, DeBusschere 18, and Bradley 17 as the Knicks won easily, 113–99. "The fans were just great and I didn't want to disappoint them," said Reed, who was named the MVP of the finals.[46] "Probably a lot of guys wouldn't have played in his condition," said West, a loser in the finals for a seventh time. "It was a real tribute to the man that he was out there at all."[47]

More than 40 years after the fact, the heroism of an injured Reed walking onto the court in May 1970 is an indelible memory for all sports fans, not just those in New York. Three years later, after trading for Earl Monroe and Jerry Lucas, the same core of players won a second title, which as of 2015 was the team's last championship. That certainly is legacy enough, but why has this team been so enshrined in the league's mythology? "They are a good team, a solid team, a fine team, a smart team," *Sports Illustrated* wrote at the time, "[but] they are not a great team."[48] Yet, in some quarters, the Knicks are more revered that the 1960s Boston Celtics teams that won eight straight championships.

Certainly, playing in the nation's media center and a basketball mecca played a role, as did the fact that the city was so starved for a championship. Winning had become blasé in Boston, and perhaps fans had just gotten tired of seeing Bill Russell and the Celtics win every year. The Knicks were something new, something exciting. It also didn't hurt that the Knicks won as the NBA was becoming more television friendly. ABC, which had the rights to the league at the time, built Reed's "will he or won't he?" decision into a national melodrama, with game analyst Jack Twyman giving regular updates and then breathlessly announcing, "I think we see Willis coming out!"[49]

Reed, Frazier, and the Knicks embraced the limelight and enjoyed it. After the championship, the players cashed in with endorsements, and each member of the team—all 12 players—went on to write a book. Aside from the happiness of winning championships and watching Red Auerbach light up his victory cigar, the Celtics did not seem to be having much fun. That was certainly true for Russell, who had a tortured racial relationship with the city of Boston, especially when he decided to move his family into the white suburb of Reading. Russell would eventually make peace with the city but at one time said, "I have never seen a more segregated city in my life. I don't care if I never go to Boston again."[50]

There appeared to be fewer such issues in melting pot New York, for fans or players. Born in tiny Hico, Louisiana, Reed was at age nine picking cotton. He came to New York from Grambling College, a historically black school, and had never played with white players until he made an exhibition tour of South America as a sophomore. By contrast, Bradley grew up the son of a banker in lily-white Crystal City, Missouri, and played with an all-white starting five at Princeton.

None of that mattered. In an era dominated by the divisiveness of civil rights, there was no black or white, no sub or starter on the Knicks—only 12 men who came together and played as one. It was basketball at its most sublime, the way it should be played but rarely is. "There is no other way to describe those years on our Knicks teams," Bradley said. "How it felt to know the satisfaction of a play well-executed, to feel the chills of winning a championship, to share the brotherhood of working in an environment of mutual trust, with people you respect, each of whom has the courage to take the last-second shot."[51]

How would the 1970 Knicks fare against one of today's teams, such as LeBron James's Miami Heat or Cleveland Cavaliers? There is no doubt that the players in today's NBA are much better athletes and there is virtually no one from that time who could match up with James, Kobe Bryant, or Kevin Durant. But it's a bit like comparing apples to oranges. Thanks a great deal to athletes like James, today's NBA is a dunking and three-point shooting league that tries to put the best players in one-on-one situations. "The players are faster, they jump higher and the game has progressed dramatically as far as ability," said DeBusschere after his retirement. "The Knicks didn't have the greatest talent of any group, but there was a unique chemistry, a special attitude and feeling that made us winners."[52]

"Championship teams share a moment few others know," added Bradley. "The overwhelming emotion derives from more than pride. Your devotion to your teammates, the depth of your sense of belonging, is like blood kinship but without the complications. In the nonverbal world of basketball, it's like grace and beauty and ease, and it spills into all areas of your life."[53]

"They were an exquisite art form for people that loved basketball," said longtime NBA reporter Bob Ryan. "They played a certain style to a perfection that has seldom, if ever, been matched again."[54]

"HE *IS* SUPERMAN"

The image of Willis Reed hobbling around Madison Square Garden bare-ly had time to settle in the sporting consciousness before a similarly famous scene took place in Boston on May 10. It did not involve the Celtics, but rather the hockey Bruins, who were on the verge of winning their first Stanley Cup in 29 years.

The fact that the Bruins were about to win the Cup was not a big surprise, as their finals opponents were the St. Louis Blues, an expansion team that had been in existence only three seasons. St. Louis was part of the NHL's growth in 1967 that doubled the size of the league from the "Original Six" teams to 12. The 1960s was a time of expansion in all the major sports leagues and the NHL wanted in on the television windfall enjoyed by football and baseball.

St. Louis had been placed in the Western Division along with the other expansion teams—the Pittsburgh Penguins, Minnesota North Stars, Oak-land Seals, Philadelphia Flyers, and Los Angeles Kings. Since the Original Six remained in the East, it meant that the East versus West Stanley Cup Finals would automatically feature an expansion team regardless of its record, a plan that was controversial from the beginning.

In the first expansion season the top five teams in the East all had more points than the Philadelphia Flyers, who won the West with a losing record. That year, St. Louis beat the Flyers in the opening round of the playoffs, knocked out Minnesota in the semifinals, and then advanced to the finals against the powerful Montreal Canadiens. "Montreal may be the first team in history to win the Stanley Cup in three games," said one writer before the finals opened.[55] It did take the Canadiens four games, although each game was decided by a single goal and two games went to overtime. The Blues returned the following spring and again the Canadi-ens administered a quick sweep in the finals.

So here were the Blues, back again in 1970 for a third try at the Cup. Glenn Hall was a brilliant goaltender who won the playoff MVP Award in 1968 despite losing all four games in the finals, and Scotty Bowman was developing the coaching style that would eventually win him a record nine Stanley Cups. "We're going into it against the best," Bowman said as the finals prepared to open, "[but] we've got 14 players back from our first team, and I think experience means something."[56]

The best, in this case was Bobby Orr and the Boston Bruins.

It is tempting to look at Orr like Chamberlain in basketball or Jim Brown in football—physical marvels who simply overpowered everyone else in their sport—and that argument can be made. "He's the fastest and strongest skater the National Hockey League has ever seen," raved St. Louis goalie Jacques Plante. [57]

But Orr was also a transformational figure whose skills were so unique that he changed the very nature of hockey itself. Before Orr made his NHL debut with the Bruins as an 18-year-old in 1966, the defensive game began and ended at the blue line. Defensemen had one main mission—stay in their own area and prevent the other team from scoring. They were called "blueliners" because they rarely strayed beyond their own blue line to join the offensive attack. When Harry Howell of the Rangers won the Norris Trophy as the NHL's best defenseman in 1967 he scored all of five goals. "I'm glad I won it this year," Howell said. "For the next few years, at least, they'll have to rename it the 'Bobby Orr' award, because that young man in Boston will own it." [58]

Howell wasn't far wrong as Orr was named the Norris winner eight straight years starting in 1968. He certainly had the toughness and mindset to play great defense in his own end. "Orr's reflexes and anticipation allow him to block many opponents' shots before they ever reach the goal," *Sports Illustrated* wrote in Orr's second season. "It's not unusual to see him block a hard shot with his legs, knock down the shooter and skate forward with the puck." [59]

But it was his offensive skills that dazzled, even as a teenaged rookie. Orr would break up a play in his own end and then take off with the puck, weaving and wheeling around opponents as if their skates were frozen to the ice. More often than not, his end-to-end dashes would end with a goal or an assist, and the rare times they didn't Orr always managed to find a way to get back in defensive position. In the 1969–1970 season Orr led the league in scoring with 33 goals and 87 assists for a total of 120 points—marks considered unimaginable for a defenseman. "That Orr, he is impossible," said the Rangers' Rod Gilbert. "Hockey is a team game, right? One man is not supposed to beat a whole team, right? But what else can I say?" [60]

Until 1967, Boston had floundered in a six-team league, missing the playoffs eight straight years. It all changed when Orr debuted and when the Bruins "pulled off hockey's biggest heist"—a huge trade with Chicago that brought Phil Esposito, Ken Hodge, and Fred Stanfield. [61] Esposito turned into the big prize—a hulking forward that defenders found almost impossible to move from the slot. "I don't know how many goals he scored from eight feet or less," said NHL coach Harry Neale, "but it was a pile of them."[62] In 1970, Esposito collected 43 goals and 56 assists, and the next year would break the NHL record for goals in a season with 76.

The Bruins also got 20-goal seasons from Hodge, Stanfield, John Bucyk, and John McKenzie and scored the most goals in the league. Boston struggled a bit in the first round of the playoffs before dispatching the Rangers in six games but then really showed its muscle against Chicago in the division finals. The Blackhawks and Bruins had tied for the most points in the NHL, but Orr "moved through the Chicago club this series almost at will," as Boston swept in four straight.[63]

So the Stanley Cup Finals opened in St. Louis on May 3 with the young Blues definite underdogs, just as they had been the previous two years. After two blowout Boston victories by scores of 6–1 and 6–2, writers were beginning to call it another Boston Massacre. "They ought to give us danger pay," said Bowman, whose team let Orr and Esposito break records for playoff scoring. "Of course I'm unhappy, but I'm not depressed because I'm a realist."[64]

Boston easily won the third game 4–1 and now had a chance to clinch the Cup at home. "I don't want to take anything away from St. Louis, because they are a good hockey team," said Esposito, "but this final is anticlimactic, the same as last year after Montreal beat us. We've just got too good a hockey club."[65] Game 4 on Mother's Day, May 10, turned out to be the best one of the series, and the Blues even managed a 3–2 lead in the third period. But Bucyk scored midway through the period and now the game was headed to overtime tied at three. Bruins' coach Harry Sinden knew that most overtime games were settled quickly, and to keep St. Louis in check he wanted Orr on the ice.

Just 40 seconds into overtime, Orr flashed down the right wing and passed to Derek Sanderson behind the St. Louis goal. As Orr split defensemen Jean-Guy Talbot and Noel Picard, Sanderson fed him with a beautiful return pass. Orr took the give-and-go, and, just as he was tripped by Picard, slid a shot under Glenn Hall for the Cup-clinching goal. As the shot was released, Orr seemed to fly through the air as he jumped over Picard's stick. "I don't know what I did," he said later. "I saw it go in the net as I was flying through the air. Then I hit the ice and before I could get up the rest of the guys were on top of me."[66]

What he had done was not only win Boston's first Stanley Cup since 1941, but also provide one of the most iconic images in sports history. Photographer Ray Lussier of the now-defunct *Boston Record-American* was assigned a spot down at the other end of the ice by the Boston net, but like Sinden he figured things could end quickly. If the Bruins won, he wanted a close-up shot, so Lussier took a chance and walked down by the St. Louis goal where he found a vacated photography stool. Lussier didn't know who was supposed to be there, but he sat himself down in perfect position for Orr's winning goal. "I never would have got the picture if that other photographer didn't go running off to get a beer," he said. When the photographer returned, he complained that Lussier was in his spot. "I told him, 'It's all yours. I've got what I need.'"[67]

The photo was prominently featured in the *Record-American* and also appeared in most newspapers the next day—Orr about three feet in the air, his body parallel to the ice and with both arms over his head. As Picard looks on with disgust and a beaten Hall tries to regain his balance, Orr's face is a picture of pure jubilation, his mouth wide open to let loose in celebration. Behind this trio the crowd at the Boston Garden is already standing, arms similarly raised over heads, to celebrate the Cup-clinching goal.

Bobby Orr would go on to an incredible Hall of Fame career that may have ranked him as the greatest player of all time if not for a series of knee injuries that forced his early retirement. He changed the nature of defensive play, pulling defensemen out of their own end and into the offense. The 100-point seasons that became routine from later defenders such as Paul Coffey and Brian Leetch trace directly back to Orr, who still holds the single-season mark for defensemen with 139 points in 1971.

He also sparked a mini Bruins' dynasty. "This is the happiest day of my life," he said after the clinching win over St. Louis. "We have a hell of a team and let's hope we can do it all over again next year."[68] During that season, Orr swept all four major awards categories, taking home the league MVP, scoring title, Norris Trophy, and Conn Smythe Trophy for playoff MVP. Just two years later, Orr tallied 37 goals and 117 points in leading Boston to another Cup win, this time over the Rangers. He also took the Bruins to the finals in 1974, and ended his career a three-time league MVP.

Yet for all those accomplishments, it is that moment in 1970 when he flew through the air for which Orr is best remembered. There is something about it that suggests the perfect athletic moment—a player at the pinnacle of his power, soaring above the opposition to reach for greatness. In 2011, more than 40 years after the goal, it was voted by NHL fans as the greatest moment ever in Stanley Cup history. The year before, the moment had been immortalized outside the Bruins' arena with an 800-pound bronze statue. Harry Weber, ironically a St. Louis native, sculpted the piece, which also included the names of the Boston players from that Stanley Cup team.

Lussier sold the negative of that moment to a man named Dennis Brearley, a longtime newspaper photographer who in 1978 opened up a gallery of historical Boston images. Today, the Brearley Collection is run by his son Matt, and its centerpiece remains Lussier's picture of Orr in flight.

"People will come in and they remember the picture," said Matt Brearley. "It's the main attraction. A little kid might say, 'Oh, that guy's flyin'; he looks like Superman,' and the dad will say, 'That's Bobby Orr—he *is* Superman.'"[69]

THANKS, BUT NO THANKS

The fight between cities to host an Olympics has become a competition almost as entertaining as the games themselves. To land an Olympics brings prestige, international media attention, and, it is believed, a huge economic boost in terms of tourism dollars. Cities now prepare bids years ahead of time and make their best pitch to the International Olympic Committee (IOC), which makes the final decision. When a city is selected by the IOC, its citizens typically gather in joyous revelry to celebrate the moment, such as when Rio de Janeiro was picked to host the 2016 Summer Games. As thousands gathered at the famous Copacabana beach in Rio to hear the announcement, Brazilian president Luiz Inácio Lula da Silva was brought to tears with happiness.

A similar moment took place on May 13, 1970, when the IOC met in Amsterdam to award sites for the 1976 Games. The Summer Olympics were given to Montreal in a close vote over Moscow. Moscow led in the IOC voting through the first round, but after Los Angeles dropped out, Montreal gained enough support to carry the day, 41 votes to 28.

Montreal's selection hurt Vancouver, because that city was pushing for the Winter Olympics. Since the IOC didn't want both games in the same country in the same year,[70] Denver ultimately won the prize, edging out Sion, Switzerland, on the final ballot. The city had been pushing for an Olympic bid since 1954, and when the victorious Denver contingent returned home from the Netherlands, it was greeted with a brass band and a downtown parade. Mayor William McNichols said Denver would stage the games in the real meaning of the Olympic movement and profusely thanked those who had placed their faith in the city.

That faith would be severely tested in the coming years in light of the fact that the Winter Olympics never made it to Colorado.

In their rush to grab the Olympics, the members of the Denver Olympic Organizing Committee (DOOC) had overlooked several substantial issues. Denver, on the eastern slope of the Continental Divide, had a high elevation, but not adequate mountains for skiing and other alpine events. Those were west of the Rockies, more than 100 miles away. The DOOC had promised the IOC that all the events would be held within 45 minutes of the Olympic Village at the University of Denver, but one proposed venue in Steamboat Springs was more than 150 miles away, and a good three hours' travel given the conditions. Another proposed site, Mount Sniktau, wasn't good for skiing and typically didn't have enough snow cover.

To get Denver and the surrounding area ready for the games would also take a lot of construction, which did not sit well with either environmentalists or local homeowners. The Nordic events were to take place in Evergreen, Colorado, where residents found out that some construction would literally run through their backyards. Wrote *Sports Illustrated*, "The Denver Organizing Committee faces the embarrassment of manufacturing snow for the downhill racers, maybe cutting eight-foot gaps in private backyard fences for cross-country skiers, bulldozing an entire hillside for jumpers, [and] packing throngs of spectators into tiny locations."[71]

And then there was the issue of money. Olympic Games are always costly for the host city, which has to build infrastructure, including modern venues and adequate transportation. Even in 1970, the tab ran into the millions and had effectively crippled the economies of previous host nations, saddling them with enormous debt. Squaw Valley, California, which hosted the 1960 Winter Games, spent $13.5 million—more than 13 times original estimates—and ten years later the state of California was still trying to pay off an annual related debt of $300,000. The IOC wanted Denver and Colorado to share in the cost of the games—estimated at around $35 million—and made it clear that if they would not, the games would go elsewhere. The DOOC agreed, and with a pledge of some $17 million from the federal government, promised that the burden to Colorado taxpayers would not exceed $5 million. Colorado leaders, including McNichols and Governor John Love, pushed ahead despite the obstacles.

But they severely underestimated the growing opposition. "We got very complacent," said Sidney Bullene of the DOOC. "Nobody really realized we might lose this whole thing and disgrace ourselves in the eyes of the whole world."[72] The citizens of Evergreen created a protest group called Protect Our Mountain Environment, which appealed to environmentalists. Another group called Citizens for Colorado's Future (CCF) alarmed taxpayers by calling the $35 million cost unrealistic and way too low. Bumper stickers began to pop up—"Don't Olympicate Colorado," and "The Olympics—$100 Million Snow Job." The protest movement gained more legitimacy with the support of State Representative Richard Lamm, a Democrat from Denver who compared the Olympics to expensive dinosaurs.

Lamm and the CCF, which collected 77,000 signatures, were both instrumental in getting an initiative put on the state ballot in November 1972. The exact wording of the initiative was confusing in that a "yes" vote meant a rejection of funding the Olympics, while "no" would be a vote of support. State officials and DOOC members flew to Munich to assure worried IOC members that the vote was secure. "I can remember Bill McNichols and me telling them there was nothing to worry about," said Lieutenant Governor John Vanderhoof, "we were going to win it by 2-to-1. I sat there and told [them] that, and learned a hard lesson."[73]

In the same election in which Richard Nixon overwhelmed George McGovern in the presidential race, Colorado voters rejected the Olympics by a similarly impressive margin. The final vote total was 514,228 to 350,964, which comes out to a whopping three-to-two margin. Governor Love said the result made clear that the people didn't want the games, and the Denver Olympics were officially dead. Salt Lake City made a hasty pitch, but the IOC felt that given the late hour it needed a site with previous experience, so it chose Innsbruck, Austria, which had hosted the Winter Games in 1964.

The U.S. Olympic movement, and especially the DOOC, was mortified. Henry Kimbrough, director of Citizens for the 1976 Winter Olympics, called it "a tremendously poor reflection on the United States. We've frequently heard the term 'Ugly American.' We'll, we've proved it again. We've said 'no' to the world."[74] Clifford Buck, president of the U.S. Olympic Committee, was no less angry. "I think it's a tragedy for the state and a tragedy for the nation that the people of Colorado were not aware of the great privilege and great honor to host the 1976 Winter Games."[75] To date, Denver is the only site that has ever refused an invitation to host an Olympic Games.[76]

But in the long run, was it truly a tragedy? In one sense, Denver has had trouble getting serious consideration for future games, and its expression of interest in hosting the 2018 Winter Games was shot down, but the IOC insists there are no grudges held. The growth and despoiling of the environment that many feared—condo developments, strip malls, and ski resorts—came anyway without the Olympics, proving that banks and developers were a much tougher enemy than the DOOC.

Financially, Colorado's decision still makes sense. It took 30 years for Montreal to pay off the debt just on its new Olympic Stadium—derisively called "The Big Owe"—and other cost overruns gave the 1976 Summer Games the name "the Bankrupt Olympics."[77] London spent $15 billion on its Summer Games in 2012, and while an official government report in Great Britain called it a great economic success, many objective observers complained that the report amounted to a whitewash.

The IOC, which once had salivating cities lining up for a chance to host the games, now often has to go begging. When consideration for the 2022 Summer Games began in earnest, Oslo, Norway, dropped out after politicians declined to give financial support, and Krakow, Poland, said no thanks after 70 percent of residents rejected the bid in a referendum. When Lviv, Ukraine, pulled its bid over security concerns, it became "the third contender to drop out of the race for a games that no one seems to want."[78]

Still, there is something about the prestige of hosting an Olympic Games that keeps Denver calling. In addition to the abbreviated attempt to land the 2018 Games, Denver officials are now talking about a formal application for the 2022 Winter Olympics. A group of Colorado business, health care, tourism, and political leaders are now considering whether to move forward in the bidding process. "The opportunity to pursue the

Games is an endeavor worth taking very seriously," said Governor John Hickenlooper in 2012. "We've asked this exploratory committee to explore all issues relevant to Denver potentially submitting a bid."[79]

If they do win the bid, chances are this time they won't give it back.

6

JUNE

"HIGH AS A GEORGIA PINE"

June was not a good month for the San Diego Padres, but then again, neither was April nor May. The Padres were only in their second year of existence and, after losing 110 games in 1969, were on their way to another difficult season. San Diego would lose 99 games in 1970, with poor hitting the main culprit. Aside from Nate Colbert, who belted 38 home runs, and Cito Gaston, who hit .318, the Padres ranked near the bottom of the National League in hits, runs, and batting average.

They also led the league in striking out, and on April 22 whiffed ten consecutive times against Tom Seaver of the Mets, a record that still stands. Seaver struck out the last ten hitters, 19 for the game, and allowed only two hits in a 2–1 win. Gaston, Van Kelly, and Jerry Morales each fanned three times. "He was like a machine," marveled Mets' first baseman Ed Kranepool of Seaver. "Whump, whump, whump."[1]

On June 12 the Padres opened a series at home against the Pittsburgh Pirates, who had Dock Ellis scheduled to pitch. Just ten days before, Ellis had beaten San Diego 5–1, going the distance and limiting the Padres to six hits. Twenty-five years old at the time, Ellis was a promising right-hander who had the reputation as a hothead and an agitator, often criticizing what he perceived as racism in baseball. "I was outspoken," he admitted. "Baseball wasn't ready for me."[2]

What only a few people knew was that Ellis had a serious dependency on drugs.

It started in Gardena, California, where Ellis was found in the high school bathroom drinking wine and getting high. School administrators told him he wouldn't get kicked out if he played for the baseball team. Arrested for grand theft auto shortly before signing a contract with the Pirates, Ellis began drinking more heavily in the minors and began popping more pills. How many did he take during a game? "Who knows?" he said. "I just reached into a bag until I got tired."[3]

He said he needed it all to deal with the stress of trying to reach the majors, and Ellis sure showed the signs of stress. During his minor league career he chased a heckler in the stands with a baseball bat, and when he got sent down to Macon, Georgia, he claimed he was being punished for the length of his hair. In 1968 he was called up to the Pirates. He was also addicted to amphetamines.

With a lifetime record of 21–26, and a season mark of just 4–4, Ellis was still not considered a major league star as the Pirates prepared for their series with the Padres. The team landed in San Diego on Thursday, June 11, and Ellis headed for the home of a friend's girlfriend. "We had the day off so I took LSD at the airport," he said. "She asked, 'What's wrong with you?' I said, 'I'm high as a Georgia pine.' The next day, what I thought was the next day, she said, 'You better get up, you've got to pitch today.' I said, 'What are you talking about? I don't pitch until tomorrow. Because I had gotten up in the middle of the morning and took more acid. She brought me the paper and showed me [that I was starting], and I said, 'Oh, wow. What happened to yesterday?'"[4]

Ellis reportedly got more drugs at the ballpark, including the amphetamine Benzedrine, and sitting in the dugout before the first game of a doubleheader he could feel his teammates looking at him. He suspected they knew he was high, but his behavior did not seem out of the ordinary, at least for Dock Ellis. Second baseman Bill Mazeroski later said he had no idea if Ellis was on drugs, admitting only that the pitcher usually behaved oddly.

As the game progressed, Ellis was not pitching sharply but still managed to retire the hitters. It was a difficult job considering that he was hallucinating, imagining Jimi Hendrix in the batter's box and Richard Nixon as the umpire calling balls and strikes. After one play in which he covered first base to record the out, he was convinced that he had just scored a touchdown.

Aided by a pair of home runs from Willie Stargell and a sensational defensive play by Mazeroski that took away a hit in the seventh, Ellis carried a no-hitter into the ninth. Despite walking eight batters and hitting another, he finished the job by striking out the last batter in a 2–0 win. "You're supposed to mature at 21," he told reporters in the noisy clubhouse. "I'm four years late."[5]

The no-hitter promoted Ellis from prospect to bona fide star. He finished 13–10 in 1970 and then, after a terrific start the next season, started the All-Star Game, where he got the loss and gave up a mammoth home run to Oakland's Reggie Jackson. Despite suffering an injury late in the season he had a record of 19–9 and helped the Pirates win the World Series. To most baseball writers and fans, Dock Ellis had turned a corner.

Except that he never stopped taking drugs.

"It was easy to pitch on LSD because I was so used to medicating myself," he admitted. "That's the way I was dealing with the fear of failure; the fear of losing, the fear of winning. It was part of the game. You get to the major leagues and you say, 'I got to stay here; what do I need?'"[6]

Attempting to enter Pittsburgh's Three Rivers Stadium in 1972, Ellis appeared drunk and was maced by a security guard. In 1974, he faced Pete Rose, Joe Morgan, and Dan Driessen in the first inning and deliberately hit them with pitches. After a trade to the Yankees, he blasted owner George Steinbrenner and earned himself another trade, this time to Oakland. He was labeled a malcontent, a big mouth, and a head case. "What's wrong is his head," wrote New York columnist Dick Young. "It's not screwed on right. He is profane, even bigoted, churlish, troublesome and irreverent."[7] When his career finally ended in 1979 with a lifetime record of 138–117, Ellis was labeled an underachiever—someone who could have been so much more if only he had worked harder.

Those perceptions changed when Ellis started to come clean with his drug problem. He was hospitalized for dependency in 1980, and then in 1984 he confessed to using drugs in the no-hitter. Even more details came out in 1989 with the second edition of *Dock Ellis in the Country of Baseball*, cowritten by Ellis and future U.S. poet laureate Donald Hall.

Baseball reacted with a mixture of fear and loathing. "That's crazy," said Tony Bartirome, who was a trainer with the Pirates during the Ellis years. "I don't know why he's saying that, but if he was standing right here, I'd tell him to his face what a liar he is."[8] The *Los Angeles Times* said that Dock Ellis boasting about pitching a no-hitter under the influence of LSD showed "he does not care about the drug problems in sports."[9]

Baseball, it seemed, now understood. Ellis was not simply a crazy, misunderstood guy who threw at players' heads or showed up at the ballpark in hair curlers—he was a drug abuser, capital D, capital A. So there would be no helping hand from baseball, but rather a finger figuratively poked in Ellis's eye.

Like certain parts of American society in the 1960s, baseball had a growing problem with drugs. While some players like Ellis may have experimented with the harder stuff, the bigger issue was stimulants such as Benzedrine, Dexedrine, or other amphetamines that players took as a means of providing quick pick-me-ups during the long season. By the time Ellis threw his no-hitter, common amphetamines in baseball were known as "greenies" and "a lot of players couldn't function without them."[10] Pitcher Pat Dobson said of one game, "I had to pitch with the flu, so I took a greenie and pitched a shutout. If [Commissioner Bowie] Kuhn says we can't use them, well, I just want to see him put on a uniform for 162 games in 180 days and see what he says then."[11]

As baseball's drug dependency gradually became public knowledge, Kuhn took a very hard line. When pitcher Ferguson Jenkins was arrested for cocaine possession in 1980, he did not wait for the outcome of any potential trial but suspended Jenkins for the rest of the season. In his letter to Jenkins, Kuhn said he would be willing to reconsider the suspension if Jenkins agreed to respond fully to questioning, suggesting that the commissioner was interested in casting a wider net in search of other users.

The net would eventually grow to include some of the most accomplished and publicized stars in the game, many of whom would testify in a shocking trial that showed just how pervasive drug use in baseball really was. In 1985, the players appeared before a Pittsburgh grand jury and were granted immunity in exchange for their testimony against drug dealers. Their testimony was compelling, to say the least. The Pirates' Dave Parker said two dealers were so well known to the team that one flew on road trips and the other attended a team party. Commissioner Peter Ueberroth suspended 11 players and allowed others to play only after drug-related community service and random drug testing. When two years later Ueberroth claimed baseball was free from drugs, one of the suspended players, Lonnie Smith, called the statement "a joke and a farce."[12]

Not long after Smith's comments, baseball entered the steroid era, a period that saw flagrant use of harmful, undetectable performance-enhancing drugs. Ken Caminiti, who had never hit more than 13 homers in a season, saw his home run totals jump to 18, 26, and finally 40 in 1996 when he won MVP honors in the National League. "It's no secret what's going on in baseball," Caminiti said later when he admitted to using steroids. "At least half the guys are using steroids. They talk about it. They joke about it with each other. I've got nothing to hide."[13] Caminiti died from drug complications at the age of 41.

Ken Caminiti was the first baseball player to publicly admit to steroid use, which seemed to open up a Pandora's box. Books chronicling rampant steroid use were published, and they implicated some of the game's biggest stars, including Barry Bonds and Mark McGwire. Congressional hearings in 2006 and baseball's own Mitchell Report in 2007 further confirmed that the problem only seemed to be spreading while baseball hid its head in the sand. A limited form of drug testing was approved by baseball and its players' union, but as of 2015 the problem is still very real.

What has transpired over the past generation in baseball has somewhat rehabilitated the image of Dock Ellis. After his 1980 stay in drug rehab, he became a drug counselor, working with patients in California and at a prison in Pittsburgh. He counseled minor leaguers against drug abuse and helped troubled Yankees pitcher Pascual Perez try to beat his addiction. "The guy had special leadership qualities," baseball executive Dennis Gilbert said. "He was always telling people, 'Don't mess up the way I did,' and they'd listen."[14]

Sadly, it was too late for Ellis himself. The years of drinking and drugs had taken a toll, and in December 2008 he died at the age of 63 of complications from cirrhosis. Of all his accomplishments, both inside of baseball and out, certainly the most defining is the night in June of 1970 that he threw a no-hitter on LSD.

Or did he?

"Dock could have done it," said Al Oliver, a teammate on the field with him that night. "I wasn't shocked about it. I'm not that familiar with how LSD affects a person, but I understand that you have trouble standing up, let alone pitching a ballgame.

"Dock had the talent to get away with it."[15]

BRIAN'S SONG

He received only two football scholarship offers coming out of high school and the team he chose went 6–24 during his three-year career. His skills and reputation were so underwhelming that after leading the nation in rushing and scoring his senior year, no pro team drafted him, even with separate AFL and NFL drafts at the time. He tried out as a free agent, finally made it, and then his team had three losing seasons in four years.

By June 1970, Brian Piccolo had been overcoming obstacles his entire life.

A six-foot, 200-pound high school star from Ft. Lauderdale, Florida, Piccolo was not considered fast enough to make it as a college running back. He got to Wake Forest only because the school was interested in a high school teammate and his coach convinced them to give Piccolo a chance. After sitting out his first year because freshmen were ineligible, Piccolo played sparingly the next two seasons. "We played 20 games and lost 19," he said. "There's a good reason why I didn't have any statistics—we never had the ball."[16]

But Piccolo still made his presence felt in a telling incident. When Maryland visited in 1963, the Terps had the Atlantic Coast Conference's first black player, Darryl Hill. Hill had been subjected to terrible abuse that season and the situation at Wake was just as tense. Before the game, Piccolo came over to the Maryland sideline and put his arm around Hill's shoulder. "When he did that," said Maryland assistant coach Lee Corso, "it got eerie silent and there wasn't another word that day about Darryl."[17]

Piccolo finally made his mark his senior year in 1964, leading the nation in rushing and scoring with 1,044 yards and 15 touchdowns. He helped Wake Forest to a 5–5 record, not bad for a school that won only one game the previous two years, and won ACC Player of the Year honors. But none of that was enough to make a difference in the draft. On the same day the Jets offered top pick Joe Namath of Alabama a record contract worth around $400,000, Piccolo sat through the entire draft—all 450 picks and 20 rounds from NFL and AFL teams—without having his name called. Piccolo had hopes of signing as a free agent with Green Bay and Vince Lombardi, but the Bears made the strongest push, and owner/ coach George Halas was so happy to get Piccolo that he held a news conference at the swank Mid-America Club in Chicago's Prudential Building to announce the signing. "I don't know what made the Old Man do it," Piccolo said of the news conference. "Naturally, the big question was why hadn't I been drafted?"[18]

The Bears draft in 1965 included Gale Sayers and Dick Butkus, and Piccolo watched from the practice squad as the two stars began their Hall of Fame careers. Piccolo called Butkus the most complete football player he had ever known, but it was Sayers, named the NFL's Rookie of the Year that season, who would have the greatest impact on his life and career.

When Piccolo finally made the team in 1966 he carried only three times all season and played mostly special teams, but he continued to impress Halas with his desire and work ethic. He got more time at running back in 1967, rushing for 317 yards and catching another 13 passes. More importantly, that season he began rooming with Sayers, making them the first players to integrate the Bears. "I had never had a close relationship with a white person before," Sayers said, "except maybe George Halas, and Pick had never really known a black person. I remember him telling me that he wondered at first, 'Are they really different?'"[19]

When the Bears made the choice to integrate they wanted Sayers to room with running back Ronnie Bull, but Sayers instead chose Piccolo. It was an interesting choice considering the star Sayers knew little about the backup, other than that Piccolo had a sense of humor. "There was something about Brian," Sayers admitted. "I don't know what it was, but he could call you 'nigger' and you'd know he was kidding. A black guy on the team, he can call anybody a nigger, but Pic was the only white guy who could get away with it. We never had much of a racial problem on the Bears, and Pic went about it backwards, but he really made things better."[20]

When Sayers tore up a knee against San Francisco in 1968 and feared his career was over, Piccolo was there to help him through the difficult rehabilitation. After Sayers returned from his injury, Piccolo moved to fullback and for a while the two started in the same backfield. In 1968, Piccolo had his best season, rushing for 450 yards, catching 28 passes, and scoring a couple of touchdowns. But by the fall of 1969 it was becoming obvious that something was wrong. First, Piccolo developed a cough, and then he began having trouble breathing. Finally, on November 16 he removed himself from the game against Atlanta. A stunning diagnosis followed—embryonal cell cancer that had spread into his chest. Immediate surgery and chemotherapy followed.

The Bears, and especially Sayers, visited him in the hospital as much as they could. "He showed me his scar," said Sayers, "[and] it made my knee look like nothing. Brian's attitude after the operation was so phenomenal it made me feel all the worse about how I had acted just after my knee surgery. Here was Brian Piccolo, after probably the most critical moment in his whole life, in fine spirits, cool and hopeful and so positive about things."[21]

But no amount of positivity could stop the disease. "What does a football player do who can't play football?" mused Piccolo."[22] Another operation followed in May 1970, and now it wasn't a matter of playing again, it was a matter of life and death. At an awards ceremony to honor Sayers as the Most Courageous Athlete for his comeback from the knee injury, he told the crowd, "Brian Piccolo is the man of courage who should receive this award. It is mine tonight. It is Brian Piccolo's tomorrow. I love Brian Piccolo and I'd like all of you to love him too."[23]

The end came three weeks later on June 16. Brian Piccolo was 26 years old.

Much has been said and written about the short life of Brian Piccolo. Parks, scholarships, and awards have been named in his honor. He has been held up as the ultimate example of courage in the face of death. Sayers wrote in his own autobiography that "my life was enriched by Brian Piccolo's friendship, by his warmth, and his love."[24]

All of it is true, but sometimes such analyses miss the forest for the trees. Over the years, Piccolo has been turned into a maudlin symbol, particularly through two immensely popular movies, both called *Brian's Song*. Such treatments tend to sanctify Piccolo and obscure the most basic elements of the man. He was sorry that Sayers got hurt but also admitted that he was happy to get the chance to play. When Sayers returned, Piccolo's pride would not let him simply head happily back to the bench. "When training camp opens I feel I'm going back as the regular. I started the last five games of the season and I think I proved I can do the job."[25] And while he did put on a brave face for family and friends while in the hospital, he knew the situation he was in and it scared him. "Can you believe this, Joy?" he asked his wife when he found out his condition. "Can you believe this is happening to me?"[26]

Frustration, fear, disappointment. Piccolo had overcome them all to play the game he loved. He just could not beat the last one.

"I think I fulfilled my real ambition in pro football," he said not long before he died. "My idea of success is to be established, to know that I could play for almost anybody, to have the respect around the league of other players and coaches. This I felt I accomplished.

"Of course, I didn't plan on having it end this soon."[27]

THE BLACK PEARL

While baseball dominated the headlines for most of June, the biggest sports story of the month was virtually ignored in the United States. The ninth annual World Cup tournament, a four-year gathering of the best national soccer teams in the world, was taking place in Mexico. Sixteen teams, including the host Mexicans and defending champions from England, took part in the month-long tournament.

The competition did not include a team from the United States.

The history of international soccer in the United States goes back to the 19th century, and the Americans won both the silver and bronze medals at the 1904 Olympics in St. Louis. The United States finished third in the 1930 World Cup in Uruguay, and then in 1950 recorded what is considered by many the greatest upset in the history of sports, beating a powerful English team 1–0 in a Cup match in Brazil. The Americans were part-time amateurs who practiced after work or on weekends, while the English were culled from the best professional teams in Europe. The soccer world reacted with disbelief, and legend has it that at first English newspapers were reluctant to print the score because they believed it to be a typo—they thought England had won 10–0.

The upset barely registered in the United States. Of the 400 reporters covering the World Cup that year, only one was from America. "The only person who met me at the airport when we flew [back] was my wife," said Walter Bahr, a high school teacher from Philadelphia who was a U.S. center back.[28] In the television age, soccer was simply too slow to attract much American interest. Boxing, baseball, and later football ideally fit the television screen and came to define U.S. sports in the electronic era.

After the win over England, no American team would even qualify for a World Cup for the next 40 years.

But American soccer interests were determined to keep trying. In 1967, FIFA (the Fédération Internationale de Football Association), which sanctioned the World Cup, started a professional league called the United Soccer Association. It soon combined with the much smaller National Professional Soccer League to form the North American Soccer League (NASL), which featured 17 teams during the 1968 season. From the outset, the NASL was beset with problems, including not enough American players, low attendance, and financial issues. Television ratings were so bad that CBS canceled its NASL contract; by 1970 the league was down to just five teams.

As soccer interest was dwindling to almost nothing in the United States, it was peaking elsewhere as teams gathered for the World Cup in Mexico. Most of the attention centered on Brazil and its superstar, Edson Arantes do Nascimento, better known as Pelé. Pelé began playing for the Brazilian Santos team at age 15 and the next year joined the Brazilian national team. His combination of strength, fluidity, and goal scoring, along with an engaging personality, turned him into an international superstar. He was the "Black Pearl," a man for whom Nigerians called a cease-fire in the midst of their brutal civil war so they could watch him play in an exhibition match.

After leading Brazil to the World Cup title in 1958, professional offers from around the world began to pour in for the "wonder forward. The bidding for him won't start under half a million dollars, and how much he will eventually realize is anyone's guess."[29] But even as his Santos club was becoming rich by showcasing Pelé in international matches, the government of Brazil declared him an "official national treasure" to prevent him from leaving the country to play with another team. Not that it mattered much to Pelé, at least financially. A Brazilian magazine pegged his salary at around $720,000 annually, which included salary, endorsements, and outside business interests.

Such was Pelé's ability and reputation that defenders found the only way to stop him was through rough play. Brazil managed to win another Cup in 1962, but both that year and in 1966 Pelé was severely limited by injury because of hard fouls. In 1966, Brazil never made it out of the first round and afterward it was announced that Pelé would not play in future Cup matches because the rugged play of opposing teams made it impossible for him to play. A newspaper account of Brazil's 3–1 loss to Portugal reported that Pelé "was chopped to the ground by a defender in a savage tackle. The injury left him out of the game for the last 60 minutes."[30]

The retirement did not last long, whether it was a change of heart on the part of the Brazilian government, the entreaties of coach Mario Zagallo, or simply Pelé's own competitiveness and love for the game. It also helped that for the 1970 World Cup, FIFA had approved the use of red and yellow cards, which included the possibility of ejecting flagrant offenders, as a means of curbing rough play. Stricter officiating also cleaned up the play, and no players were actually ejected during the tournament.

The Brazilians had stormed through qualifying matches the previous year, winning all six games and outscoring opponents by a combined score of 23–2. Pelé played with his usual brilliance, scoring five goals, but the real star was Tostão, who notched six goals in the six games. The Brazilians came to Mexico on May 1, the first of the finalists to arrive, and spent a month under strict training, protected by private guards. They had more than 250 crates of equipment, food, and medicine shipped in as part of their regimen.

Brazil was placed in group three with the defending champion England, and the two teams met in the second game. In the second half, English keeper Gordon Banks made a stop that Pelé called the greatest he had ever seen. Pelé had already started to celebrate his perfectly timed header when Banks appeared from nowhere to knock the ball over the crossbar. Brazil still managed to win the game, 1–0, on a goal by Jairzinho. After the breathtaking match, a shirtless Pelé swapped jerseys with Banks as a sign of respect.

Jairzinho was quickly becoming yet another Brazilian star of the tournament, and by the time it was over he had scored a goal in every game, an unheard-of feat that earned him the nickname "The Hurricane." Brazil stormed through group play unbeaten and kept its mastery going through the quarterfinals and semifinals. In the quarters against Peru, both Tostão and Jairzinho scored in a 4–2 win, and in the semifinals Brazil knocked off Uruguay 3–1. The wins set up a World Cup Final against Italy.

The final was played before 112,504 fans at Azteca Stadium in Mexico City on June 21, and they were treated to another graceful exhibition of soccer from the Brazilians. Pelé opened the scoring with a header in the 18th minute and then Brazil clinched the Cup with rapid-fire goals in the second half. Jairzinho scored his seventh goal in six games, and then Carlos Alberto added what many called the "wonder goal" of World Cup play, streaking down the right side and blasting a perfectly timed kick in the far side of the net. After Brazil's impressively easy 4–1 win, fans rushed the pitch to carry off on their shoulders Pelé, named the winner of the Golden Ball Trophy as the tournament's most outstanding player. "He had his clothes ripped off him. Tiny Tostão raced across the field followed by supporters who had torn off his shirt. The crowd [also] tore off his shorts."[31]

To those who had watched the match in person, or for the estimated 800 million that had watched on television around the world, something sublime had happened, as if the Brazilians had elevated the play of the entire sport. "The Brazilians played as if they had wings," said Italian coach Ferruccio Valcareggi, and few could disagree.[32] Brazil had won 12 straight games—six in the qualifying round and six at the finals—and in Mexico outscored its opponents by 19 goals to seven. By winning the World Cup for a record third time they also earned permanent possession of the Jules Rimet Trophy.

Even today, both the 1970 World Cup and the performance of the Brazilian team are revered by soccer historians. Italy's 4–3 semifinal win over West Germany was voted by a panel of experts from *World Soccer* magazine as the greatest single match in World Cup history. In the same poll, the 1970 Brazilians were voted the greatest team of all time, their play of "such style [that they] have become a myth, a team to be held up as the ultimate exponents of the beautiful game."[33] Others hailed them as "a team that raised the game to a level of panache and elegance that outstripped even their own renowned standards."[34]

At the head of the class, of course, was Pelé. Now 30 years old, he announced his retirement from World Cup play and played his last international match in 1971. His incredible totals are world records in almost every category: 1,283 goals in 1,367 games, 77 international goals, 92 hat tricks, and four goals in a game no fewer than 30 times. He had seemingly accomplished everything there was to do in the world of soccer.

Except conquer America.

The NASL was still hanging on, just barely, at the time of Brazil's historic run through the World Cup. That same year, the New York Cosmos team was founded and began play in the NASL in 1971. Almost from the time the team kicked its first ball, owners Ahmet and Nesuhi Ertegun had sought to bring Pelé to New York, reasoning that the world's most famous soccer player should be able to pump some life into the moribund American sport. Complications from his contract with Santos made negotiations difficult until Pelé finally retired from the Brazilian team in 1974 after 19 seasons. The contract he signed with the Cosmos was eye-popping—three years for $4.7 million, or about $20 million today—and helped convince the 34-year-old star to come out of retirement yet again.

Cosmos' officials knew they were not getting the dynamic scoring "Black Pearl" of Pelé's youth, and were quick to note that Pelé was not being paid just to play soccer. He was brought in to be a goodwill ambassador and perhaps lift American soccer to a place equal with football or baseball. "I reminded him that he had conquered the world," said Cosmos general manager Clive Toye when Pelé signed his contract, "but the single greatest marketplace is North America and he hasn't tapped that yet."[35]

That signing took place on June 10, 1975, before hundreds of media members at the 21 Club in New York. A few days later he played in his first match, an exhibition meant merely to introduce the new star, but Pelé flashed both his ability and his drawing power. In a 2–2 tie with the Dallas Tornado, he scored one goal and assisted on another. More importantly, the game drew more than 21,000 fans to New York's Downing Stadium, a dumpy old relic on Randall's Island, as chants of "Pelé! Pelé!" rang across the East River. Another 20,000 showed up in Philadelphia just to see him introduced in street clothes. Every time he had a chance to address the crowd Pelé would say the same thing: "I came to your country because I realized I was the only one who could help soccer here. Spread the news that soccer has finally arrived in the U.S."[36]

For a while, it certainly worked. Ten million people watched that first exhibition match on television, and by the following season the league had secured a national contract with ABC. Cosmos' home attendance tripled in that first season, and the team eventually moved to modern Giants Stadium in New Jersey where it was not unusual for the team to draw crowds of 40,000. The Cosmos enticed other international superstars, such as Franz Beckenbauer of West Germany and Giorgio Chinaglia of Italy, and by Pelé's last season in 1977 won the NASL championship.

In October of that same year, Pelé closed out his career in an exhibition match between the Cosmos and his former Santos team before 76,000 fans at Giants Stadium. Playing one half for each side, Pelé scored his final goal on a free kick as the Cosmos won 2–1. Afterward, as he was lifted on the shoulders of several Cosmos' players and carried around the field, he carried a Brazilian flag in one hand and a U.S. flag in the other. "I am very happy to be with you at this moment in my life," Pelé said to the crowd. "I want to ask you in this moment when the world looks to me, to take more attention to the kids all over the world. We need them so much." He then asked the crowd to repeat the word "love" with him three times, which they did, and then he said, "Thank you very much."[37]

The next year, even without Pelé, the Cosmos won the title again before more than 73,000 home fans, and by the end of the decade overall league attendance had increased 8 percent. It seemed Pelé had done exactly what he set out to do, and earned every penny the Cosmos had paid him.

But the shine soon wore off. Giddy with the Pelé success, the NASL had grown too far, too fast, and added too many teams that weren't on solid footing. By 1980, the league was bleeding money, and even the relatively wealthy Cosmos found it difficult to pay all those high-priced imports such as Beckenbauer and Chinaglia. Trying to compete with the Cosmos, teams started running up debts of millions of dollars, and after the 1984 season the NASL finally called it quits.

Professional soccer in America has moved in fits and starts since then. At one point, there was a pinball-like indoor league because organizers figured fans wanted to see more scoring. The most current incarnation is Major League Soccer, which in 2015 had 19 fairly stable clubs in the United States and Canada. Thanks in part to a television contract with ABC/ESPN and then NBC, as well as assorted marketing deals such as uniform sponsorships, the league has shown signs of financial stability and even growth. Much like the NASL did with Pelé, the MLS lured English superstar David Beckham of Manchester United and Real Madrid to the United States. Like Pelé, Beckham earned a huge salary and brought championships to his team, the Los Angeles Galaxy.

Given the rather middling success of professional soccer in the United States, one could argue that Pelé had little impact on the American game, but that ignores his effect on youth soccer. Up to the 1970 World Cup, American Little League sports programs were most heavily concentrated in football, baseball, and basketball. The success of the Brazilian national team, and especially Pelé's triumphant tour with the Cosmos, inspired a new generation of kids to play soccer. According to U.S. Youth Soccer, registration for the organization increased from 103,000 in 1974 to 810,000 in 1980. That number doubled by 1990 and nearly doubled again just five years later.[38]

It took a while for what Pelé started to bloom, but soon FIFA noticed the astounding growth and awarded the 1994 World Cup to the United States.[39] The total attendance of nearly 3.6 million and the average attendance of 69,000 are still World Cup records. Fittingly, Brazil won its fourth Cup, beating Italy in a penalty shootout, 3–2.

Brazil over Italy in the finals had a familiar ring, for it was those same two teams that had met in Mexico City in June 1970 in what is still considered the best World Cup ever played. If anything, the achievements and impact of Pelé and the Brazilians are even more appreciated today. Their brilliance, like that of a black pearl, only increases over time.

BASEBALL'S BLACK EYE

Only a year into his tenure as commissioner, Bowie Kuhn already had the reputation of someone who would go to great lengths to protect what he called "the best interests of baseball." Kuhn and his allies saw him as the guardian of the game and someone not afraid to take swift action to protect baseball's integrity. Those on the wrong end of Kuhn's often arbitrary decisions called him "stiff-necked, hammer-handed, and uncompromising."[40] He had a long-running feud with Oakland A's owner Charley Finley, who publicly called him the village idiot.

In other words, Kuhn did not lack for stubbornness or enemies, as would become quite evident in June 1970. It all came to light in a showdown between the puritanical Kuhn and iconoclastic pitcher Jim Bouton, author of the book *Ball Four*.

Ball Four was Bouton's diary of the 1969 season when he pitched for the expansion Seattle Pilots and the Houston Astros. A successful pitcher with the New York Yankees who won 21 games in 1963 and two games in the 1964 World Series, Bouton suffered an arm injury that severely reduced his effectiveness. Eventually landing with the woeful Pilots and then traded to Houston, Bouton recorded his observations of the season in a diary.

The idea of a player writing a diary book was not new, as evidenced by *The Long Season*, Jim Brosnan's account of the 1959 season he pitched for the St. Louis Cardinals and Cincinnati Reds. Brosnan's work was hailed by critics as "crisp, compact and expressive. [Brosnan] put the same effort into sentence structure as he did into his slider."[41] Brosnan attempted to portray players accurately, as opposed to the fawning and idolatrous coverage they usually received.

But while the book became a best seller, it barely registered a blip on the baseball Richter scale. Perhaps it was the timing, as Vietnam, civil unrest, and various liberation movements had yet to take hold in 1960. Perhaps it was the fact that Brosnan did not seek to become an instigator, but merely wanted to give readers an honest look at baseball. "I wasn't aware I was breaking any taboos or attacking the establishment," he said. "Or feel as if I were a social revolutionary."[42] For whatever reason, *The Long Season* would be always be considered a superior artistic work but would have nowhere near the cultural impact of its younger cousin.

That cousin debuted on June 24 and immediately became a national sensation. In lurid detail, Bouton described players who were obsessed with foul language, sexual promiscuity, and voyeurism. It wasn't quite a no-holds-barred portrayal—Bouton admitted that he withheld some of the more salacious material to protect the players' marriages—but it was enough to make the players seem like little more than emotionally stunted adolescents. That many of the stories and quotes came from players who either didn't even know Bouton was writing a book or felt he had invaded their private lives only added to the controversy.

Before the book came out, several excerpts appeared in *Look* magazine, which was enough for Bowie Kuhn to call in Bouton for a special meeting. The commissioner, always looking for a place to wield his disciplinary hammer, realized he had little legal recourse other than to give Bouton a stern lecture about not doing it again. If one believes Bouton, the commissioner also asked for a signed statement repudiating the book as a pack of lies. "When I politely told the Commissioner what he could do with his statement, he turned a color which went very nicely with the wood paneling. He then spent the next three hours extracting a promise that I would never reveal what went on at our meeting."[43]

Much to the commissioner's dismay and Bouton's good fortune, the meeting and advance publicity only made the interest in *Ball Four* that much greater. It became a quick best seller and interviews with Bouton appeared in newspapers, television, and radio. But not all the publicity was good, especially from the players about whom Bouton had written. They could not complain about the truthfulness of the book, but many were upset that he had violated what they called "the sanctity of the clubhouse" by exposing their private behavior. They were also angry about his less than flattering portrayals of several baseball heroes, including Yankee icon Mickey Mantle. "Jim Bouton is a very selfish and self-centered man," said Elston Howard, a former Yankees teammate of Bouton and Mantle. "He got angry with the Yankees for trading him. No matter what he says, he wrote in anger."[44] Sportswriters called him a "social leper," while players taunted him from the dugout yelling, "Fuck you, Shakespeare!"[45]

Still, Bouton remained defiant, saying that the players who turned on him hadn't read the book. He never backed down and never apologized for *Ball Four*, even at the height of the controversy. "I'm glad I wrote the book," he told reporters after his meeting with Kuhn. "I did it because I wanted to entertain people, and I did it because I wanted things told from the inside, and because—let's not kid ourselves—I wanted to make some money."[46]

Bouton also admitted that there was very much a part of him that was a provocateur—someone who wanted to shake things up. Even as a successful pitcher, Bouton had always seemed out of step with baseball, and in one of his later books referred to himself as a "deviant," saying, "[Other players] think I'm weird and throw a weird pitch. What I ought to do is take up chewing tobacco and let the dark brown run down the front of my uniform, and say things like 'shit' and 'let's get these guys.' Then, instead of being weird, I'd be rough and tough."[47]

Ball Four gave Jim Bouton a fame that far outstripped what he accomplished as a pitcher. Sent down to the minors a month after the book came out, Bouton instead decided to retire. He unretired at age 39 to pitch in a comeback with the Atlanta Braves, and finally left the game for good in 1978. After ten major league seasons, Bouton finished with 62 victories and a losing record.

After the initial meeting with Kuhn, Bouton said he had no plans to write any more books, but four more followed. None of them had the impact of *Ball Four*, especially on the practice of sports journalism. Before the book came out, sportswriters and sports organizations had an unwritten understanding that they would publish nothing private or unflattering. There is a story, possibly apocryphal, of reporters covering Babe Ruth during the baseball star's height of popularity in the 1920s. While the team was riding the train between cities Ruth ran through one of the cars stark naked. Right behind Ruth was a similarly naked woman chasing him with a knife. One reporter who witnessed the scene turned to another and said, "It's a good thing we didn't see that, otherwise we'd have to report on it."[48]

For better or worse, *Ball Four* ended that type of reporting forever. Part of it was due to the book's overwhelming commercial success, including more than 5 million copies sold in hardcover and paperback. Robert Lipsyte of the *New York Times* called it the "most important sports book ever written [and] the best piece of sports journalism ever written."[49] It turned out that fans really wanted the truth, salacious as it was, rather than a sanitized version that Bouton called "the milk and cookies image."[50]

Part of it also was that once the truth got out there was no stuffing it back in the box and going back to a simpler time. Players who had been critical of Bouton and *Ball Four*, such as Mickey Mantle and Pete Rose, soon rushed to publish their own tell-all books, and the New York Yankees' "Bronx Zoo" era a few years later ended any pretensions people had about what went on inside a baseball clubhouse. In 1970, when Bouton wrote that some ballplayers cheated on their wives, people reacted in shock. Twenty years later, Wilt Chamberlain helped pump up sales of his autobiography by bragging that he slept with more than 20,000 women, an admission that seemed to shock only for its sheer size. Roger Kahn, the award-winning author who often wrote about the romantic side of baseball, said *Ball Four* "began the peeping-tom journalism; the *National Enquirer* journalism that is such a blight on the country today."[51]

It's not known how many of those books Kuhn ever read, but he spent the next 14 years trying to put out the fires started by *Ball Four*. Every year seemed to bring new revelations of indiscretions on the part of players and managers, who grew increasingly more willing to defy the commissioner's authority. Long after he retired as commissioner in 1984, Kuhn continued to insist that he never read *Ball Four*. "I read excerpts from it," he admitted, "and what I looked at I found fairly dull."[52]

Dull is hardly a word to describe either Jim Bouton or *Ball Four*. "Mostly I did it," Bouton said, "because I wanted to go down in history as the guy who wrote the book you absolutely have to read if you want to understand about this American subculture called baseball."[53]

Mission accomplished.

DEATHS IN THE FAMILY

On June 24, the Cincinnati Reds closed down Crosley Field with a 5–4 win over San Francisco. Immediately after the game, the bases were given away to fans, and home plate was dug up and presented to Cincinnati mayor Eugene Ruehlmann, who delivered it by helicopter to the Reds' new home, Riverfront Stadium. Four days later, the Pirates swept a doubleheader from the Cubs in the last games played at Forbes Field in Pittsburgh. Unlike Cincinnati, the fans in Pittsburgh never gave an opportunity for any postgame ceremonies. They mobbed the field, digging up dirt and pulling apart the scoreboard for souvenirs. "In a sense, I'm glad to leave," said Pirates' manager Danny Murtaugh. "The new stadium will be better for the fans. The people will enjoy the games more, and the more they enjoy them, the more they will come out to see us."[54]

Both parks dated back to baseball's Deadball Era, as Forbes opened in 1909 and Crosley in 1912. "For architectural beauty," the *Reach American League Guide* said of Forbes Field when it opened, "imposing size, solid construction, and for public comfort and convenience it has not its superior in the world."[55] But six decades later, both ballparks seemed small, antiquated, and inadequate to accommodate modern baseball. Their somewhat unsentimental farewells suggested that it was time to move on.

Forbes and Crosley represented the first modern age of ballpark construction. Most parks in the early years of the 20th century were made of wood and subject to destruction by fire, as happened to the Polo Grounds in New York and the South End Grounds in Boston. The Boston fire of 1894 was started by careless children playing with matches while a game was in progress, and "the flames licked up the sun-dried bleachers like so much tinder."[56] New ballparks were made of steel and concrete and built to last, as evidenced by the fact that Fenway Park (1912) and Wrigley Field (1914) are still in use.

During a time of industrialization, most fans lived in the cities, and that's where the parks were built. The geography of city and neighborhood boundaries limited what architects could do, and thus several parks had odd configurations. The Polo Grounds was shaped like a bathtub, with a massive center field area and short foul lines, while in Boston the Red Sox made up for a small left field area by building a 37-foot wall that came to be known as the Green Monster.

The park was usually accessible by foot or train, and many were built near mass transportation stations. Such proximity created a ballpark that became part of the social fabric of the community. "Wrigley Field is like an apartment building or home in a community," said longtime Cubs' infielder Ernie Banks. "As a player you have to be a part of that community."[57] As a 20-year-old rookie for the New York Giants in 1951, Willie Mays would often play stickball with the kids in his Harlem neighborhood. "I play ball every day in my neighborhood," he said. "Sometimes I play in the evening and other times in the afternoon. Sure, I play every day when the Giants are home. Why not?"[58]

But in the 1950s the city neighborhoods began to change as fans left for the suburbs. As the public street gave way to the private mall, people couldn't walk or train to the games anymore—they had to drive. At roughly the same time, television was making it easier for these fans to simply stay home and watch the game. Suddenly, ballparks needed parking, ease, and access. So by 1958, Crosley Field had become such a liability that Reds president Powel Crosley Jr. threatened to move the team unless more parking could be added.

For some, the threat became reality. Ebbets Field in Brooklyn was the most famous casualty, despite the legendary attachment between Dodger fans and the stadium. "You would walk around the lake on a balmy summer evening, and fathers and sons, hundreds of kids would be chattering," said Brooklyn fan Joe Flaherty. "Then you would get to maybe within two hundred yards of the ballpark . . . and all of a sudden the sky would be lit up. My God, it was like the Emerald City."[59]

But Ebbets had room for only 35,000 fans and no place to park, so in 1958 owner Walter O'Malley took the team to the greener pastures of Los Angeles. The Braves had already left Boston for Milwaukee and then Atlanta, the Giants followed the Dodgers to California, and the Senators abandoned Washington for Minnesota. In each case, new suburban parks were built with plenty of parking and easy access to freeways. The older parks, including Ebbets, the Polo Grounds, and Shibe Park in Philadelphia were torn down, and a simpler way of life seemed to be going down with them. When the Giants left New York for San Francisco in 1958, "It's one of the most tragic things that ever happened to me," said Mrs. John McGraw, widow of the Giants' legendary manager. "I guess all I have left now is memories."[60]

In their place rose gleaming, sterile palaces that could accommodate both football and baseball. They were usually perfectly symmetrical with uniform distances and conditions, leading Richie Hebner, who played for several teams during the 1970s, to say, "When I go up to bat, I can't tell if I'm in Cincinnati, Philadelphia, Pittsburgh or St. Louis. They all look alike."[61] The most extreme example was the Houston Astrodome, the first domed, climate-controlled stadium that opened in 1965. The Astrodome cost $45 million to build, could seat nearly 70,000 for football, and had parking for 30,000 cars. Almost all who visited said it would change the whole concept of sports arenas.

The success of the Astrodome helped persuade the Reds and Pirates to build their own multipurpose stadiums. With the opening of Riverfront Stadium in Cincinnati and Three Rivers Stadium in Pittsburgh, baseball attendance increased in both places and the initial reaction was mostly positive. Newspapers noted that "already visitors are calling [Riverfront] the ultimate in stadia. [It] scores top points in location, access, design, comfort, and most importantly, profitability."[62]

Profitable, yes, but also somewhat plastic, antiseptic, and soulless. There was often little connection between the fans and players other than the action on the field, and even that was often strained. When the Astrodome crammed in 52,693 fans for a college basketball game between Houston and UCLA in 1968, the nearest seats to the action seemed miles away. "The lighting was real strange and nobody was within 100 yards of the court," said UCLA's Lew Alcindor. "It was strange circumstances with this huge crowd so far away."[63]

Ironically, the most recent trend in ballpark construction has seen a return to the cities. Parks in Baltimore, Detroit, and Cleveland, among others, have risen in downtown areas as a means of urban renewal and revitalization. There may not be as much parking, but the new stadia, complete with unique configurations and modern amenities, have been tremendously successful in terms of attendance. The Indians, Orioles,

Tigers, Twins, and Giants have all set franchise records for attendance since opening their downtown ballparks.

Interestingly, many of the newer ballparks are actually smaller than their predecessors. The Astrodome could seat more than 55,000 for baseball, while Minute Maid Park in Houston barely holds 40,000. The idea seems to be replacing volume with quality of experience, and many fans are returning to places like Camden Yards in Baltimore because of greater intimacy and community. That need to reconnect, to go back to a time of childhood and the primacy of baseball, was seemingly lost for good at Crosley and Forbes. Both stadiums were demolished, with only a few historical markers to indicate a collective 119 years of baseball memories.

Yet fans will not let the memories die.

Part of the Forbes Field wall still exists on the University of Pittsburgh campus, and it's where Saul Finkelstein gathered every year starting in 1985 to sit and listen to a recorded radio broadcast of the seventh game of the 1960 World Series—the game that featured the dramatic, walk-off home run by Bill Mazeroski to lift the Pirates over the Yankees. At first, Finkelstein made a solitary pilgrimage, but soon other fans began joining him. Even after Finkelstein passed away, fans continued to gather every October 13, the anniversary of the home run, to listen to the game broadcast. In 2000, on the 40th anniversary, more than 600 people showed up, including Mazeroski. "This is something," he marveled. "I never thought there'd be something like this going on 40 years later."[64]

While the people of Pittsburgh have part of a wall, the Cincinnati suburb of Blue Ash, Ohio, has *all* of Crosley Field, or at least a full-scale replica. Blue Ash decided to build the replica both as a memorial to Crosley and as a place for local teams to play. The reproduction is stunning and includes the sloped terrace in left field, original Crosley Field seats along the third base line, and a scoreboard with all the information intact from when the final game was played at the stadium. The batting order, lineups, and out-of-town scores are just as they were on June 24, 1970. A crowd of some 7,500 showed up for the park's dedication and an Old Timers' game in 1988.

"Looking at the old scoreboard and the terrace was a mind-boggling experience," said former Reds' infielder Johnny Temple. "First I got goose pimples, and then I started to cry."[65]

A DEAD CITY REBORN

Among the many lessons learned in the aftermath of the 9/11 attacks was the healing power of sports. With New York City, along with all of America, reeling from unprecedented terrorist attacks, the Mets, Yankees, Giants, and Jets helped bind the wounds. Perhaps the most dramatic moment came on September 21 in the first sporting event held in the city after the attacks. Trailing the Braves in the eighth inning at Shea Stadium, the Mets won the game 3–2 on a dramatic home run by Mike Piazza. After the game, Piazza met with the families of firemen who had lost their lives trying to save victims from the World Trade Center. "When Mike hit that home run, the release of everyone around us was just incredible," said Carol Gies. "We never thought there would be a light at the end of the tunnel. But I saw my boys jumping up and down and screaming and smiling again for the first time. Like it was OK to live and enjoy life again. I truly believe in my heart that I have Mike and the Mets to thank for that."[66]

That same kind of healing was on display on a night in June 1970 in the west Texas city of Lubbock. The weather that evening of June 27 was typical Lubbock—hot and dry, with temperatures hovering around 100 degrees. The saying among the locals is that Lubbock gets about nine inches of rain a year, but it all comes in one day. Just two months earlier, the city got all that and more.

On May 11, a pair of tornadoes ripped through the area, with the second by far the most devastating. It would be later identified as an F5 tornado (the Fujita scale had yet to be developed) with winds of nearly 100 miles an hour. It swept through the city around 9:27 p.m. as evidenced by the frozen clock face at a local junior high school, and tore through the Texas Tech University campus, twisting light poles at the football stadium and severely damaging the Lubbock Municipal Coliseum where the university's graduation was scheduled five days later. Instead, graduation was canceled and the building was turned into an emergency shelter for the hundreds injured and homeless. In some places, water in the streets stood a foot high. "We have a disaster plan in place," said mayor Jim Granberry, "but Lubbock at this time is a dead city." [67] The actual death toll stood at 26, which made it the deadliest tornado attack since a storm in Waco, Texas, killed 114 people in 1953, ironically also on May 11.

Lubbock was crippled, with drinking water scarce and 2,500 blocks of the city severely damaged or destroyed. As emergency supplies were brought in from nearby Muleshoe, residents began the cleanup, their attitude a mixture of defiance and typical west Texas optimism. Granberry imposed a curfew and police chief J. T. Alley sternly announced that any looters would be shot, but there was no need. There were no incidents. "Our first priority is to tend to the living, bury the dead and clean up the city," said Granberry.[68]

By June, a semblance of normalcy had returned to Lubbock, and the city prepared to show its brave face to the sporting world. On June 27, Lubbock would host the tenth annual American Football Coaches Association All-America Game. It was an exhibition game that featured recently graduated college players against each other in an East versus West format, with profits going to fund scholarships. The first nine games were played in Buffalo and Atlanta, and they struggled to draw crowds and interest. After only 17,008 showed up for the 1969 game, organizers began looking for a new home, and Lubbock stepped in.

Thus, the city had two goals for the game—to show that it belonged in the big time, but more importantly, to show that the devastation of May could not keep Lubbock down. Game organizers could not even reach anyone in Lubbock for four days after the tornado because of downed telephone lines, but those in the city reassured them that in the best west Texas tradition the show would go on. "It gave us something to work for, a chance to show the country the kind of hard-working, God-fearing, close-to-earth sort of people we have out here," said Granberry, and he could not have been disappointed when a game-record crowd of 42,150 turned out.[69]

The game itself was a little short on star power, at least in terms of future NFL stars, and most of the scoring was done by names like Gordon Slade, Carter Campbell, and Frank Foreman. However, future offensive Rookie of the Year Dennis Shaw threw a touchdown pass, while Bruce Taylor, who would win defensive Rookie of the Year honors, scored the winning points on an interception return, as the East beat the West 34–27. Running back Jim Otis, who would go on to a long NFL career, was named the game's most valuable player after rushing for 145 yards. "Oh, man, these people are unbelievable," he said afterward. "They wanted this game so bad you could feel it."[70]

And that, more than anything else, was the headline that came out of the game. The event stayed in Lubbock until it ended in 1976, the victim of injury concerns, growing rookie salaries, and dwindling interest in college all-star exhibitions. The people of Lubbock never stopped supporting the game, which averaged around 40,000 throughout its stay. But the signature moment remained June 27, 1970, when a ravaged city reminded everyone that it would not go quietly into that good night.

In August 2000, Texas Tech invited back members of the class of 1970 to a special graduation, and more than 200 returned to campus to take part in a ceremony that was blown away by a tornado 30 years before. The ceremonies were held at the new United Spirit Arena, not the Coliseum, but it was still a happy moment of closure. "How often do you get the chance to complete the past in this way?" asked Holmes Brannon, one of the returnees. "Back in 1970, it was an uncool, establishment thing to go to graduation. I was going to skip it anyway, but after 30 years your focus changes. The idea of completing the past, I think, is a little bit spooky, but a little bit fun, too."[71]

7

JULY

THE PEACOCK AND THE BEAR

July means only one thing to the golf world—the British Open, or simply "The Open" in deference to its position as the oldest and most prestigious championship. In 1970 the tournament would return to one of its oldest courses, St. Andrews in Scotland. "It turns a golfer on," said Jack Nicklaus of the course. "You suddenly want to play. When you ride up to St. Andrews, it's like going through the gates of Augusta National here in America."[1]

Like going through the gates of heaven if you win. And the gates of hell if you lose.

Nicklaus knew all about the heaven part. Coming to St. Andrews he already had seven major championships under his belt on his way to a record 18. By 1970, he was the "Golden Bear," considered the best golfer in the world, thanks to a combination of powerful and accurate shot making. He was the "blond young goliath with awesome power" who hit the ball farther, better, and more consistently than anyone else.[2] When he won the 1965 Masters by a record nine shots, golfing legend Bobby Jones called it the greatest tournament performance in golf history.

But what really separated Nicklaus from everyone else were nerves of steel and the seeming uncanny ability to stand over a putt to win or tie a tournament and make it more often than not. He stalked a course with a confidence and coolness under fire intimidating the field with his mere presence. Nicklaus, who admitted to getting nervous, especially in big tournaments, didn't believe all the stories about intimidation, but he didn't necessarily discourage them, either. It was like having another club in the bag, and in some ways it was his most important club. "Inner certitude about one's abilities is a golfer's primary weapon," he had said. "There have been many players in my time who have possessed all the attributes necessary with the single exception of sufficient confidence in themselves."[3]

That was going to be borne out at the 99th British Open.

Among the challengers at St. Andrews was Doug Sanders, a Georgian who grew up picking cotton as a teenager to help his family. Despite a painful neck injury that would bother him for years and force him to shorten his backswing, Sanders was an excellent golfer who won the Canadian Open as an amateur in 1955. Coming into the British Open he had won 18 PGA tournaments, a figure that certainly put him in the upper echelon of professional golf. In 1965, he had even stared down Nicklaus, beating him in a playoff for the Pensacola Open title. "I hope 'Baby Beef' doesn't miss the $4,000," Sanders joked, referring to the money difference between first and second place.[4]

"Baby Beef," "Baby Dumpling," and "Blobbo" were some of the unflattering nicknames the young Nicklaus had picked up in his early years on the tour. Fans poked fun at his heavyset physique and for his daring to challenge Arnold Palmer as the best golfer in the game. Nicklaus answered by quitting smoking, slimming down, and taking the crown from Palmer as golf's king by beating him in a series of major championships. "Nobody likes to be called fat," he said after a diet helped him shed 20 pounds. "Personally, I don't think I was fat. I was big. There is a difference."[5] It had taken nearly a decade, but by 1970 fans had warmed up to the new Nicklaus, appreciating him for his skill and his battles with Palmer and Gary Player.

Sanders never quite reached the level of the "Big Three." There was a sense that he liked to have too much fun out on the course for his own good, engaging fans with jokes and conversation when he should have been concentrating on the next shot. "I must admit I don't work at my golf as much as most of the fellas," he said that July. "I like to enjoy my life and that comes first with me these days."[6] One time on the practice tee a fan asked him how to hit a fade. Sanders took a few minutes to patiently explain not only the fade, but also the hook. After he finished he looked at the fan and said, "If Arnold Palmer had answered that it would have cost you $200."[7]

He was also "The Peacock of the Fairways" who always dressed to put on a show. He admitted to owning nearly 300 pairs of shoes, taking four dozen with him to tournaments. Sportswriter Dan Jenkins admitted that Sanders was one of the inspirations for the lead character in his book *Dead Solid Perfect*, the story where "an unknown touring pro finds love and laughter on and off the fairways, as well as in various bedrooms, and finally conquers his self-doubt and wins a big tournament."[8]

That big tournament began on July 8 in Fife, Scotland, with Sanders only able to play after successfully going through qualifying rounds. The Old Course sits hard by the North Sea, which sends the wind in gales from seemingly every direction, but day one brought calm conditions and low scoring. Tony Jacklin, the defending champ who had won the U.S. Open a month earlier, shot an eight-under 29 on the front side and was nine-under through 13 holes when the elements finally decided to show up in the form of a torrential rainstorm. Play was halted for the day, and when Jacklin returned the next morning "his luck was gone and he ended up losing the title by the three strokes he had slept on."[9]

Nicklaus and Sanders were in a large group three back after the first round, and both moved up to two behind heading into Saturday's final round. That final round was played in true British Open weather—raw and blustery with winds hitting up to 50 miles per hour—and the scores reflected it. Lee Trevino led going into Saturday, but a five-over 77 ended his hopes and he finished tied for third with Harold Henning. Jacklin had his troubles as well, shooting a 76 that left him three strokes out. Every other contender was having similar trouble, so Nicklaus and Sanders were essentially the last men standing.

Playing one hole ahead and a shot behind Sanders, Nicklaus drove the shortish finishing hole. But he seemed overanxious, rolling his eagle putt 12 feet past and then missing the comeback for birdie. His three-putt par left him at five-under, and as he walked off the green, Nicklaus had the look of a man who thought he had just lost the tournament. "I was completely dejected," Nicklaus admitted. "My caddie had tears in his eyes. Neither of us imagined that Sanders would make anything worse than par on the 18th."[10]

Sanders looked every bit ready for a coronation, dressed in royal purple from head to toe, including sweater, pants, socks, shoes, and golf glove. As Nicklaus finished, Sanders stood in a pot bunker on the famous Road Hole 17th. It was a bunker so notorious that in a later Open, Tommy Nakajima would take five shots just to get out, costing him a nine on the hole. Someone asked Nakajima if he had lost his concentration. "No," he said, "I lost count."[11] Steadying his nerves, Sanders hit one of the greatest pressure shots of all time, blasting out to within inches for an easy par. As he walked to 18 he learned about Nicklaus. All he needed to win the Open was par on the final hole.

Sanders hit his tee shot comfortably in the fairway, but cautious of the "Valley of Sin"—a natural depression that lurked in front of the green— he flew his second shot on the green, 30 feet past. "He looks absolutely exhausted," said BBC television commentator Henry Longhurst after the shot. Crowds now rushed the fairway, pressing in on Sanders and his playing partner Trevino.

Two putts and 30 feet to win the Open.

Sanders would putt first, but not before backing off and complaining that a camera click had distracted him. He settled back and rolled it short, leaving himself another downhill putt. "Not a shot that I would like to have," Longhurst told his audience. Trevino finished out with a birdie leaving Sanders center stage. Standing next to Nicklaus and watching from behind the green, Jacklin turned and said, "Hey Jack, you're still alive."[12]

One putt and 30 inches to win the Open.

Sanders got over the putt and stood for what seemed like an eternity— actually ten seconds—before stopping to pluck an imaginary pebble from his line. He got back over the ball again and this time the wait was even longer—12 seconds. He moved his head from the hole to the ball and back to the hole, and then repeated the process several times. It was pressure one could almost feel, like a blast coming in off the North Sea, and it appeared to finally pull the club right out of Sanders's hand. As soon as his putter hit the ball, he knew it was lost.

Sanders stabbed a putt that rolled through the break and slid by to the right side, and almost as soon as he made contact he pulled up and started after it with his club as if trying to bring it back for a second try. "There but for the grace of God," intoned Longhurst. "I knew it when he hit that second so far past. I knew that was coming. Everybody who plays here does." Sanders made the bogey putt, but had the ashen-faced look of a man who had just survived a multicar pileup. While an 18-hole playoff with Nicklaus loomed, there was an inescapable feeling at St. Andrews that the fates had given Sanders his one great opportunity and that he had thrown it away.

Sanders returned for the playoff the next day, this time resplendent in orange and white, but somehow the peacock seemed less flashy. He hadn't slept all night and looked sluggish at the start, trailing by two at the turn. Down four after 13, Sanders could have packed it in, but he gamely rallied to win three straight holes and trail by only a single shot heading to the dramatic 18th.

This time, Sanders played the hole perfectly, laying up and getting his birdie, while Nicklaus drove through the green. "Jack is at the back of the green and in what could be tough grass," said Sanders. "So I'm thinking if I get a birdie and he gets a five, then I'm the champion."[13] Instead, Nicklaus chipped to seven feet and faced a putt to win the Open. Sanders had no doubt. "As soon as that happened, I'm dead. The championship has gone."[14]

Nicklaus curled it in, the ball disappearing at the last possible instant in the right side of the hole. To add insult, as soon as the ball dropped, Nicklaus flung his club high in the air and Sanders had to cover his head with his arms to avoid getting beaned. The two embraced warmly and Nicklaus put his arm around Sanders's shoulder. "How lucky can you get?" asked Nicklaus. "I never expected to be here now. Doug had it all wrapped up on the final hole Saturday."[15]

The newspapers described Sanders as "disappointed," which had to be an incredible understatement. "Let's give Jack full credit," he said gracefully.[16] He had lost to Nicklaus in a British Open in 1966 and now lightning had struck again. At age 37, there didn't figure to be too many more chances, and there weren't. He would never win a major championship, never again challenge for one, and win only one more PGA tournament the rest of his career.[17]

Some players go through disasters in crucial situations and become objects of ridicule. Jean van de Velde blew up on the last hole of the Open in 1999, giving away a three-shot lead and the tournament in one of the biggest debacles in golf history. When Greg Norman lost a six-shot lead to Nick Faldo in the final round of the 1996 Masters, sportswriter Jim Murray called it "not a choke, it's a goiter. He went down like the Titanic. Calling what he did losing is, as someone said, like calling the Johnstown Flood a leak."[18]

Maybe it was a kinder, gentler time or maybe the genial Sanders had built up enough goodwill during his career, but he was viewed more with sympathy than scorn. Fans seemed to connect with him, understand him in some elemental way. They were frustrated with him when his motel room was robbed three years in a row at the Crosby Invitational Tournament in California, on one occasion costing him $25,000. They laughed with him when Vice President Spiro Agnew skulled him with an errant shot during a pro-am event. Agnew hooked his first shot into the rough and shanked his second into Sanders's head. Sanders's first words to Agnew were, "I hope you've got a lot of insurance."[19]

Now, the image of a purple-clad David tragically unable to finish off Goliath struck a chord with anyone who saw it. Every golfer, from pro to hacker, understood exactly how Sanders felt after the missed putt on 18. When he appeared at a tournament in Philadelphia the next week, one spectator yelled out, "We ran out of handkerchiefs, Doug."[20]

Sanders moved on and tried to put the putt behind him, but it became a tragic, defining moment of his career. In terms of money, he estimated that the loss cost him some $200 million in endorsements, speaking engagements, and publicity, but it was the trophy that he wanted most of all. A recently as 2012, someone asked him if he ever thought about the 30 inches that could have changed his life. Replied Sanders, "Sometimes I can go five minutes without thinking about it."[21]

Nicklaus, of course, would go on to have one of the greatest careers in the history of professional golf, and his final resume included three Open titles. At the age of 65 he returned to St. Andrews to play the Open one more time. Jack gave the crowd one final thrill by sinking a curling birdie putt on the final hole, much like he did against Doug Sanders in 1970.

Among the spectators at that 2005 British Open was none other than Sanders, this time just a 72-year-old face in the crowd and not the man standing over a putt to dethrone the game's greatest player. Sanders went almost unnoticed until recognized by golf course architect Robert Trent Jones II.

"There he is," said Jones of Sanders, who was intently watching Nicklaus on the course. "Looking at the man who took his golfing life away."[22]

THE COLLISION

By the first week of July, Cincinnati's new Riverfront Stadium was less than a week old and there were still worries that it was not quite finished. The stadium was scheduled to host the annual baseball All-Star Game on July 14, and there was enough concern that commissioner Bowie Kuhn had a backup plan in place to move the game to Atlanta. On July 1, to the relief of everyone in Cincinnati, Kuhn decided that the game would take place in Riverfront after all. With that announcement, he set the stage for one of the most dramatic games in All-Star history.

At the time, baseball interest was peaking in the city. The Reds were running away with the National League's Western Division, piling up a record of 62–26 by the All-Star break, and they led the league with five players on the National League squad. Catcher Johnny Bench and third baseman Tony Perez would start, while the reserves included pitchers Jim Merritt, Wayne Simpson, and a former infielder now playing outfield named Pete Rose.

The Reds could not quite figure out what to do with Rose when he reached the majors in 1963, starting him at second base, shifting him to third, and then moving him back to second. Built like a squat linebacker, Rose didn't have the fluidity to play the infield and lacked the typical power or speed of an outfielder. He seemed like a man without a position.

But every time he was in the lineup, Rose hit, and by 1970 he was in the midst of a streak that would see him hit .300 or better for nine straight seasons. He moved to the outfield, playing well enough to win Gold Gloves for defensive play in 1969 and 1970, and while he never did hit for power, with just 16 homers in his best season, he made up for it with lots of singles and doubles. Rose told reporters he wanted to be the first singles hitter to make $100,000 in salary, and he reached that mark with the new contract he signed back in March. "It proves that an individual doesn't necessarily require size or have to be a home run hitter to earn an outstanding salary," said Reds' general manager Bob Howsam, "although it takes a tremendous lot of work."[23] In addition to the raise, the Reds rewarded Rose by naming him captain, the first for the team in 30 years.

Rose worked hard to overcome his physical shortcomings, but there was also a childlike enthusiasm for the game that endeared him to fans. He ran to first base after walks, slid headfirst into bases, and earned a new nickname from Yankees' stars Whitey Ford and Mickey Mantle in 1963.

"Ford saw Rose running around in spring training and asked Mickey Mantle who it was. Mantle answered 'Pete Rose.' Ford said, 'Pete who? I got a name for that thing. That's Charlie Hustle.'"[24]

The American League squad, which had lost seven straight in the All-Star series, was loaded with players from the Baltimore Orioles, a team on its way to 108 wins and the World Series. Seven Orioles were on the squad, which was managed by Baltimore's Earl Weaver. By contrast, the Cleveland Indians were in the middle of a seven-year period in which they finished under .500 ever year, and they placed only pitcher "Sudden" Sam McDowell and catcher Ray Fosse on the All-Star team.

Just 23 years old, Fosse was having a breakout season in his second full year in the majors. He came into the All-Star Game hitting .313 with 16 home runs, and at one point hit safely in 23 straight games. Fosse was a tough-as-nails catcher who gave no quarter and came honestly by his nickname "Mule." When Fosse felt that Tigers' pitcher Bill Denehy was throwing at him in a game, he started a bench-clearing brawl described by one umpire as one of the bloodiest fights he had ever seen on a baseball field. "I'm a catcher and lots of things can happen around the plate," said Fosse. "Denehy will be coming in to score on me some time and I'm going to remember him and go get him."[25]

In the days before the Home Run Derby, each team had a workout in the stadium on the Monday before the game. The practices were low key and informal, and more than anything they gave players from both squads a chance to socialize a bit. During the National League practice, American League president Joe Cronin stopped by to chat with players and singled out Rose, telling him he was risking serious injury by sliding into bases headfirst. Pete respected the advice but told Cronin that's the only way he knew how to play.

The socializing continued after the workouts at the players' hotel. As Fosse and teammate McDowell were in the lobby and looking for something to do, they were approached by Rose who invited them and their wives out to dinner. After the meal, the three couples returned to Rose's home where they stayed up late talking about baseball.

There would be plenty to talk about after the game as well.

President Nixon threw out the first pitch before another capacity crowd, as both Rose and Fosse started on the bench, and the game was still scoreless when both players entered in the fifth inning. In the top of the sixth, Fosse singled to Rose in right field and eventually scored on a hit by Carl Yastrzemski. Then in the seventh, Fosse got up again with the bases loaded and just missed a home run, but the sacrifice fly made it 2–0. In the bottom of the inning Jim Perry nailed Denis Menke with a pitch that got away from him up high. "An awfully tough night for Denis Menke," Sandy Koufax said on the national radio broadcast, referring to the fact that Menke also took a ball to the face on a throw in the infield earlier in the game. "There have been so many players hurt in the All-Star Game and possibly ruined their careers. It would be a shame to have anything happen to any of these great players here tonight."[26]

Going to the bottom of the ninth the American League led 4–1, and it had been a disappointing night for the hometown Reds players, all of whom had gone hitless, including Rose who had struck out and walked. The National League suddenly rallied with three runs and Rose had a chance to be the hero, but he again struck out, this time stranding the winning run on base. The game was tied 4–4, but so far it did not look like Pete Rose's night

Fosse had a similar chance to drive in the go-ahead run in the 11th but grounded out with Tony Oliva on second. So now the game went to the bottom of the 12th, where the National League got two quick outs. Rose finally got on base with a clean single to center off of Clyde Wright, and after a single by Billy Grabarkewitz, Rose moved to second as Jim Hickman came to the plate. Hickman lined a single to center, and as Amos Otis fielded and threw home, third base coach Leo Durocher frantically waved Rose around. There was no need—Pete was already at full speed and had no intentions of stopping.

Lots of things can happen around the plate, Fosse once said.

Now they were happening to him.

After a strong throw by Otis, the ball, Pete Rose, and Ray Fosse all arrived at the same time about three feet up the third base line. Pete was going so fast he appeared to stumble, but he was actually crouching to deliver a blow. His left shoulder hit Fosse full force, sending the catcher spinning backward in a somersault while the ball careened toward the backstop. It was a body block of which any NFL player would be proud. "I was 195 pounds, the son of a football player, charging toward the end zone with a full head of steam," said Rose. "Ray was standing still. Do the math."[27] It added up to an exciting 5–4 National League victory and a prostrate Ray Fosse. Fosse, dazed and in obvious pain, grabbed his left shoulder while National League players celebrated. As teammates rushed to congratulate him, Rose, caught in the moment, did not react other than to stare hard at Fosse—the conqueror standing over the vanquished.

A collision at the plate is one of the most dangerous plays in the game, especially for the catcher, who is often keeping his eye on the ball and not the player charging down the line. The Yankees' Bill Dickey was knocked unconscious and hospitalized for ten days after a 1936 run-in with Boston's Eric McNair. Johnny Bench would later require shoulder surgery after a collision with Gary Matthews of the Giants.[28] "I don't care if someone is 150 pounds or 300 pounds," Fosse said. "If they are coming full blast at you while you are standing still and they hit you, you are going to feel it."[29] Pete Rose well knew the collision with Fosse could end up with someone getting hurt—he just didn't care. "I knew I had to score," he said. "I didn't care about hurting myself if we could win."[30]

In the immediate aftermath of the game, that kind of attitude was applauded as good, hard National League baseball. Before free agency and interleague play, each league had its own distinct personality, and with players like Rose the National League was viewed as far more aggressive. Frank Robinson played ten years with the Reds before a 1966 trade sent him to Baltimore, and he brought the same kind of play with him, often upsetting infielders with his hard slides into second base to break up a double play. Fans liked that kind of effort, especially from a player making a big salary, and they appreciated that players like Pete Rose played to win at all times, even in meaningless exhibition games. "Hell, can you imagine what would have happened if Ray had caught the ball and tagged me out?" Rose said. "He would have been the hero and I would have been the goat."[31]

It turns out the goat had both fractured and separated his left shoulder, injuries that simple X-rays at the time couldn't find. So Fosse kept playing. "We didn't have MRIs back then, but I couldn't lift my arm," he said. "And the next game, I check the lineup card and I'm batting fourth and catching, so I just changed my swing and played. I didn't miss a game until I broke a finger about a month and a half later. In my mind I never got my swing back after that."[32] After hitting 16 homers before the All-Star break, Fosse hit just two the rest of the season. His homer production went down every year after that and his career batting average skidded to .231. Fosse played seven more years in the majors and won some championships in Oakland, but statistically and physically he was never the same player.

Dizzy Dean had broken a toe in the 1937 All-Star Game and the injury wrecked his career, and Ted Williams broke an elbow crashing into a wall in the 1950 game. But at least Williams and Dean played long enough to eventually make it into the Hall of Fame. Fosse never got that chance. "Could I have hit 30 home runs a year if [the collision] doesn't happen?" he once asked. "Maybe not. I'll never know."[33]

In the public mind, Fosse became a tragic figure—a luckless loser in the wrong place at the wrong time. To Rose, the hard-nosed hustler, the 1970 All-Star Game was just another of the highlights in a 26-year career that would undoubtedly land him in the Hall of Fame.

Then Pete became a hustler of a different kind.

When his gambling problems became public in 1989 and Rose was banished from baseball, including possible election to the Hall of Fame, a different, unsavory side of his life emerged. As the details threatened to destroy his career and reputation, Rose became a desperate, lying, say-anything, do-anything operator determined to get back in the game. Rose denied for years that he had bet on baseball games and then finally came clean in a 2004 autobiography that disappointed those who had staunchly supported him. His admission was viewed as little more than an attempt to make himself eligible for the Hall.

Rose's book talked about all parts of his career, including the 1970 All-Star Game. And that's what bothers Ray Fosse.

Fosse says Rose has changed or made up a lot of details about the incident, going back to their dinner the night before the game. Rose claims Fosse and McDowell were at his house until four in the morning, while Fosse says it was closer to midnight. Rose also wrote that he never set out to run into Fosse, but because the plate was blocked "if I had slid in there I would have broken both legs," which seems to suggest Rose did indeed care about getting hurt.[34] "He said I was blocking the plate, which I wasn't," Fosse answered. "You could almost say I was blindsided. He was starting to dive, but then he just kind of came after me. I never touched the ball."[35] Newspaper accounts suggested that Rose could have slid around Fosse, leg-first instead of headfirst.

Rose always maintained that the collision was inadvertent, but that story has changed over the years as well, with Rose writing in his book that he couldn't have faced his father if he hadn't run over Fosse. "That's the thing that bothered me most," admitted Fosse. "That still bugs me."[36]

Time, which is supposed to heal all wounds, has apparently done just the opposite.

But it has reversed that indelible image of the last play of the 1970 All-Star Game. Fosse has spent nearly 30 years broadcasting games for the Oakland A's, winning an Emmy Award and a nomination for the Ford C. Frick Award from the Hall of Fame. Rose, of course, can't get anywhere near the Hall, except to visit or sign autographs, which he occasionally does. In fact, Rose earns his money now in Las Vegas signing autographs and other baseball memorabilia.

In a real-life sense, it is Fosse now crouched over a stunned and injured Pete Rose.

Pete Rose spent five months for federal income tax evasion at a minimum security facility in southern Illinois. Baseball's all-time hits leader—4,256 hits, but known in prison as number 01832061—earned 11 cents an hour in the facility's welding shop.

When Rose left prison in 1991 he could have made an easy ten-mile drive up Illinois Highway 37 to nearby Marion. If he had turned right on Highway 13, he would have passed Ray Fosse Park. Said Marion's favorite son and the park's namesake, "There was a little irony that he ended up there."[37]

"I'm one of those guys, when I'm gone, you can think about me in nine different ways," Rose said later in life. "You can think about me getting all the hits. Or you can think about me going to prison or getting divorced or sliding headfirst or knocking catchers down. You can think of me being brash. Or you can think about me being the biggest winner in the history of sports. That's the best record I've got."[38]

THE VALLEY OF DEATH

Brian Piccolo's death in June was not the first for an athlete in 1970 and unfortunately, it would not be the last. A series of tragedies would continue to mar the sports landscape, no more so than in the fall when dozens of college football players would lose their lives in two separate airplane crashes (see chapter 11). On July 21, Bob Kalsu, a lineman for the Buffalo Bills, was serving as a second lieutenant with the 101st Airborne in Vietnam. At a time when many athletes were protesting or otherwise avoiding the Vietnam War, Kalsu made the decision to go. "I'm no better than anybody else," he said. "I gave 'em my word. I'm gonna do it."[39] Kalsu's unit came under heavy fire near the A Shau Valley, and the 25-year-old became the only active NFL player killed in action in Vietnam.

With so much death around, it's hard to believe someone would seek it out—would willingly stare death in the face, not once, but several times. But a lot of things were hard to believe about Karl Wallenda and his family. "It is what our lives have been about," said Karl's brother Herman. "The smell of death, that is what we are about. Death has become good business for the Wallendas."[40]

Born in Germany in 1905, Karl and Herman were part of the "Flying Wallendas," a family group that had specialized in dangerous high-wire acts in and around Europe since the 1700s. The Wallendas learned to cross the wire almost as soon as they could walk, and in some cases, before. Karl's sister-in-law Rietta, who represented the eighth generation of performing Wallendas, was carried across the high wires while still in her pregnant mother's belly. "There is no other life for me," said Karl, speaking for the entire family. "I'll keep doing it as long as I can."[41]

It wasn't just a matter of walking a high wire. Karl and the Wallendas had to keep making the act bigger, better, and more entertaining, and that meant more dangerous. They started with a four-man pyramid but soon developed an even riskier seven-man, three-tier pyramid that included a bicycle. Bicycles, handstands, headstands—anything and everything that could possibly draw the audience's attention—soon became part of the act. "I feel I have to do more to impress the audience," said Rietta, who began using a larger steadying pole so it would sway more. "I get a little reckless. My husband will always bawl me out when I come down. I just say, 'Who works up there, you or me?'"[42] As the ultimate act of danger, the Wallendas refused to use a safety net going back to when Willie Wallenda died in 1936. Willie fell on his bicycle, bounced off the net and onto the concrete floor, so the family never bothered with one again. Karl reasoned if the family started using a net, someone else would do a show without one.

Working without a net meant the Wallendas were courting disaster, and their list of tragedies was startling. In January 1962, the seven-man pyramid crashed in Detroit, four stories above the concrete floor at the state fairgrounds. It killed two and paralyzed Karl's adopted son Mario. Karl and Herman managed to hold on to the wire and in doing so, caught one of the acrobats and prevented her from falling. Rietta died the following year in Omaha when she fell 50 feet during her solo act, and Karl's son-in-law Chico Guzman died during an outdoor walk when his pole touched an electrical wire. Near misses included the performance when a cable snapped and Karl had to catch the head of wife Helen with his ankles.

Karl grieved for the losses, but as his family had for hundreds of years, he picked up the pieces and looked for the next wire, keeping his family, and the act, together. "We must go on," he said after Rietta's death. "What can we do? Fold up the act? It is our living."[43]

So on July 18, Karl Wallenda, now 65 years old, kept doing what he knew best. This time it would be a solo act—crossing a gorge 1,000 feet across on a wire less than two inches in diameter. The attempt would take place in Tallulah Falls, Georgia, a remote spot in the northeast part of the state, and if Wallenda fell this time, it would not be the matter of a simple 30-foot fall, but rather some 750 feet into a rocky abyss. As he always did, Karl promised to look straight across, and not down. When Helen looked out over the gorge, she told him, "If you gonna fall, I jump too."[44] As always, there would be no net.

The walk took place on Saturday, July 18, and it seemed to confirm Herman's belief that death was good business. A crowd of nearly 35,000, paying $5 a ticket, looked on as did several skeptical reporters. "When he falls off," a photographer asked a bystander, "what's the best way to get down to the bottom?"[45] Maybe he had no reason to be, but Wallenda was supremely confident, saying God was with him. Several people were praying for him as he began his walk, including Georgia governor Lester Maddox.

Wallenda took his first steps on the wire shortly after three in the afternoon. About 250 feet in, he put down his 40-pound pole across the wire, braced himself, and stood on his head. As the gathered crowd thundered its applause, Wallenda acknowledged it by waving his feet. He had only planned to stand on his head once, but a letter from servicemen he had received back in the spring asked him to stand on his head twice for the men in Vietnam. When Wallenda repeated the headstand later in the walk, he briefly lost balance and lurched to the side but quickly recovered. The rest was easy, or rather, Wallenda made it look so easy, that his 17-minute walk seemed nothing more than a brisk morning constitutional. After signing some autographs and receiving a plaque from Governor Maddox, Wallenda went back to his tent to finish his day with a martini, energized by the success of the walk and the attention it brought him. "He does not need this," said Herman, "but the applause, ah, the applause. It is his whole life."[46]

Wallenda later broke a world skywalk record when at the age of 69 he walked 1,800 feet at Kings Island, Ohio.[47] He was still going at age 73 when the story ended the only way it could. On a 1978 walk between two buildings in San Juan, Puerto Rico, Wallenda fell 120 feet to his death. High winds and faulty wiring were considered factors in the fall, which was captured in grisly detail by cameramen at the scene. Only hours after the fall, 17-year-old granddaughter Rietta Wallenda performed her own tightrope act in San Juan, while in Oakland, California, nephew Steve Wallenda walked a high wire over the Oakland Zoo in what he called a tribute to his uncle.

"My uncle taught me from the age of three to go on with the show," said Steve. "There's no way I'd quit. I will do the same as my uncle Karl did. I will probably die on the wire."[48]

"We say that what has to happen has to happen," Karl once said. "We realize in our business that it is dangerous. We have always said that God is with us."[49]

THE NFL'S HARD HAT

On July 30, a few NFL players reported to their respective training camps. That list included Bobby Walden and Curtis Gentry with Pittsburgh, Don Alley and Rick Eber for San Diego, and Tim McCann with the Giants. The players were not considered stars, but their reporting to camp made news across the country.

That's because they were about the only veterans in the entire NFL to show up.

NFL players were on strike in an attempt to get the league to improve its pension plan. The National League Football Players Association (NFLPA) began in 1956 as a largely ineffectual group, although it did stage a brief strike in 1968 that forced owners to accept a collective bargaining agreement and a minimum salary of $10,000 per year. That agreement had expired in the spring of 1970, and efforts to reach another agreement had so far failed. In June, the NFLPA filed an unfair labor practice charge against the owners. NFL owners responded by locking out the players and threatening to start the season with replacements. "You can't let them drive you out of business, can you?" asked Kansas City Chiefs' owner Lamar Hunt.[50]

Hunt's Chiefs had to receive special permission from the league to play the annual exhibition game matching the Super Bowl champs against a team of college all-stars. After Kansas City won the game 24–3 on July 31, its veterans did not report to camp and the impasse resumed, leading some owners to predict that the season was already lost. Tensions escalated even further when owners opened their training camps, but only for certain players. "We knew that would happen," said Chiefs' player representative Jim Tyrer. "The owners are trying to weaken the players and bust the Players Association."[51]

There was some weakening. Buffalo quarterback Dan Darragh originally agreed to report, changed his mind "in an effort to preserve unity in our group," and then reported anyway.[52] Browns' running back Leroy Kelly didn't show up but said he remained undecided about whether he would report later. As more veterans began trickling in, including Steelers' running back Rocky Bleier, Bengals quarterback Sam Wyche warned about possible retaliatory injuries. "Just think if we had been the only team to report," he said. "Every team we faced after the settlement would remember that we had bucked the Association. I don't have to tell you that memories like that would make for a long season."[53]

Amid the chaos and uncertainty, one player stood resolute—Mike Curtis.

Curtis was an All-Pro linebacker with the Colts and certainly the biggest name of the reporting veterans. "I have one job," he said about his decision to come to camp. "This game. I have to prepare myself. And to prepare properly, I have to be here."[54] When Curtis walked into the Colts' training facility at Western Maryland College, he received a round of applause from the rookies. "I'm here," he told reporters, "and be sure you spell my name right. It will probably be the last time you use it until I'm busted out of the league."[55]

That Curtis broke the strike and came to camp surprised absolutely no one. In an age of longhairs, free spirits and political radicals, Mike Curtis was truly a throwback—a clean-cut, unabashed conservative who openly idolized John Wayne. Even as the Nixon administration was denouncing protestors and creating an "enemies list," Vice President Agnew praised Curtis as an example of hard work, determination, and humility.

Add on top of all that a no-holds-barred, take-no-prisoners style of play that earned Curtis two nicknames—"Mad Dog" and "The Animal." In a game against Miami in Baltimore, when a fan ran onto the field and tried to make off with the football, Curtis leveled the intruder with a ferocious hit. "That's the way the cat's programmed," said one Colt player, "and you can't turn him off."[56] Not even in practice, it seems. Curtis was the only player with the courage, or foolhardiness, to tackle Johnny Unitas during drills. When Unitas threw a ball at him one day in retaliation, Curtis threatened the legendary quarterback to his face. "I told him that if he ever did that again I would kill him and none of his offensive linemen would be there to protect him."[57]

The Colts were a team threatening to come apart at the seams even before the strike. Hard-driving coach Don Shula had produced a winner on the field but few friends in the locker room. "Maybe everybody hated Shula and that's what he wanted," said Curtis. "Maybe he felt it would translate into making us a close team because we hated him. It was a bad situation."[58] Shula had solved the problem by jumping ship to Miami back in February, but even that was contentious. Team owner Carroll Rosenbloom, perhaps more out of spite than anything else, contested the move and ended up with a first-round draft pick as compensation. He then elevated assistant Don McCafferty to head coach.

On top of this turmoil, an unrepentant Mike Curtis had defied the strike. His Colts' roommate, Bill Curry, was the team's player representative and in charge of keeping the veterans united behind the union position. Another Colts' teammate, John Mackey, was president of the entire NFLPA. When Mackey told reporters that player support for the strike was close to 100 percent, it had to be embarrassing that the most notable player to break ranks was on his own team.

Yet such was the respect for Curtis that neither he nor the Colts expected any sort of repercussions. Mackey insisted that the veterans who did report would not be penalized, and as the team held informal workouts waiting for the strike to end, Curry added, "He's doing what his conscience dictates as the right thing. They'll be no resentment on my part. I realize that he made a decision, and while we didn't agree on it, we don't agree on a lot of things. We're still friends and we'll be roommates when training camp starts, if Mike wants me."[59]

With the players not drawing a salary, and reports that the NFL could lose up to a million dollars for every preseason game canceled, pressure mounted for the two sides to reach a deal. After an all-night meeting in New York, a new collective bargaining agreement was announced on August 3. Both sides compromised in order to cut a deal. "In a situation like this," said Mackey, "there is no winner, only agreement."[60]

The players reported to training camp immediately, with exhibition games scheduled to start in just a few days. Curry returned to his familiar room at Western Maryland and his familiar roommate. "I don't like you," Curtis said upon greeting him. The tension lasted all of a few seconds before Curtis broke out in a grin. "There are no hard feelings between us," he said. "Nothing could be further from the truth. You don't build a friendship over a three-year period and then split over a policy matter."[61]

Mike Curtis went on to play until 1978, and he remained uncompromising until the end. When the NFL players went out on strike again in 1974, this time with the slogan "No Freedom, No Football," Curtis was as adamant as ever. "Hell, yes, I plan to report. I'm not a member of the union. I don't plan on paying any attention to the strike and I don't think they can stop me."[62]

By that time, Bill Curry was gone from the Colts and playing the last season of his career with the Rams. But he was still not surprised. "What Mike is more than anything else is a pure football player," said Curry. "Totally dedicated to football and obsessed by winning. Excellence is more important to him than acceptance."[63]

The year began with a dramatic Cotton Bowl game between Texas and Notre Dame. Billy Dale scores with less than two minutes to play to win it for the Longhorns, 21–17. Texas became the last all-white team to win a national championship.

Curt Flood's odyssey against Major League Baseball began in January and ended with his defeat in the U.S. Supreme Court in 1972. Here, Flood (far right) and union leader Marvin Miller (second from right) enter U.S. Federal Court in New York on May 21.

Larry Owings (right) upsets Dan Gable 13–11 in the final of the NCAA Wrestling Championships on March 28 in Evanston, Illinois. It was Gable's only loss stretching back 118 matches in college.

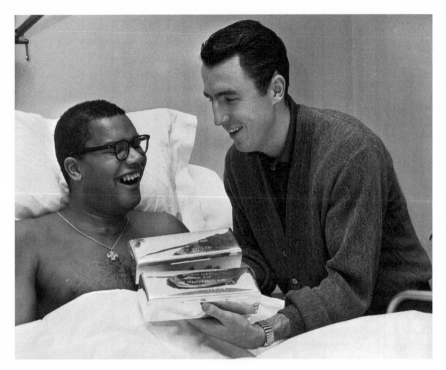

The friendship between Maurice Stokes (left) and Jack Twyman ended in April with Stokes's death from a heart attack. Here, Twyman presents Stokes with the award they shared as "Most Courageous Athletes" from the Philadelphia Sports Writers Association in 1962.

Morganna the Kissing Bandit surprised ballplayers all across the major leagues in 1970. Here, she tracks down a reluctant Wes Parker (28) of the Dodgers on June 30.

The moment of impact at the All-Star Game on July 14. Pete Rose crashes into Ray Fosse to score the winning run in the National League's 5–4 victory. Onlookers include third base coach Leo Durocher, on-deck hitter Dick Dietz (2), and home plate umpire Al Barlick.

On July 18, Karl Wallenda crosses Tallulah Gorge in Georgia before 35,000 onlookers. As usual, there was no net to protect Wallenda from a potential 750-foot fall. He not only crossed successfully, but made two headstands on the way over.

Gary Gabelich poses with the Blue Flame at the Bonneville Salt Flats on September 25. Less than a month later, Gabelich and the Blue Flame took the land speed record away from Craig Breedlove at 622.4 miles per hour.

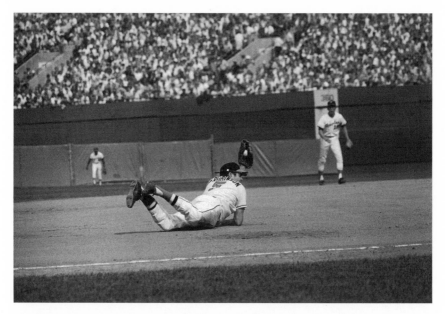

The World Series was a personal showcase for Baltimore's Brooks Robinson. Here he takes away a hit from Cincinnati's Johnny Bench in Game 3 on October 14. Robinson hit .429, made several spectacular plays in the field, and was named MVP of the Series, which the Orioles won in five games.

Two plane crashes in the fall devastated the football programs at Wichita State and Marshall University. Here, rescue workers comb through the wreckage of the November crash in Kenova, West Virginia, that killed everyone on board.

8

AUGUST

"IT'S TOO DAMN LATE FOR EVERYBODY"

As July turned to August, some bad things were happening on college campuses. A manhunt was under way for UCLA professor Angela Davis, an avowed communist who had fled the state after an August 7 courtroom shooting that killed a presiding judge and three other persons in San Rafael, California. Davis had purchased the guns but not taken part in the killings. After the FBI found her and brought her into custody she was eventually found not guilty of any complicity. On August 24, a bomb with greater force than the shells used in Vietnam exploded at the Army Math Research Center at the University of Wisconsin in Madison. The blast killed researcher Robert Fassnacht and injured three others. The four students responsible for the bomb—Karleton Armstrong and his brother Dwight, along with Leo Burt and David Fine—came to be known for the "New Year's Gang" for a series of campus bombings in the state. All but Burt were apprehended and convicted; the group said it wanted to bring home the horrors of the Vietnam War.

There were concerns that the violence on college campuses would spill over onto the athletic fields, and as students and athletes returned to school from summer break that's exactly what happened. At Kent State, just three months removed from the shooting deaths of four students at the hands of National Guardsmen (see chapter 5), returning football players were issued identification cards to show security guards patrolling the campus. "We feel that football can help bring these people together," said Kent football coach Dave Puddington.[1]

Any such hopes at Syracuse University were quickly dashed.

As the Orangemen returned for fall football practice, seven black players were conspicuous by their absence. Back in the spring, nine of the ten blacks on the squad had boycotted practice because they said the school had reneged on its promise to hire a black assistant coach. After Syracuse acquiesced and hired Carlmon Jones from Florida A&M, coach Ben Schwartzwalder sent a letter to the players who had skipped spring practice, advising them that if they had any interest in returning they needed to make amends with him before August 1. When only two of the nine players were invited back for the fall, all hell broke loose.

The snubbed players filed a complaint with the local Human Rights Commission against Schwartzwalder and the coaching staff, claiming "racial difficulties." "It is clearly a team problem," said defensive back Dana Harrell, "but we have been declared wrong. Coach Ben Schwartzwalder, instead of dealing with the team problem, has eliminated us."[2] Another player said that the white players agreed with the blacks but were too afraid to speak up. Those whites that did talk did not agree. "Most of us were for Ben's choice," said defensive tackle Ray White. "The idea was that we weren't against the demands of the blacks. It's just that they quit."[3]

The incident polarized the football team, if not the university and surrounding community. Syracuse chancellor John Corbally Jr. denied the charges made to the Human Rights Commission and offered to reinstate the players if they would sign an agreement that among other things required a cooperative attitude in all drills and other assignments. Other black students joined the cause and threatened to boycott the first home game, citing concerns for the safety of the players if they did not return to the squad, and complaining that they had been used as pawns. A series of meetings ensued after which the blacks returned to the team following a vote by the remaining players. But the vote was hardly unanimous and its results were released tersely in one sentence saying that the suspended players would return for the Kansas game. Even then, some white players threatened their own boycott for allowing the players to return. "We don't want them back," said guard Ted Lachowicz, "not because they're black, but because they walked out on us."[4]

Not surprisingly, a conflicted Syracuse team lost that game to Kansas 31–14 and started the season with three straight losses. Even before the first game, the situation seemed hopeless. "It's too damn late for everybody," said one Syracuse player who wanted to remain anonymous. "For the black players, for Ben Schwartzwalder, for the university. And it's only going to get worse."[5]

That such an ugly situation could take place at Syracuse was puzzling given the school's football history. Schwartzwalder was recruiting and playing blacks when the NFL still had a quota system. Jim Brown, Floyd Little, and Ernie Davis had all starred at the school, with Davis winning a Heisman Trophy. Schwartzwalder publicly stood up for Davis in the face of racism, often accusing opponents of unnecessarily rough play against the running back. He also supported Davis during a contentious Cotton Bowl win in 1960, when the Orangemen accused University of Texas players of spitting and using racial epithets. According to his players, "Schwartzwalder would never swear at a player, never drink alcohol in front of his team, never tolerate inequalities. The coach kept a strict honor code, and nobody ever overruled his edicts."[6] It was that Cotton Bowl win that gave Schwartzwalder and Syracuse an unbeaten season and the national championship.

So what exactly happened?

In August 1970 Schwartzwalder was 61 years old and had been at Syracuse for 21 years. He was a former captain in the 82nd Airborne who had fought with distinction during the invasion of Normandy in World War II. In every way, he represented the old-school authoritarian coaches—a group described by one psychiatrist in 1969 as "the remaining stronghold of the archaic family structure"—who demanded absolute obedience from their players.[7] Such coaches were not by nature racists or even bad people; they were just caught in changing cultural tides they could not control or even understand. During the height of the controversy, Schwartzwalder told one reporter, "I [don't] talk to Communists, draft dodgers, flag burners or people trying to destroy our country."[8]

Maybe it was such rigidity that led Jim Brown to call his former coach an "old fool" for the way he handled the situation. "I have no dislike for Ben," Brown had said, "but he is a lot older now and totally inflexible. I don't know if Ben has the ability to change to deal with the young men of today. I went through things here 14 years ago that the kids nowadays won't stand for."[9]

Schwartzwalder was not alone. The "Black 14" had already been suspended at the University of Wyoming, which would cost coach Lloyd Eaton his job at the end of the season (see chapter 1). Eaton was described as someone who "all his life has lived by the rules. He is a stern disciplinarian who can neither understand nor forgive a breakdown in team unity."[10] That sounds a lot like Jack Mitchell, who during his tenure as football coach at the University of Kansas learned that some of his players had taken part in a campus sit-in to protest discrimination. "You're not here to demonstrate," he told them flatly. "You're here to play football."[11]

While inflexibility certainly played a part, so did confusion and misunderstanding. At Indiana University, John Pont had built a solid program that took the school to its only Rose Bowl appearance after the 1967 season. Just two years later, nine black players—claiming that the program was "mentally depressing and morally discouraging to blacks"—quit the team.[12] The program collapsed as Indiana lost 22 of 25 games. According to one sportswriter, "Keeping the team together would be difficult and recruiting would be impossible—other coaches would use the incident against Pont. And for the life of him, Pont couldn't think of anything he had done wrong."[13] He was fired after the 1972 season.

A lot of coaches, it seems, could not adapt to the expressive athlete that had grown up in the tumultuous period of the 1960s, and had experienced war protests, race riots, and an assortment of personal freedom movements. "You're dealing with a new breed of young people today," said Florida A&M coach Jake Gaither. "I began to see it three or four years ago. Kids who didn't have anything better to do than rebel against discipline, rebel against the Establishment, rebel against the status quo. Kids with their hands out, kids who want everything on a silver platter."[14]

It was also a generation that had been taught to "turn on, tune in and drop out," a philosophy often incompatible with the demands of modern athletics. In Philadelphia, Eagles' linebacker Tim Rossovich "eats light bulbs. He wears tie-dyed shirts and shower-of-hail suits, Dracula capes and frontier buckskins and stands on his head in hotel lobbies."[15] In Oakland, Chip Oliver walked away from the Raiders a year after starting in the AFL Championship Game. He joined a commune in Larkspur, California, gave away his possessions except for some old clothes and a small camera, and scrubbed tables at a nonprofit health food restaurant. And in Chicago, the Bears drafted a defensive end from Stanford named

Bill Nicholson. "He was supposed to be a very good football player," said Bears' running back Gale Sayers. "Well, he reported to camp with long hair wearing leather pants and no shoes. He was there a couple of days, then told Coach [Jim] Dooley he didn't need that kind of life. 'I want to be a hippie,' he said, and walked out of camp. Last I heard the guy was working as a mailman out West."[16]

While some needed no reason to drop out, others took up a specific cause. Black athletes in particular seemed no longer willing to suffer in silence, such as Muhammad Ali, who had refused induction into the U.S. military (see chapter 1). Tommy Smith and John Carlos, who both had brief pro football careers, protested racism at home and abroad by raising gloved fists on the podium after winning medals in the 200-meter sprint at the 1968 Olympics. Before the games even began, a professor at San Jose State University named Harry Edwards attempted to organize a boycott by black athletes. "We have the numbers and can pull off the boycott anytime we like," he said two months before the games opened. "We are in the driver's seat now and we can call the tune. The black people have had no victories in this country but I think we have one now."[17] Dr. Martin Luther King Jr. supported the boycott, and while Lew Alcindor and Elvin Hayes cited other reasons, they decided against playing basketball at the games.

The boycott never really materialized as fully as Edwards intended, and black athletes helped the United States win more overall medals, and more gold medals, than any other country. Carlos and Smith were suspended from the games and sent home. The traditionalists, it appears, decided it was much easier to marginalize the players rather than deal with them. "The whole problem is that no one understands us," said Wyoming's Joe Williams, one of the Black 14.[18] One college football coach said in reply, "We've always got to understand *them*. Well, maybe I can't. I can't know what it's like to be a Negro. Or live in a ghetto. But that doesn't mean I don't try, and I sure think trying works two ways: they've got an obligation to understand me."[19]

About the same time Edwards was organizing his Olympic boycott, Schwartzwalder addressed the American Football Coaches Association. "The subordination of individual freedom to representative responsibility is a factor of prime importance in football and in our American way of life," he told the coaches.[20] He fully believed that just as much as he believed that he had not done anything wrong in dealing with his black players.

Syracuse rallied to finish the 1970 season at 6–4, but the team never again had a winning record during the remainder of Schwartzwalder's tenure and his last squad in 1973 won only two games. Schwartzwalder retired after that year and coached for the last time in 1974 in the American Bowl college all-star game. After his North team beat the South 28–7, a reporter asked Schwartzwalder how his team played so well after practicing together only four times. "They were good kids to start with and they got along."[21]

If only the same thing had happened that fateful August at Syracuse.

THE NEW BREED SERVES NOTICE

August also opened with the finals of the U.S. Clay Court tennis championships, won by Cliff Richey who defeated Stan Smith in four sets. Richey's victory on August 2 was not nearly as interesting as what happened in other matches, such as when Brian Fairlie walked off the court and sat in the grandstand because he said Richey was toweling off too much. In another match, Ilie Nastase of Romania got so upset with a call that he hit a ball at umpire Al Buman. When Nastase later knocked a ball out of the arena, Buman shouted at him and called for the referee. Threatened with disqualification, Nastase cooled down but lost the next three games and the match.

What exactly was happening to the genteel game of tennis?

For generations, tennis was played by white-suited country clubbers on manicured lawns like Forest Hills in New York. The game grew up amid the amateur ideal that flourished at the turn of the 20th century. In 1896, Baron Pierre de Coubertin organized the modern Olympics as an amateur competition, going so far as to propose that athletes swear an oath on their national flags as a means of ensuring their amateur standing. At roughly the same time, a series of books and serials chronicled the athletic exploits of fictional Frank Merriwell, who was described as "courteous, clean, patriotic and respectful of his elders; he loved God and country and private enterprise. He was athletic, brave, chaste and competitive. He neither smoked, drank nor swore. He loved women, but from afar. His heart was pure."[22]

Tennis players were expected to live up to the same ideal, as were spectators. A list of rules for the international Davis Cup tournament advised spectators not to move around, make noise, or applaud bad shots. Even in the era of florid sportswriting of the 1920s, when football players were called "behemoths" and baseball players were often "rowdies," tennis players were still referred to as "ladies" and "gentlemen," designations that hold to this day at Wimbledon. "Tennis was the last of the old-fashioned sports where amateurs played for the love of the game and victory's honor," according to writer Bob Greene. "In every other sport, the pros had taken control and stolen the glory. Not tennis."[23]

Actually, yes, tennis.

There had been a professional element in the game since the 1920s, but it was sneered at as uncouth by the tennis establishment. When Don Budge turned pro in 1939 he was criticized for playing for money rather than championship trophies, which were only for amateurs. Pros usually signed a contract with a promoter who toured them around the country in invitational matches against other professionals. It was a situation not unlike the early years of professional baseball and football in the United States. In both sports, the college game and its players were initially considered morally and athletically superior, while "the public's dubious regard of professional baseball players—'you're all right, but please don't try and join the family'—continued for the better part of the century's first two decades."[24]

It was a difficult, knockabout life for tennis professionals until 1968 when Wimbledon, the French Open, and the U.S. Open first began allowing professional players and awarding prize money.[25] The growth of sports in general, and tennis in particular, increased the demand to see the best players in the premier events. Other sports such as football had ridden television to new heights of popularity and riches, and tennis was in danger of getting left behind. Thus, 1968 ushered in the "open era" of tennis in which professionals and amateurs competed together for fabulous amounts of prize money. When Ken Rosewall won the U.S. Open in 1956, he received a gold tennis ball and a handshake. When he won again in September 1970, he left $20,000 richer.

It was not so easy for the amateurs, who did not want to give up their privileged position. For years, many players had been amateurs in name only, receiving envelopes filled with "expense" money—often thousands of dollars—at tournaments. The governing United States Lawn Tennis

Association didn't approve of the payments but didn't work very hard to stop them, either. "I've received $4,500 in expenses for competing in one tournament," said women's star Billie Jean King. "Well, we've had enough of that."[26]

An amateur circuit continued to exist, but as the professional game became more popular it threatened to overwhelm tennis. Particularly hurt was the Davis Cup, which had been one of the most prestigious events in the sport, but soon became virtually insignificant. In 1968, U.S. Davis Cup captain Donald Dell called the fighting between the amateurs and pros "a senseless war. The pros are playing into the hands of the old conservative groups who never wanted to change a blade of grass in the game. These forces against progress point to the present troubles and say, 'See, we told you.' Here the pros are trying to take over."[27]

Dell, a former Yalie whose main job was as an attorney in Washington, DC, epitomized the old order that eventually gave way. No longer would the top players be part-timers who played only on weekends. Tennis now demanded the same year-round attention that football and baseball were getting. A young tennis phenom named Jimmy Connors was 18 years old at the time and had already moved from his childhood home in Illinois to Southern California where he could train under former professional Pancho Segura.

Actually, moving to California was the idea of Connors's mother, Gloria, whose micromanagement of her son's career and life led to the coining of the term "tennis mother." A former tennis pro herself, Gloria Connors gave up the game to marry, but with her husband now dead she turned her full-time attention to Jimmy. She was his coach, mentor, and business manager, even though she had no formal business training. In all areas, she relentlessly pushed her son to be the best. "I know what people say about me and I don't care," she said unapologetically. "When he was young and didn't play well, I'd wait till we were off the court and then I'd give him a good kick. It's a tough sport that needs discipline. And I believe in discipline."[28]

Jimmy Connors responded and in September would break through with his first big professional win, defeating Roy Emerson in the Pacific Southwest Open. He would go on to win 110 tournaments in his career, including eight Grand Slam singles titles, and for several years rank as the number-one player in the world. He is remembered as a fiery competitor who introduced and perfected the two-handed backhand.

But Connors is also remembered as an emotional powder keg liable to go off at any minute. His matches were exhibitions of raw power, both physical and emotional, and his temper tantrums were legendary. It was Connors, seemingly pushed to the edge and beyond by his mother, who ushered in the era of the "tennis brat"—the prima donna who needed constant success, flattery, and attention. As Connors broke racquets, swore at umpires, and generally engaged in a scorched-court policy across tennis, the old guard recoiled in horror. Their ideal was the gentlemanly Arthur Ashe, who had won the U.S. Open in 1968, or the demure rising star Chris Evert, a 16-year-old who was often referred to in stories as "the exciting little court princess."[29] But when anyone complained about her son, Gloria was quick to dismiss it. "Everyone can't like you," she would say. "He was taught to be a tiger on the court and a gentleman off it and he has been."[30]

Meanwhile, everyone else seemed to love this new and exciting breed of player. Fans flocked to the courts, as much for a possible blowup or altercation as for the skill. Even when they weren't winning, players like Connors and Nastase, another famous bad boy often referred to as "Nasty" or the "Terror of Tennis," made headlines, and tennis needed headlines. Television soon began to get interested, the prize money got bigger, and players soon got rich.

It was a lesson not lost on a generation of new tennis players who looked at Connors and Nastase as role models of a sort. Soon, every kid big enough to hold a racquet was leaving home to get private tutoring from a renowned coach. Home, school, and social life were all considered secondary, as was proper court behavior; winning was the only thing that mattered. The age of the tennis brat reached its zenith—or nadir, depending on the point of view—with the arrival of John McEnroe, a quick-tempered prodigy whose antics made Connors look like a Sunday school teacher. McEnroe was even more athletically gifted than Connors but also more volatile, and his legendary temper tantrums, including foul language and broken racquets, soon became must-see television.

Other tennis brats and parents followed. Teenage wunderkind Jennifer Capriati won three Grand Slam titles but also went through early burnout that led to highly publicized incidents of shoplifting and marijuana use. Another teenaged prodigy, Mary Pierce, was so pushed and abused by her father that she eventually filed a restraining order. "You never know what he's capable of," said Pierce, who hired bodyguards for protection. "One reason I hesitated to break away was that you just don't know what he might do."[31]

As the game and money got bigger, tennis literally and figuratively moved away from its roots, abandoning the sedate grass courts for the synthetic surfaces that produced a faster game. The U.S. Open finally left the country club atmosphere of Forest Hills in New York for the new U.S. Tennis Center in bustling Flushing Meadow, the site of a previous World's Fair. "Tennis changed from a tradition-bound, little-understood sport to a billion-dollar-a-year industry. The gentlemen's game had turned into a boom town," wrote Greene. "Success is the most intoxicating potion you can find, and if the success of new tennis meant some of the old ways had to go . . . well, that was the price tennis had to pay."[32]

Not everyone was willing to pay it, especially the old guard. Jack Kramer, a Grand Slam champion and leading proponent of the open era, created the men's Grand Prix points system and in 1972 helped found the Association of Tennis Professionals. But even Kramer felt the game's growth was creating problems. "It's disturbing and disheartening," he said. "I get sick when I think of how much others have sacrificed to promote the game only to have their efforts fouled by a bunch of selfish, short-sighted guys with no regard at all for the system."[33] "They are getting too big for their britches," added Budge. "All they do is take out of the game and put nothing back in—it's a shame."[34]

Once the genie got out of the bottle there was no putting him back in. The quiet Sunday afternoons on the tennis lawn are as dead at wooden racquets and long white pants. Like any change, it came with the good and the bad. It's hard to argue for the "good old days" when the U.S. Open now awards $2.6 million to the winner and players can make additional millions in endorsements.

In 1915, the *New York Times* observed, "It is no longer an 'afternoon tea' sport, but as played now is a fast, grueling game which requires all the vigor that can be put into it. Tennis, as it is played today, has found a new place in the field of sports."[35]

Plus les choses changent, plus elles restent les memes: "The more things change, the more they stay the same."

TWO JEWELS IN THE TRIPLE CROWN

Aside from Diane Crump and the three big races, horse racing in 1970 was bookended by a pair of magnificent Triple Crown winners. On August 8 at Calumet Farm in Kentucky, Citation passed away from old age at 25. He swept the Kentucky Derby, Preakness, and Belmont in 1948, but it was by no means an easy ride. After opening the 1948 season with wins in the Seminole Handicap and Flamingo Stakes, Citation lost his jockey Al Snider, who drowned while fishing off the Florida Keys. Eddie Arcaro replaced Snider and in their first race together the duo lost the Chesapeake Trial Stakes.

Citation would not lose again for nearly two years.

He and Arcaro won the Kentucky Derby in the mud, coming from behind to overtake his unbeaten Calumet stablemate Coaltown by three and a half lengths. Sportswriters called him the "Calumet Comet" and predicted no one could beat him in either in the Preakness or Belmont Stakes.[36] No one did, as Citation and Arcaro won the Preakness by five lengths and the Belmont by eight, tying Count Fleet's Belmont record at 2:28 1/5, and "running like he was romping at a Sunday school picnic."[37]

Citation finished 1948 by winning 19 of 20 races, and all told had won 27 of 29, in taking home Horse of the Year honors. Before he finished his career at stud, he was the first horse to take home more than a million dollars in winnings, and at one point won 16 consecutive races. "I've tried to fault him, but I just can't find any holes," said Citation's trainer, Ben Jones. "He's the best. Maybe we'll never see his likes again in our time. He was the best horse I ever saw. Probably the best horse anybody ever saw, I expect."[38]

From 1948 to his death, Citation ruled as the last Triple Crown winner and one of the best Thoroughbreds of all time. As the 1970 racing season passed, those in the racing community began to wonder if there would ever be another Triple Crown champion. No one could have guessed that the next great winner had been born just four months before.

On the drizzly, damp, early morning of March 30 at the Meadow Stud in Doswell, Virginia, just north of Richmond, the foal of Somethingroyal and Bold Ruler came into the world. Bold Ruler was the preeminent sire in the Thoroughbred industry at the time, and his newest foal was a big, majestic-looking chestnut. "I never saw perfection before," said Charles Hatton, a writer for the *Daily Racing Form*. "I absolutely could not fault him in any way."[39] Given the racing success of Somethingroyal's off-spring, this newest addition came with great expectations.

Secretariat would not disappoint.

The horse, also known as "Big Red" for his color, won seven of nine races as a two-year-old and was voted Horse of the Year by the Thoroughbred Racing Association. Then came the transcendent racing season of 1973, which began with two victories prior to a stunning loss. In the Wood Memorial in New York, a traditional warm-up for the Kentucky Derby, Secretariat started last as usual and simply could not make up the distance, finishing third behind Angle Light and Sham, a finish that stunned even the winner. "Are you kidding?" Angle Light owner Edwin Whittaker asked after the race.[40]

Secretariat's stumble in the Wood made it a very nervous time for owner Penny Tweedy, who had sold shares of the horse worth $6.8 million to 32 different investors. "Everybody's blamin' everybody else," wrote racing reporter Dink Carroll. "Mrs. Tweedy blames Lucien Laurin, the trainer, and he blames Ron Turcotte, the rider. Turcotte blames Secretariat, claimin' he didn't have it when he called on him. The turf writers suddenly remember that he's a son of Bold Ruler, who had trouble above a mile and a quarter, which is the Derby distance. Maybe he's just a sprinter."[41] That kind of concern caused many writers and horseplayers to switch their derby pick to Sham, considered Secretariat's top competitor, especially when rumors flew that Secretariat was either injured or ill and would be scratched from the race.

Instead, on a bright, sunny day at Churchill Downs, Secretariat blazed to a derby record, his time of 1:59 2/5 making him the first horse to eclipse two minutes for the mile and a quarter. Sham ran a respectable race but still finished comfortably two and a half lengths behind, with Our Native third. "The horse had to redeem himself and he did," bubbled Laurin after the race. "I had more pressure on me today than I ever had in my life, [but] I knew all along he could do it."[42]

The next test came two weeks later at the Preakness in Baltimore, and breaking last as usual, Secretariat went for the lead by the first turn. In almost a carbon copy of the derby, Big Red held off Sham by two and a half with Our Native once again finishing third. Secretariat missed another race record only because the track's electronic timer had malfunctioned. The official time was listed at 1:54 2/5, although several hand timers at the event clocked Secretariat in 1:53 2/5, which would have been a Preakness record.

After the Preakness, Secretariat had three weeks to get ready for the Belmont, where a win would make him the first Triple Crown winner since Citation. By now, the handsome horse had captured the imagination of the entire nation, appearing on the covers of *Time*, *Newsweek*, and *Sports Illustrated*. Certainly, Secretariat was news because he was going for a record feat on the track, but his appeal seemed to go far beyond that. In a country that seemed split right down the middle on race relations, the war in Vietnam, and Watergate,[43] Secretariat was the one thing everyone could agree on. People bought pennants and buttons bearing his name, and flocked in record numbers to see him in person. Some sent postcards or letters, many of which asked for pictures. Instead of getting spooked by the attention, the horse actually seemed to embrace it. Those who knew him best called him a ham. "If Secretariat were a person, you'd say he was aware of his public image," said Tweedy. "He knows how to behave. When the cameras click, the ears go up."[44]

It was a one-horse revival of the racing industry, which had lagged in the doldrums since the ascendance of pro football and basketball. People crowded around him in workouts, hoping to get perhaps a closer look, or in a true flight of fantasy, maybe a quick touch as if somehow Secretariat would rub off on them. "If he were to lose the Belmont," said sportswriter Larry Merchant, "the country may turn sullen and mutinous."[45]

Fat chance of that. Perhaps in recognition of the inevitable, only four challengers entered the last and longest of the Triple Crown races, and of that small field only Sham was considered to have any chance against Secretariat, who went off as a one-to-ten favorite. Secretariat ended the suspense early, pulling away from Sham at the six-furlong mark, methodically stretching his lead to the point that race caller Chic Anderson noted that he was "running like a tremendous machine."[46]

Faster and faster went Secretariat, and with each snap of the hooves the lead continued to grow. Twelve lengths, 15 lengths, 18 lengths. And still more than half the race to go. Many trackside observers thought that the horse was running too fast and might totally collapse in the stretch, but Secretariat never tired and never let up. As he came into the stretch, victory assured, the crowd rose as one in the stands and along the rail, many of them weeping as he stormed by. Curiosity finally got the better of jockey Ron Turcotte, who turned around to see just how far ahead he really was. "At the quarter pole," said Laurin, "I thought, 'Good Lord, just don't let him fall down.'"[47]

He didn't and the final margin of victory was an astounding 31 lengths, the largest in Triple Crown history. His final time of 2:24 flat shattered the Belmont record by more than two seconds, a record that has not been threatened since. For the record, Twice A Prince finished second with Sham last, a full 45 lengths behind, but that was just bookkeeping. All anyone could talk about was the stunning athletic achievement they had just seen. Charles Hatton, who had covered horse racing for some sixty years, said simply, "His only point of reference is himself."[48]

After a few more races, Secretariat retired to stud, his owners fearing that a racing injury would diminish his value as a sire. He never produced another champion like himself, but he enjoyed his retirement life, siring and relaxing at Claiborne Farm in Kentucky, where he finally passed away at the age of 19 on October 4, 1989. Years after his death, fans still come to see the fields where he roamed and many leave flowers at his former stable. When doctors performed the autopsy they were shocked; all of Secretariat's organs were of normal size except the heart. "We just stood there in stunned silence," said Dr. Thomas Swerczek. "We couldn't believe it. The heart was perfect. There were no problems with it. It was just this huge engine."[49]

Maybe it shouldn't have been a surprise. No one who ever saw Secretariat run could doubt the size of his heart.

That leaves the big question: Who would have won a match race of Secretariat and Citation if both were in their prime? "I thought Citation was the best racehorse I ever saw," said longtime sportswriter Jim Murray. "His edge was courage and will."[50] Arcaro said the question really couldn't be answered. "That's great barroom talk," he said, "and you could argue it forever. I will say this, though. I don't think any horse could have beaten Secretariat on Belmont day. I've never seen a horse do the things he did that day."[51]

FICKER IS QUICKER

By the summer of 1970, Bill Ficker was an established architect in Newport Beach, California. His Ficker Group was responsible for designing the $55 million Orange County Correctional Facility, the engineering research laboratory for the University of California, Irvine, and many retail shopping malls. "It's a huge managerial task," Ficker said. "The coordination of people and jobs is endless. But organization is something I've always prided myself on."[52]

In this case, he was not talking about architecture.

Ficker's real love was sailing, where his planning, strategy, and organization had led him to championships in several classes, including the Star class world championship in 1958, and later the Congressional Cup. In August 1970, he had his sights set on an unofficial Triple Crown of yachting and the 12-meter America's Cup.

The Cup—the "Auld Mug"—was the oldest international sporting trophy in the world and had been held by the Americans since the first race in 1851. Twenty straight international challenges—including five from Scottish tea baron Sir Thomas Lipton—failed to wrest it from the Americans. The type of sailing yachts, the location, and the crews changed, but the results stayed the same: America held the Cup so long that it was actually bolted to an oak table in the New York Yacht Club. No West Coast skipper had ever challenged for the Cup, and to get ready, Ficker had led his crew in a rigorous three-month training program that included five hours on the water and another seven hours each day in calisthenics. At night, he and the crew viewed videotapes of the day's performance. "He leaves nothing to chance," said a crew member. "It's his attention to detail and his control over his emotions."[53]

For the first time, there would be multiple challengers. The Australian entry *Gretel II* turned back a challenge from the French in a seven-race series, while Ficker's *Intrepid* crew had little difficulty in beating another American hopeful, *Valiant*. "The boats are close together in speed and time," said Ficker, "but it's clear that we are winning the races. We think we have demonstrated that we are capable of winning the Cup."[54] After *Intrepid* had won the right to sail in the finals by beating *Valiant* for the sixth straight time, a crew member of the vanquished boat lamented, "It's Ficker's organization," he said. "It's just better than ours."[55] Ficker was now only one step from the goal he called the "holy grail" of yachting.

While admitting to being a perfectionist and insisting on silence during a race except for commands, Ficker was no Captain Bligh. He allowed the crew to play cards between races and was more likely to respond with a compliment than a criticism. "He knew exactly what kind of people he needed to support him, and he knew how to bring it all together," said his tactician, Steve Van Dyck. "He made a lasting impression that way."[56] Ficker also good-naturedly put up with the green-and-white "Ficker Is Quicker" buttons that began popping up in Newport during the trials. "I was embarrassed about them at first," Ficker said. "None of the sailors wanted to do anything to flaunt himself."[57] Jackie Onassis had no such reservations, sporting one of the buttons as she watched the finals get under way.

The truth of the matter was that Ficker was not necessarily quicker and *Gretel II*, skippered by Jim Hardy, would present a formidable challenge. "I was out to watch him beat *Valiant* and there's no doubt *Intrepid* is a fine boat," said Hardy. Ficker and *Intrepid* jumped out to win the first three races, but all were close, exciting, and in the case of the second race, unforgettable.

Hardy and *Gretel II* took a gamble at the start of the second race that resulted in the challenger bumping into the defender. *Gretel II* overcame an early lead by *Intrepid* to cross first, 1:04 ahead, but a protest by the Americans was upheld, giving the race to Ficker. Depending on the point of view, the protest was either justified or just mean spirited. "*Gretel* had not only failed through poor timing to accomplish her tactic of squeezing out *Intrepid*," read one American account, "but was guilty of the nautical equivalent of sliding with spikes high when caught off base, or, after being outsmarted, of roughing a receiver who has already caught the football."[58] The Aussies countered vigorously, including one commentator who stretched the limits of hyperbole in saying "everything the U.S. did for American-Australian good will in the Battle of the Coral Sea in 1942 was undone."[59] The race also featured a helicopter rescue of Van Dyck, who went into shock after getting stung by a bee, and a delay over fear of a mine floating among the spectator fleet. Van Dyck was treated and released at a local hospital, and the mine turned out to be a fisherman's buoy, but such was the race that, according to one report, "if *Intrepid* had been swallowed by a whale after crossing the finish line, few onlookers would have been surprised."[60]

Hardy and the Australians did manage a clean victory in race four and certainly had a boat capable of mounting a comeback, but in the end it was a triumph of crew, navigation, tactics, and helmsmanship. The final race, in which the speedier *Gretel II* took an early lead, resulted in a 1:44 win for Ficker and *Intrepid*. Barely had the *Intrepid* put across the finish line when her crew hoisted a flag to the masthead that read "Ficker Is

Quicker." "We played ducks and drakes up the last leg hoping for a miracle," said Hardy, "but it didn't happen. [Ficker] sailed a great race today."[61] "By most views, *Gretel II* should have beaten us," said Van Dyck. "But we simply outsmarted them by protecting a very small lead for a very long way. That race illustrated Bill at his best."[62]

For yet another year, and at least until the next challenge in 1973, the America's Cup would stay in America. Not until 1983 would a challenger take the Cup, when the Australians ended a winning streak that had reached 132 years and 26 challenges. Ficker continued to stay active in sailing and in 1980 was honored by the Long Beach Yacht Club with the Ficker Cup, an annual event that draws international competition. His accomplishments in sailing, and his accolades, have continued to grow over the years.

"You're my hero, Bill," U.S. Sailing president Gary Jobson told him during a testimonial in 2012, "and the saying 'Ficker is Quicker' is still as apt today as it was in 1970."[63]

9

SEPTEMBER

DEATH OF AN ERA

As sailing yachts gathered off the coast of Newport for the America's Cup, a different kind of struggle was taking place in Washington, DC. At Georgetown University Hospital, Vincent Thomas Lombardi was nearing the end of a life that had dominated pro football for a decade. Fans, players, and coaches were shocked to hear about Lombardi's condition—at 57, he seemed too young, too vibrant, too dominating to be beaten, even by cancer.

Both Lombardi and pro football had captured the American imagination in the 1960s. A native New Yorker, he had served as an assistant at Army and with the New York Giants before taking over the Green Bay Packers in 1959. The Packers were a moribund team that had not had a winning record in 12 years, but almost immediately Lombardi transformed them into winners, then champions, and then legends. "I cannot make any predictions on what kind of team I'll have," he said that first season, "but I know this much: You will be proud of the team because I will be proud of them."[1]

Pride, devotion, honor. They were the cornerstones of his life as well as his coaching philosophy. Lombardi's football strategy was not complicated. His teams ran only a few basic plays that opponents had prepared for well in advance, but they ran those few plays to perfection. Lombardi was a fanatic about fundamentals, discipline, and especially teamwork. It was not so much the football strategy that won games, but the pride and devotion he had instilled in the players who executed the strategy. "I don't think he ever taught me any football," said Packers' defensive tackle Henry Jordan. "What he'd do three times a week was preach on life."[2]

The Packers had a winning record that first season, went to the championship game the next year, and then won the title in 1961, the first of five NFL championships during the decade under Lombardi. He turned a losing franchise in a small, backwater Wisconsin town into "Titletown, USA," a name the city trademarked as its own. Eleven players from those Packers teams eventually made the Hall of Fame, and almost to a man, each one credited Lombardi for his success. Lombardi made quarterback Bart Starr a special project, turning over his team to a 17th-round draft choice who had languished on the bench for three seasons. Under Lombardi's guidance, Starr launched his own Hall of Fame career. "I told him personally that I think he's made me as a man and as a football player," said Starr. When asked if he could ever have made it without the coach, Starr replied, "I honestly don't know. Naturally, I'd like to think so, but I can't say for sure. The man has had a great impact on me."[3]

Almost every player he ever coached, especially from Green Bay and then his last team, the Washington Redskins, said much the same thing. "I learned to love that man," said Redskins quarterback Sonny Jurgensen. "I benefitted tremendously as a football player and as a person."[4] His teammate, receiver Charley Taylor, had played in the NFL five years before Lombardi arrived, yet it was Lombardi who "taught me how to play football. I never really knew before."[5]

Such devotion was unusual given that Lombardi was often a harsh, demanding taskmaster with his players, who often said that he "treats us all the same—like dogs."[6] "My No. 1 job is doing away with the defeatist attitude I know is here," he told that first Green Bay team. "Defeatists won't be with the club very long," and they weren't.[7] Lombardi cleaned house, often keeping less talented players who nonetheless had the attitude, leadership, and willingness to sacrifice that he was looking for. One victim was ten-time Pro Bowl center Jim Ringo, who tried to use the help of a lawyer in negotiating a contract. During their meeting Lombardi excused himself for five minutes and then returned to tell Ringo, "You and your lawyer have been traded to Philadelphia."[8]

When Lombardi stepped down as Packers coach to become the general manager in 1968, the team finished with a losing record. The roster was much the same, the system was the same under Lombardi's former assistant Phil Bengtson, the practices were the same—but the Lombardi magic was gone. "There are three things that made the Packers great," said linebacker Ray Nitschke, "A belief in God, a belief in Vince Lombardi and teamwork."[9] Perhaps the genius, or at least part of it, was in Lombardi's ability to take a group of 40 disparate men, a collection of separate individuals from different backgrounds and with different abilities, and turn the whole into something more than the sum of its parts. "We're all different," he had once said. "We all have our own interests, our own preferences, and yet we go down the same road, hand in hand."[10]

Now the road was ending, slowly and painfully from colon cancer. Back in June, doctors had removed two feet of the colon, and Lombardi was making plans to return and coach the Redskins for a second season. But by July the disease was back and spreading quickly, prompting Lombardi to turn over the team to assistant Bill Austin. Lombardi returned to the hospital on July 27 with what was described as an extraordinarily virulent form of cancer. By August, it was apparent how things were going to end, and a litany of players came to say good-bye. Many were shocked at his appearance—the seemingly always-robust Lombardi now gaunt and frail. "I can't face the reality of it," said longtime Packer Willie Wood.[11] "I got a long lunch hour to go to the hospital," said Redskins' receiver Bob Long, "and I tried to thank him for all he'd done. He just reached out and squeezed my hand."[12] Like many who visited in those final days, Long wept as he left the hospital room.

The end came on September 3, Lombardi telling a priest that he was not afraid to die, but that he regretted he had not accomplished more in life. His last words, spoken to his wife, Marie, at 7:12 a.m., were "Happy anniversary. I love you."[13] The two had observed their 30th wedding anniversary only three days before.

The death was announced in page one, bold print in newspapers across the country. His funeral on September 6 at St. Patrick's Cathedral in New York attracted no less attention, and an estimated 5,000 people filed by the day before to view the casket. Cardinal Terence Cooke delivered the eulogy and quoted from one of Lombardi's favorite Bible verses, and one that he often used with his teams, when he advised them to "run to win"—"Do you not know that in a race all the runners run, but only one gets the prize? Run in such a way as to get the prize."[14] Among the dozens of other tributes that appeared in the following days, Robert Lipsyte of the *New York Times* wrote, "[His players] bled for Lombardi because he offered them the opportunity to be the best. It all worked only because he came to his people offering them more than he asked."[15]

There was sense that an era had ended—the "Lombardi era" as it came to be known—a decade of hard, tough football coached and played by hard, tough men. The NFL of 1970 was about to embark on a new era, one in which the former AFL and NFL teams would play in a new merged league. It would be an era of artificial surfaces, player unrest, and league turmoil.

The death of Vince Lombardi seemed to signal the death of a simpler time—a time in which ordinary men could rise up to become heroes by doing extraordinary things. No single game spoke to the Lombardi mystique more than the 1967 Ice Bowl NFL Championship against Dallas, when the Packers overcame 15-below temperatures to mount a winning drive in the last few minutes of the game. "Those last five minutes are what the Packers are all about," said Lombardi afterward. "They do it because they respect each other. They are selfless."[16] Tackle Bob Skoronski added, "This game was our mark of distinction."[17]

Two weeks after the Ice Bowl, Lombardi coached the Packers to a Super Bowl win over the Raiders. After his death, the Super Bowl trophy was named in his honor. He also has had streets and hospitals named after him, and he has been the subject of countless books, movies, and a successful Broadway play. Even the home where he lived in Green Bay has become something of a shrine, with visitors still today walking up uninvited and unannounced as if on a religious pilgrimage.

The Lombardi name represents many things, but for many fans, many of whom never saw him coach, it has become a synonym for a romanticized slice of professional football. For those who play and coach, and even for those who simply watch, Lombardi still speaks as the voice of the game.

"Football is not just a game," he once said, "it's a game of courage, stamina and coordinated efficiency, of sacrifice, dedication, self-denial and love."[18]

CARBURETOR ROULETTE

On Labor Day, September 7, in Indianapolis, Don "The Snake" Prudhomme faced off against Jim Nicoll in the Top Fuel Dragster Finals at the National Hot Rod Association (NHRA) championships. "I remember thinking as we came up on the lights, 'I'm going to win this SOB,'" said Nicoll, "then I felt the clutch slipping and thought, 'Oh, no. Here it comes.'"[19]

Almost as soon as Nicoll crossed the finish line, in 6.48 seconds compared to Prudhomme's winning time of 6.45, his overheated clutch disintegrated and cut the car in two at 225 miles per hour. Almost unnoticed, Nicoll and the roll cage went over the guardrail and landed in a soft spot on an embankment. Meanwhile, the front half of the car spun wildly into Prudhomme's lane, causing the Snake and the millions more watching on television to assume the worst and guess that Nicoll had been killed. Climbing out of his car as the new champion, a visibly shaken Prudhomme surveyed the wreckage and tearfully announced that he was quitting the sport. But Nicoll had only a concussion and a swollen foot, and after a brief stay in the hospital returned to racing and went on to win Top Fuel Driver of the Year honors from *Drag News*. Although memory of the incident stayed with him for years, Prudhomme did not retire and went on to win seven NHRA national titles in top fuel dragster and funny car.

Nearly 5,000 miles away, another spectacular crash did not end as well.

On September 5, Austrian Grand Prix driver Jochen Rindt was in Monza, Italy, for the Italian Grand Prix. The Saturday before the race, he chatted idly with other drivers as his car was rolled out for a practice run. Rindt had developed the habit of kissing his wife, Nina, right before he climbed into his car for a practice run or race, and superstition or not, it must have helped because Rindt was dominating the Formula One circuit. On this particular day, he hurried to the car and did not have time to find Nina, who would watch the run from the pits.

She would not see him again until she collected his body a few hours later in the morgue.

Shortly after Rindt had climbed into his car, Nina had watched in horror as it veered off the dangerous Monza course. Witnesses said the car swerved left, hit the guardrail, and then came back to the center of the track where it overturned. Although the car did not catch fire, a doctor pronounced Rindt dead at the scene. "I lay there thinking how stupid the whole business is, how futile and painful," said defending Grand Prix champion Jackie Stewart. "I kept seeing Jochen lying in the ambulance and I saw his left foot and I remember Nina screaming that we were all mad when we wouldn't let her go to him and then her sitting all alone, with her eyes empty."[20]

Rindt's death was just the latest in what had become an incredibly tragic year on the Formula One circuit. On June 2, New Zealand driver Bruce McLaren was killed while testing in England. In an experimental car, and at speeds estimated at 180 miles an hour, McLaren spun out of control and ran off the course. His car split in two and exploded on impact. Three weeks later at the Dutch Grand Prix, a race that Rindt ended up winning, the aptly named Piers Courage of England died on the 23rd lap when his car left the road, rolled over, and burst into flames. A public announcement reassured the large crowd that Courage had escaped injury, but shortly afterward reporters were handed slips of paper telling them of the driver's death.

The string of fatalities renewed concerns about Formula One safety practices. It had always been a dangerous sport, even back to the time of famed German driver Bernd Rosemeyer, who in 1938 got his Auto Union Special up to more than 200 miles per hour before a gust of wind lifted him airborne and smashed his car into a bridge abutment. Rosemeyer became one of the growing ranks of casualties of the "dead-or-glory era." There were 30 fatalities in the 1950s and '60s, making Formula One a dangerous game not only for drivers, but spectators as well. Dan Gurney, whose own devastating wreck at the Dutch Grand Prix had killed a spectator, said that after he retired he would lie awake in bed at night counting up all the people he had known who died in racing. "After a while," said Gurney, "maybe an hour, I counted up fifty-seven."[21]

In response to safety concerns, drivers formed the Grand Prix Drivers Association (GPDA) in 1961, and even before Rindt's death the organization had become alarmed. Prior to the German Grand Prix in August, Rindt visited the track at Nurburgring and with the GPDA developed a list of suggestions to make the track safer. When organizers ignored them, Rindt and the group, meeting in London for the memorial services of McLaren and Courage, voted not to race at Nurburgring. That finally got the attention of Formula One officials and the race was quickly moved to Hockenheim, where Rindt won for the final time in his career.

Despite its small victory in getting the German Grand Prix moved, and the fact that the 1970 season gratefully ended with no more casualties, the GPDA still had very grave concerns over safety. Drivers were well aware that "despite the adulation, the action, the romance of the sport and its tangential advantages, it seems like a game of carburetor roulette. Eventually the whole thing will explode in your face."[22]

No one knew that better than Jackie Stewart, who quit school at age 15 to pump gas in his father's garage in Scotland and would eventually win three Grand Prix titles. Yet Stewart, who more than anyone epitomized the suave yet daring caricature of the Formula One driver, had now seen two very good friends in Rindt and Courage die within a couple of months. He was especially close to Rindt, who lived just up the hill from Stewart in Begnins, Switzerland. "I had sworn I would never get close to another driver again," he said, "not after Jochen, but I cannot control my affections as well as I can a car. It hurt, it hurt so very much."[23] Stewart took his despair and funneled it into safety, and it was his concerns over track conditions that led to a boycott and eventual cancelation of the Belgian Grand Prix in 1969. When the crashes and fatalities continued on into 1971, Stewart warned that some F1 events would have to be canceled.

Impatient for change and on the heels of the death of yet another driver, teammate François Cevert, Stewart announced his retirement from racing after winning his third championship in 1973. "Somewhere along the line I'm going to make a mistake," he said, "whether it be a small mistake or a big one; a mechanical failure beyond my control or someone else's mistake, and then . . ."[24] Stewart didn't finish the sentence, but he didn't have to. He quit at the relatively young age of 34.

The problems in Formula One seemed to go on the back burner until another spate of crashes and deaths in 1994, including the death of three-time champion Ayrton Senna, killed in the San Marino Grand Prix. Senna's death led to the reestablishment of the GPDA, which had been disbanded in 1982, and the indictment and manslaughter trial of six people connected to Senna's Williams Renault team, including team owner Frank Williams.[25] Medical experts blamed the crash on a badly done modification of the steering column, which broke and caused Senna to crash. More importantly, at least for GPDA drivers, the accident led to more safety measures, including narrower cars and grooved tires.

The tradeoff was slower speeds and a more predictable race. Gone were the glory days of reckless abandon and dramatic passes on the final turn. The idea was to replace reckless with wreck less, and the result was a Formula One circuit that became "a high-tech, high speed parade where passing is virtually impossible and finishes almost predictable."[26] Driver Eddie Irvine once commented that the racing had become so dull "I wish I'd had a stereo in the car to keep me amused."[27]

Formula One continues to work on the delicate balance between safety and speed, as do organizers in open-wheel and stock car racing. NASCAR, another group that had come under scrutiny for dragging its feet on safety issues, used the 2001 death of superstar Dale Earnhardt to enact new rules related to seat belts along with head and neck restraints. "It made us all aware that everyone in our business is at risk and we needed to do things to lessen that risk," said NASCAR driver Brett Bodine. "NASCAR had to react and react now."[28]

Formula One did not react in time to save the lives of McLaren, Courage, and Rindt in the deadly summer of 1970. Despite his death in Italy, Rindt had accumulated enough points to win the Formula One championship despite missing the last three races. He became the first, and last, driver to posthumously win the Grand Prix title.

"Last year I had a lot of bad luck," he said the day of his fatal crash. "But this year it has changed."[29]

THE KING AND HER COURT

If anyone ever had a perfect name for tennis it was Margaret Court. And if anyone ever played tennis perfectly, at least in 1970, it was still Margaret Court. On September 12, the Australian beat Rosie Casals in the finals of the U.S. Open 6–2, 2–6, and 6–1 to complete a Grand Slam of women's singles titles. "The tension was especially hard on me going for a grand slam," she said after the match. "Thank God I won in the end."[30] The victory added to her previous titles at Wimbledon, the French Open, and the Australian Open. Court had previously won a mixed doubles slam, and there was very little doubt that at the age of 28 she was the best women's player in tennis, and maybe of all time.

It was a lofty position, but one not quite as high as some would have liked. The problem Court had at the time was a problem shared by other women's tennis players and female athletes in general: a lack of recognition and equal opportunity, especially when compared to the men. As Court chased the Grand Slam, *Sports Illustrated* noted that "for the ladies, Grand Slams are all but impossible to achieve. The female of the species seems to be more vulnerable than the male to such things as fatigue, physical ailments, and just plain shattered nerves."[31] Earlier in the summer at Wimbledon, when Court beat Billie Jean King 14–12, 11–9 in one of the greatest matches in the history of the event, newspaper accounts referred to both players as "girls." Perhaps those kinds of attitudes were the reason that Court won $7,500 for her U.S. Open Championship, while men's winner and fellow Aussie Ken Rosewall pocketed $20,000.

In an age of women's liberation, such discrepancies were becoming harder to tolerate. King split time between the circuit and her home, but her husband eventually convinced her to devote her full-time energies to tennis, where she faced battles of a different kind. "Success for me is hitting a great shot and knowing the public appreciates it, but money is the measuring stick by which people decide whether or not to appreciate you. In 1967, I had my greatest tournament year, but I didn't have that measuring stick, and no one came to see those beautiful shots. I'd like to help women [athletes] get purses equal to men."[32]

That seemed unlikely. In 1970, the men's singles winner at Wimbledon got twice as much as the women's champion, and the other Grand Slam tournaments were about the same. The Pacific Coast International tournament initially offered $12,500 to the men's singles winner and only $1,500 to the women's winner, before pressure forced tournament organizers to increase the women's award to $11,000. But that largesse aside, the future did not look promising.

Until a hustler named Bobby Riggs showed up.

Riggs was formerly a world-class tennis player who had won three Grand Slam titles and been ranked number one in the world in 1939. But now in his 50s, long past his prime and pretty much out of competitive tennis, Riggs had spent the past several years making a living by betting on himself in unofficial matches against various opponents. Gambling was simply a part of Bobby's personality, and he later acknowledged that he couldn't play his best unless he had a bet going on the match. At some point, perhaps spurred by either Court or King, the lightbulb went on.

Riggs would challenge the best women's players in the world. "Women's tennis is so far beneath men's tennis," he boasted. "I wasn't scared before, but after watching the girls at Wimbledon I may even be overconfident."[33]

It's unlikely that Riggs actually believed all his bluster and was simply trying to increase public interest in an exhibition match. At first he set his sights on King, but when she refused Riggs continued his grandstanding, hoping to catch someone else in his promotional net. By 1973 he finally hauled in Margaret Court, still ranked number one in the world. The two agreed to a $10,000 winner-take-all match at the San Vicente Country Club near San Diego, although CBS, which would televise the event, agreed to pay the players win or lose. It generated a tremendous amount of publicity, certainly with the general public, but especially among the tennis pros of the day. Opinion was divided on whether the 55-year-old Riggs could keep up with the younger Court, but Bill Talbert noted presciently, "Bobby would never agree to the match if he wasn't sure he would win."[34]

Before a national television audience Riggs humiliated Court 6–2, 6–1 in what came to be known as the "Mother's Day Massacre." Before the match, Court promised that she would not let Riggs psych her out, but she seemed nervous and shaky throughout. "Her nerves are her only weak point," said fellow Aussie pro Kerry Melville of Court. "Put her under pressure like that and she gets rattled."[35] Among those in attendance was Karen Hantze Susman, a former Wimbledon champion. "To beat Bobby, you have to serve and go to the net," she said. "Margaret wasn't doing that. I don't know why."[36]

Among those not in attendance, the most interested was Billie Jean King, fuming that the result was both outrageous and demeaning to women. "There was no point in this in the beginning," she went on, the anger rising within her, "but now I think that since Margaret really got waxed, I think I can do a lot better. I think I thrive on pressure more than Margaret does."[37]

Bobby Riggs had hooked his next big fish.

The match was a $100,000 winner-take-all event scheduled for September 20, 1973, at the Astrodome in Houston, Texas, which allowed plenty of time for buildup. Riggs delightedly assumed the role of the male chauvinist, and said he was determined to "keep our women at home, taking care of babies where they belong. Women's lib will be set back 20 years."[38] Twenty-six years younger than her opponent, King returned serve by saying Riggs had better take extra vitamins and that she would handle the pressure much better than Court. Few believed her, including Vegas oddsmaker Jimmy "The Greek" Snyder who installed Riggs as the eight-to-five favorite.

The 30,472 who came to the Astrodome, still a record audience for a tennis match, and the millions watching on television saw quite a spectacle before the match even started. Riggs came out wearing a yellow "Sugar Daddy" warm-up jacket, carried on a rickshaw by beautiful young women. King countered by entering on a chariot carried by bare-chested young men dressed as Egyptian attendants to Cleopatra. As a final touch, King presented Riggs with a squealing piglet before the match began.

The match itself failed to live up to the hype, as King methodically ran Riggs ragged, easily winning in straight sets, 6–4, 6–3, and 6–2. There was no bluster or bravado in Bobby's game that night and he looked very much like the older man he was. When the match mercifully ended, Riggs summoned enough energy to jump over the net and congratulate the winner. "I underestimated you," he whispered to King.[39]

There has been speculation in recent years that Riggs, the consummate hustler and gambler, actually threw the match. A man named Hal Shaw claims that he overheard a conversation between Riggs and a group of mobsters months before the match took place. According to Shaw, Riggs would beat Court and then lose to King, even while making it appear that the loss was on the level. While certainly plausible, such allegations are otherwise unsubstantiated.

The real effect of King's victory was not to set back women's lib 20 years, but rather to push it forward. King went on to launch the Women's Tennis Association, which still remains the governing body of women's professional tennis, and was an instrumental factor in helping women achieve equal pay with the men. Whatever dislike she had for Bobby Riggs at the time melted over the years and the two became good friends. Before Riggs died in 1995, King called him at his home and said she loved him. After Riggs responded in kind he said, "We really made a difference, didn't we?"[40]

And what of Margaret Court, the 1970 Grand Slam winner who eventually turned over the throne to King? She retired in 1976 at age 33, her place in tennis history secure. Court finished with 64 total Grand Slam titles—singles, doubles, and mixed doubles—still a record for men or women. Part of her biography from the International Tennis Hall of Fame reads, "For sheer strength of performance and accomplishment there has never been a tennis player to match [her]."[41]

But she is not remembered in the same light as King or the other pioneering players who pushed women's tennis to the forefront. She was not a trailblazer but was instead described "as an exemplary sportswoman, a player who never resorted to gamesmanship, a champion who won with honor."[42] "If I was involved in the tennis area like Billie Jean King and Martina Navratilova are now," she later said, "I would probably get a lot of publicity. I don't think the younger people today really know what I have done. Personally it doesn't affect me. It is probably a bit sad for the history of the game, but I am not upset about it."[43]

Instead, Court focused on her family and her religion, and her stance as a Pentecostal minister in Australia put her on the court facing Billie Jean King one more time. Court has been an outspoken critic of homosexual rights, and suggested that lesbianism has been harmful to the women's tennis tour. Such a position has made her extremely unpopular in several quarters, including with openly gay former players such as King and Martina Navratilova. Yet the two remain friendly rivals who often dine together during Wimbledon and debate political topics. When a protest arose to have Court's name removed from the Australian Open arena because of her views, King was quick to respond. "Get rid of her for that?" King said. "Because you don't agree with her? Are you kidding? Please. She deserves it. She's a great player."[44]

Margaret Court showed that greatness in September 1970. "I still play tennis and enjoy it, and it is a part of my life that I loved. I wouldn't have had the opportunities I have had in life without tennis. It opened doors for me in life and brought honor and fame. But I feel I fulfilled all of my goals and dreams and now I am fulfilling another part of my life and I love that."[45]

MOTHER LOVE'S TRAVELING FREAK SHOW

The NFL that Vince Lombardi left behind at his death was undergoing massive change. The war between the leagues had finally ended with a merger, and in 1970 the new league would feature head-to-head competition between teams from the NFL and old AFL in the regular season for the first time. The NFL was also moving into a new era as far as its playing surfaces, which were quickly transitioning from grass to synthetic turf. The Orange Bowl in Miami, site of the upcoming Super Bowl V, added the turf in 1970, meaning that seven of the league's 26 teams were using it. NFL commissioner Pete Rozelle boldly predicted that the turf would be on all NFL fields within ten years.

The legacy of artificial surfaces is still with the NFL today, the biggest change during the season by far would take place on Monday nights. The NFL had experimented with games on days other than Sunday for years, and in Detroit the annual Thanksgiving game had been a tradition since 1934.[46] More recently, games had been scheduled on Friday and Saturday nights to avoid scheduling conflicts in cities where NFL teams had to share a stadium with the local baseball team. In fact, the first game of the 1970 season took place on Friday night, September 18, when the Rams beat the Cardinals 34–13 in Los Angeles.

The NFL started thinking about Monday nights in 1964 when Detroit set a home attendance record of 59,203 against the Packers on Monday, September 28. The success of that game prompted the NFL to stage a limited number of Monday night games from 1966 to 1969, and the AFL added some Monday games in 1968. But no one had seriously considered putting on a game *every* Monday night.

That thinking changed when the NFL renegotiated its television contracts in 1964. Despite offering the league more than $26 million for two years of Sunday football, ABC was shut out of the negotiations in favor of CBS and NBC. "I couldn't get it through my mind," said Ed Scherick, ABC's vice president in charge of programming at the time. "Do you realize our whole blasted *network* had cost only $15 million in 1951?"[47] It was a clear signal, said William Johnson in *Sports Illustrated*, that "whatever pro football did in the future, decisions would have to be made in terms of the economic needs of television."[48]

The man who had made television such a force in football and understood its power was Pete Rozelle. He was the one who ended the practice of teams cutting their own individual television deals and prodded Congress to allow a league-wide contract with money shared by all the teams. The deal made the NFL incredibly rich, and Rozelle saw even more money could be made by putting the game in prime time.

Rozelle realized that prime time was different than Sunday afternoon, and he needed a network willing to reach new audiences. Desperate to get in the game, ABC had the money ($8.6 million for the 13-game schedule) and the man to make it happen—president of ABC Sports Roone Arledge. "What we set out to do," Arledge explained, "was get the audience involved emotionally. If they didn't give a damn about the game, they might still enjoy the program."[49]

Arledge had successfully used that formula in his work at ABC with college football, the Olympics, and *Wide World of Sports*, winning multiple Emmy Awards along the way. Now he was going to try and bring the same type of coverage—personalizing the athletes and giving audiences an extremely close-up look at them—to the NFL. By doing so, Arledge hoped to shift the emphasis of the game from the competition to what *Wide World*'s opening theme would famously describe as "the human drama of athletic competition." "It is not just a football game," Arledge insisted. "It is an event."[50]

To make it an event, Arledge rethought the concept of the television announcer booth, using three people instead of the traditional two. His play-by-play man would be Keith Jackson, a solid, if unspectacular choice, who would be replaced after the first year by Frank Gifford. Joining Jackson was the unlikeliest combination of pro football broadcasters—Howard Cosell and Don Meredith.

Meredith had just retired at the relatively young age of 31 after spending a decade at quarterback for the Cowboys. He had a quick wit and engaging personality but had absolutely no experience in the booth. When he stumbled badly during an exhibition telecast he told Arledge, "Look, fellas, this really isn't my bag, and I don't even know that much about football. I think I'll just leave."[51] Meredith was eventually persuaded to stay by Cosell.

Cosell was an even stranger choice than Meredith. A sports reporter for ABC, he had mostly covered boxing and had little football background. Cosell had a nasal voice, odd appearance, and delighted in showcasing what he considered his superior intellect and ability. "What you saw was what you got," said fellow ABC sportscaster Jim McKay. "That wasn't a character he devised to smoke cigars, be bombastic and use big words. That was him."[52] Critics carped about his looks, his voice, and mostly his demand to be in the spotlight, and one went so far as to say that he was someone "who can no more keep his mouth shut than a porcupine can sing opera."[53]

Those same critics predicted that the Monday night experiment would fall flat on its face when it debuted on September 21, 1970. The game itself seemed attractive enough—the New York Jets and popular star Joe Namath playing a talented Browns team in Cleveland. "No one else wanted the game because they thought it would die at the gate," said Browns' owner Art Modell, "but I was willing to take a chance. All I said was, 'Give me the Jets,' because I figured having the New York market would give the game a jump."[54]

An all-time Cleveland record crowd of 85,703 jammed the old stadium to be a part of history and to watch the Browns rally to beat the Jets 31–21. "I don't know if I made the right move," Modell said smugly after the game. "Did you hear the crowd? Did you hear the din? They loved it."[55] Jackson was professional, but it was Meredith and Cosell that produced the chemistry. "Dandy Don," as Cosell called him, had an aw-shucks, country bumpkin demeanor that played perfectly against Cosell's pomposity. Just as Arledge had hoped, Cosell became the conduit through which everything flowed—a man whom audiences could love or hate but could not ignore. Millions of football fans tuned in to watch the game, but it was not the game that kept them watching, it was Howard Cosell.

The mail poured in, much of it critical of Cosell, but Arledge was unfazed. "Worried?" he said. "That's exactly what I'm looking for!"[56] "Maybe I am abrasive," said Cosell. "But it is not entirely my fault that some people react the way they do. I am simply trying to bring the tenets of good journalism to television. It is difficult because sportscasting is a bottle that was put to sea many years ago and has been lost."[57]

Meredith and Cosell became overnight stars and television cult figures, with Cosell eventually hosting his own short-lived prime-time variety show. "It was a carnival," said Gifford. "Every city we went to. Don [Meredith] had a great name for it. He called it 'Mother Love's Traveling Freak Show.'"[58] Monday night bowling leagues, bingo parlors, and poker games either shut down or moved to a different night. *Variety* reported a significant decline in movie attendance, while restaurant and bar business fell off some 25 percent.[59] Herb Rushing, who owned a steakhouse in Montclair, California, noted, "Monday's the worst night of the week, period. It's been terrible the past few months but since the NFL telecasts began it's atrocious."[60]

What some were convinced would flop vividly demonstrated both the power of television and the demand for more NFL product. A league that for decades played only on Sunday afternoons now offers a regular schedule of games on Sunday, Monday, and Thursday nights. No matter what the time slot, the NFL ratings continue to climb and dominate almost all other competition. It is seemingly bulletproof to competition, audience fragmentation, and the challenges of new technology.

The legacy of *Monday Night Football* is also its staying power. ABC aired the franchise until 2006 and then handed over the program to sister network ESPN, which paid an astonishing $15 billion for its television rights. *Monday Night Football* deserves a lot of credit for changing the way football is telecast, and it pioneered many innovations beyond the three-man broadcast booth. "*Monday Night Football* would change the face of sports in America forever," said NFL author Michael MacCambridge, "both in the way games were portrayed, but it also moved all of American sports into a much more central role in American culture."[61]

10

OCTOBER

IN THE ZONE

The 1970 Baltimore Orioles came into October mad. In fact, they had been mad almost the entire season. The previous fall an underdog New York Mets team had brushed aside an Orioles squad that had won 109 games and was considered among the best in baseball history. New York humbled Baltimore in the World Series four games to one and held the powerful Orioles' lineup to a meager three home runs and .146 batting average for the five games. While the Mets became the darlings of baseball, the Orioles suffered through a long winter of discontent. "After the last game, I was in a daze," said catcher Elrod Hendricks. "I'm sitting out in the bullpen saying, 'I don't believe this.' Then all of a sudden it sunk in. Even though I had to go to Puerto Rico and play winter ball, all I could think about was next year."[1]

When next year came, Baltimore took its frustrations out on the American League, winning 108 games and losing only 54. The team had the best hitting, pitching, and fielding in the league, leading manager Earl Weaver to understandably call it the best team in baseball. The headlines went to sluggers Boog Powell and Frank Robinson, and to the team's trio of 20-game winners—Jim Palmer, Dave McNally, and Mike Cuellar—and they helped Baltimore to an easy three-game sweep of Minnesota in the American League Championship Series.

One player flying under the radar was third baseman Brooks Robinson. Robinson had another solid season, hitting .276 with 94 RBI, but he often seemed to get lost among the big names on the team. Aside from his MVP season in 1964, Brooks Robinson never hit higher than .303 or collected more than 23 homers in any season. His hair already thinning, at 33 he looked like a much older man, especially with his slow, stiff-legged way of running. When the Orioles' Gene Woodling was asked by manager Paul Richards to watch and evaluate the young Robinson in a workout, "I thought Paul was kidding," said Woodling. "He couldn't hit, he couldn't run, and his arm wasn't that strong."[2] Even Robinson's old high school coach thought he was too slow and couldn't hit well enough. It took several years of bouncing between the majors and minors before Robinson finally stuck with the Orioles for good in 1960.

Robinson struggled all his career with his hitting, but it was his fielding that finally established him at third base. He helped the Orioles to a shocking four-game World Series sweep of the Dodgers in 1966, but he hit only .214 in the series and again it was Frank Robinson who got most of the headlines. Frank came over to Baltimore in a trade before the season and won the American League MVP with a .316 average, 49 home runs, and 122 RBI. First baseman Boog Powell would win the MVP in 1970 with 35 homers and 114 RBI.

The Orioles' opponent in the World Series would be a Cincinnati Reds team that had won 102 games on the strength of a powerful lineup that included National League MVP Johnny Bench (45 homers and 148 RBI), Tony Perez (40 homers and 129 RBI), and Lee May (34 homers and 94 RBI). Cincinnati did not have near the pitching depth of Baltimore, but the Reds led the National League in batting average and homers as they came to be known as the "Big Red Machine." "'Are you awed by them?' a reporter asked Earl Weaver. 'I dunno,' he replied. 'Are they awed by us?'"[3]

The World Series began on October 10, 1970, at Cincinnati's Riverfront Stadium, making it the first series game ever played on artificial turf. "I'll play a little deeper than normal," Robinson said, "behind the dirt part, and just hope a ball doesn't hit the edge of the turf."[4] With the score tied 3–3 in the sixth, May hit a scorching two-hopper that skipped over the dirt and appeared to be headed into the left field corner for a double. Robinson reached out at the last minute, got to the ball fully extended and in foul territory, and somehow managed to get off a throw to first while his body was headed the opposite direction. Helped by a friendly bounce from the artificial surface, the ball hopped to Powell just in time to beat May to the bag. It was an astounding piece of defensive artistry, which Robinson later punctuated by hitting a game-winning home run in a 4–3 Orioles win. "I'd put it in his top 100 plays," Weaver said afterward, but he then corrected himself. "Those hundred," he said, "are only since I've been here."[5]

Robinson's play would have been all the talk of Game 1, if not for a play at the plate in that same inning. With teammate Bernie Carbo on third, Cincinnati's Ty Cline bounced a dribbler in front of the plate, which was collected by catcher Elrod Hendricks. Pitcher Jim Palmer alerted his catcher that Carbo was trying to score, so Hendricks turned to tag the sliding Carbo. Home plate umpire Ken Burkhart, who should have been behind Hendricks for the play at the plate, had moved out front to see if the ball was fair or foul. Burkhart was now out of position with his back to the play and trying to look over this shoulder at the action, and when he signaled out, it prompted a furious reaction from Carbo and Reds' manager Sparky Anderson. "I'd like to see pictures of that play," Anderson yelled at Burkhart, who replied, "I'd like to see it too."[6] What the pictures would later reveal was that Carbo missed the plate with his slide, but it didn't matter because Hendricks tagged him with an empty glove—the ball was still in his throwing hand. "I knew I tagged somebody on that play," Hendricks joked, "but I didn't realize it was the umpire."[7] Burkhart later admitted that he was in a bad position, but there was nothing he could do about it. Neither could the Reds.

The Burkhart-Carbo-Hendricks troika was pushed off the front pages the following day by Robinson, and again he robbed May, this time stopping another hard smash to start a double play in the bottom of the third. Robinson also singled in a five-run Orioles fifth, as Baltimore won 6–5. As the series prepared to move to Baltimore, Robinson was now being called "Hoover," and the "Vacuum Cleaner," for his defensive play. "That little bit of old lady luck and Brooks Robinson beat us," said Anderson. "Brooks is the finest third baseman I've ever seen. That's two days in a row he's done that to us. It's great to see, except it's happening to us."[8]

It did not take long for Robinson to continue his magic in Game 3, as in the top of the first inning he took away a hit from Johnny Bench, diving to his left to snare a low line drive. In the bottom of the inning he doubled home two runs, and added a later hit to raise his series batting average to .458. Baltimore won 9–3 to take a commanding 3–0 lead in the

Series. In Game 4, May finally solved his problem by hitting one way over Robinson's head, a three-run homer that won the game 6–5 and ruined a day in which Robinson went four-for-four and hit another home run of his own. In the top of the eighth, after the Reds had put two men on and right before May came to bat, a fan yelled out from the stands, "Get three, Brooks."[9]

By Game 5, such was his reputation that when rain threatened to delay or cancel the game, catcher Andy Etchebarren told him, "Brooksie, make it stop raining." When Robinson asked the rain to stop and it did, Etchebarren said in mock amazement, "I'm getting out of here."[10] The spell continued into the game as Brooks singled in the Orioles' clinching 9–3 victory. Just for good measure, he iced the cake with a diving stop of a Bench line drive in the ninth, once again going into foul territory. "I hope we can come back and play the Orioles next year," Bench said in the losing clubhouse. "I also hope Brooks Robinson has retired by then."[11]

Robinson easily won series MVP honors after hitting .429 and tying a series record with nine hits in the five games,[12] but it was his defensive play that demoralized the Reds. As he was being interviewed on television in the postgame celebration, Robinson was interrupted by Sparky Anderson. "As for this guy," Anderson said, "somebody ought to shoot him."[13] When Pete Rose found out that Robinson would get a new car as part of his MVP award, he replied, "If we knew he wanted a car so badly, we'd have bought one for him ourselves."[14]

Even before the term existed, Robinson spent five games in the "zone," that pinnacle of athletic performance that players visit infrequently. Players in all sports, from the great to the mediocre, sometimes lift themselves beyond their own capabilities or expectations for a period of time. They can't explain it or sometimes even understand it; all they hope is that they can keep it going for as long as possible. "There is no doubt that the experience is real," said sports psychologist Dr. John Silva. "Being 'in the zone' is something that has been described by many athletes in different sports, in different levels of sport. It has been experienced by athletes from Little League through high school, college, professional sports and the Olympics. Something definitely takes place, something powerful."[15]

Sometimes the zone is short, such as when Reggie Jackson hit three home runs on three consecutive pitches during the 1977 World Series. Sometimes it can last a whole season. A career .271 hitter, Norm Cash of the Tigers spent the entire 1961 season in the zone, leading the league in hits (193) and batting average (.361), while smacking a career-high 41 home runs. The following season, Cash's average fell to .243, still the biggest one-year drop for a batting champion in major league history. Robinson's zone really started during the American League Championship Series when he hit .583 in the three games against the Twins. His combined postseason numbers for eight games that October were 16 hits in 33 at bats (.485 average), eight RBI, four doubles, and three home runs.[16]

But it's his defensive work that still stands out all these years later. Robinson's fielding in the World Series was so spectacular that an official from the Baseball Hall of Fame in Cooperstown, New York, asked him for his glove. Thirteen years later, Brooks joined his glove in the Hall, and he is still acknowledged as one of the greatest third basemen in baseball history. "You can watch him here and there and see him make a great play," said Tom Seaver, whose Mets had beaten the Orioles the year before. "But to really appreciate a player like Robinson you've got to see him for a full series. Then you can understand the true value of Brooks Robinson. It was truly watching genius at work."[17]

ARCHIE'S ARMY

A joke making the rounds in the fall of 1970 went something like this: A man in northern Mississippi was despondent and threatened to jump off a bridge.

"Wait," said a friend. "Think about your family and your religion."

"Don't have any family," the jumper said, "and I don't believe in religion."

"Well," said his friend, desperately, "then think about Archie."

"Archie who?"

"Jump, you s.o.b., jump."[18]

No one, especially in Mississippi, should have had to ask "Archie who?" Before Peyton and before Eli, there was Archie Manning, who by the age of 21 had achieved cult-figure status as the senior quarterback at the University of Mississippi. In hanging a picture of Manning in his office, a local doctor asked, "Is it really wrong for a 40-year-old man to be in love with a 21-year-old boy?"[19]

Who couldn't love the hometown kid from little (population 2,674) Drew, Mississippi—a freckle-faced Huck Finn in shoulder pads—who came to the big city, overcame adversity, married a beauty queen, and returned Ole Miss to the national football conversation?

The adversity came in the summer before his sophomore year when his father committed suicide and Archie was the one who discovered the body. He also took care of it so that his mother and sister would be spared the sight. "He grew up in a matter of two minutes," said sister Pam. "Any decision made in our household after that, Archie was the one to make it."[20] Archie later admitted that the event motivated him to play even harder to honor his father's memory.

That fall, Manning completed less than half his passes and threw more interceptions than touchdowns but still led Ole Miss to a 7–3–1 record, including a Liberty Bowl win over Virginia Tech. The legend of Archie was likely born his junior season in a shootout loss to Alabama. In a game that shattered numerous NCAA and conference records, Manning completed 33 of 52 passes for 436 yards and two touchdowns, and also ran for 105 yards and three more scores. Several Alabama players swear that coach Bear Bryant fired his defensive coordinator Ken Donohue three times that night before the Tide finally prevailed, 33–32. Ole Miss coach John Vaught called it the greatest performance by a quarterback he had ever seen.

Tennessee was not convinced, and when the unbeaten and third-ranked Volunteers hosted Ole Miss a few weeks later, fans wore "Archie Who?" buttons, and All-America linebacker Steve Kiner openly taunted the Rebels. "Hee-haw," said Kiner, "them's not horses, them's mules."[21] The Rebel mules ripped Tennessee 38–0 with Manning throwing for one touchdown and running for another. Ole Miss turned around the ridicule and created its own buttons that read, "You Know Damn Well Who!" and "Super Mules." Archie's season ended with a fourth-place finish in the Heisman voting, a Sugar Bowl win over Arkansas, and even a higher fever pitch for what he might do his senior season.

If any state or university needed a hero like Archie Manning in the fall of 1970, it was Mississippi. In 1962, two people died when Ole Miss erupted in a riot trying to prevent the first black from enrolling. That same weekend, as a giant Confederate flag covered the field, Governor Ross Barnett addressed the crowd at the Ole Miss–Kentucky game in

Jackson and proclaimed his love for the state, its people, and particularly its heritage and customs.

Ole Miss won the Kentucky game, finished the year unbeaten, and captured a version of the national championship, but such heroics were getting drowned out. That fall, the football team shared its practice field with federal troops stationed there to keep the peace. A year later, civil rights activist Medgar Evers was gunned down in his own yard; a year after that, the bodies of three murdered civil rights workers were discovered buried in a Neshoba County field. Jackson television station WLBT was so vehemently opposed to integration and civil rights that the Federal Communications Commission revoked the license of its owners. Even during Archie's senior year, seven black students were kicked out of Ole Miss after taking part in a racial protest on campus. "It's difficult, if you will," said Don Cole, one of those expelled and later an Ole Miss administrator, "to change some memories, especially when they've sunk in so deep, hit so hard, been so personal."[22]

It was a beaten and battered Mississippi that fully embraced its native son. Here was someone fresh faced and seemingly unstained by the dark issues plaguing the state. The problems themselves would take a long time to work out, but in the meantime, Archie could take your mind off them for a few hours every Saturday. In a state where no one could seem to agree on politics, civil rights, Vietnam, and desegregation, everyone could agree on Archie Manning.

The love-in included buttons (Archie for Heisman), bumper stickers (Archie's Army), posters, dolls, T-shirts, and even a record. A group called the Rebel Rousers cut a song called "The Ballad of Archie Who." A poor copy of Johnny Cash's "Folsom Prison Blues," it still sold 50,000 copies. Part of the lyrics of the song went, "Just ask ol' Hee-Haw Kiner if he's not a real stud hoss." The university got so many requests for his autograph that the athletic department made a stamp out of it and hired a secretary to handle all the mail. "The only thing I can figure out," said the soft-spoken kid at the center of the storm, "is that Archie is a different name. Maybe if it were Bill or something, none of this would have started."[23]

Archie and Ole Miss started 1970 ranked number five in the nation, and entered October with wins over Memphis State and Kentucky. On October 3, the Rebels got their first big test of the season in a rematch with Alabama, this time in Jackson. "I've never seen him like this," said his fiancée, Olivia Williams, the week of the game. "Even before the Tennessee game last year he wasn't this fired up. Why, I think he wants to hurt somebody, and that's not like Archie."[24] Nursing a pulled groin muscle, Archie mused, "I haven't had good games statistically; I'm not even in the top 10 in total offense. But that doesn't bother me."[25]

It certainly bothered Alabama, and if there were still any people left asking "Archie who?" by game's end they could probably be counted on one hand. Before a huge television audience, Manning threw three touchdown passes in leading Ole Miss to a 48–23 rout of the Tide. The Rebels had beaten Alabama only twice in the last 21 meetings and both times it was Archie Manning at quarterback. The following week at Georgia, Manning led the Rebels to 17 points in the fourth quarter as Ole Miss rallied to win 31–21. "I'm just glad we won't have to see Archie Manning anymore," said Georgia coach Vince Dooley. "He should win the Heisman Trophy."[26] At that moment, it all seemed possible for Archie and his army—the Heisman, an unbeaten season, and maybe even a national championship.

But as the October leaves changed from red and orange to brown, so too did Manning's season turn cold. On October 17, the Rebels hosted Southern Mississippi and played for the first time at their home stadium in Oxford instead of in Jackson. Ole Miss got two quick touchdown passes from Archie but never scored again in losing 30–14. The real star of the game was Ray Guy, a future NFL Hall of Fame punter who kicked three extra points and a 47-yard field goal and intercepted a Manning pass. It was the first time Ole Miss had ever lost a game to Southern Miss.

Three days later, Vaught suffered a mild heart attack. The 62-year-old coach was hospitalized for a few days and hoped to return, but assistant Frank "Bruiser" Kinard, a former Ole Miss All-American, would finish out the season in his place.[27] In Kinard's first game played in a downpour in Nashville, Ole Miss looked sluggish but still beat Vanderbilt 26–16. Manning threw only 17 times and completed nine.

The pall that settled over Oxford with Vaught's hospitalization became funereal at the homecoming game against Houston. It started well enough—Manning completed 14 of 26 passes for 188 yards and a couple of touchdowns as Ole Miss took a 14–7 lead. But with 10:46 left in the third quarter, Houston linebacker Charlie Hall caught up with Manning as he faked a handoff and rolled to his right. Manning stuck out his left arm to break his fall, and the result was a broken ulna, the long bone that goes from the elbow to the hand. Manning had pushed interest in the Ole Miss program to new heights, and the university had installed artificial turf at Hemingway Stadium during the summer. That turf, ironically called "Archie's Carpet," may have contributed to the injury. "My hand didn't slip when it hit," Manning said. "On that stuff, you don't slip."[28] The Rebels went on to win 24–13, but it hardly seemed to matter.

Manning had broken the same bone in high school in almost the same place, but that did not require surgery. This time, surgery would be needed and Archie settled in to Baptist Hospital in Memphis, just across the street from Methodist Hospital where Vaught was still recuperating. When asked if the two had talked, Manning said yes, but his voice trailed off and he could not finish. The head of Archie's Army, and the general who trained it, were no longer on the front lines, and as *Sports Illustrated* observed, "without Archie, Ole Miss is about as dangerous as the Confederate Army without Lee."[29]

Ole Miss didn't need Manning in a 44–7 blowout of Chattanooga, as the wonderfully named backup Shug Chumbler threw four touchdown passes. "He's got a lot of talent," Manning said of Chumbler, "but he just hasn't had the chance to get out and show it."[30] But great name or not, Chumbler was no Manning, and the next week the Rebels lost their annual Egg Bowl rivalry game to Mississippi State 19–14.

Originally, doctors said Manning's arm would be in a cast for three months, but coaches and trainers thought some kind of harness or sleeve would allow him to keep playing, especially since the break was in his nonthrowing arm. The week of the last game of the season against another rival, LSU, Manning went to Memphis to get outfitted for a special protective device. Even though the device was approved for play, LSU coach Charlie McClendon warned that his team would not be responsible if Manning reinjured himself.

Manning didn't get hurt, unless you count two interceptions and a safety he suffered in a little over two quarters of play. Tommy Casanova ran back two punts for touchdowns as LSU clinched an Orange Bowl bid by destroying Ole Miss 61–17. With a few more weeks to recover, Manning played much better in the Gator Bowl, but Auburn beat the Rebels 35–28. "I don't think that old hospital bed ever got off my back," said Manning, who had to sit on the bench the final few minutes from exhaustion. "I never really got my wind back after I went into the hospital, and I felt it today."[31] Despite the injury and three straight losses to end the season, Manning finished third in the Heisman Trophy voting behind Jim Plunkett of Stanford and Joe Theismann of Notre Dame.

The exhilaration of October wins over Alabama and Georgia, the talk about a Heisman Trophy and an unbeaten season, and the passion that people from Mississippi and all around the South felt about their native son did not have the happiest of endings. In fact, 1970 was really a microcosm of Archie Manning's star-crossed football career. There was always so much promise, so much potential, but something always seemed to get in the way.

In 1971, Manning was the number-one draft choice of the Saints, a dreadful team that was hoping to bring the passion of Archie's Army to New Orleans. In eleven seasons, Archie played for seven head coaches, none of whom had a winning record, and took a beating behind terrible offensive lines. Somehow, he became a two-time Pro Bowl quarterback. Had the circumstances been different, had Manning played for the Cowboys, Rams, or Vikings during his prime, his talent would have likely landed him in the Hall of Fame. "Archie was a very good quarterback for a long time," said former teammate John Hill, "a very hard-working, very dedicated athlete. It was a shame we couldn't put a better team around him. Nobody can play the game by themselves."[32]

Archie Manning is now better known as the father of two Super Bowl–winning quarterbacks, and perhaps his sons have eclipsed his ability. But for all their greatness, neither Peyton nor Eli ever generated the passion and excitement that their old man did in the fall of 1970. It was a glorious time when an innocent kid with a thick Mississippi drawl could make the state forget about its problems for a while. And all these years later, especially on the Ole Miss campus where speed limits are set at 18 in deference to a particular football jersey number, no one needs to ask "Archie who?"

"IT'S BETTER THAN SEX"

It sits about 100 miles west of Salt Lake City, the largest of the many salt flats that are remnants from the Great Salt Lake. It is dry, arid, and smooth as glass—in short, perfect for racing powerful cars—and for years, those in search of speed had come to this part of northwestern Utah to test the limits of vehicular speed and human bravery. In many ways,

Bonneville was like the Old West, where gunslingers rode into town, but now with the horses under the hood.

On October 23, a former astronaut trainee named Gary Gabelich peered out at the Bonneville Salt Flats from a three-wheeled, rocket-powered car he had named the Blue Flame. Gabelich had spent ten years at Rockwell, working himself up from the mail room to test guinea pig, and the experiments he went through helped scientists better prepare astronauts for space travel. But even as those astronauts landed on the moon, Gabelich had fixed his sights closer to home. "I was interviewed by NASA for a spot on the astronaut team," he said, "but if I had the choice of setting a land speed record or going on a space flight to the moon, I'd rather have the speed record. I'd rather be a hero here for life than a hero for one day or a week."[33]

That land speed record belonged to Gabelich's friend and rival Craig Breedlove, who had owned it for the better part of a decade. Breedlove first grabbed the record in 1963 at Bonneville at 407.45 miles per hour and kept inching the speed higher. He broke it twice in 1965, the second time breaking the 600-mile-per-hour mark in the "flying mile"—the average of his two best runs over a mile distance from a running start.

Breedlove and Gabelich, both growing up as teenagers in car-crazy California, began to challenge British domination of the land speed title in the 1950s. In 1959, having just turned 19, Gabelich hit 356 miles per hour at Bonneville. Three years later, Breedlove put a surplus jet from a Navy F-4 Phantom on a car he called the Spirit of America to break Englishman John Cobb's record. Breedlove became so associated with speed records that the ultimate California band, the Beach Boys, sang about him in "Spirit of America."

It had not come without cost. Strapping a rocket to a vehicle may push the speed record, but it also strains the laws of mechanics and physics. Englishman Donald Campbell set eight speed records on both land and water, but in 1967 at Coniston Lake in England his Bluebird craft lifted, somersaulted, and killed him instantly on its impact with the water. In 1964, at more than 500 miles per hour, Breedlove had his parachute snap off. While the car smashed through some telephone poles and sank in a canal filled with 18 feet of water, Breedlove somehow walked away wet but uninjured. "And for my next act," he said breezily upon emerging, "I'm going to set myself on fire."[34]

But once Breedlove had the record, public interest—and more importantly, sponsorships—began to wane. There seemed to be a sense of "been there, done that" as five years passed before any serious challenge rose. While Breedlove fell into debt and slipped from the limelight, Gabelich bided his time, racing on water for a while and setting a speed record for drag boats. He skydived, played tennis, jumped out of airplanes, and raced go-karts. No adrenaline rush was too great, especially if it meant going fast. "It's better than sex," he once said. "It's better than anything."[35] Finally, after more than five years, it was finally time, and Gabelich and crew headed to Bonneville.

The quest started on September 19, and in fits and starts—not to mention 20 tries—the team inched toward the record. Now, on October 23, Gabelich climbed in the Blue Flame believing he had a chance. He had two goals: to take the record away from Breedlove—who held the mark at 600.6 miles per hour—and to break the sound barrier at 760-plus miles per hour. His relationship with Breedlove was relaxed and friendly, the younger Gabelich often tweaking his friend about their four-year age difference, calling Breedlove the Old Man who needed a "rocket-powered wheelchair."[36] But here was an attempt to finally step out of Breedlove's supersonic shadow. To become the first one to break the sound barrier would make it that much better.

Gabelich carried with him almost every form of good-luck charm he could find, including a St. Christopher medal, a Mexican peso, and even a lock of his girlfriend's hair. Then it was time to get down to serious business and talk to the car itself. "Let's do it together, baby," he told the Blue Flame, patting its long nose cone. "Give me a good ride. We can do it together."[37]

Most racers like to get out close to dawn when the weather is cooler on the flats, but Gabelich waited until later in the morning. As he climbed into the Blue Flame, he admitted that "you're scared before a race begins, but then the adrenaline that goes through you with the car's acceleration overcomes it all."[38] At 37 feet in length, 6,500 pounds, 58,000 horsepower, and powered with liquefied natural gas, the Blue Flame would give Gabelich plenty of both adrenaline and acceleration.

He took off like a rifle shot on one of his early runs but tore a parachute, forcing him to abort at 500 miles per hour. Technicians got the chute fixed, but the failure cost precious fuel. Even with larger fuel tanks, the team had only enough left for eight more runs, and even then the weather forecasts were not promising. Finally, just as the sun broke through the clouds, Gabelich seemed ready for a record run. "I usually like to have the sun shining," Gabelich said. "It wasn't at first, but later on it came out and I knew we would have a good day."[39]

With fuel and patience almost exhausted, Gabelich hit 630.388 miles per hour on one pass. He still needed another run in the opposite direction to qualify for the record, and he got it, even though he only had enough fuel to get halfway through. Gabelich coasted home to the record, averaging 622.407 miles an hour for the two passes. As he climbed victoriously out of the Blue Flame, his father, a U.S. Marshal from Los Angeles, greeted him in tears. "I guess I got a little emotional back there," Len Gabelich said later. "It's just a relief that it's all over."[40] The new speed demon had shattered his old rival's mark by nearly 30 miles per hour. Breedlove did not come to Bonneville to watch, but when he heard about Gabelich he silently vowed to regain the crown.

Hailed as the new champion, Gabelich basked in his new fame with a series of interviews and television appearances, and for 13 years he held the title as the fastest man on land. But in many ways, the historic run was the beginning of the end for both Gabelich and the flats. Gabelich seriously injured himself in a funny car racing accident in 1972, requiring six operations on his hands and legs. "I've been in racing one way or another since I was 18, so I guess I was due for a good one," he said somewhat philosophically.[41] But the injuries were so severe that Gabelich never raced again competitively. He died as one might expect: at the age of 43, the victim of a crash when his motorcycle hit a truck in San Pedro, California. "Racing is my whole life," he had once said. "The faster you go, the more thrilling it is."[42]

Gabelich's record run was the last ever set at the flats. As early as 1975, patches of dirt began appearing on the salt table along with other buckling and cracking, and the area shrank from 15 miles in length to ten. Some of the salt was the victim of natural erosion, while much of it had been collected and used in the making of fertilizer. In 1997, a project began to pump salt back onto the flats and that has helped restore some of its condition, but by then the racing was gone. That same year, an Englishman named Andy Green broke both the speed record and the sound barrier by reaching 760.343 at Black Rock in Nevada. The sonic boom rattled windows as far as 13 miles away. "Well," Breedlove told reporters when he heard the news, "they've certainly raised the bar on us."[43] His public relations director, Cherie Danson, was more downcast. "We were devastated. This is not the way the script was supposed to end."[44]

If Breedlove has his way, it will end with him holding the record again, not as driver but as team owner. Now in his 70s, he is still chasing the dream, which for him is to become the one to break 800 miles an hour. "Most people can't understand why we do this," he once said. "The land-speed record quest is a unique, exclusive thing. Some assume it's for ego, and maybe it is the first time, but the tug is a far more deep-seated thing."[45]

Were Gary Gabelich still alive, he would no doubt agree.

BACK FROM THE DEAD

Tales of courage are common in the NHL. Most professional sports are physically demanding, but hockey players seem to take extraordinary pride in their ability to play hurt and under adverse conditions. Six weeks after rupturing a bowel and undergoing emergency surgery in 1958, Canadiens' star Bernie "Boom Boom" Geoffrion returned against the advice of doctors and helped Montreal win the Stanley Cup. In the 1964 Cup final, Bobby "Boomer" Baun of the Maple Leafs broke his leg during Game 6 but stayed on the ice and scored the winning goal. Baun refused to have the leg X-rayed until after the series had ended and the Leafs had beaten Detroit.

This particular story of courage climaxed on October 25, but in a roundabout way it began all the way back in 1933.

On December 13, 1933, the Bruins' Eddie Shore came from behind on a check of Toronto's Ace Bailey. Bailey, a star in the league and future Hall of Famer, flew backward and hit his helmetless head on the ice, fracturing his skull. Bailey's teammate Red Horner rushed to his defense and knocked out Shore with one punch, so both men were carried from the ice on stretchers.

Shore quickly recovered, but Bailey hovered near death for days and required two operations to relieve the pressure of blood clots. He would also recover yet would not be able to play hockey again. The NHL staged a benefit game two months later in his honor that netted around $20,000, as the Leafs beat a team of league all-stars that included Eddie Shore. The highlight of the 7–3 win for Toronto was a pregame handshake between

Bailey and Shore. "White-faced and visibly nervous in the All-Star dressing room before the game," went one newspaper account, "Shore skated into a rousing, spontaneous welcome with Bailey. Doubtful about the reception he would receive, the big Bruin defenceman . . . met a Toronto audience that fairly shrieked forgiveness."[46]

Bailey went on to college coaching and also served as penalty timekeeper at Maple Leaf Gardens for nearly 50 years. His son, Garnet Bailey—also nicknamed "Ace"—went on to an 11-year career with five different teams, including the 1970 Boston Bruins. Unlike his father, Ace the son was never a star, but he was with the Bruins to contribute to the Stanley Cup championship the team had won back in May and chipped in during the regular season with 11 goals and 22 points.

One player not on the ice to celebrate the Bruins' Stanley Cup was defenseman Ted Green. A solid if unspectacular player like his teammate Bailey, Green had missed the entire championship season as a result of the most dangerous on-ice incident since Bailey's father was nearly killed nearly 40 years before.

Ted Green was a tough defender who had played eight seasons in the NHL and had earned a nickname he hated—"Terrible" Ted. "I didn't like the name or the reputation," he admitted. "I played hockey hard and I hit because it was my job to hit. I hit back when I got hit. But that was to protect my part of the ice, my goalie, my partner and myself."[47] Others in the league were less understanding and called Green "the meanest, rottenest player in hockey. Wielded his stick like a machete. Stalked heads instead of pucks. Lived by the sword for eight violent seasons in the NHL."[48]

Until one day, he almost died by the sword.

During a preseason game against the Blues on September 21, 1969, in Ottawa, Green got into a stick-swinging fight with Wayne Maki. It started about 12 minutes into the first period in the Bruins' defensive zone, with Green shoving Maki in the face and sending him down to the ice. Maki responded by spearing him, prompting Green to hit Maki on the head with his stick. Maki retaliated with a full swing at Green's head, hitting him with the hardest part of the stick, where the blade meets the shaft. "The next thing I knew, I was lying on my stomach with my head turning violently," said Green. "I remember trying to stop it from moving, but I couldn't because I had no control over it. Everything else that followed is vague in my memory—little snatches of action, dim pictures of guys around me."[49] With no helmet, Green collapsed to the ice with a fractured skull and at least a mild form of brain damage. The sight of Green trying to get off the ice, his legs buckled and his face contorted in pain, made Blues' broadcaster Dan Kelly almost physically ill. Even as he was carried from the ice and speaking almost unintelligibly, Green wanted to go after Maki to finish the fight. To keep him away from the enraged Bruins, Maki was eventually hustled off the ice and watched the rest of the game in street clothes. The league later suspended him for 30 games.[50]

Green went to a local hospital where he finally recognized the severity of his injury and asked for the last rites. Dr. Michael Richard worked for two hours to remove the bone fragments that had been driven into Green's brain and to insert a protective plate. Despite the fact that Green was experiencing some paralysis on his left side, Richard told reporters that he could make a complete recovery and might even play later in the season provided he wore a helmet. Green did not return, but when the Bruins went on to win the title he was given a full share of the playoff money and had his name engraved on the Stanley Cup.

Now, more than a year after the incident, Ted Green was back on the ice with the Bruins. He played sparingly in the early part of the 1970 season, trying to regain his old form, and admitted that "an awful feeling of inadequacy had possessed me. I wasn't afraid, just unsure of myself. That doubt was killing me, killing my game, making me wonder what I was doing out on the ice."[51] But on October 25 against the Flyers, Green showed how far he had come. With Boston down 2–0 in the second period, Green pushed in his first NHL goal since the injury. The capacity Boston crowd gave Green a standing ovation of more than a minute's length, and his goal played a big part in Boston's 4–3 victory. A few weeks later Green passed another test when he got into his first fight since the injury. Chicago players seemed reluctant to engage him, but Green insisted, removing his helmet to get a better shot at Blackhawks' rookie Dan Maloney. A series of solid punches knocked Maloney to the ice and put Green in the penalty box. Afterward, an almost euphoric Green said, "They're not afraid of hurting me anymore. They're afraid of me hurting them."[52]

Ted Green went on to have a productive season with five goals and 42 points. He helped the Bruins win the Cup again in 1972, then after moving to the fledgling World Hockey Association the following year, he captained the New England Whalers to the league title. After the stick-

swinging incident that nearly took his life, Ted Green went on to play ten
more seasons.

It was a much happier ending than the one for Wayne Maki, who
eventually became a consistent scorer with the Vancouver Canucks. But
in 1972, Maki began suffering terrible headaches. "They were real bad,
like a knife stabbing into my head," he said. "They'd last a minute, go
away, be gone five minutes, and then come back. They kept getting
worse."[53] The diagnosis was a brain tumor, and while some believed it
may have been caused by his years of rough play, doctors told Maki it
was likely he was born with the condition. Among the hundreds of get-
well cards Maki got in the hospital was one from Ted Green, although
Maki admitted that because of the injury and operations he could not
remember it. He died in 1974 at just 29 years of age.

Maki and Green are forever linked by one of the most violent incidents in NHL history. Both players faced criminal assault charges, the
first time league violence had spilled off the ice and into the court system.
Although both players were acquitted, the incident traumatized the
league. Bruins' chairman of the board Weston Adams Sr. was so disturbed that he ordered the players to begin wearing helmets, at least in
practice, and the Boston farm team in Oklahoma City obliged. But the
Bruins themselves refused. "When they tried to force all defensemen to
wear helmets, the guys walked out on them," said Boston center Derek
Sanderson. "They weren't going to take anything like that. If they pass a
rule about it, I'd have to balk, too."[54]

Change came slowly, in part because those old attitudes were so firmly entrenched. Not even the death of Minnesota's Bill Masterton in
1968—caused when he hit his head on the ice after a legal check—could
move the needle toward greater safety. Interestingly, one player whose
attitude had changed was Ted Green. "The big shots who run the NHL
and the WHA haven't got the guts to do what should be done," he said in
1974. "They're gutless. They think high-sticking and slashing is a part of
hockey. Adds color. Yeah, it adds color all right—the color of blood
running."[55] The NHL finally mandated helmets for all new players in
1979, although the rule excluded veterans who didn't want to wear them.
Another bloody incident, when the Rangers' Marc Staal took a slap shot
to the eye, prompted the league to make visors mandatory in 2013.

Violence in the NHL has become a paradox. The league has taken
great pains to curb extralegal activity, yet there is no doubt that violence

and fighting remain popular with a certain segment of fans. There is also no doubt that the potential for another Maki-Green incident remains, despite the league's best intentions. In February 2000, the Canucks' Donald Brashear was slashed in the head by Boston's Marty McSorley. Even with a helmet, Brashear crumpled to the ice with a grade three concussion; McSorley was suspended and charged with assault but avoided jail time by serving 18 months of probation.

Donald Brashear was just the latest in a long line going back to Ace Bailey and Ted Green. Each could have received an award for courage, but the NHL didn't have such an award back then. It does now, though. In 2009, the league created an award for the player who shows exceptional courage and determination.

It's called the Ace Bailey Award of Courage, named for the younger Ace Bailey. On September 11, 2001, Ace Bailey, then a scout for the Los Angeles Kings, died on board United Airlines Flight 175, which crashed into the World Trade Center.

11

NOVEMBER

"QUARTERBACKS ARE ALWAYS READY"

The midterm elections held on November 3 did not offer much in the way of surprises. President Nixon and the Republicans lost 12 seats in the U.S. House of Representatives, and while they picked up three seats in the Senate, Democrats still controlled both houses of Congress. The fact that the Republicans lost fewer seats than expected in the House and added strength in the Senate allowed Vice President Spiro Agnew to claim that the party had gained ideological control of Congress. Tom Wicker of the *New York Times* disagreed and used a football analogy to suggest that the president "had lost ground at halftime" of his first term.[1]

The analogy was an appropriate one given Nixon's love for sports and his description by most newspapers as the "nation's number-one fan." Nixon especially liked baseball, and would occasionally attend Washington Senators games. He was an honorary member of the Baseball Writers Association of America and said he would have enjoyed being a sportswriter. When he named an all-time baseball team in 1972 the article appeared in newspapers across the country under his own byline.

But Nixon's real love was football, going back to the days when he played as an undersized scrub on the Whittier College team in California:

> As a 150-pound seventeen-year-old freshman I hardly cut a formidable figure on the field, but I loved the game. . . . There were only eleven eligible men on the freshman team, so despite my size and weight I got to play in every game and to wear a team numeral on my sweater. But

for the rest of my college years, the only times I got to play were in the last few minutes of a game that was already safely won or hopelessly lost. [2]

Nixon had made a highly publicized visit to the Texas-Arkansas "Big Shootout" in 1969 (see chapter 1) and took great delight that his halftime prediction of a Texas comeback came true. [3] In the winning Texas locker room, he presented the Longhorns with a plaque "to the no. 1 college football team in college football's 100th year," which got him in hot water with fans of undefeated Penn State. More than 100 Penn State students called the White House after the game to protest Nixon's decision. "If the president insists that he play politics with football," said Ted Thompson, head of the undergraduate student government, "he should at least play fairly." [4]

It was noted that the White House "hurriedly huddled to decide whether to punt, pass or run" with the controversy. [5] Nixon also had an obvious interest in the Washington Redskins and the Miami Dolphins, as he had a presidential retreat in Key Biscayne. He even suggested a play for the Dolphins in Super Bowl VI against Dallas, a down-and-in pass to Paul Warfield. The play failed and Miami lost 24–3.

Even though he was not running, Nixon did not sit on the sidelines for the midterm elections and campaigned vigorously for Republican candidates. One of his pet projects was a neophyte politician running in New York's 39th Congressional District in Buffalo. The candidate had no experience but did have the next best thing in politics—name recognition. According to his Democratic opponent Tom Flaherty, "When I began my campaign I would tell people, 'I'm Tom Flaherty. I'm running for Congress.' I drew blank stares. So I started saying, 'I'm running for Congress against Jack Kemp,' and people would light up immediately." [6]

The people of Buffalo knew Kemp primarily as the quarterback who had delivered them their greatest moments of sporting glory—back-to-back AFL championships in 1964 and 1965. The 1964 game was played in Buffalo against the defending champion San Diego Chargers, a team considered one of the best in AFL history. But led by Kemp and a tough defense, Buffalo won its first pro football title 20–7. Just a year earlier, Buffalo fans had booed Kemp when the team failed to win the Eastern Division title. Now, as the clock ticked down, Buffalo fans broke through the police restraining line, tore down both goalposts, and hoisted Kemp on their shoulders. The next year, Kemp threw a touchdown pass and the Bills did it again, this time shutting out the Chargers 23–0 in San Diego. In his ten years in the AFL with Buffalo and the Chargers, Kemp played in the title game five times and made the All-Star team seven times.

A native Californian, Kemp was political long before he decided to become a politician. He actively campaigned for Nixon's losing gubernatorial bid in 1962 and Barry Goldwater's presidential run in 1964 and served on Ronald Reagan's staff when Reagan was governor of California. Groups such as the Buffalo Jaycees and the Western New York Americans for Freedom invited him to speak, and one of his common themes was "The Struggle of Communism for Control of the Minds of our Youth." His political philosophy, which included support for the Vietnam War and cutting taxes, sounded like it was created by a Nixon speechwriter: "After going into the highly competitive business of pro football, I gained an even deeper appreciation of the competitive free-enterprise system to which this country owes its past, present and future progress and freedom."[7]

Kemp struggled a bit in the heavily Democratic 39th District but ended up edging Flaherty 51.6 percent to 48.4. The win prompted a congratulatory phone call from the White House, with Nixon aide Herb Klein telling reporters that the president considered Kemp a rising national figure. Klein certainly had that right, as Kemp's victory launched the former quarterback on a political career that would see him win nine terms in Congress, serve as secretary of housing and urban development under President George H. W. Bush, and run unsuccessfully for both president and vice president. When asked by Bob Dole to run as his vice presidential candidate in 1996, Kemp accepted by saying, "Quarterbacks are always ready."[8]

Certainly, athletes before Kemp had ventured into politics, and even in the same 1970 elections voters in Bakersfield, California, returned former Olympic decathlete Bob Mathias to his third term in Congress. Almost all who made the transition credited their athletic background with helping them in political situations. "Pro football gave me a good sense of perspective to enter politics," Kemp said. "I'd already been booed, cheered, cut, sold, traded and hung in effigy."[9] Gerald Ford, a former football star at the University of Michigan, and just four years away from the presidency, recalled a losing game against Minnesota in his 1934 senior season. "During 25 years in the rough-and-tumble world of politics, I often thought of the experiences before, during, and after that game," he said. "Remembering them has helped me many times to face a tough situation, take action, and make every effort possible despite adverse odds."[10]

Ford was an outstanding college player but never played professionally and as a lineman never really achieved much public recognition. By contrast, Kemp had one of the highest profiles of the new crop of athlete-politicians, and his steep career ascent seemed to open the door to other athletes looking for new horizons after retirement. When his career with the New York Knicks ended in 1977, Bill Bradley won three terms in the U.S. Senate and ran unsuccessfully for president in 2000. He was quickly followed by baseball pitcher Jim Bunning (U.S. House of Representatives and U.S. Senate from Kentucky), Nebraska football coach Tom Osborne (U.S. House of Representatives from Nebraska), and NBA star Kevin Johnson (mayor of Sacramento, California). Arnold Schwarzenegger and Jesse "The Body" Ventura combined their athletic careers with movie and television roles to further their political ambitions. Both served as governors—Ventura in Minnesota and Schwarzenegger in California.

Writer Frank Deford made the interesting observation that most of these athlete-politicians, with notable exceptions such as Bradley and Detroit mayor Dave Bing, are Republicans. Even former Pittsburgh Steeler Lynn Swann ran as a Republican in his bid for governor of Pennsylvania in 2006, a rarity in that so few blacks identify themselves as Republicans. "When the Republicans do make inroads into blue states, they do it with football players," Deford noted. "The governor of Maryland and the governor of Rhode Island were Ivy League players. And then, when a Democrat Ivy leaguer does something athletic, everybody laughs at him. Remember John Kerry windsurfing? And what are the Kennedys famous for? Touch football. Touch . . . the Republicans play tackle, man."[11]

That is not to suggest that former athletes can simply call themselves Republicans and punch their ticket to political office. Swann lost decisively to incumbent Ed Rendell, winning only 40 percent of the vote. In 1964, popular University of Oklahoma football coach Bud Wilkinson resigned to run for the U.S. Senate but narrowly lost to Democrat Fred Harris. A decisive 28–7 loss to archrival Texas the previous season may have figured in the defeat. "I would say that the loss to Texas easily cost Bud 50,000 to 75,000 votes," said Oklahoma state representative Tim Dowd. "Oklahomans take their football just as seriously as they do their politics."[12] In the 1970 midterms, Wilkinson's son Jay, a former football player at Duke, also lost in his bid to win a congressional seat in Oklahoma.

And it may be, too, that former athletes with Democratic leanings prefer to exercise their power in a different way. Jim Brown, Roberto Clemente, and Bill Russell were very outspoken in their political views yet were not seriously tempted to run for political office. They instead used their celebrity-athlete status as a platform for reform that became increasingly powerful in the television age. Brown has been especially active in minority and underprivileged areas, trying to end gang violence. "No one today," wrote his biographer Mike Freeman, "especially with the scared, frightened likes of Michael Jordan and Tiger Woods, gorged with corporate money and afraid to take a stand on anything—not a soul, is like Jim Brown."[13]

Jordan was somewhat symbolic of the modern athlete who had grown rich on free agent contracts and shoe endorsements and seemed to have more concern about stock portfolios than social issues. When Jordan refused to campaign for Harvey Gantt, a black Democrat running for the U.S. Senate in North Carolina in 1990, he somewhat famously said, "Republicans buy sneakers, too," a reference to his lucrative association with Nike.[14] "The advent of agents has supplanted the players' own consciences," said Reggie Williams, who played linebacker for the Bengals in the 1980s while also serving on the Cincinnati City Council. "Their consciences became how much money they could make."[15] Yet, in 2012, Jordan hosted a $20,000-per-person dinner for President Barack Obama that raised $3 million. Jordan also appeared with several other NBA stars in a fund-raising "Obama Classic" basketball game that offered courtside seats for $5,000 apiece, while special VIP packages went for $35,000.

Among the winners and losers in the 1970 elections, former NFL linebacker Sam Huff may have had the best perspective. Recently retired from the Washington Redskins, Huff returned to his native West Virginia to run for the U.S. Congress from the First District, an area that included his home town of Farmington. Huff spent $50,000 and wore out his car crisscrossing the area he had made famous as a star at West Virginia University and as an NFL Hall of Fame player. Even the signs heading into tiny Farmington read, "Home of Sam Huff, All-America." None of it seemed to help, as Huff never even made it out of the Democratic primary.

"I became very angry at the end," he admitted. "I could take the slanders, the innuendos. I could take everything but what they did to me in my home town of Farmington. Two days before the primary, the mayor of Farmington held a free pig roast for my opponent. In sports, your opponent always faces you eyeball to eyeball. In politics you are fighting shadows. You never know where your enemy is."[16]

Sam Huff never ran for political office again.

STUMPY HAS HIS DAY

When Archie Manning's son Eli finished his senior season as Ole Miss quarterback in 2003, everyone expected him to be one of the first players taken in the NFL Draft. The Chargers had the top pick that year, but Archie made it publicly known that Eli had no desire or intention to play in San Diego. When San Diego picked Eli number one overall in the 2004 draft, the team quickly traded him to the Giants for draft picks and New York's top selection, quarterback Philip Rivers. It worked out wonderfully for Eli Manning, who in his first ten years in the league led the Giants to two Super Bowl championships.

The decision to steer Eli from San Diego to New York created a great deal of controversy at the time. San Diego linebacker Donnie Edwards admitted, "I was born and raised here in San Diego. It's almost like a slap in the face to us. I think a lot of people took it that way."[17] The Mannings seemed unrepentant, especially after reports surfaced that some in the San Diego organization told Archie to keep Eli away from the team. The Chargers disputed that claim, but there may have been a more compelling reason for Archie to keep Eli clear of San Diego—his own personal history. The 2003 Chargers finished last in the NFL with a record of 4–12,[18] and perhaps Archie had visions of Eli repeating his tortured career with the New Orleans Saints (see chapter 10).

In 1970, the year before Archie Manning joined the Saints as their number-one draft pick, the team was considered one of the worst in the NFL and a model of how not to build an expansion team. New Orleans came into the league in 1967 with high hopes, and optimism rose to giddiness when on the very first play in franchise history, Saints' receiver John Gilliam returned the opening kickoff of the season 94 yards for a touchdown against the Rams.

But the Saints eventually lost that game and then lost a lot more. While other expansion teams such as the Cowboys and Vikings eventually became respectable by building with younger players, the Saints stuck with washed-up veterans and castoffs and became known for their comic futility. In the inaugural season, owner John Mecom Jr., as young as his players and about as big, jumped off the sideline to join a bench-clearing brawl and decked a Giants' player with one punch. "If I had wanted a seat in the stands," he said, "I could have bought one each Sunday for $6. I own the club and I want to be where the action is."[19]

There was something about this team suggestive of the 1962 Mets, as the fans kept coming out even as losses piled up. When the Saints hosted the Rams on November 1, 1970, the game attracted a near-capacity crowd of 77,861 despite the home team's record of 1–4–1. Once again, their patience was not rewarded. An antique cannon misfired prematurely during a halftime show re-creation of the Battle of New Orleans, and then the Saints blew a 14-point lead and lost 30–17. That was the end of the line for coach Tom Fears, who was fired after the defeat. "The funny thing is," Fears observed, "that our record when I was fired was better than our record [0–6–1] at the same stage last year."[20]

As the Saints prepared to host Detroit on November 8, J. D. Roberts would take over for Fears. There was nothing to suggest that this game would be any different than other Saints games, especially considering that the Lions were one of the better teams in the league and came to New Orleans with a record of 5–2, but a good crowd of 66,910 filled old Tulane Stadium. As the teams warmed up before the game, New Orleans' kicker Tom Dempsey tested out a leg that had been injured almost all season. The injury had severely affected Dempsey, and through the first seven weeks he had hit only five of 15 field goals.

At six two, 255 pounds, Dempsey looked more like a young Santa Claus than a professional athlete. Most noticeable were birth deformities of both his right hand and foot that earned him the nickname "Stumpy" but did not keep him from playing college football as a two-way lineman for Palomar College near San Diego. Almost by accident did he get into kicking, as the team was struggling to find someone who could kick off and get the ball into the end zone. "The coach lined up the whole team and said, 'Kick,' and we all went down the line. I kicked it out of the end zone and he said, 'Do it again.' It went out of the end zone again and he says, 'You're on for Saturday night.'"[21]

Dempsey began his NFL career in 1968, kicking with a taped bare foot for the San Diego practice squad. The Chargers helped him develop a special leather, squared-off shoe that looked, and sounded, like a sledge-hammer. It struck with such force that San Diego coach Sid Gillman marveled, "That guy is going to hit one 90 yards one day."[22] By the time he had moved on to New Orleans in 1969, Dempsey had corralled his power to the point that he made 22 field goals in 41 attempts to earn both Pro Bowl and All-Pro honors.

With his injury finally healed, Dempsey looked forward to returning to all-star form against Detroit. In the first half, Dempsey hit a pair of field goals from inside 30 yards. He felt so good, he was disappointed that Roberts chose later to punt and did not let him try one from 55 yards. "We didn't let him kick that one," Roberts said. "He was upset and I said, 'Well, if you think you can get a high trajectory on it we'll kick a long one a little later.'"[23] In the second half, a third Dempsey field goal gave the Saints a brief 16–14 lead, but Detroit responded with a late drive and field goal to take a 17–16 lead with only 11 seconds to play. Once again, it seemed that Saints fans would go home disappointed.

Al Dodd returned the ensuing kickoff out to the 30-yard line as only three seconds elapsed, leaving eight still on the clock. Dodd then made a sensational catch of a Billy Kilmer pass, dragging his feet to stay in bounds and then falling across the sidelines to stop the clock at the Saints' 45-yard line. "Tell Stumpy to get ready," said Saints offensive coordina-tor Don Heinrich. "We're going to try a long field goal."[24] The Dodd catch took six seconds, leaving time for just one final play. "I knew I could kick the ball that far," said Dempsey, "but whether I could kick it straight that far kept running through my mind."[25] Broadcaster Al Wester was calling the game for the Saints on the radio: "Dempsey will have to kick one 62 yards to win the ballgame. Holy daylight, I've seen 'em all, but this is the most exciting moment in Saints history!"

The kick should have been from 62 yards, but holder Joe Scarpati set up eight yards behind the line of scrimmage instead of seven, figuring Dempsey needed the extra distance to allow for more loft. The added yardage made the attempt seem even more foolish, and the Lions were laughing as the Saints lined up for the kick. Warned by his assistants to look for a fake, Detroit coach Joe Schmidt sent defensive back Lem Barney deep downfield to guard against a long pass. "Fellas," Dempsey told his blockers, "give me just a moment longer. This one is kind of long."[26]

"Dempsey will try the longest kick he's ever attempted. Two seconds left. . . . Here's the snap, the ball is down. . . ."

Up in the press box, sportswriter Jerry Green, who covered the Lions for the *Detroit News*, figured the Lions had the game won. "I was standing next to the elevator waiting to go down to the locker room," he said. "Saints' owner John Mecom was standing with me and said, 'Hold on, I want to watch this.'"[27] Scarpati snapped the ball, and when Dempsey swung his squared-off foot those on the field said it sounded like a rifle shot. "He really got into it," Scarpati said. "It was a cannon."[28]

"Dempsey kicks, it's on the way . . . it iiiiiiiiiiiiis . . ."

"I couldn't see where the ball came down, that far away," Dempsey admitted.[29] It had, in fact, just barely limped over the crossbar for a new NFL record.[30]

"Good! Good! It's good! The Saints have won! The Saints have won!"

The crowd went crazy, as did the Saints. "I jumped the fence behind our bench, ran into the stands and began shaking hands," said defensive back Doug Wyatt, "and someone stole my helmet."[31] Off the field on their shoulders the Saints carried their hero as fans rushed the field.

"The stadium is wild! Dempsey is being mobbed! Time has run out . . . the Saints have won, 19–17! Dempsey with a 63-yard field goal . . . the longest field goal in the history of the National League! The Saints are being mobbed now! The new coach is being taken off on the shoulders of his team! The Saints have beaten the Lions, 19–17!"

A team and a town that had suffered so much frustration finally had something to celebrate. "If you're going to set a record, this is the town to do it in," Dempsey said. "I didn't get home until about 7:30, 8 o'clock the next morning."[32] The Lions were much less jubilant, and when they got to the locker room Schmidt knocked a hole in the blackboard with his clipboard. When he calmed down a bit, he said the field goal was "like winning the Masters with a 390-yard hole-in-one on the last hole."[33] Added Detroit linebacker Wayne Walker, "Tom Dempsey didn't kick that field goal; God kicked it."[34]

It may have been the greatest day for kickers in NFL history, as later that afternoon the Raiders' George Blanda kicked a 52-yard field goal in the dying seconds to help beat the Browns 23–20. The ageless Blanda, at 43 the oldest player in the league, had also come off the bench to throw a touchdown pass and kick two other field goals. In four straight games culminating on November 22 against San Diego, Blanda kicked or passed for a tying or winning score in the final minutes. "The guy almost embarrasses you," said Raiders' center Jim Otto. "He's out there, 43 years old, running the wind sprints, yelling all the time, coming in to pull it out for us."[35]

Back in New Orleans, J. D. Roberts was enjoying a win in his first game as an NFL head coach. "I just hope everyone can get down off the clouds," he said.[36] Unfortunately, there was nothing but storm clouds for the Saints the rest of the season. The win over Detroit marked their last of the year and they finished at 2–11–1. Right before the next season started, when rookie quarterback Archie Manning was set to debut, Roberts released Dempsey, a move that created some hard feelings for the onetime toast of Tulane Stadium. Dempsey went to Philadelphia where he led the league in field goal percentage, and kicked until 1979 with three more teams.

But his heart never really left New Orleans, and after retirement he returned for good to the city where he enjoyed his greatest triumph. He started a family, built a home, rebuilt it after Hurricane Katrina, and to this day still enjoys talking about the Sunday afternoon when he was the greatest kicker who ever lived.

"I wouldn't change a thing," he said, "but people expected me to smack it 60-some yards every time I went out there."[37]

GONE IN AN INSTANT

By the fall of 1970, college football had already mourned two airplane disasters. The most notable came in 1931 when Notre Dame's Knute Rockne, perhaps the most famous coach in America, died in a commercial flight that fell from the sky in rural Kansas. In 1960, 16 members of the Cal Poly–San Luis Obispo team died when their team flight crashed near Toledo, Ohio. Graduate assistant John Madden stayed behind that weekend to coach a junior varsity game, and while he may have missed the crash, its emotional impact led to his decision many years later to bus to games as a broadcaster.

Now, college football would suffer two crashes within the span of six weeks that would essentially wipe out the programs at two universities.

On November 14, following a 17–14 loss to East Carolina, 75 members of the Marshall University football program, including 36 players and eight coaches, boarded a Southern Airways DC-9 for the trip back home. About 12 miles from the campus in Huntington, West Virginia, the plane attempted to land at the Tri-State Airport in conditions that included rain, smoke, and fog. Shortly after 7:30 p.m. and on its final approach, the plane missed the runway completely and crashed into a nearby Kenova hillside, exploding on impact.

A later report by the National Transportation Safety Board concluded that the plane dipped to the right, almost inverted, and had crashed nose-first into a hollow, flying too low to successfully land. The plane was some 300 feet too low, although pilot Frank Abbott may not have known that as the airport had no instruments to advise pilots of their altitude. Abbott, a 20-year veteran, did not communicate any danger or problem in his last radio transmission before the plane went down. The best guess was that the plane's engines got clogged from the trees that were clipped during descent.

The report went on to say that the crash was "unsurvivable," which was a fact already known—everyone on board had died. Besides players and coaches, the victims included five air crewmen, a team trainer, and some university boosters. Firemen, police, and National Guardsmen hacked through trees just to get to the crash site and then worked for 12 hours trying to pull bodies from the wreckage; all the victims were taken to a temporary morgue at the local armory. So violent was the impact that identification of the bodies was nearly impossible, and a special FBI disaster team spent days sifting through charred personal effects.

The victims who could be identified were returned to their families for private burial, but six players became something like the "Unknown Soldiers" of Marshall football. The university held a public funeral, and for two hours some 2,500 mourners, half of them students, filed past the six identical silver-and-gray coffins. They were buried in a common grave about two miles from campus, the graveside ceremony somewhat brief due to the subfreezing weather. "Our lives will never be the same," said Alfred Walker, the Methodist minister who conducted the services. "They dare not be."[38]

Back on October 2, a plane carrying the Wichita State football team had crashed in Colorado, killing 31 people, including 13 players and head coach Ben Wilson. Despite the grim coincidence of more than a hundred deaths, federal investigators found little or no similarity between the Wichita State and Marshall University disasters.

The week before the Wichita State tragedy, the Shockers remained winless on the season after a 43–0 loss at West Texas State. The school did not have its own aircraft, so to get back to Kansas it rented a plane through Jack Richards Aircraft of Oklahoma City. For the flight, Richards Aircraft pulled an old Martin 404 out of mothballs from Las Vegas, where the 20-year-old plane had sat unused for three years. The pilots came from Golden Eagle Aviation, also out of Oklahoma City.

As that flight left Oklahoma the landing gear on the Martin 404 failed, causing the plane to veer off the runway and bend a propeller. No one was hurt, but the damage was extensive enough that the pilots had to find another plane to pick up the Wichita State team. The damaged plane was left in Oklahoma City for repairs and the Shocker team got home without further incident.

A week later, Wichita State had another long trip scheduled, this time to Utah State. Two planes were needed—one called "Gold" and the other "Black" for the school's colors. "Gold" would fly the team's coaches and starting players, while "Black" had the substitutes and other team officials. Either unaware of the minor mishap from the previous week, or undeterred, school officials again went through Jack Richards Aircraft and Golden Eagle Aviation. When they boarded on Friday, October 2, for the flight to Utah, "Gold" was once again a Martin 404, registration number N464M.

The exact same plane that had crashed the week before.

Richards Aircraft had repaired the plane and sent it out for Wichita State to use. This time, the failure was not simply a matter of broken landing gear. After a refueling stop in Denver, first officer Ron Skipper announced the plane would detour on a sightseeing trip of the Rockies while "Black" stayed on its original flight plan. Around 1:14 p.m. local time near Loveland Pass, the pilots flew into a blind canyon, discovered that the plane was too heavy to escape a towering ridge that suddenly appeared, and crashed at the foot of the Continental Divide.

Several passengers, most of them in the rear of the plane, initially survived the crash, but others were trapped inside and unable to escape as the fuel tank exploded. "It was like if you cut the cord on an elevator," said one of the fortunate survivors, linebacker Gene Kostal. "We dropped that quickly. All our clothes had been blown off or torn off, and I was buried up to my chest in debris. As we walked down the hill [to get help], a fireball swept through the plane and it exploded."[39] The "Black" plane landed without incident in Utah, where its passengers were taken to a local hotel and immediately put under sedation.

It appeared to be a simple case of pilot error, but federal investigators found the plane nearly 4,000 pounds overweight at the time of the crash. It was not loaded down with too much luggage or too many passengers, but rather mechanical issues. While a government investigation suggested some kind of wrongdoing, Skipper, who survived the crash, later testified, "The only thing I can think of is that something mechanical happened to the airplane in the last few moments of the flight."[40] Even the "Black" plane, which landed without incident, was found to have 16 maintenance defects, including oil leakage and a corroded battery. "I don't see that I have a responsibility," said Jack Richards, "since the planes were leased to the university and the university was the operator. I'm awful sad about the lives that were lost, but I don't see anything I could have done."[41]

Federal officials revoked the air taxi and commercial flying licenses for Golden Eagle and grounded the entire fleet of Jack Richards Aircraft to go along with a $50,000 fine. The Federal Aviation Administration issued a nationwide warning to all universities and colleges to start checking with its regional offices for advice on the safety records of the flight companies they used for travel. Utah State canceled the game and held a memorial service on the field for the stricken Wichita State team. Instead of a spirited game, those in attendance saw a mostly silent, empty stadium with but a single funeral wreath of black and gold placed on the 50-yard line. The Shockers resumed the season, getting special permission from the NCAA to use freshman players at a time when such players were ineligible. Wichita State lost all nine of its games and was outscored by opponents 381–99.

Part of Wichita State football died that October day in 1970; the other part died in 1986 when the school officially abandoned its varsity program. How much the crash affected that decision is unclear, but the school obviously struggled to rebuild its program. Wichita State had just two winning seasons in the following 16 years, which led to declining interest. When the school pulled the plug in 1986, attendance had dwindled to fewer than 10,000 per game and the program lost nearly a million dollars. Head coach Ron Chismar used a debatable analogy upon hearing the news, telling reporters, "Gentlemen, I'm not real good at funerals and that's where I am right now. What happened to me today and what happened to my kids was the worst thing I've ever been through."[42]

The Wichita State crash was the worst athletic air disaster on record for only about six weeks. Marshall University was not used to traveling by plane and bused to most of its games, which were relatively close. After the Wichita crash, Marshall officials reconsidered their decision to fly to East Carolina, which was nearly 500 miles away. School officials did change their mind, but instead of switching back to a bus they opted for what they considered a bigger, safer jet instead of a smaller propeller plane.

It was the first, and last, plane flight for the Marshall football team that year.

Unlike Wichita State, Marshall was determined to keep its football program. The rest of the 1970 season was canceled and the Herd did not have another winning season until 1984, but the determination eventually paid off. Marshall won I-AA (now FCS) national championships in 1992 and 1996, and the school has sent numerous players to the NFL, including such stars as Randy Moss, Byron Leftwich, and Chad Pennington. In 1997, it moved up to Division I (now FBS) and regularly plays in bowl games.

There have certainly been other tragic plane crashes involving college teams. A 1977 crash killed the entire University of Evansville basketball team, while in 2011 a similar fate befell the Oklahoma State women's basketball program. But for sheer emotional impact, it's hard to match what happened that November evening in West Virginia. The tragedy has become part of popular culture thanks to the successful 2006 movie *We Are Marshall*, which depicted both the devastation of the crash and the resiliency of the school and surrounding community in its aftermath. Nearly 50 years later, that spirit still lives on.

"I'll never forget it," said *Huntington Herald-Dispatch* reporter Jack Hardin, a resident of Kenova who was one of the first on the scene. "Lord knows I've tried to, but I just can't."[43]

12

DECEMBER

SPINNING OUT OF CONTROL

For a trophy with so much history and significance, the Stanley Cup has been sorely mistreated over the years. The players from the winning team get some time each summer to spend with the Cup, and in 1992 one of the Pittsburgh Penguins threw it into Mario Lemieux's swimming pool. An older story about the Cup goes back to the days of the great Red Kelly in Toronto. When the Cup came to Kelly's house, he placed his three-month-old son right in the bowl. "Conn broke out in a wide grin," said Kelly. "[He] made a big dump right in the bowl. I think about that every time I see players drinking out of that bowl each spring."[1]

Perhaps the harshest treatment came on December 5, 1970, when someone broke into the Hockey Hall of Fame in Toronto and stole three NHL trophies, including the venerated Stanley Cup. It took seven years, but acting on a tip, police finally recovered part of the trophy wrapped in a brown paper bag in a Toronto cleaning store. "There are marks on there that I don't remember," said Maurice Reid, curator of the Hall of Fame, "but I think it can be restored to 98 percent of the way it looked when it was stolen."[2] A Toronto man was arrested and charged with possession of stolen property.

But the sadness of the NHL over the stolen Cup was nothing compared to what happened just a week later. On Saturday, December 12, *Hockey Night in Canada*, a national institution that stretched back into the days of radio, was set to broadcast the game between Toronto and Chicago at Maple Leaf Gardens. More than 2,000 miles away in Fort St. James, British Columbia, no one looked forward to the game more than Roy Spencer. A local farmer, mechanic, and gravel-pit operator, Spencer was finally going to get to see his son Brian play in an NHL game.

A left winger, Brian Spencer was just 21 years old and already nicknamed "Spinner" for his daring play on the ice. The fifth player taken by the Maple Leafs in the 1969 draft, he had spent most of that first season hurt, and was just now getting his chance after a call-up from minor league Tulsa. Fort St. James was a rough-and-tumble place in the wilds of British Columbia, and Spencer had already charmed his teammates with tales of his youth in a dirt-floor hovel, without electricity or running water, and having to shoot his own dinner. In actuality, there was electricity, which came from an outdoor generator that also powered his father's oxygen machine after he developed emphysema. Roy Spencer was no less a character, and would often visit the local bar on Saturday nights to watch hockey on television. Not only would he now get to see his son play, but Brian had also been picked for a live intermission interview with host Ward Cornell.

Except that when Roy Spencer went to watch the game, it wasn't there. *Hockey Night* producers figured the viewers on the West Coast would want to watch the local Vancouver Canucks, an expansion team playing in its first season, so the game between the Canucks and California Golden Seals was regionally televised to British Columbia. Roy Spencer, by now with a few drinks in him and steaming mad, decided to do something about it. He got in his truck and drove the 100 or so miles to Prince George, site of CKPG Television, the Canadian Broadcasting Corporation affiliate showing the game. As the Maple Leafs and Blackhawks continued play in Toronto, the real drama was now unfolding on the other side of the continent.

Roy Spencer reached CKPG and accosted the first person he saw, newsman Tom Haertel, who was entering the building. Spencer demanded to know why the Toronto game was not on the air, pulled a gun, and then forced Haertel inside. As Spencer moved to the switchboard to rip out the phones, Haertel ran into the newsroom warning colleagues to call the police. Spencer made his way to the television studio and forced a technician to switch the station off the air. As the Canucks and Seals vanished from CKPG, Spencer then lined up seven station personnel and made the cryptic remark, "There's going to be a revolution soon in Canada."[3] Apparently satisfied he had accomplished his mission, he then headed for the front door and back outside.

By this time, the Royal Canadian Mounted Police had arrived to confront Spencer and demanded he drop his gun. Instead, Spencer fired three shots from his Belgian-made pistol, hitting one policeman in the foot and nicking the holster of another. The police had no alternative but to shoot back, and one hit Spencer with a shot to the chest. Still alive at the scene, he never made it to the hospital, and died at 59 years old. At almost the exact moment Roy Spencer was killed, his son was being interviewed on *Hockey Night in Canada*, dedicating the game to his father.

Leafs officials told Spencer about his father as he came off the ice after Toronto beat Chicago 2–1, and he insisted on playing the following night. Just as many across Canada were becoming aware of the tragedy, Brian Spencer recorded his first two NHL points—assists—and got in two fights in a 4–0 win over Buffalo. Thereafter, he carried in his wallet the names of the three police officers involved in the shooting.

A police inquest returned a no-blame verdict against the police officers, saying they had probable grounds to return fire and protect themselves. Brian Spencer finished his season with nine goals, 24 points, and 115 penalty minutes in 50 games. He went on to play parts of ten seasons with three different teams, never scoring more than 14 goals in one year but still widely popular as the "Spinner." In 1973 with the Islanders, fans voted him the most popular player. "I loved the travel, the people," he said after his retirement. "I loved it all."[4]

That should have ended the story, and Brian Spencer should have finished his career as an undeserving, and underachieving, figure. But unfortunately, the story did not end there.

For better or worse, and mostly for worse, Brian Spencer inherited a lot from his father. Maybe it was that rough-and-tumble upbringing in the backwoods of western Canada, or maybe the blood just ran too deep. Maybe it was simply the crushing enormity of what had happened in December 1970. As one sportswriter noted, "Spinner Spencer was never anything more than a hard-scrabble kid whose talent yielded to the lies of his heart. He never stopped trying and he never stopped throwing the fists, but [he] never does anything beneficial."[5]

After he left the NHL, Spencer drifted. His marriage ended, and he got into drugs. Just as he had on the ice, he liked to use his fists, and a series of fights and altercations followed him around, including accusations he beat up a girlfriend. He settled out of court in a civil suit in which a driver claimed Spencer assaulted him after a traffic accident. It all crashed down around him in 1982 when he was jailed on murder and kidnapping charges in the death of a Florida man named Michael Dalfo. Spencer's ex-girlfriend claimed that he had shot Dalfo twice and left him for dead, and West Palm Beach police were convinced they had the right man. "This was a revenge killing, maybe involving drugs," said John Conklin of the homicide squad. "We've been getting quite a few calls from Canada. Was this guy a hero up there?"[6]

But it was a shaky case, based in large part on testimony from prostitutes and shady characters, and in 1987 a jury returned an acquittal. "It's been a trying ordeal," said Spencer. "I just want to thank all the people who've stood behind me. The support has been incredible, but it's all over now."[7] Except that it wasn't over, and that the Spinner's life had clearly spun out of control.

The following year, Spencer was apparently out buying crack cocaine when he was robbed at gunpoint. The one thing the robbers wanted was his wallet, which Spencer refused to hand over. It's not that the wallet had any great amount of money in it, but it did contain something Spencer had carried for 18 years—the names of the three police officers involved in the death of his father. A shot was fired and Brian Spencer, 39 years old, had died just like his old man. The tragedy had come full circle.

It was a descent few could have predicted in December 1970 when a fresh-faced kid from the western wilds made his debut on *Hockey Night in Canada*. Maybe if Roy Spencer hadn't held a television station hostage, the Brian Spencer story would have turned out differently. Others who knew him best say the story ended the only way it could.

"Maybe he was just destined for this," said former teammate Mike Robitaille when he heard of Brian's death. "He lived on the cutting edge, whether it was hockey or life."[8]

ONE TOUGH SON OF A BITCH

By December, it had become clear that 1970 had not been kind to Joe Kapp. In 1969, he had quarterbacked the Minnesota Vikings to the Super Bowl and earned Most Valuable Player honors in the NFL. Along the way, he had tied a league record by throwing seven touchdown passes in a 52–14 win over the Baltimore Colts. "If you look at the film, I looked almost as good as Johnny Unitas," Kapp said. "In fact, after that game, I asked Johnny for his autograph."[9]

Kapp's troubles started in January when the Kansas City Chiefs beat heavily favored Minnesota 23–7 in the Super Bowl. Losing was bad enough, but the Chiefs also beat up the Vikings physically and knocked Kapp out of the game with a shoulder injury. It turned out to be the last game Kapp ever played for Minnesota. He had refused to sign a contract extension with the team and played out his option, meaning that as of May 1 he was free to sign with any other team. Minnesota originally wanted to re-sign Kapp, but the negotiations quickly turned acrimonious. Kapp asked for a five-year, $1.25 million deal, which prompted the Vikings to respond with a much lower take-it-or-leave-it offer. Kapp refused to report to training camp. "Damn it," he said, "I don't answer ultimatums. I'm not some kind of slave."[10]

It was unthinkable for Vikings fans that the team would not re-sign the man who had become a folk hero in Minnesota. Kapp was not the prototype of the strong-armed, gunslinging quarterback, but what he lacked in artistry Kapp more than made up for with toughness. "You won't see me ducking out the window when somebody wants to tangle," he once said, and he came to symbolize the Vikings' motto of "Forty for Sixty"—40 men playing together for 60 minutes.[11] "Joe Kapp," Vikings safety Karl Kassulke said simply, "is one tough son of a bitch."[12]

While Kapp returned to his native California and waited, the Vikings began making plans to play without him. Journeyman Gary Cuozzo was given the starting job, and he responded with a solid performance in a redemptive, season-opening win over the Chiefs. "Kapp?" said Mick Tingelhoff, the Vikings' center. "We'd like to have Joe back, sure. But Cuozzo's our quarterback."[13] Safety Paul Krause shared the opinion. "Everybody looks to Cuozzo as the leader now," he said. "He proved it. If Kapp comes back, he'll have to beat Gary out."[14] Kapp watched the game with relatives in California and admitted, "Man, was I proud."[15]

Proud, but still out of work. "Under no circumstances was Joe going to play with the Vikings in 1970," said Minnesota general manager Jim Finks. "We decided this in mid-August when he refused to report. He couldn't play for us—for the good of the organization and the good of the players."[16] In October, Kapp finally found a team willing to pay him close to what he wanted—the lowly Boston Patriots, who signed him to an agreement worth a reported $500,000 for three years, making him the highest-paid player in the league. Ticket sales immediately jumped, as did the value of publicly traded shares in the Patriots. One hotel owner in Boston gushed, "Joe Kapp is the biggest thing to hit Boston since Bobby Orr, and Bobby Orr is the biggest thing to hit Boston since Paul Revere."[17]

It was not destined to be a happy union. Kapp was going from one of the best teams in the NFL to one of the worst, as Boston won only two games all season while scoring the fewest points in the league and giving up the most. After watching the Patriots lose to the Colts from the sidelines, and then sitting out another half behind Mike Taliaferro, his first action came in the second half against a familiar foe—the same Chiefs who had beaten the Vikings in the Super Bowl. The Chiefs again made life miserable for Kapp, whose final stat line read—11 attempts, two completions, 16 total yards, and two interceptions in the 23–10 loss. "Kapp will help Boston," Chiefs' coach Hank Stram said charitably after the game.[18]

He did not. Kapp was sacked eight times and threw three interceptions in another loss to the Colts. In a five-game stretch starting in Kansas City, all losses, Kapp threw one touchdown pass and ten interceptions. Now in December, he had one more humiliation to endure. On December 13, Kapp led the Patriots against his former Minnesota team. The crowd at Harvard Stadium was in an ugly mood, throwing a barrage of snowballs during the game as fights broke out throughout the stands. It got no better on the field as Kapp threw three interceptions to Ed Sharockman in a 35–14 loss. "It would have been nice to beat the old team," Kapp said. "This has been a change-over year. It's been a mess. I'm looking forward to a whole new ball game next year."[19]

Except that there would be no next year for Joe Kapp. Not with the Patriots and not with any team. After a 45–7 loss to Cincinnati, he had played his last game in the NFL.

Kapp wanted to stay with Boston, but technically he had never signed a standard NFL player contract. The Patriots had worked out a legal agreement that allowed him to play while they tried to negotiate an official deal. But after its disastrous 2–12 season, Boston had the number-one pick in the NFL Draft and used it to select Heisman Trophy quarterback Jim Plunkett from Stanford. Perhaps stung by Plunkett's presence, Kapp again refused to sign the standard contract. "This is unbelievable," said

Patriots' general manager Upton Bell, while president Billy Sullivan called it "a monumental disappointment."[20] Once again, Joe Kapp was playing hardball.

When Kapp originally signed with Boston in the fall, Vikings general manager Jim Finks noted, "Joe Kapp is now a Patriot. Isn't that ironic?"[21] In a sense, Kapp *had* become a patriot, fighting the NFL system that restricted player freedom. When Kapp left Minnesota for Boston, the league was under the "Rozelle Rule," named after Commissioner Pete Rozelle. If a player refused to sign a contract and play out his option, his new team would have to compensate his old one with players, money, or draft picks. If the teams could not agree on the compensation, Rozelle would step in and decide the issue, as he did in this case when he awarded Minnesota a future number-one draft pick and defensive back John Charles from New England.

Now, Rozelle demanded that Kapp sign the standard contract, and just as Kapp did when the Vikings issued him an ultimatum, he stiffened his neck. He sued the NFL for $12 million in back pay and damages from the Patriots, claiming that he was prevented from honoring the three-year agreement he already had with the team, and that he would be forced out of football. Win or lose, much like Curt Flood did in challenging Major League Baseball back in February, Kapp had signed his own death warrant in terms of playing again in the NFL.

After winding through various courts, the final verdict came down in 1976 with a six-member jury in California ruling against Kapp and refusing to award damages. U.S. District Court judge William Sweigert said that even though the courts had determined the NFL was guilty of restraint of trade, Kapp had not necessarily been damaged. "I'm disappointed, of course," said Kapp, 38 and out of the NFL for six years. "I only hope it doesn't hurt the players overall."[22]

But in fact, he had helped the players. In his ruling, Sweigert had noted that the NFL's ability to perpetually restrain a player's movement was both unreasonable and illegal. Kapp may have lost the battle, but his fight ultimately helped win the war and set in motion player free agency. In many ways, the million-dollar contracts of the modern NFL can be traced back to the man often called the "Curt Flood of football."

When Kapp's case against the NFL was nearing its end, one of the NFL lawyers, James McKay, argued, "If Joe Kapp has been damaged by leaving football it is a self-inflicted wound."[23] Most of Kapp's wounds throughout his career were self-inflicted. Stories abounded of his fights, near fights, and other misdemeanors. His basketball coach at the University of California recalled Kapp leading the team in a New York street brawl, while another brawl in Canada left him with a 100-stitch gash in his chin. He got into a fight—complete with fists and cane swinging—with Canadian Football League rival Angelo Mosca. The incident took place at a CFL reunion in 2011 when Kapp was 73 years old. [24]

In the last NFL game of his career, down 45–0 to the Bengals, Kapp picked himself off the turf and threw his last touchdown pass, a 12-yard effort to Ron Sellers. For one last time, in the December of his career, he had stared down an opponent and metaphorically punched him in the face.

"Nobody had more fun playing quarterback than I did," Kapp said. "It's hugely possible that nobody had more fun doing anything." [25]

IN OR OUT?

On the final weekend of the NFL regular season, the St. Louis Cardinals were a desperate team. After the Cardinals crushed the Cowboys 38–0 on November 16, they led Dallas by a full two games in the NFC East and seemed a shoo-in for the playoffs. Two losses and a tie later, they trailed both the Cowboys and Giants by a half game. The season would come down to the final game on December 20, 1970, in Washington against the Redskins, a team still reeling from the September death of coach Vince Lombardi, and given its losing record, one with nothing to play for.

Even so, it was the Redskins that played like a desperate team and took a 28–13 lead in the second half. St. Louis gamely fought back and trailed only 28–27 when it recovered a fumble deep in Washington territory with just minutes to play. Washington held and forced a very makeable 26-yard field goal attempt from Jim Bakken, one of the better kickers in the league. But with all the momentum, and a season riding on the outcome, Bakken somehow missed the chip shot wide left, and St. Louis lost 28–27. End of game, end of season, end of playoff hopes. The loss cost coach Charley Winner his job, [26] and players later admitted they choked. "You press to prevent it, then you're pressing too much," said offensive tackle Ernie McMillan, "and that's it. Definitely, I think we were waiting for something like that to happen." [27]

Aside from the playoff and coaching implications, the game was notable for featuring two of the best tight ends in the NFL. Jackie Smith of the Cardinals finished his fifth straight Pro Bowl season catching three passes for 29 yards and a touchdown. At six four, 235 pounds, he had the size and strength to run the tough patterns over the middle, but with four-seven speed in the 40-yard dash, he was also frequently used as a deep receiver. By today's pass-happy standards his final numbers—480 catches for 7,918 yards and 40 touchdowns—don't seem impressive, but at the time of his retirement they made him the top receiving tight end in history, and he won induction into the Hall of Fame on his second try in 1994.

The other tight end in the game was an unrelated Smith, Jerry. At six three, 208 pounds, Jerry Smith was often described as too big for a wide receiver and too small for a tight end, and he often split time between the positions. Eventually settling at tight end, he made two Pro Bowl teams and was named All-Pro in 1969. But he always seemed overshadowed by other players, including Jackie Smith. He was not brash or cocky, and he seldom seemed to stand out, even on his own team. The summer before his sophomore season when he caught 54 passes for six touchdowns, he said, "I think I stink, and that's the truth. I didn't know a thing, even this year. I just went out to catch a pass. I had no moves to speak of."[28]

Yet, on this particular December Sunday, he outshone Jackie Smith, catching three passes for two touchdowns, and running an end around for another 20 yards. He also has career numbers that compare favorably to Jackie, and his totals for 13 years included 421 catches for 5,496 yards and 60 touchdowns. So how is one Smith in the Hall of Fame and not the other?

Quite possibly because Jerry Smith was gay.

It was not something many people knew during his playing career, although his teammates certainly had their suspicions. But such was the climate at the time that a public admission of homosexuality would have either killed Smith's career or made it incredibly difficult to continue. "I believe there were players who would have cared, and I believe there are players who would have demanded he be kicked off the team," said gay rights advocate and author David Mixner. "I believe there are players who would have participated in the oppression of him if they knew, and I believe he knew all of that. He faced fear every day that he played."[29]

The first openly gay player in the NFL waited until three years after his retirement in 1972 to come out of the closet. Dave Kopay played for five teams in a nine-year career, and knows what Smith went through. "Smith never acknowledged his homosexuality outside of gay bars," Kopay wrote. "[But] it wasn't as if the Redskins didn't know it. Most of the team ignored Smith's homosexuality because the wide receiver scored 60 touchdowns over 13 years."[30]

After his retirement following the 1977 season, Smith moved to Austin, Texas, where he co-owned a gay bar. By the time he returned to the Washington area he was exhibiting alarming signs of high fever, drastic weight loss, and constant illness. In the summer of 1986 he was diagnosed with the AIDS virus, which at the time was considered fatal. Confined almost exclusively to homosexuals, it had created a wave of mass hysteria, with victims often quarantined, and some states considered legislation to brand sufferers like Holocaust victims. In the midst of this fear, Smith took the opportunity to go public with his illness, saying, "Maybe it will help people understand. Maybe it will help with development in research. Maybe something positive will come out of this."[31]

But Smith would not go so far as to admit his homosexuality. When asked how he contracted the disease, he would only say, "It just happened. It just happened."[32] But as Mixner later said, "Everyone knew how he got it. He knew everyone knew how he got it."[33]

Smith checked into Holy Cross Hospital in Silver Spring, Maryland, where his condition quickly worsened, and his weight dropped to 130 pounds. Friends and former teammates visited him before the end, including his best friend on the Redskins, Brig Owens. "One message he always left with young people," said Owens, "was that regardless of the situation, no matter how hard, never give up. He was a fighter, a person who never gave up."[34]

Jerry Smith, only 43 years old, died on October 15, 1986. He was the first former professional athlete to die from AIDS, and his decision to go public with his illness may have made it easier for other gay athletes such as Michael Sam and Jason Collins. In 2014, Sam, a standout defensive player at the University of Missouri, announced his homosexuality before the NFL Draft. Collins became one of the first male professional athletes to come out during his playing career and was profiled on a 2013 cover of *Sports Illustrated*. Even though both decisions received widespread praise, there was still plenty of resistance. Despite his desire to continue playing basketball, it took almost a year before any team would take a chance on Collins, and even when the New Jersey Nets signed him in 2014, it was only to a ten-day contract. Sam failed to stick with any NFL team in his first two years and tried to hook on with a team in Canada.

The question still remains: If cultural attitudes have changed so much since 1970, why isn't Jerry Smith in the Hall of Fame, and is his homosexuality playing a part in keeping him out? There are other reasons, of course. Smith played for some bad teams in Washington and made just the one All-Pro team. "I'm sure his homosexuality has never come up," one longtime Hall of Fame voter said. "He was a very good player. He just never stood out."[35] Smith became eligible for the Hall in 1983 but never received serious consideration, making the first cut for inclusion only twice in 25 years. After his candidacy moved to the seniors division, he received a similar lack of support. "He needs somebody to speak up for him," Owens said. "The numbers speak for themselves."[36]

Smith may or may not become the first gay player in the NFL Hall of Fame. But even if that one day happens, his more lasting legacy is that of someone who suffered greatly, both physically and emotionally, to make it easier for the players that would follow him. Unfortunately, it is a legacy that cost him his life.

"I know this isn't politically correct," said Kopay, "but I wish I had outed Jerry. He might be alive today."[37]

A MAN

As the world gathered to celebrate New Year's Eve, former heavyweight champion Charles "Sonny" Liston lay dead in his Las Vegas home. No one would know that fact until a few days later when his wife Geraldine and authorities discovered the body. The death date was officially listed as December 30, but how Liston died was as much a mystery as how he lived.

No one was sure exactly how old Liston was because he had no formal birth certificate. The most reliable accounts suggest he was born in Arkansas in 1928 to an abusive man who reportedly fathered 24 other children. "I had nothing when I was a kid but a lot of brothers and sisters, a helpless mother and a father who didn't care about any of us," he said. "We grew up with few clothes, no shoes, little to eat. My father worked me hard and whupped me hard."[38] Sonny finally made his way to St. Louis where his mother had relocated, but with no job or education, he quickly took to crime. Convicted of armed robbery, he began boxing in prison and decided to pursue it professionally after his parole in 1952. His handlers were shadowy underworld types who often made money by fixing fights.

As a boxer, Liston was raw, but powerfully built and with tremendous reach and punch. From his debut in 1953 through 1960, he won 31 of 32 fights, most of them by knockouts or technical knockouts in the early rounds. After Liston knocked out Zora Folley to become the number-one contender for the heavyweight title, *Sports Illustrated* asked, "How good is he? His body is so awesome—arms like fence posts, thighs like silos— it is reassuring to hear him speak and not utter some terrible atavistic growl."[39]

Liston was often described as a kind and decent man, especially by Geraldine, but his intimidating size and underworld connections gave him a certain aura. The best way to describe it is menacing—Liston looked like he could inflict serious pain and enjoy doing so. A famous *Esquire* magazine cover in December 1963 depicted a sullen Liston wearing a Santa Claus hat. George Lois, who had arranged the photo shoot, had to drag Liston away from the craps tables to get the picture shot. "By now he was known by everyone as the meanest man in the world," said Lois. "[He] flaunted his surly, menacing image at a time when rising racial fever dominated the headlines."[40]

Liston cultivated that image well, especially in the ring, and it finally helped him get a title shot against Floyd Patterson. In their first meeting in 1962, and in their rematch a year later, Liston simply overwhelmed the smaller champion, bullying him all around the ring and knocking him out in just over two minutes in both matches. "He barely let Floyd Patterson out of the dressing room Monday before he began almost without enthu- siasm to drop him on the floor like a sack of soiled laundry," wrote sportswriter Jim Murray. "Two more knockdowns and Floyd would have got housemaid's knee."[41]

Flying to Philadelphia the morning after the fight, Liston expected a waiting crowd of fans and reporters, and even had a speech prepared in which he promised to be a good champion. When no one showed up to greet the plane, Liston realized that he was never going to escape his role as the villain. White America was scared of his raw power, mob connections, and criminal record, while blacks were concerned Liston's image would set back the emerging civil rights cause. The NAACP had begged Patterson not to take the fight, and Manhattan branch chairman Percy Sutton admitted, "Hell, let's stop kidding. I'm in for Patterson because he represents us better than Liston ever could or would."[42] The rebukes only seemed to make Liston even more brooding and sullen.

Two famous fights with Muhammad Ali followed, both of which ended in controversy. Liston believed he could intimidate his younger opponent and did very little training for the first fight in February 1964. Overconfident and out of shape, Liston was way behind when he refused to come out for the seventh round. Many who watched the fight, including former heavyweight champ Rocky Marciano, felt that Liston had committed the unpardonable sin for an athlete—he had simply quit. "How could that big stiff sit there on the stool and let them take his title away?" asked Marciano. "How could he care so little about it? The man was heavyweight champion of the world!"[43]

The second fight the following year was even stranger, with Ali knocking out Liston early in the first round with what some described as a "phantom punch" (see chapter 1). Almost immediately, speculation began that Liston's mob connections had ordered him to throw the bout. While officials with the World Boxing Association called it a disgrace, Liston denied a fix, saying, "Me? Sell my title? Those dirty bastards!"[44]

The FBI investigated the fight for months, and despite testimony from several witnesses who indicated the fight was fixed, and evidence that Liston was controlled by mobster Frank "Blinky" Palermo, the bureau never pushed the issue. It is possible that Liston had been the victim or beneficiary of dives for most of his professional career. "As a boxer, he was mob controlled from day one," wrote author Brian Tuohy, "so much so that untangling which mobster owned which piece of Liston is nearly impossible."[45]

With the second loss to Ali, Liston mostly disappeared from the public consciousness, even though he did keep fighting. His last fight came just six months before he died when he battered Chuck Wepner for five rounds before finally winning by technical knockout. The fight took place in Jersey City, and true to form, there were rumors that Liston had been approached to throw the fight in favor of Wepner, a local Jersey kid whom the mob wanted to promote. Instead, Liston pummeled the appropriately named "Bayonne Bleeder" whose face was so badly cut that the ring doctor stopped the fight.

Liston's final months were filled with more of his high-rolling Vegas lifestyle, including gambling and drinking. Two days before he died Geraldine had a dream in which Liston was falling in the shower calling out to her for help. When she returned from a Christmas visit to her mother's in the first week in January, she noticed a bad smell coming from the master bedroom of their home, which she originally believed was food that had been left out too long. Sonny Liston, once the biggest, baddest man on the planet, was dead, his body quickly decomposing. Although Liston was found with fresh needle tracks on his arm, the coroner listed the cause of death as "natural causes stemming from poor oxygen and nutrient blood supply to the heart."[46]

That report only raised more questions than it answered, and various explanations have arisen as to what killed Sonny Liston. Was it of his own doing? A drug overdose? Did the mob do him in and cover it up? If it was natural causes, why were traces of morphine and codeine found in his system, and why would the official police report list the cause of death as a heroin overdose? And for a man who never had a drug problem and was also afraid of needles, why were there needle marks in Liston's arm?

As with any good mystery, the answers to such questions remain unknown. Geraldine refused to believe the rumors and insisted that a heart attack killed him. Others, including his publicist Harold Carson, thought Liston needed the money and got mixed up with more bad characters. His sparring partner Gary Bates believed that Liston was collecting for a shylock in town and got into trouble, while others said he had been given what was called a "hot shot" (of heroin) by the mob, or some element of gangsters to whom he owed money.

Mystery permeates Liston's life, all the way from birth to death—the exact date of either no one knows for sure. His final resting place in a Las Vegas cemetery is marked with a stone that reads only, "A MAN."

Perhaps there is no more fitting requiem than one written by Carson—"I think he died the day he was born."[47]

EPILOGUE

The year in sports 1970 unofficially ended with the Astro-Bluebonnet Bowl college football game on New Year's Eve night in Houston, and it went out with a bang. Oklahoma's Bruce Derr kicked a field goal with less than a minute to play as the Sooners tied Alabama 24–24. A wild fourth quarter included not only the last-minute field goal, but also a throwback touchdown pass to Alabama quarterback Scott Hunter and a missed field goal by the Tide's Richard Ciemny that would have won the game with just one second remaining.

As 1970 ended and the New Year began, there was a sense that things would be different, and that the old order of things was passing away. Notre Dame and Texas met again in the Cotton Bowl on New Year's Day, but this time the Irish won 24–11, ending the Longhorns' winning streak at 30. More importantly, Julius Whittier suited up in the game after lettering for Texas in the fall.[1] The following year, the Associated Press published a five-part series on the Longhorns' reluctance to recruit blacks, a series that coauthor Robert Heard said "cried out to be written."[2]

While the Texas streak was impressive, less than a week later the Harlem Globetrotters lost to a team called the New Jersey Reds, ending the 'Trotters win streak at 2,495 games. Reds' player/coach Red Klotz, 50 years old at the time and a veteran at losing to the Globetrotters in the staged exhibitions, hit the winning shot. "They couldn't believe the game was over," Klotz said of the crowd in Martin, Tennessee. "Beating the Globetrotters is like shooting Santa Claus."[3] The 'Trotters didn't take the loss too hard and immediately embarked on a new streak that lasted for 8,829 games and 24 years.

After an 89–82 loss to Notre Dame on January 23, UCLA would begin its record 88-game winning streak. John Wooden then led the Bruins to another national title, his seventh, with a 68–62 win over Villanova. The Notre Dame upset was engineered by rookie coach Digger Phelps, who had come over from Fordham. He was one of an incredible class of new coaches around the country that included Bob Knight at Indiana, Denny Crum at Louisville, and Chuck Daly at Penn. It would be Phelps and Notre Dame again, three years later, who would also end the UCLA winning streak. By that time, Wooden had won two more titles.

A year older and wiser, and now with help from the legendary Oscar Robertson, Lew Alcindor helped dethrone the Knicks in the NBA. Alcindor's Milwaukee Bucks won 20 straight games at one point and squashed the Baltimore Bullets in the finals, four games to none. The difference was Oscar, who had come to Milwaukee in a trade after a decade languishing with noncontenders in Cincinnati. The man considered by many the greatest player of all time had never won a championship since his high school days at Crispus Attucks in Indianapolis. "This is the first time I've ever had champagne in the dressing room," he said after the clinching win. "We only got soft drinks when we won in high school, but this is the big time."[4]

From the high of his dramatic win over Muhammad Ali in March, things spiraled down for Joe Frazier. A devastating loss to George Foreman in 1973, in which Frazier was knocked down six times in less than two rounds, and the two subsequent losses to Ali, took something from the heavyweight champ. He kept going until 1981 and wanted to go even longer but eventually retired to train fighters, including his son Marvis. Joe Frazier's later years were characterized by health and financial problems as well as his ongoing, ever-complex relationship with Ali. When Ali got to light the Olympic flame at the 1996 Games in Atlanta, Frazier said, "If it had been me there, he'd have been pushed in the fire." [5] But by the end of his life, Frazier acknowledged the need to mend fences. "We got to do it, before we all close our eyes, because I want to see him in heaven."[6]

The yearling Secretariat had yet to run a race, and another horse almost beat him to the Triple Crown. Canonero II won both the Kentucky Derby and Preakness before finishing fourth in the Belmont. Racing primarily in Venezuela, and unimpressive even there, Canonero II's success may have been one of the most surprising victories in the 97-year history of the Kentucky Derby. Margaret Court started the year quickly by winning the Australian Open, but it was another Aussie, Evonne Goolagong, who broke through with wins at Wimbledon and the French Open. Billie Jean King won the U.S. Open and reached one of her goals, becoming the first female athlete to earn $100,000.

Bobby Orr and the Bruins shattered all kinds of scoring marks in trying to defend their Stanley Cup but were upset in the first round of the playoffs by Montreal. The difference was rookie Ken Dryden, who played in only six games during the regular season but showed enough promise to take over the top goaltending spot for the playoffs. "That guy just baffled us," said Boston's Ken Hodge. "We were really surprised to see him play the way he did under playoff pressure."[7] Dryden keyed playoff wins over the Bruins, North Stars, and finally the Blackhawks in winning playoff MVP honors and leading the Canadiens to yet another Cup.

Gary Player, Billy Casper, and Doug Sanders all finished out of the money in golf's major championships, while Lee Trevino won the U.S. and British Opens on his way to Player of the Year honors. Nicklaus rebounded to win the PGA Championship and the tour money title, but perhaps the best golf of the year came from astronaut Alan Shepard, who whacked two golf balls on the moon during his trip on *Apollo 14*. "Hey!" he said after the second shot. "That one made it to the second crater. Miles and miles and miles."[8]

As Curt Flood finished his career with the Washington Senators, the Senators themselves were finished in Washington. This was the second incarnation of the American League team—the first version had already moved on to Minnesota. These new Senators were much like their predecessors and lost an average of 90 games per season, a futility that persuaded ownership to relocate to Dallas and become the Texas Rangers. In typical Senators' fashion, the team was one out from beating the Yankees in its Washington finale when "hundreds of rowdy youngsters and adults charged onto the field to begin mobbing the players [and] ripping up the scoreboard."[9] The game was officially forfeited to New York, and baseball disappeared in DC until the Nationals moved from Montreal in 2005.

Pete Rose hit .304, but the Reds could not repeat a trip to the World Series. Brooks Robinson had another typical season for him with a .272

average and 92 RBI, but it was the Orioles' four 20-game winners—Jim
Palmer, Pat Dobson, Dave McNally, and Mike Cuellar—that headlined
their return to the Series. Baltimore lost in seven games to the Pirates and
their often underappreciated star Roberto Clemente. Clemente had a hit in
every game, made spectacular plays in the field, and finished with a .414
average. "This means so much to me," he said. "Now people in the whole
world know how I play."[10]

The main Cold War battlefield remained Vietnam, but the minor skir-
mishes moved from the chessboard to the Ping-Pong table. A trip to
China by U.S. table tennis players for a series of exhibition games proved
enormously popular and helped thaw relations between the two countries,
including a relaxing of trade restrictions. Chinese leader Chou Eu-lai told
the visiting American players that their trip to China had "opened a new
page in the relations of the Chinese and American peoples."[11] The United
States reciprocated by inviting the Chinese team to play in the States, and
within a year President Nixon would make his historic trip to Peking.

The NFL career of Gale Sayers did not last much longer than that of
his friend Brian Piccolo. In a preseason game, Sayers wrecked his other
knee and although he attempted another comeback, this time he couldn't
do it. In his last two years in the league, Sayers had just 36 carries for 90
yards and no touchdowns. As the *Chicago Daily News* aptly observed,
"Gone are that instant acceleration from medium to top speed and the
incomparable ability to change directions on a dime without hesitation or
loss of speed."[12] Before the year ended, ABC would introduce the world
to the Sayers-Piccolo friendship with the premiere of *Brian's Song*, a
movie that got an enthusiastic endorsement from President Nixon. "Believe me, it was one of the great motion pictures I have seen. Some will
say it's corny," but the president was clear that he was not part of the
"some."[13]

Another movie, *Patton*, the favorite of Ohio State coach Woody
Hayes, won Oscars for Best Picture and Best Actor for George C. Scott.
On a different battlefield, Hayes resumed his "Ten Year War" with Bo
Schembechler and Michigan, losing in Ann Arbor 10–7. Protesting an
official's call in the game, Hayes rushed on the field and then tore up a
sideline marker. The outburst drew widespread condemnation, with
newspapers across the country calling Hayes "a raving lunatic," "horse's
rear end," and "a clown act."[14] Michigan athletic director Don Canham,
well aware that Woody's antics drew attention and paying customers,

laughed off any criticism. "I'll buy all the down markers Hayes wants to break," he said, "because Ohio State without Hayes would mean 30,000 less people in the stands."[15]

Wichita State and Marshall tried to pick up the pieces of their shattered football programs but could only win five games between them. Even so, those wins were extremely satisfying. In their first home game since the crash, and playing mostly with freshmen and sophomores, Marshall rallied to beat Xavier University 15–13 by scoring a touchdown on the game's final play. Players and coaches were mobbed by elated fans, and after an hour in the locker room "the players and coaches emerged to find most of the fans still in the stands, many crying, many hugging and some almost afraid that if they left, it might not have been true."[16]

There were plenty of tears shed for the sports figures who left the scene. Freddie Steinmark, who bravely watched the Cotton Bowl from the sidelines on one leg (see chapter 1), was unable to beat cancer and passed away on June 6 in Houston. Legendary sportscaster Bill Stern died in November, and golfing great Bobby Jones, first winner of the Grand Slam and creator of the Masters Tournament, went in December. A painful disease called syringomyelia first crippled Jones and then reduced his weight to around 60 pounds at the end. Sportswriter Herbert Warren Wind eulogized, "As a young man, he was able to stand up to about the best that life can offer, and later he stood up with equal grace to just about the worst."[17]

FINAL THOUGHTS

An argument could be made that 1970 represented a crossroads in America—a transition from the grim problems of the 1960s to the indulgent "me decade" that was to follow. The term was coined by writer Tom Wolfe, who was fascinated by "how people treated themselves; dramatized their own lives. Now, all sorts of middling folk could take part in what the upper classes had been doing, putting themselves on stage."[18]

That stage, at least in a sports sense, was a grand one in 1970. Maybe it's just the sentimentality of old men recalling the glory days, but things did seem simpler and more elemental. Athletes focused on winning and playing hard, not on their next shoe contract or rap album, and we still looked at them as examples of the best of us. Today's athletes are seldom heroes and even less likely to be role models, as former NBA star Charles Barkley so frankly admitted. Where is the Willis Reed of today, someone who "reminded [us] of El Cid, strapped dead to his horse to lead his men to victory against the Moors. Who plays so hurt now?"[19]

Perhaps money, and especially television money, killed him. The short-lived NFL players' strike of 1970 presaged an era in which players saw the millions of dollars being made and began to demand their fair share. The most competitive battles in sports moved from the playing fields to the boardrooms and courtrooms.

Sociologists called this the "corporatization" of sport, where "attracting spectators and media sponsorships becomes more important than the playing process because sport is now driven by profit and the market."[20] In the 1960s, professional sports were still very much "games," often played in smaller parks and arenas, and very closely attached to the neighborhoods in which they took place. Now, they were becoming big-ticket "events" that required larger stadiums, sterile atmospheres, and more businesslike approaches. "I think 1970 is a line of demarcation for professional sports in America," said author Michael MacCambridge. "A lot of the most charming, eccentric, unusual realities of football in the 60s would disappear. Professional sports, namely the NFL, became much more corporate, much more homogenized, [and] much more sophisticated."[21]

The athletes of 2015 are so financially successful that many of them—including Michael Jordan, Magic Johnson, and John Elway—have transitioned directly into team ownership or other forms of management. Aside from the few superstars at the top, the athletes of 1970 typically worked off-season jobs as teachers, salesmen, and businessmen. "All of our guys worked," said Cleveland Browns' guard John Wooten, who was a math teacher. "Nobody just sat around and 'worked out.'"[22]

While money has played a role, the change is also cultural and sociological. The same Harry Edwards who in 1968 tried to organize a black boycott of the Olympics has long predicted "the street culture of the so-called underclass would eventually transform sports."[23] The blacks who were simply fighting for recognition in 1970 are now predominant in almost every sport, at least as athletes, and their ascendance has radically transformed how games are played and understood.

Overwhelmingly, this has been a positive development on many fronts, but it has not come without backlash. Sportswriter Jason Whitlock, himself black, said that "African-American football players caught up in the rebellion and buffoonery of hip-hop culture have given NFL owners and coaches a reason to whiten their rosters. That will be the legacy left by Chad [Johnson], Tank [Johnson], Pacman Jones, Terrell Owens, Michael Vick, and all the other football bojanglers."[24] Critics were quick to respond that "within such reactionary diatribes, 'hip-hop' has become another raced euphemism for black criminality and deviance."[25] There were a lot of problems in 1970, including crime, pollution, and 339,000 U.S. troops still fighting in Vietnam at year's end, but without a doubt, race remained the biggest problem in the United States at the end of 1970. That still seems to be the case today.

In a similar way, women continue to struggle to achieve equality with men. The pay differences have largely been eliminated, at least for major individual sports such as golf and tennis, and the athletes aren't called "girls" anymore, but important discrepancies still remain. Media coverage of female sporting events has been virtually nonexistent. Despite the presence of more female athletes and sports reporters, female athletes still receive only around 5 percent of the national airtime devoted to sports. In an assessment of content on ESPN, CNN, the *New York Times*, and *USA Today*, men's coverage was greater than women's coverage by a ratio of 15 to 1. The Internet and social media could level the playing field, but while "the technology has presented liberating possibilities for women's sports, those possibilities aren't being met. Instead, the new media platforms are replicating the discrimination and bias that has always been a part of old-media framing of women's sports."[26]

Thus, the problems of 1970 remain in 2015, only in different guises. And a new set of issues, impossible to foresee so many years ago, define what we understand as modern sport. In a sporting sense, are things today better than in 1970? Worse? That is a personal decision, just as surely as the music one listens to. The great teams of 1970 have been compared to a piece of classical music—all the parts of the orchestra working together to create a harmonious whole. Things in 2015 are a bit cacophonous, and the brass section might go off on an unscheduled five-minute riff, but maybe the end result is just as good. Says Robert Lipsyte of the *New York Times*, "Rap replaces classic rock. The melody and the harmony are gone, but maybe rhythm is enough these days."[27]

NOTES

INTRODUCTION

1. "1970 Nikita's Year to Beat Out U.S.," Associated Press, *Vancouver Sun*, June 26, 1961, 9.

2. Norman Mailer, "Ego," *Life*, March 19, 1971, 19.

3. Ecclesiastes 1:9 (New International Version).

4. Jim Bouton, *Ball Four plus Ball Five* (New York: Stein & Day, 1980), 428.

I. JANUARY

1. "No. 1 Chant Rings Loud among Lions," Associated Press, *Pittsburgh Post-Gazette*, January 2, 1970, 17.

2. Tom Loomis, "Michigan Demolishes Ohio State, 24 to 12," *Toledo Blade*, November 23, 1969, D1.

3. Kaye Kessler and William F. Reed, "Bye-Bye, No. 1," *Sports Illustrated*, December 1, 1969, 20.

4. John Henderson, "Spirit of the Black 14," *Denver Post*, November 8, 2009. Retrieved August 16, 2013, http://www.denverpost.com/ci_13739558.

5. "Wyoming Loses 14 Players in Dispute," Associated Press, *Eugene (OR) Register-Guard*, October 18, 1969, 2B.

6. Pat Putnam, "No Defeats, Loads of Trouble," *Sports Illustrated*, November 3, 1969, 26.

7. Putnam, "No Defeats," 26.

8. Jay Drew, "BYU Football: Remembering the Black 14 Protest," *Salt Lake City Tribune*, November 6, 2009. Retrieved August 17, 2013, http://www.sltrib.com/byucougars/ci_13728556.

9. Rick Gosselin, "Spartans Recruited Black Texans before State Schools Did," *Dallas Morning News*, December 25, 2014, http://www.dallasnews.com/sports/columnists/rick-gosselin/20141225-gosselin-spartans-recruited-black-texans-before-state-schools-did.ece.

10. "Ole Miss Recruits Negroes, Vaught Admits 'Kiddingly,'" Associated Press, *St. Petersburg Times*, September 8, 1966, C1.

11. John Westbrook walked on at Baylor in 1964 but had nowhere near the career or impact of LeVias. In 1953, Benjamin Kelly played at San Angelo College, making him the first black player at a previously all-white Texas school.

12. Morton Sharnik, "Too Small to Be Overlooked," *Sports Illustrated*, November 30, 1970, 26.

13. Ivan Maisel, "Dr. King Meeting Lasts a Lifetime," *ESPN*, February 21, 2014. Retrieved February 22, 2014, http://espn.go.com/college-football/story/_/id/10491694/meeting-martin-luther-king-remains-smu-jerry-levias.

14. Roger Springfield, executive producer. *Rites of Autumn: The Story of College Football*, Lions Gate Films, 2002.

15. "Jerry LeVias Opened Door for Blacks in Southwest," United Press International, *Beaver County (PA) Times*, December 26, 1968, D3.

16. Robert Heard, *Oklahoma vs. Texas: When Football Becomes War* (Austin, TX: Honey Hill, 1980), 285.

17. Richard Pennington, *Breaking the Ice: The Racial Integration of Southwest Conference Football* (Jefferson, NC: McFarland, 1987).

18. Dan Jenkins, "A Sane Conclusion in a Cockeyed Conference," *Sports Illustrated*, November 7, 1966, 45.

19. "First Black Letterman Remembers DKR," *KUT* radio, November 13, 2012. Retrieved August 17, 2013, http://kut.org/2012/11/first-black-letterman-remembers-dkr/.

20. Joe Drape, "Changing the Face of Texas Football," *New York Times*, December 23, 2005. Retrieved August 17, 2013, http://www.nytimes.com/2005/12/23/sports/ncaafootball/23texas.html?_r=4&.

21. Dan Jenkins, "Texas Hangs On to Its No. 1," *Sports Illustrated*, January 12, 1970, 28.

22. Springfield, *Rites of Autumn*.

23. A 14–14 tie with Notre Dame prevented the Trojans from playing for the national championship.

24. Ross Greenburg, producer, *Against the Tide* (television documentary), Showtime, 2013.

25. Jon Saraceno, "Bad Judgment Doomed Eagles, Not QB Sickness," *USA Today*, February 10, 2005. Retrieved November 6, 2013, http://usatoday30.usatoday.com/sports/columnist/saraceno/2005-02-10-saraceno_x.htm.

26. Springfield, *Rites of Autumn*.

27. Springfield, *Rites of Autumn*.

28. "First Black Letterman."

29. William F. Reed, "The Other Side of 'The Y,'" *Sports Illustrated*, January 26, 1970, 38.

30. Drew, "BYU Football."

31. "Afros against Crew Cuts," Associated Press, *Spokane (WA) Spokesman-Review*, January 11, 1970, 8.

32. "Jayhawk and Tiger Football Teams of 1891 Started Rivalry Now an Annual High Spot," *Lawrence (KS) Journal-World*, November 22, 1937, 8.

33. "Has Best Mustache," *Milwaukee Journal*, December 24, 1913, 3.

34. William Glover, "'Hair' First Platform for Hippie Movement?" Associated Press, *Nevada Daily Mail*, July 16, 1970, 5.

35. "Afros against Crew Cuts," 8.

36. John Underwood, "Concessions—and Lies," *Sports Illustrated*, September 8, 1969, 37.

37. Peter King, "The AFL," *Sports Illustrated*, July 13, 2009. Retrieved February 20, 2010, http://sportsillustrated.cnn.com/vault/article/magazine/MAG1157664/3/index.htm.

38. Jim Bouton, *Ball Four plus Ball Five* (New York: Stein & Day, 1980), 215.

39. Underwood, "Concessions—and Lies," 39.

40. Greg Jayne, "Wooden Left an Impression on All," *Vancouver (WA) Columbian*, June 5, 2010. Retrieved September 7, 2013, http://www.columbian.com/news/2010/jun/05/wooden-left-an-impression-on-all/.

41. John Underwood, "Shave Off That Thing!" *Sports Illustrated*, September 1, 1969, 23.

42. Blaine Newnham, "What Went Wrong?" *Eugene (OR) Register-Guard*, October 12, 1979, B1.

43. "Money Is the Reason as Joe Namath Shaves," Associated Press, *Meriden (CT) Morning Record*, December 12, 1968, 15.

44. "Curt Flood's Reserve Clause Challenge Begins," Associated Press, *Sarasota Journal*, May 19, 1970, 1C.

45. Eliot Asinof, *Eight Men Out* (New York: Henry Holt, 1963), 22.

46. Federal Baseball Club v. National League, 259 U.S. 200 (1922).

47. Toolson v. New York Yankees, 346 U.S. 356 (1953).

48. "No. 1 'Draftee' Endorses System," Associated Press, *St. Petersburg Times*, June 7, 1966, C5.

49. "Baseball Players Show Signs of Bending," Associated Press, *Eugene (OR) Register-Guard*, February 20, 1969, 1C.

50. "Carl Yastrzemski Asks Poll of Major League Players to Determine Opinion on Flood's Reserve Clause Challenge," Associated Press, *Gettysburg (PA) Times*, January 19, 1970, 9.

51. Curt Flood and Richard Carter, "My Rebellion," *Sports Illustrated*, February 1, 1971, 27.

52. "Average Salaries in Major League Baseball, 1967–2009," Major League Baseball Players Association, 2009. Retrieved from http://hosted.ap.org/specials/interactives/_sports/baseball08/documents/bbo_average_salary2009.pdf.

53. Roger Angell, *Five Seasons* (New York: Warner, 1977), 316.

54. Allen Barra, "How Curt Flood Changed Baseball and Killed His Career in the Process," *Atlantic Monthly*, July 11, 2011. Retrieved August 18, 2013, http://www.theatlantic.com/entertainment/archive/2011/07/how-curt-flood-changed-baseball-and-killed-his-career-in-the-process/241783/.

55. Flood and Carter, "My Rebellion," 26.

56. "Modifying Reserve Clause Would Ruin Game—Kuhn," *Milwaukee Journal*, May 28, 1970, part 2, p. 17.

57. George Willis, "Flood Opened Gates," *New York Post,* July 4, 2011. Retrieved August 19, 2013, http://www.nypost.com/p/sports/more_sports/flood_opened_gates_nCLaNnWIKEXKO97J7YdLON.

58. Paul Dickson, *Bill Veeck: Baseball's Greatest Maverick* (New York: Walker, 2012), 276.

59. "Curt Flood Needs Reserve Clause," Associated Press, *Pittsburgh Post-Gazette*, October 30, 1970, 21.

60. "Baseball Reserve Clause Upheld," Associated Press, *Regina (SK) Leader-Post*, June 20, 1972, 25.

61. "Seitz Waves Magic Wand Again, Messersmith, McNally Cut Free," Associated Press, *Ocala (FL) Star-Banner*, December 24, 1975, 2B.

62. Roger Angell, *Late Innings* (New York: Random House, 1982), 22.

63. Howard Cosell, "Flood's Courage Brought Baseball Out of the Slave Era," *Pittsburgh Press*, July 16, 1986, C6.

64. "'Phantom Punch' Beats Liston; Clay Wants Floyd Patterson," Associated Press, *Nashua (NH) Telegraph*, May 26, 1965, 15.

65. "Clay, Terrell Put On a Show," Associated Press, *Charleston (SC) News and Courier*, December 29, 1966, D2.

66. Joe Flaherty, "Ali-Terrell: The Sadistic Game of 'What's My Name?'" *Village Voice*, February 9, 1967, 3.

67. Ray Grody, "Will Real Clay Please Stand Up?" *Milwaukee Sentinel*, February 9, 1967, part 2, p. 2.

68. Grody, "Real Clay," part 2, p. 2.

69. William Johnson, "And in This Corner . . . NCR 315," *Sports Illustrated*, September 16, 1968, 34–49.

70. "Ali vs. Marciano vs. a Computer," *Windsor (ON) Star*, February 17, 1979, 13.

71. "Ali and the Rock: Super Fight Filmed," *Baltimore Afro-American*, January 6, 1970, 19.

72. Michael Ryan, "Phantom Bout Was Real Fix," *Melbourne Age*, January 22, 1970, 24.

73. Ryan, "Phantom Bout," 24.

74. Scorecard, *Sports Illustrated*, September 15, 1969, 18.

75. Eriq Gardner, "NFL Draft Dodgers," *Slate*, April 22, 2010. Retrieved November 29, 2013, http://www.slate.com/articles/news_and_politics/recycled/2010/04/nfl_draft_dodgers.html.

76. "Yazoo Smith Awaits Cash, Says Decision Was Inevitable," *St. Petersburg Times*, September 10, 1976, 3C.

77. Roy McHugh, "Smoke Rings," *Pittsburgh Press*, January 28, 1970, 60.

78. Milton Richman, "Last Draftee Thinks He Could Make Good," United Press International, *Lexington (NC) Dispatch*, February 7, 1970, 7.

79. Roscoe Nance, "2013 NFL Draft Class Includes Most HBCU Players in a Decade," *BlackAmericaWeb.com*, April 24, 2013. Retrieved November 29, 2013, http://sports.blackamericaweb.com/index.php?option=com_content&view=article&id=10175:2013-nfl-draft-class-includes-most-hbcu-players-in-a-decade&catid=92:nfl&Itemid=452.

80. "Black College Players Vie for Attention in NFL Draft," Associated Press, *CBS Sports*, April 24, 2007. Retrieved November 27, 2013, http://www.cstv.com/sports/m-footbl/stories/042407aac.html.

81. "Players from HBCUs Ignored in the NFL Draft," *Journal of Blacks in Higher Education*, May 26, 2012. Retrieved November 29, 2013, http://www.jbhe.com/2012/05/players-from-hbcus-ignored-in-the-nfl-draft/.

82. Nance, "2013 NFL Draft Class."

83. "Black College Players Vie for Attention."

84. Darren Rovell, "The Dark Cloud over Black Colleges," *ESPN*, February 25, 2004. Retrieved November 27, 2013, http://sports.espn.go.com/espn/blackhistory/news/story?id=1743388.

85. Thomas Henderson and Peter Knobler, *Out of Control: Confessions of an NFL Casualty* (New York: Pocket, 1987), 62.

86. George Schroeder, "Grambling Players Provide Shocking Details, Reason They Ended Boycott," *USA Today*, October 22, 2013. Retrieved November 29, 2013, http://www.usatoday.com/story/sports/ncaaf/swac/2013/10/21/grambling-players-provide-shocking-details-former-coach-swayed-them-back-out-of-protest/3144353/.

87. "Five Reasons Why More HBCU Players Aren't Taken in the NFL Draft," *HBCU Digest*, May 6, 2012. Retrieved November 29, 2013, http://hbcudigest.com/five-reasons-why-more-hbcu-players-arent-taken-in-the-nfl-draft/.

88. Schroeder, "Grambling Players."

89. "Federal Judge Rules Against Football Draft," Associated Press, *Charleston (SC) News and Courier*, September 9, 1976, C1.

90. "New Trouble for Grid Pact?" Associated Press, *Spokane (WA) Spokesman-Review*, February 23, 1977, 16.

91. "Judge Bryant's Decision That Snafued NFL Draft," *Baltimore Afro-American*, September 11, 1976, 12.

2. FEBRUARY

1. Murray Rose, "Frazier Defeats Quarry, Challenges Jimmy Ellis to Fight between Titlists," *Gettysburg (PA) Times*, June 24, 1969, 11.

2. "Ellis Ready for Action," *Nevada Daily Mail*, February 11, 1970, 6.

3. Pat Putnam, "One Round of Boxing Was More Than Enough," *Sports Illustrated*, November 30, 1970, 21.

4. Frazier had a lifelong flirtation with music and singing, and during the 1970s fronted a band called "Joe Frazier and the Knockouts."

5. Bob Johnson, "My Nickel's Worth," *Spokane (WA) Daily Chronicle*, February 17, 1970, 13.

6. Ira Berkow, "Frazier-Ali Bout Transcends Sports," Newspaper Enterprise Association, *Owosso (MI) Argus-Press*, March 6, 1971, 9.

7. "Big Rematch Looms," United Press International, *Palm Beach Post*, March 10, 1971, D4.

8. "Ali: Like Being Close to Death," Associated Press, *Pittsburgh Post-Gazette*, October 2, 1975, 20.

9. "Ali-Frazier III—Finale of Boxing's Greatest Rivalry," *Charlottesville (VA) Cavalier Daily*, October 2, 1975, 5.

10. "Boxing Legend Joe Frazier Dies," *ESPN*, November 8, 2011. Retrieved August 19, 2013, http://espn.go.com/boxing/story/_/id/7206261/joe-frazier-former-heavyweight-champion-dead-67.

11. Joe Jares, "Up, Up and Away Go Artis and New J.U.," *Sports Illustrated*, January 5, 1970, 20.

12. Jares, "Up, Up and Away," 20.

13. "Look, We've Still Got to Finish the Game," Associated Press, *Spartanburg (SC) Herald-Journal*, February 2, 1970, 13.

14. "We've Still Got to Finish," 13.

15. "Pistol Pete Maravich's Top College Games," *PistolPete23.com*. Retrieved August 19, 2013, http://www.pistolpete23.com/top_college.htm.

16. Pete Maravich and Curry Kirkpatrick, "I Want to Put On a Show," *Sports Illustrated*, December 1, 1969, 39.

17. Lisa Twyman, "Pete Maravich Used to Be a Hot Dog; Now He Won't Even Eat One," *Sports Illustrated*, October 29, 1984, 106.

18. Maravich and Kirkpatrick, "I Want to Put On a Show," 46.

19. Leonard Koppett, "McLain Is All Business, But Baseball Is Pleasure," New York Times News Service, *Miami News*, September 2, 1968, 2B.

20. Dan Martin, "Denny McLain Knows Exactly What Wainwright Was Thinking," *New York Post*, July 16, 2014. Retrieved July 16, 2014, http://nypost.com/2014/07/16/denny-mclain-knows-exactly-what-wainwright-was-thinking/.

21. Harold Seymour, *Baseball: The Golden Age* (New York: Oxford University Press, 1971, 288).

22. Scorecard, *Sports Illustrated*, February 23, 1970, 10.

23. Scorecard, February 23, 1970, 10.

24. Peter Carry, "McLain: With Love and Hisses," *Sports Illustrated*, July 13, 1970, 42.

25. Spoelstra's grandson Eric has coached the Miami Heat to multiple NBA titles.

26. Arthur Daley, "Denny McLain: To Know Him Is to Dislike Him," *Miami News*, May 18, 1972, C1.

27. "Denny McLain Gets 23-Year Prison Sentence," Associated Press, *Los Angeles Times*, April 26, 1985. Retrieved August 21, 2013, http://articles.latimes.com/1985-04-26/sports/sp-20974_1_denny-mclain.

28. "Star of the Past Is Charged with Stealing Small Town's Hope for the Future," *New York Times*, December 1, 1996. Retrieved August 21, 2013, http://www.nytimes.com/1996/12/01/us/star-of-the-past-is-charged-with-stealing-small-town-s-hope-for-the-future.html.

29. Mike Christopulos, "MU Spurns NCAA for NIT," *Milwaukee Sentinel*, February 25, 1970, part 2, p. 1.

30. Scorecard, *Sports Illustrated*, June 16, 1975, 14.

31. Christopulos, "MU Spurns NCAA," part 2, p. 1.

32. Roger Jaynes, "McGuire's Bell Tolls for Rupp," *Milwaukee Journal*, December 13, 1977, part 2, p. 7.

33. Mark Wiedmer, "NIT Title Formerly a Big Deal; 1970 Marquette Team Spurned NCAA and Won," *Chattanooga Times-Free Press*, March 30, 2007. Retrieved January 30, 2014, http://www.timesfreepress.com/news/2007/mar/30/NIT-title-formerly-a-big-deal-1970-Marquette/.

34. "Rupp Scoffs at MU Anger," *Milwaukee Journal*, February 26, 1970, part 2, p. 13.

35. Joe Jares, *Basketball: The American Game* (Chicago: Follett, 1971), 48.

36. Michael Rapaport, director, *When the Garden Was Eden* (television documentary), ESPN, 2014.

37. Wiedmer, "NIT Title."

38. "Marquette vs. Fordham in College Hoop Feature," Associated Press, *Schenectady (NY) Gazette*, February 25, 1971, 41.

39. Bill Dwyre, "Time for Tears . . . of Joy," *Milwaukee Journal*, March 29, 1977, part 2, p. 9.

40. William F. Reed, "The Upstaging of Pistol Pete," *Sports Illustrated*, March 30, 1970, 22.

3. MARCH

1. "Palmer, Player Head Open Field," Associated Press, *Regina (SK) Leader-Post*, June 15, 1961, 33.

2. They Said It, *Sports Illustrated*, July 20, 1970, 11.

3. Ayesha Durgahee, "Gary Player: Staying in Shape with 'World's Most Traveled Athlete,'" *CNN*, August 28, 2012. Retrieved August 22, 2013, http://www.cnn.com/2012/08/28/travel/golf-gary-player.

4. Durgahee, "Gary Player."

5. Cecil Eprile, "Olympic Tangle: Apartheid Splits Nations at Games," *Ottawa Citizen*, March 1, 1968, 7.

6. Tim Glover, "Golf: The Paradox That Is Gary Player," *(UK) Independent*, July 16, 1996. Retrieved August 22, 2013, http://www.independent.co.uk/sport/golf-the-paradox-that-is-gary-player-1329010.html.

7. Glover, "Golf."

8. Glover, "Golf."

9. "Gary Player Stands Up for South Africa Home," Associated Press, *Vancouver Sun*, June 9, 1970, 22.

10. "Gary Player Wants Blacks in Masters," Associated Press, *Gettysburg (PA) Times*, April 6, 1972, 14.

11. Will Grimsley, "Player Overcomes Apartheid Situation," Associated Press, *Ludington (MI) Daily News*, April 6, 1978, 7.

12. Daniel E. Ginsburg, *The Fix Is In: A History of Baseball Gambling and Game Fixing Scandals* (Jefferson, NC: McFarland, 1995), 30.

13. Marty Ralbovsky, *Super Bowl* (New York: Hawthorn, 1971), 74.

14. "Nobody Likes Haber, but He's a Winner," *Boca Raton (FL) News*, December 31, 1970, 11A.

15. Pat Putnam, "A Win for Booze and Nicotine," *Sports Illustrated*, March 31, 1969, 22.

16. "Nobody Likes Haber," 11A.

17. "Paul Haber," United States Handball Association. Retrieved January 24, 2013, http://www.ushandball.org/content/view/414/427/.

18. Putnam, "Booze and Nicotine," 22.

19. Jim Stingl, "Filmmaker Hopes to Flesh Out Handball Legend Paul Haber," *Milwaukee Journal-Sentinel*, January 26, 2013. Retrieved January 24, 2014, http://www.jsonline.com/news/milwaukee/filmmaker-hopes-to-flesh-out-handball-legend-paul-haber-o38h3j9-188505131.html.

20. Stingl, "Filmmaker Hopes."

21. Pat Putnam, "Just Like a Green Bay Tree," *Sports Illustrated*, December 1, 1969, 29.

22. Dave Seminara, "Vinko Bogataj and the Ecstasy of Defeat," *RealClearSports.com*, March 20, 2010. Retrieved August 24, 2013, http://www.realclearsports.com/articles/2010/03/20/vinko_bogataj_and_the_ecstasy_of_defeat_96904.html.

23. Bob Verdi, "Agony of Defeat," *Pittsburgh Press*, February 13, 1984, C5.

24. Rich Hofmann, "'Agony of Defeat' Cherishes Moment," *Boca Raton (FL) News*, February 15, 1984, D1.

25. Seminara, "Vinko Bogataj."

26. "And the Agony Continues. . . ." *Sarasota Herald-Tribune*, December 9, 2002, 2C.

27. "Says Wooden: We're Starting a New Season," Associated Press, *Eugene (OR) Register-Guard*, March 18, 1964, 5B.

28. The University of Connecticut women's team holds the all-time record with 90 consecutive wins between 2008 and 2010.

29. "The First Champion," *Newsweek*, January 31, 2007. Retrieved September 14, 2013, http://www.thedailybeast.com/newsweek/2007/01/31/the-first-champion.html.

30. Richard Sandomir, "Searching for Mat Glory in a Sweaty Gym in Iowa," *New York Times*, April 10, 2007. Retrieved September 14, 2013, http://www.nytimes.com/2007/04/10/books/10sand.html?_r=0.

31. Wright Thompson, "The Losses of Dan Gable," *ESPN*, August 21, 2013. Retrieved September 14, 2013, http://espn.go.com/espn/feature/story/_/page/Dan-Gable/the-losses-dan-gable.

32. Herman Weiskopf, "A Good Littler Man Wins Big," *Sports Illustrated*, April 6, 1970, 72.

33. Weiskopf, "Good Littler Man," 72.

34. "Dan Gable Defeated in Finale," Associated Press, *Fredericksburg (VA) Free Lance-Star*, March 30, 1970, 6.

35. "Dan Gable Defeated," 6.

36. "Gable Predicts He Will Win Gold Medal," Associated Press, *St. Joseph (MO) News-Press*, August 28, 1972, 3B.

37. "Hawkeyes Ease to 16th Title," Associated Press, *Dubuque (IA) Telegraph-Herald*, March 24, 1996, 1B.

38. "Gable Continues to Dominate Wrestling," United Press International, *Lodi (CA) News-Sentinel*, March 17, 1986, 17.

39. "Gable Continues to Dominate," 17.

40. Thompson, "Losses of Dan Gable."

4. APRIL

1. "Apollo 13 Reports Trouble," United Press International, *Palm Beach Post*, April 14, 1970, A1.

2. As of 2015, the silver medals remained unclaimed and have been kept in a bank vault in Lausanne, Switzerland.

3. "Young U.S. Cagers Take Setback Hard," Associated Press, *Schenectady (NY) Gazette*, September 11, 1972, 27.

4. John Linklater, "Spassky at Peace after Years of Chess Warfare," *Glasgow Herald*, September 18, 1987, 15.

5. Scorecard, *Sports Illustrated*, December 13, 1971, 16.

6. Larry Evans, "The Enigma Tries a New Role," *Sports Illustrated*, October 12, 1970, 85.

7. Harold C. Schonberg, "Bobby Fischer Lives Only to Win at Chess," New York Times News Service, *Milwaukee Journal*, December 5, 1971, part 4, p. 1.

8. "1970 USSR vs. Rest of the World," *Chessgames.com*. Retrieved August 30, 2013, http://www.chessgames.com/perl/chesscollection?cid=1024274.

9. Evans, "Enigma Tries a New Role," 86.

10. Evans, "Enigma Tries a New Role," 87.

11. Robert Cantwell, "How to Cook a Russian Goose," *Sports Illustrated*, August 14, 1972, 25.

12. Pal Benko and Burt Hochberg, *Winning with Chess Psychology* (New York: Random House, 1991), 87.

13. Marty Ralbovsky, *Super Bowl* (New York: Hawthorn, 1971), 74.

14. Roger Ebert, "Searching for Bobby Fischer," *Chicago Sun-Times*, August 11, 1993. Retrieved September 2, 2013, http://www.rogerebert.com/reviews/searching-for-bobby-fischer-1993.

15. Linklater, "Spassky at Peace," 15.

16. Ed Wilks, "Maurice Stokes Steals Show in NIT's Semifinal Action," Associated Press, *Florence (AL) Times*, March 18, 1955, sec. 2, p. 5.

17. After Stokes died in 1970, the game continued in various forms until 1999 when it was dropped because of insurance issues. It was replaced by a golf pro-am. The money raised went to help several charities, including indigent former NBA players.

18. "The Man behind the Stokes Benefit Game," *Newburgh (NY) Evening News*, August 2, 1984, 4B.

19. "Man behind the Stokes Benefit Game," 4B.

20. Jeff Zillgitt, "Chauncey Billups Wins First Twyman-Stokes Teammate of the Year Award," *USA Today*, June 9, 2013. Retrieved August 26, 2013, http://www.usatoday.com/story/sports/nba/2013/06/09/chauncey-billups-jack-twyman-maurice-stokes-teammate-of-the-year-award/2406383/.

21. "Fans Rally Again on Behalf of Paralyzed Pro Cage Star," United Press International, *Altus (OK) Times-Democrat*, June 29, 1959, 6.

22. Zillgitt, "Chauncey Billups."

23. Frank Litsky, "Twyman Lives Role of 'Brother's Keeper,'" New York Times News Service, *Miami News*, August 18, 1966, 11A.

24. Zillgitt, "Chauncey Billups."

25. "Stokes Steals Show in NIT Tournament," *Baltimore Afro-American*, March 20, 1955, 14.

26. People, *Sports Illustrated*, April 20, 1970, 50.

27. People, April 20, 1970, 50.

28. "Diamonds Have Been a Buss, Not a Bust, for Morganna," *Reading (PA) Eagle*, May 4, 1986, C2.

29. A self-described born-again preacher, Stewart was given three life sentences for taking a hotel maid hostage in 1992.

30. John Eisenberg, *Cotton Bowl Days* (New York: Simon & Schuster, 1997), 175.

31. John Kunda, "Stars Are Shining Brightly," *Allentown (PA) Call-Chronicle,* May 13, 1984. Retrieved September 2, 2013, http://articles.mcall.com/1984-05-13/sports/2414179_1_two-man-teams-better-ball-amateur.

32. Peter Curry, "To a Stripper, Boyer's Hipper," *Sports Illustrated*, July 20, 1970, 47.

33. Curry, "Boyer's Hipper," 47.

34. Steve Rushin, "Where Are They Now? Morganna," *Sports Illustrated*, June 30, 2003. Retrieved September 2, 2013, http://sportsillustrated.cnn.com/2004/pr/subs/siexclusive/07/09/flashback.morganna/index.html.

35. Dan Raley, "An All-Star Memory Sealed with a Kiss," *Seattle Post-Intelligencer*, July 5, 2001. Retrieved September 2, 2013, http://www.seattlepi.com/news/article/An-All-Star-memory-sealed-with-a-kiss-1058973.php.

36. "Kissing Bandit In Demand," Scripps Howard News Service, *Youngstown (OH) Vindicator*, April 28, 1991, G5.

37. Jim McCabe, "Upset? Not Quite," *Golf Week*, June 10, 2012. Retrieved August 25, 2013, http://golfweek.com/news/2012/jun/10/casper-66-open-i-think-i-won/.

38. Arnold Palmer and James Dodson, *A Golfer's Life* (New York: Random House, 2010).

39. Robert F. Jones, "Has Anybody Here Seen Billy?" *Sports Illustrated*, June 14, 1969, 25.

40. Frank Litsky and Bruce Weber, "Tommy Bolt, a Top Golfer Who Was Known Better for His Temper, Dies at 92," *New York Times*, September 3, 2008. Retrieved August 25, 2013, http://www.nytimes.com/2008/09/04/sports/golf/04bolt.html?_r=0.

41. Dan Jenkins, "After the Others Had Gone, George Was Left," *Sports Illustrated*, April 21, 1969, 28.

42. "It's Masters Green for 'Cowboy' Archer," *Vancouver Sun*, April 14, 1969, 20.

43. Dan Jenkins, "All Yours, Billy Boy," *Sports Illustrated,* April 20, 1970, 19.

44. It would be the last 18-hole playoff in Masters history, as the tournament later changed to a sudden death format.

45. "Masters Golf, Casper, Littler Pals to the End," Associated Press, *St. Petersburg Evening Independent*, April 13, 1970, C1.

46. Gil Capps, *The Magnificent Masters: Jack Nicklaus, Johnny Miller, Tom Weiskopf and the 1975 Cliffhanger at Augusta* (Boston: Da Capo, 2014), 139.

47. Billy Casper, James Parkinson, and Lee Benson, *The Big Three and Me* (Columbus, MS: Genesis, 2012).

48. Bob Harig, "Odd-Man-Out Casper Deserved More," *ESPN*, February 8, 2015. Retrieved February 8, 2015, http://espn.go.com/golf/story/_/id/12295052/odd-man-billy-casper-deserved-more-golf.

49. Joe Jares, *Basketball: The American Game* (Chicago: Follett, 1971), 136.

50. The NBA rule was the reason Wilt Chamberlain had to play a year with the Harlem Globetrotters after leaving a year early at the University of Kansas. The league ended the restriction in 1971.

51. Jares, *Basketball*, 145.

52. Bert Rosenthal, "Officials Still Hoping for NBA-ABA Merger," Associated Press, *Reading (PA) Eagle*, February 6, 1972, 63.

53. William Rhoden, "Remembering Big O's Legacy amid the Glitter," *New York Times*, February 12, 2007. Retrieved January 6, 2014, http://select.nytimes.com/2007/02/12/sports/basketball/12rhoden.html?n=Top%2fNews%2fSports%2fColumns%2fWilliam%20C%20Rhoden&_r=0.

54. Frank Deford, "Serious Contenders for a Funny City," *Sports Illustrated*, December 9, 1968, 28.

55. Antonio R. Harvey, "Robertson Put Up Unmatched Numbers," *Milwaukee Journal-Sentinel*, January 6, 2002, 5C.

56. Jares, *Basketball*, 81.

57. David Leon Moore, "Legendary UCLA Volleyball Coach Leaves Rich Legacy," *USA Today*, April 5, 2012. Retrieved November 17, 2013, http://usatoday30.usatoday.com/sports/college/volleyball/story/2012-04-05/al-scates-leaves-rich-legacy-at-ucla/54063330/1.

58. Mike Miazga, "Al Scates Retires," *Volleyball Magazine*, May 3, 2012. Retrieved November 17, 2013, http://volleyballmag.com/articles/42680-al-scates-retires.

59. Joe Jares, "Spiking the Punch at UCLA," *Sports Illustrated*, May 4, 1970, 24.

60. Mike Bresnahan, "Kirk Kilgour, 54; Volleyball Standout," *Los Angeles Times*, July 12, 2002. Retrieved November 17, 2013, http://articles.latimes.com/2002/jul/12/local/me-kilgour12. During a training exercise in 1976, Kilgour broke his neck and became a quadriplegic. He died in 2002 after complications from pneumonia.

61. In NCAA history, the total ranks only behind North Carolina women's soccer coach Anson Dorrance, who won 20 titles.

62. Alan Shipnuck, "Legendary UCLA Men's Volleyball Coach Al Scates Shoots for 20th Ring," *Sports Illustrated*, April 20, 2012. Retrieved November 17, 2013, http://sportsillustrated.cnn.com/2012/writers/the_bonus/04/19/al.scates/.

63. Miazga, "Al Scates Retires."

64. Wendy Soderburg, "Al Scates: 50 Years of Bruin Volleyball," *UCLA Magazine*, April 2012. Retrieved November 17, 2013, http://magazine.ucla.edu/features/al-scates-50-years-of-bruin-volleyball/index2.html.

65. Soderburg, "Al Scates."

5. MAY

1. Marty Ralbovsky, *Super Bowl* (New York: Hawthorn, 1971), 123.

2. "Other Views," *Virgin Island Daily News*, August 22, 1970, 5.

3. Brian Landman, "Diane Crump Reflects on Her Derby Day," *ESPNW*, May 7, 2011. Retrieved September 6, 2013, http://espn.go.com/espnw/news/article/6472779/kentucky-derby-diane-crump-reflects-derby-day.

4. "Diane Crump," *Femalejockeys.com*. Retrieved September 3, 2013, http://www.femalejockeys.com/crump.html.

5. Sheena McKenzie, "Jockey Who Refused to Stay in the Kitchen," *CNN*, October 2, 2012. Retrieved September 3, 2013, http://edition.cnn.com/2012/09/26/sport/diane-crump-first-female-jockey.

6. A teenager named Barbara Jo Rubin could have been the first female jockey, but in January of 1969 at Tropical Park in Florida male jockeys refused to ride against her and she was replaced. A month after Crump rode in Florida, Rubin became the first female to win a race, taking home a 13-to-one shot named Bravy Galaxy at Aqueduct in New York.

7. "Diane Crump Gets Jockey OK in Florida," Associated Press, *Dubuque (IA) Telegraph-Herald*, February 11, 1969, 21.

8. Landman, "Diane Crump Reflects."

9. Landman, "Diane Crump Reflects."

10. High Echelon won the Belmont on a muddy track by less than a length over Needles N Pens.

11. McKenzie, "Jockey Who Refused."

12. A state grand jury initially absolved the National Guard of any blame and indicted 25 students for deliberate criminal conduct. Eight Guardsmen were eventually indicted for violating the civil rights of the victims, but they and state officials were cleared of any responsibility in 1975.

13. They Said It, *Sports Illustrated*, March 16, 1970, 12.

14. At one point, Broncos coach Lou Saban required his new players to enlist in the Guard. Unfortunately, some of those rookies who did not make the team later saw action when their Guard units were called up.

15. Peter Golenbock, *Cowboys Have Always Been My Heroes* (New York: Warner, 1997), 419.

16. "Walton Arrested in Protest," *Milwaukee Journal*, May 12, 1972, 19.

17. "Wife Stands by Soldier Husband," *Svoboda*, August 22, 1970, sec. 2, p. 1.

18. "Vietnam War Is Personal Challenge to Lieutenant," Associated Press, *Spartanburg (SC) Herald-Journal*, June 27, 1970, 1.

19. Christine Brennan, "Keeping Score," *USA Today*, November 18, 2004. Retrieved September 7, 2013, http://usatoday30.usatoday.com/sports/columnist/brennan/2004-11-18-brennan_x.htm.

20. He also became one of the most tragic figures in Michigan football history. Lantry missed game-winning field goals at the end of games against archrival Ohio State in 1973 and 1974.

21. "Coach Hayes Delivers Speech, Dominates Award Ceremony," Associated Press, *Pittsburgh Press-Courier*, February 20, 1976, 18.

22. "Hayes Brings Roses to Boys in Vietnam," *St. Petersburg Times*, January 6, 1969, C6.

23. "'Hypocritical Bunch of Jerks' Chargers Ohio State Alumnus," Associated Press, *Meriden (CT) Journal*, November 28, 1961, 4.

24. Michael Rosenberg, *War as They Knew It* (New York: Hachette, 2008), 65.

25. Mike Harden, "Will We Remember Jackson State?" *Milwaukee Journal-Sentinel*, May 5, 2000, 23A.

26. "Fired Hayes Is the Same Old Grouch," *Milwaukee Journal*, January 19, 1979, part 2, p. 9.

27. "Emotional Speech and Greatest Day of His Life," Associated Press, *Portsmouth (OH) Daily Times*, March 14, 1987, 5.

28. The Bucks won a coin flip with the Phoenix Suns for the rights to the top overall draft pick and selected Alcindor. Lew turned down an offer from the ABA's New York Nets, who also made him a first-round draft pick.

29. "Alcindor Unanimously Named Rookie of the Year," Associated Press, *Meriden (CT) Morning Record*, April 15, 1970, 16.

30. Mike Recht, "Knicks Defeat Bucks; Face Lakers in Finals," Associated Press, *Waycross (GA) Journal-Herald*, April 21, 1970, 6. After trading for Oscar Robertson in the off-season, the Bucks went on to win the NBA title the very next year.

31. Joe Jares, *Basketball: The American Game* (Chicago: Follett, 1971), 122.

32. The record lasted until 1970 when broken by Austin Carr (see chapter 2).

33. "Frazier (Clyde) Leaves Rolls Home," Associated Press, *Lakeland (FL) Ledger*, April 21, 1974, 3C.

34. Mitch Lawrence, "Memory of Red Holzman Serves as Motivator for Lakers' Phil Jackson," *New York Daily News*, June 10, 2009. Retrieved September 8, 2013, http://www.nydailynews.com/sports/basketball/knicks/memory-red-holzman-serves-motivator-lakers-phil-jackson-article-1.374292.

35. The Sixers that year started the season 46–4, finished at 68–13, and swept the Celtics in the playoffs, ending Boston's run of eight straight championships.

36. Ken Rappoport, "Reed Injured, DeBusschere on Bench," *New London (CT) Day*, May 5, 1970, 17.

37. "X-Rays to Reveal Knicks Chances," United Press International, *Bend (OR) Bulletin*, May 5, 1970, 8.

38. Jim Cour, "Lakers Tie Title Series," United Press International, *Deseret News*, May 7, 1970, 1E.

39. "Horror Show for Knicks," *Milwaukee Journal*, May 7, 1970, 23.

40. "Horror Show for Knicks," 23.

41. Frank Deford, "In for Two plus the Title," *Sports Illustrated*, May 18, 1970, 16.

42. "Reed Overcomes Pain, Knicks Overcome L.A.," Associated Press, *Miami News*, May 9, 1970, B1.

43. "Willis Reed," *SportsCentury*, ESPN, 2000.

44. Deford, "In for Two," 16.

45. "Willis Reed."

46. "Knicks Respond to Reed's Play," Associated Press, *Fredericksburg (VA) Free Lance-Star*, May 9, 1970, 6.

47. "Knicks Respond," 6.

48. Deford, "In for Two," 16.

49. The same Jack Twyman mentioned in chapter 4.

50. "Rugged Individualist Russell Remains His Own Man," Associated Press, *Meriden (CT) Journal*, March 1, 1975, 4.

51. Bill Bradley, "Blood, Sweat and Magic," *Sports Illustrated*, May 26, 2003. Retrieved September 8, 2013, http://sportsillustrated.cnn.com/vault/article/magazine/MAG1028807/index.htm.

52. "Dee-Busschere," Associated Press, *Reading (PA) Eagle*, March 29, 1981, 89.

53. Bradley, "Blood, Sweat and Magic."

54. Michael Rapaport, director, *When the Garden Was Eden* (television documentary), ESPN, 2014.

55. Pete Waldmeir, "Sing No Sad Songs for Those Astonishing Blues," *Sports Illustrated*, May 13, 1968, 73.

56. Paul Le Bar, "Blues Hope Home Ice, Experience Will Help," Associated Press, *Owosso (MI) Argus-Press*, May 1, 1970, 12.

57. Mark Mulvoy, "Bobby Mines the Mother Lode," *Sports Illustrated*, January 12, 1970, 21.

58. "Norris Laurel Orr's Again," Canadian Press, *Calgary Herald*, May 18, 1973, 16.

59. Pete Axthelm, "You Gotta Have Sock," *Sports Illustrated*, December 11, 1967, 27.

60. Mark Mulvoy, "Mr. O and the Sack of New York," *Sports Illustrated*, April 27, 1970, 20.

61. Joel Feld, executive producer, *Bobby Orr and the Big Bad Bruins* (television documentary), New England Sports Network, 2010.

62. Derik Murray and John N. Hamilton, executive producers, "Phil Esposito," *Legends of Hockey* (TV), 2001.

63. Bruce Levett, "Hawks Shock Sinden, Lose 4–1," Canadian Press, *Windsor (ON) Star*, April 22, 1970, 27.

64. Paul Le Bar, "Phil Esposito and Bobby Orr Set New Records for Assists as Boston Bruins Win Second Game of Stanley Cup Finals," Associated Press, *Gettysburg (PA) Times*, May 6, 1970, 21.

65. Leo Monahan, "Got Those St. Louis Blues," *Sports Illustrated*, May 18, 1970, 59.

66. "Orr Scores Goal and Bruins Achieve One: Stanley Cup," *Milwaukee Journal*, May 11, 1970, part 2, p. 9.

67. "Bobby Orr the Goal," *BobbyOrr.net*, 2011. Retrieved February 21, 2014, http://bobbyorr.net/goal/goal.php.

68. Brian McFarlane, *Stanley Cup Fever* (Toronto: Stoddart, 1992), 161.

69. Feld, *Bobby Orr.*

70. The Winter and Summer Games were held in the same year until 1994 when the Winter Olympics were held in Lillehammer, Norway. Winter and Summer Games are now two years apart.

71. Roger Rapoport, "Olympian Snafu at Sniktau," *Sports Illustrated*, February 15, 1971, 60.

72. John Sanko, "Colorado Only State Ever to Turn Down Olympics," *Rocky Mountain News*, October 12, 1999. Retrieved February 14, 2014, http://denver.rockymountainnews.com/millennium/1012stone.shtml.

73. Sanko, "Colorado Only State."

74. "Colorado Puts Out Olympic Torch," Associated Press, *St. Petersburg Independent*, November 8, 1972, 1C.

75. "Colorado Puts Out Olympic Torch," 1C.

76. The 1908 Summer Games were originally scheduled for Rome but were hastily moved to London after the eruption of Mount Vesuvius.

77. Paula Newton, "Olympics Worth the Price Tag? The Montreal Legacy," *CNN*, July 19, 2012. Retrieved February 14, 2014, http://www.cnn.com/2012/07/19/world/canada-montreal-olympic-legacy/index.html.

78. "Does Anyone Want to Host the 2022 Olympics?" Associated Press, *New York Post*, June 30, 2014. Retrieved June 30, 2014, http://nypost.com/2014/06/30/does-anyone-want-to-host-the-2022-olympics/.

79. Howard Berkes, "Denver Reconsiders the Olympics despite Dumping 1976 Games," *National Public Radio Blog*, January 5, 2012. Retrieved February 14, 2014, http://www.npr.org/blogs/thetwo-way/2012/01/05/144728356/denver-reconsiders-the-olympics-despite-dumping-1976-games.

6. JUNE

1. "Seaver Turns 19," *St. Petersburg Evening Independent*, April 23, 1970, 2C.

2. Helene Elliott, "Dock Ellis, Former Major League Pitcher Who Counseled Drug Addicts, Dies at 63," *Los Angeles Times*, December 21, 2008. Retrieved September 11, 2013, http://www.latimes.com/news/ obituaries/la-me-ellis21-2008dec21,0,3291785.story.

3. Jerry Crowe, "Dock Ellis," *Los Angeles Times*, June 30, 1985. Retrieved September 11, 2013, http://articles.latimes.com/1985-06-30/sports/sp-266_1_dock-ellis.

4. Christopher Isenberg, producer, "Dock Ellis and the LSD No-No," YouTube video, 4:31. No Mas Productions, 2009.

5. "Dock Ellis Knew It All the Time," Associated Press, *Miami News*, June 13, 1970, 3B.

6. Isenberg, "Dock Ellis."

7. Bill Madden, "From No-Hitter on LSD to Curlers to Feuds, Dock Ellis Was a Free Spirit," *New York Daily News*, December 22, 2008. Retrieved September 11, 2013, http://www.nydailynews.com/sports/baseball/no-hitter-lsd-hair-curlers-feuds-dock-ellis-free-spirit-article-1.357470.

8. "Pirates Trainer Says Ellis Lying about Drugs," *Pittsburgh Post-Gazette*, April 9, 1984, 16.

9. Steven L. Mazza, Frank Malfitano, and John M. Stalberg, "Dock Ellis' Statement Was Not Fit to Print," *Los Angeles Times*, July 6, 1985, B3.

10. Jim Bouton, *Ball Four plus Ball Five* (New York: Stein & Day, 1980), 81.

11. "Dobson Throws Kuhn Curve by Endorsing Use of Pills," Associated Press, *Lawrence (KS) Journal-World*, February 24, 1971, 17.

12. "Smith Blast Puts Holes in Baseball's Anti–Drug Abuse Campaign," *Lewiston (ME) Daily Sun*, July 29, 1987, 21.

13. Tom Verducci, "Totally Juiced," *Sports Illustrated*, June 3, 2002. Retrieved September 11, 2013, http://sportsillustrated.cnn.com/vault/article/magazine/MAG1025902/index.htm.

14. Elliott, "Dock Ellis."

15. Bob Wolf, "Remember When: Ellis' No-Hitter against Padres Was High Drama," *Los Angeles Times*, July 18, 1990. Retrieved September 11, 2013, http://articles.latimes.com/1990-07-18/sports/sp-603_1_dock-ellis.

16. John Crittenden, "Piccolo Playing Own Tune after Pro Draft Marches By," *Miami News*, December 16, 1964, 4B.

17. Michael Hiestand, "Corso Recruited ACC's First Black Athlete," *USA Today*, November 11, 2008, 3C.

18. Mike Puma, "Piccolo Led Wake to '64 Win over Duke," *ESPN*, November 19, 2003. Retrieved September 15, 2013, http://espn.go.com/classic/s/add_piccolo_brian.html.

19. Gale Sayers, *I Am Third* (New York: Bantam, 1974), 62.

20. Jeannie Morris, "The Doctor Finally Says Those Bad Words," *Pittsburgh Post-Gazette*, January 27, 1972, 6.

21. Sayers, *I Am Third*, 74.

22. Morris, "Doctor Finally Says," 6.

23. "Courageous Brian Piccolo Dies of Cancer," Associated Press, *Lewiston (ME) Morning Tribune*, June 17, 1970, 15.

24. Sayers, *I Am Third*, ix.

25. "Brian Piccolo Back in Lineup," Newspaper Enterprise Association, *Ft. Scott (KS) Tribune*, July 11, 1969, 6.

26. Jim Murray, "Brian Battled to Bitter End," Los Angeles Times Special, *Milwaukee Sentinel*, December 1, 1971, part 2, p. 2.

27. Morris, "Doctor Finally Says," 6.

28. James Montague, "When U.S. Postmen and Miners Humbled England," CNN, June 11, 2010. Retrieved September 13, 2013, from http://www. cnn.com/2010/SPORT/football/02/23/football.us.popularity.1950/index.html.

29. Jimmy Lay, "Brazil's Pele Prime Target," *Vancouver Sun*, October 5, 1961, 27.

30. Lay, "Brazil's Pele Prime Target," 27.

31. "Pele Makes Superb Exit," *Sydney Morning Herald*, June 23, 1970, 15.

32. Dennis Redmont, "Brazil Cops World Soccer Championship," Associated Press, *Waycross (GA) Journal-Herald*, June 22, 1970, 7.

33. Mike Collett, "Brazil's 1970 Winning Team Voted Best of All Time," Reuters, July 9, 2007. Retrieved September 13, 2013, http://www.reuters.com/article/2007/07/09/us-soccer-world-best-idUSL0988846220070709.

34. "Where Are They Now? Tostao," *London Independent*, December 21, 1993. Retrieved September 13, 2013, http://www.independent.co.uk/sport/where-are-they-now-tostao-1468876.html.

35. Dave Anderson, "In 100 Years Pele May Be the Photo on the Wall," New York Times News Service, *Miami News*, June 6, 1975, 4B.

36. Jerry Kirshenbaum, "Curtain Call for a Legend," *Sports Illustrated*, June 23, 1975, 20.

37. George Albano, "Soccer & Pele, They Go Together," *Connecticut Age*, October 3, 1977, 25.

38. "Membership Statistics," U.S. Youth Soccer, 2012. Retrieved September 13, 2013, http://www.usyouthsoccer.org/media_kit/keystatistics/.

39. The impact of youth soccer also helped persuade FIFA to launch a women's World Cup in 1991. The United States won the inaugural Cup and then won again on home soil in 1999, beating China in penalty kicks. The winning kick by Brandi Chastain is considered the signature moment in U.S. women's soccer history.

40. Robert Lipsyte, "Kuhn Discusses Denny's Actions," New York Times News Service, *Milwaukee Journal*, April 14, 1970, part 2, p. 14.

41. Michael Gee, "Long Relief, Jim Brosnan Makes His Pitch," *Boston Phoenix,* October 18, 1983, 3.

42. "Jim Brosnan Gains Notoriety for Writing," Associated Press, *Youngstown (OH) Vindicator*, December 26, 1976, D3.

43. Bouton, *Ball Four plus Ball Five*, 408.

44. "Elston Howard Raps Bouton for 'Ball Four,'" *Palm Beach Post*, July 16, 1970, D11.

45. Matthew Mills Stevenson, "It Takes a Stadium: Will it Play in Pittsfield?" *Harper's*, April 2004.

46. Robert Lipsyte, "Bouton Spills the Baseball Beans," New York Times News Service, *St. Petersburg Times*, June 2, 1970, 3C.

47. Bouton, *Ball Four plus Ball Five*, 298.

48. Tim Braine, producer, *The Not-So-Great Moments in Sports*, New York: Home Box Office, 1985.

49. Mark Shapiro, executive producer, "Ball Four," *SportsCentury*, ESPN, 2002.

50. Bouton, *Ball Four plus Ball Five*, xiii.

51. Bouton, *Ball Four plus Ball Five*, xiii.

52. Shapiro, "Ball Four."

53. Lipsyte, "Bouton Spills the Baseball Beans," 3C.

54. "Forbes Field Reign Comes to an End," Associated Press, *Spokane (WA) Spokesman-Review*, June 28, 1970, 5.

55. Bill Christine, "Forbes Field Fades into Memory after 4,700 Games," *Pittsburgh Press*, June 28, 1970, sec. 4, p. 3.

56. "Fire, Havoc and Horror," *Lewiston (ME) Daily Sun*, May 16, 1894, 1.

57. Bruce Lixey, producer, *The Story of America's Classic Ballparks*, Chicago: Questar Video, 1989.

58. Joe Reichler, "Mays Bids Farewell to New York Giants," Associated Press, *Charleston (SC) News and Courier*, May 29, 1952, B1.

59. Peter Golenbock, *Bums* (New York: Penguin, 1984), 84–85.

60. "Mrs. McGraw Upset over Giant Move," Associated Press, *Lexington (NC) Dispatch*, August 21, 1957, 8.

61. Lawrence S. Ritter, *The Glory of Their Times* (New York: William Morrow, 1984), 4.

62. Ted Blackman, "Reds' New Riverfront Stadium Right in the Middle of Town," *Montreal Gazette*, August 20, 1970, 8.

63. "UCLA-Houston Game in 1968 Is Remembered as a Classic," Associated Press, *Spartanburg (SC) Herald-Journal*, January 20, 1988, D6.

64. David Cicotello and Angelo J. Louisa, eds., *Forbes Field: Essays and Memories of the Pirates' Historic Ballpark, 1909–1971* (Jefferson, NC: McFarland, 2007), 153.

65. Lawrence S. Ritter, *Lost Ballparks* (New York: Viking, 1990), 49.

66. Peter Botte, "Sept. 11 Family Will Never Forget Mets Former Catcher Mike Piazza," *New York Daily News*, September 28, 2013. Retrieved November 29, 2013, http://www.nydailynews.com/sports/baseball/mets/9-11-family-forget-mets-piazza-article-1.1470645.

67. "Tornado Rips Texas City," United Press International, *Deseret News*, May 12, 1970, 1.

68. "Tornado Rips Texas City," 1.

69. William F. Reed, "A Tornado with a New Twist," *Sports Illustrated*, July 6, 1970, 17.

70. Reed, "Tornado," 16.

71. "Class Getting Its Graduation Walk, 30 Years Late," Associated Press, *Victoria (TX) Advocate*, August 12, 2000, 4A.

7. JULY

1. "Nicklaus Predicts Return of Sanders," Associated Press, *Calgary Herald*, July 14, 1970, 15.

2. Will Grimsley, "Nicklaus Wins Masters in Record Style," Associated Press, *St. Joseph (MO) Gazette*, April 12, 1965, 7.

3. Jack Nicklaus and Ken Bowden, *Jack Nicklaus: My Story* (New York: Fireside, 1997), 269.

4. "Sanders Tops Nicklaus for Honors," Associated Press, *Sarasota Journal*, March 8, 1965, 18.

5. Mark Mulvoy, "The Trades Becalm Skinny Jack," *Sports Illustrated*, November 16, 1969, 43.

6. Joe Nagle, "Sanders on Brink Again," United Press International, *Middlesboro (KY) Daily News*, July 11, 1970, 3.

7. Ralph Bernstein, "Doug Sanders Gives Golf Lesson to a Fan during Practice at Philadelphia," Associated Press, *Gettysburg (PA) Times*, July 15, 1970, 11.

8. Dan Jenkins, *You Call It Sports, but I Say It's a Jungle Out There* (New York: Fireside, 1989), 312.

9. Dan Jenkins, "Virtue in the Valley of Sin," *Sports Illustrated*, July 20, 1970, 15.

10. Jack Nicklaus, "End of a Long, Long Drought," *Sports Illustrated*, July 27, 1970, 16.

11. Bob Harig, "The Road Hole: One Way to Disaster," *St. Petersburg Times*, July 14, 2005. Retrieved September 17, 2013, http://www.sptimes.com/2005/07/14/Sports/The_Road_Hole__one_wa.shtml.

12. Nicklaus, "A Long, Long Drought," 16.

13. "That Fatal 18th Finally Gets Sanders," Associated Press, *St. Petersburg Evening Independent*, July 13, 1970, 2C.

14. "That Fatal 18th," 2C.

15. Peter Stone, "Nicklaus Holds On to Win by Stroke," *Melbourne Age*, July 13, 1970, 22.

16. "That Fatal 18th," 2C.

17. Sanders did win a Senior Tour event in 1983.

18. Jim Murray, "'Shark' Makes Choking an Art," Los Angeles Times News Service, *Eugene (OR) Register-Guard*, April 20, 1986, 1D.

19. People, *Sports Illustrated*, February 16, 1970, 39.

20. Bernstein, "Doug Sanders," 11.

21. Bobby Pope, "Doug Sanders Had the Game to Match His Style," *Macon (GA) Telegraph*, April 2, 2012. Retrieved September 17, 2013, http://www.macon.com/2012/04/02/1972442/doug-sanders-had-the-game-to-match.html.

22. Dermot Gilleece, "I Tried to Treat the Crowd to the Real Nicklaus." *Dublin Independent*, July 17, 2005. Retrieved September 17, 2013, http://www.independent.ie/sport/golf/i-tried-to-treat-the-crowd-to-the-real-nicklaus-26210596.html.

23. "Rose Inks Six-Figure Contract," Associated Press, *Spartanburg (SC) Herald-Journal*, March 1, 1970, B2.

24. Dwight Chapin, "Charlie Hustle? He's a Baseball Player, That's All," Los Angeles Times News Service, *Tuscaloosa (AL) News*, March 4, 1969, 9.

25. "Ray Fosse Is Bitter," Associated Press, *Palm Beach Post*, June 20, 1971, E1.

26. "1970 All-Star Game," *NBC Radio*, July 14, 1970.

27. John Shea, "Rose's Words Puzzle Fosse," *Youngtown (OH) Vindicator*, July 12, 2005, C4.

28. A 2011 collision that seriously injured Giants' catcher Buster Posey led to new rules to end home plate collisions in 2014. The new rules forbid catchers from blocking home plate and runners from targeting catchers.

29. Tracy Ringolsby, "Rose's Hit, Claims Still Hurt Fosse," *Fox Sports*, July 5, 2012. Retrieved September 19, 2013, http://msn.foxsports.com/mlb/story/Cincinnati-Reds-Pete-Rose-Cleveland-Indians-Ray-Fosse-collision-home-plate-1970-All-Star-Game-070412.

30. "Fosse, Rose Will Miss Action after All-Star Plate Collision," Associated Press, *St. Petersburg Times*, July 16, 1970, 1C.

31. Shea, "Rose's Words Puzzle Fosse," C4.

32. Mychael Urban, "Where Have You Gone, Ray Fosse?" *MLB.com*, May 22, 2002. Retrieved September 19, 2013, http://oakland.athletics.mlb.com/news/article.jsp?ymd=20020522&content_id=30876&vkey=news_oak&fext=.jsp&c_id=oak.

33. Urban, "Where Have You Gone?"

34. "Rose Tells of Crashing Into Fosse," United Press International, *Lodi (CA) News-Sentinel*, July 15, 1970, 15.

35. "Rose Tells of Crashing Into Fosse."

36. Urban, "Where Have You Gone?"

37. Shea, "Rose's Words Puzzle Fosse," C4.

38. Jerry Crasnick, "Pete Rose: 25 Years in Exile," *ESPN*, August 22, 2014. Retrieved August 24, 2014, http://espn.go.com/mlb/story/_/id/11384095/mlb-pete-rose-walking-contradiction-25-years-ban.

39. William Nack, "A Name on the Wall." *Sports Illustrated*, July 23, 2001. Retrieved July 17, 2010, http://sportsillustrated.cnn.com/vault/article/magazine/MAG1023026/1/index.

40. Mark Kram, "The Smell of Death Was in the Air," *Sports Illustrated*, July 27, 1970, 18.

41. Peter Gallagher, "Spirit of Karl Wallenda Keeps Show Going On," *St. Petersburg Times*, March 19, 1979, 1D.

42. "Wallenda Family Aerialist Killed in 50-Foot Fall," Associated Press, *St. Petersburg Evening Independent*, April 19, 1963, 1.

43. "Wallenda Family Aerialist Killed," 1.

44. Tom Greene, "High Wire Artist to Attempt Daring Feat," United Press International, *Lexington (NC) Dispatch*, July 18, 1970, 8.

45. Kram, "Smell of Death," 18.

46. Kram, "Smell of Death," 18.

47. Another Wallenda, Nik, later broke that record, and in 2012 became the first person to walk a tightrope across Niagara Falls.

48. "For Flying Wallendas, 'The Show Must Go On,'" United Press International, *Boca Raton (FL) News*, March 23, 1978, 3A.

49. Robert H. Boone, "Reporter Remembers Karl Wallenda," *Norwalk (CT) Hour*, March 24, 1978, 2.

50. Terry Bledsoe, "Chiefs Owner Sees Season of Leftovers," *Milwaukee Journal*, July 31, 1970, part 2, p. 13.

51. Joe Jares, "The One Night Season," *Sports Illustrated*, August 10, 1970, 12.

52. Ken Rappoport, "Players Don't Report to Camp," Associated Press, *Hopkinsville (KY) New Era*, July 31, 1970, 10.

53. "Bleier Joins Grid Camp," Associated Press, *Milwaukee Sentinel*, August 1, 1970, part 2, p. 3.

54. Skip Myslenski, "I'm a Football Player, Not a Worker," *Sports Illustrated*, August 10, 1970, 10.

55. "Open Camps Lure Only a Few Veteran Players," Associated Press, *Michigan Daily*, July 31, 1970, 12.

56. Morton Sharnik, "For an Opening, He Might Come Out and Growl," *Sports Illustrated*, January 18, 1971, 19.

57. "Baltimore Colts," *America's Game: The Super Bowl Champions*, season 2, episode 2, NFL Films, 2007.

58. Jack Olsen, "The Rosenbloom-Robbie Bowl," *Sports Illustrated*, November 9, 1970, 27.

59. "Baltimore Colts."

60. "Football Strike Comes to an End," United Press International, *Bonham (TX) Daily Favorite*, August 4, 1970, 6.

61. "Strike Fails to Affect Roommates' Friendship," Associated Press, *Palm Beach Post*, August 7, 1970, C2.

62. "Colts Curtis Again Refuses to Strike," Associated Press, *Eugene (OR) Register-Guard*, June 27, 1974, 6B.

63. Sharnik, "For an Opening," 19, 23.

8. AUGUST

1. Sandy Treadwell, "Not Such a Bad Scene After All," *Sports Illustrated*, September 28, 1970, 54.

2. "Dismissed Black Gridders File against Syracuse," Associated Press, *Eugene (OR) Register-Guard*, August 21, 1970, 2B.

3. Scorecard, *Sports Illustrated*, August 31, 1970, 7.

4. Scorecard, August 31, 1970, 7.

5. Pat Putnam, "End of a Season at Syracuse," *Sports Illustrated*, September 28, 1970, 22.

6. Brian Cubbison, "How the Express Fumbled Real Ernie Davis Story," *Syracuse Post-Standard*, October 16, 2008. Retrieved September 27, 2013, http://www.syracuse.com/news/index.ssf/2008/10/how_the_express_fumbled_the_re.html.

7. John Underwood, "The Desperate Coach," *Sports Illustrated*, August 25, 1969, 66.

8. Putnam, "End of a Season," 22–23.

9. "Brown Takes Side of Syracuse Blacks," *Milwaukee Journal*, September 4, 1970, part 2, p. 17.

10. Pat Putnam, "No Defeats, Loads of Trouble." *Sports Illustrated*, November 3, 1969, 26.

11. John Underwood, "Concessions—and Lies," *Sports Illustrated*, September 8, 1969, 30.

12. "Irate Black Athletes Stir Campus Tension," *New York Times*, November 16, 1969, 1.

13. Michael Rosenberg, *War as They Knew It* (New York: Hachette, 2008), 42.

14. Underwood, "Concessions—And Lies," 31.

15. John Underwood, "He's Burning to Be a Success," *Sports Illustrated*, September 20, 1971, 92.

16. Gale Sayers, *I Am Third* (New York: Bantam, 1974), 48.

17. "Edwards Claims Control of Key U.S. Olympic Athletes," United Press International, *Lexington (NC) Dispatch*, July 2, 1968, 9.

18. Putnam, "No Defeats," 26.

19. Underwood, "Concessions—and Lies," 31.

20. John Crittenden, "Schwartzwalder: Too Late for Unbending Ben to Yield," *Miami News*, September 24, 1970, 1D.

21. "Schwartzwalder Wins Last Game," Associated Press, *Gadsden (AL) Times*, January 5, 1974, 10.

22. Jack Smith, "To Be Frank, Merriwell Was a Virtuous Square," Los Angeles Times Service, *Milwaukee Journal*, January 26, 1970, 5.

23. Bob Greene, "The Magic of Forest Hills Has Died," Field Newspapers Syndicate, *Fredericksburg (VA) Free Lance-Star*, September 6, 1977, 2.

24. Donald Honig, "Baseball America," in *The Fireside Book of Baseball*, ed. Charles Einstein, 4th ed. (New York: Simon & Schuster, 1987), 166.

25. The Australian Open followed in 1969.

26. Scorecard, *Sports Illustrated*, October 5, 1970, 11.

27. "Net War Senseless Says U.S. Captain," Associated Press, *Eugene (OR) Register-Guard*, December 19, 1968, D1.

28. Karen Hall, "Queen of the Connors Clan," *Windsor (ON) Star*, May 3, 1980, A7.

29. "16-Year-Old Chris Evert Adds Lesley Hunt to List of Victims," Associated Press, *St. Joseph (MO) Gazette*, September 9, 1971, 3B. As unlikely as it seems, Connors and Evert were engaged for a time in 1974 in what reporters called a "love match." Both won Wimbledon singles titles that year but soon broke off their relationship.

30. Gretchen Ziems, "Gloria Connors Talks Tennis," *Toledo Blade*, April 5, 1978, 27.

31. Sally Jenkins, "Persona Non Grata," *Sports Illustrated*, August 23, 1993, 30.

32. Greene, "Magic of Forest Hills," 2.

33. Will Grimsley, "Those Tennis 'Stars' Can't Be Bothered," Associated Press, *Madison (IN) Courier*, January 4, 1979, 7.

34. Grimsley, "Those Tennis 'Stars,'" 7.

35. "Modern Tennis," *New York Times*, September 8, 1915, 15.

36. Gayle Talbot, "Citation Led Coaltown to Wire in Kentucky Derby," *Montreal Gazette*, May 3, 1948, 18.

37. "Citation Takes Belmont Stakes Triple Winner," Associated Press, *Wilmington (DE) Morning Star*, June 13, 1948, 26.

38. Jenny Kellner, "Big Cy of Calumet Farm," New York Racing Association, 2011. Retrieved June 7, 2014, http://www.belmontstakes.com/history/citation.aspx.

39. "A Charmed Farm Gave Birth to a Champion: Secretariat," *Virginian-Pilot*, March 21, 2010. Retrieved August 24, 2013, http://hamptonroads.com/2010/03/charmed-farm-gave-birth-champion-secretariat.

40. "Secretariat Upset Opens Derby," Associated Press, *Milwaukee Sentinel*, April 23, 1973, part 2, p. 8.

41. Dink Carroll, "The Great Prognostication: Sham to Win Today's Derby," *Montreal Gazette*, May 4, 1973, 14.

42. "Speedy Secretariat Blinds Derby Field," Associated Press, *Ocala (FL) Star-Banner*, May 6, 1973, D1.

43. Less than a week before the Kentucky Derby, President Nixon had fired his top two advisers, John Ehrlichman and H. R. Haldeman, and White House counsel John Dean. The day before Secretariat's win in the Preakness, nationally televised Watergate hearings began in the U.S. Senate.

44. Milton Richman, "Secretariat's Belmont Win May Be the Greatest Ever," United Press International, *Lexington (NC) Dispatch*, June 11, 1973, 9.

45. As cited in Bill Doolittle, "Legacy," *Secretariat.com*, 2013. Retrieved August 24, 2013, http://www.secretariat.com/secretariat-history/legacy/.

46. John Goolrick, "Heart of a Hero," *Fredericksburg (VA) Free-Lance Star*, July 20, 2002, 8.

47. Goolrick, "Heart of a Hero," 8.

48. William Nack, *Secretariat* (New York: Hyperion, 2010), ix.

49. William Nack, "Pure Heart," *Sports Illustrated*, June 4, 1990, 80.

50. Jim Murray, "A Match Race for the Ages," *Los Angeles Times*, August 8, 1990. Retrieved June 7, 2014, http://articles.latimes.com/1996-08-08/sports/sp-32391_1_great-match-races.

51. "Citation vs. Secretariat," *That's the Way It Was* (television program), Gerry Gross Productions, May 8, 1977.

52. Barbie Ludovise, "California Pioneers Sailed into Picture," *Los Angeles Times*, June 17, 1988. Retrieved September 30, 2013, http://articles.latimes.com/1988-06-17/sports/sp-5354_1_west-coast.

53. Jane M. Dozier, "A Perfectionist in Yachting," Associated Press, *Southeast Missourian*, September 10, 1970, 18.

54. "Intrepid Wins but Not Picked," United Press International, *Boca Raton (FL) News*, August 27, 1970, 10A.

55. Dozier, "A Perfectionist in Yachting," 18.

56. Ludovise, "California Pioneers Sailed into Picture."

57. Ludovise, "California Pioneers Sailed into Picture."

58. Carleton Mitchell, "No Cup for the Lady," *Sports Illustrated*, October 5, 1970, 14.

59. Scorecard, *Sports Illustrated*, October 5, 1970, 10.

60. "Buoy, Bee, Protests—and Gretel," Associated Press, *St. Petersburg Times*, September 21, 1970, 1C.

61. "Gretel's Skipper Gracious in Defeat," Associated Press, *Charleston (SC) News and Courier*, September 29, 1970, 2B.

62. Ludovise, "California Pioneers Sailed into Picture."

63. Taylor Hill, "Bill Ficker, America's Cup Winner and Architect, Honored Oct. 3," *Log*, October 5, 2012. Retrieved June 5, 2014, http://thelog.com/Article/Bill-Ficker--America-s-Cup-Winner-and-Architect--Honored-Oct--3.

9. SEPTEMBER

1. Tom Seppy, "Cancer Claims Vince Lombardi," Associated Press, *Reading (PA) Eagle*, September 3, 1970, 36.

2. Ken Hartnett, "He Was Called 'God,'" Associated Press, *Reading (PA) Eagle*, September 3, 1970, 36.

3. Milton Richman, "Packers' Bart Starr Cool as a Cucumber before Tilt," United Press International, *Altus (OK) Times-Democrat*, January 14, 1968, 4.

4. "'They're All Gone,' Says Charlie Taylor," Associated Press, *Daytona Beach Morning Journal*, September 4, 1970, 15.

5. "'They're All Gone,'" 15.

6. Arthur Daley, "'This Is One Beautiful Man,'" New York Times News Service, *Daytona Beach Morning Journal*, September 4, 1970, 15.

7. Seppy, "Cancer Claims Vince Lombardi," 36.

8. Tom Silverstein, "The Center of Gravity," *Milwaukee Journal-Sentinel*, November 20, 2007, 1C.

9. Leslie Timms, "Lombardi—Happy as Coach," *Spartanburg (SC) Herald-Journal*, September 3, 1970, 35.

10. Jerry Kramer and Dick Schaap, *Instant Replay* (New York: Anchor, 1968), xvi.

11. Bud Lea, "Lombardi's Death Shocks Players," *Milwaukee Sentinel*, September 4, 1970, part 2, p. 1.

12. "'They're All Gone,'" 15.

13. Chris Higgins, "64 People and Their Famous Last Words," *Mental Floss*, August 22, 2014. Retrieved August 22, 2014, http://mentalfloss.com/article/58534/64-people-and-their-famous-last-words.

14. 1 Corinthians 9:24 (NIV).

15. Robert Lipsyte, "Vince Lombardi without Tears," *Miami News*, September 7, 1970, C1.

16. Chuck Johnson, "Packers Move 1 Foot to Miami," *Milwaukee Journal*, January 2, 1968, 20.

17. Tex Maule, "The Old Pro Goes In for Six," *Sports Illustrated*, January 8, 1968, 15.

18. Hartnett, "He Was Called 'God,'" 36.

19. Todd Veney, "Jim Nicoll: A Man Who Raced on His Terms," *Competition Plus*, February 1, 2014. Retrieved August 16, 2014, http://www.competitionplus.com/drag-racing/news/24004-jim-nicoll-a-man-who-raced-on-his-terms.

20. Robert F. Jones, "Sportsman of the Year," *Sports Illustrated*, December 24, 1973, 47.

21. "Jackie Stewart Quit Racing While He Was Ahead—and Alive," Newspaper Enterprise Association, *Owosso (MI) Argus-Press*, November 6, 1973, 13.

22. "Jackie Stewart Quit Racing," 13.

23. Jones, "Sportsman of the Year," 49.

24. "Jackie Stewart Quit Racing," 13.

25. An Italian court initially cleared all those involved in the crash, but upon appeal a second court returned a guilty verdict for technical director Patrick Head. Because the statute of limitations had expired by the time of the second verdict, Head never served jail time.

26. Stephen Wade, "Shhhhh . . . Formula One Fans Fast Asleep," Associated Press, *Lawrence (KS) Journal-World*, June 4, 1999, 7C.

27. Wade, "Formula One Fans Fast Asleep," 7C.

28. Mike Harris, "Earnhardt's Death Changes NASCAR Forever," *Ellensburg (WA) Daily Record*, December 29, 2001, A7.

29. "Austrian Driver Rindt Killed," Associated Press, *Spartanburg (SC) Herald-Journal*, September 6, 1970, B5.

30. "Little Ken King of Court," Associated Press, *St. Petersburg Times*, September 14, 1970, 1C.

31. Gwilym S. Brown, "Fierce Lass in Quest of an Elusive Title," *Sports Illustrated*, September 14, 1970, 94.

32. Phyllis Battelle, "Billie Jean King: Ms. America Fights for Women's Rights," *Boca Raton (FL) News*, July 4, 1974, B1.

33. "How Bobby Runs and Talks, Talks, Talks," *Time*, September 10, 1973. Retrieved October 2, 2013, http://content.time.com/time/magazine/article/0,9171,907843,00.html.

34. "Riggs Jabs Court in Net Preparation," Associated Press, *Spartanburg (SC) Herald*, May 11, 1973, C2.

35. Brown, "Fierce Lass," 96.

36. "Billie Jean Serves Challenge to Riggs," Canadian Press, *Montreal Gazette*, May 15, 1973, 33.

37. "Billie Jean Wants Riggs," Associated Press, *Palm Beach Post*, May 15, 1973, D3.

38. Gerald Eskenazi, "King to Riggs: 'I'm Not Margaret Court,'" New York Times News Service, *Miami News*, July 12, 1973, 2C.

39. Don Van Natta Jr., "The Match Maker," *ESPN*, August 25, 2013. Retrieved October 3, 2013, http://espn.go.com/espn/feature/story/_/id/9589625/the-match-maker.

40. Van Natta Jr., "Match Maker."

41. "Hall of Famers: Margaret Court Smith," International Tennis Hall of Fame. Retrieved October 3, 2013, http://web.archive.org/web/20061119112638/http://www.tennisfame.com/famer.aspx?pgID=867&hof_id=150.

42. Steve Flink, "Margaret Smith Court: Career Retrospective," *TennisChannel.com*, January 15, 2012. Retrieved October 3, 2013, http://www.tennischannel.com/news/NewsDetails.aspx?newsid=10190.

43. Flink, "Margaret Smith Court."

44. Leo Schlink, "Billie Jean King Says Margaret Court Shouldn't Be Punished for Opposing View," *Melbourne Herald Sun*, January 19, 2012. Retrieved October 3, 2013, http://www.heraldsun.com.au/archive/old-sport-pages/billie-jean-king-says-margaret-court-shouldnt-be-punished-for-opposing-view/story-fn77kxzt-1226248739217.

45. Flink, "Margaret Smith Court."

46. Dallas began hosting a Thanksgiving game in 1966, while the AFL played on the holiday in each of its ten seasons.

47. William Johnson, "After TV Accepted the Call, Sunday Was Never the Same," *Sports Illustrated*, January 5, 1970, 23.

48. Johnson, "Sunday Was Never the Same," 29.

49. Bill Carter, "Roone Arledge, 71, a Force in TV Sports and News, Dies," *New York Times*, December 2, 2002. Retrieved July 31, 2010, http://www.nytimes.com/2002/12/06/business/roone-arledge-71-a-force-in-tv-sports-and-news-dies.html?ref=roone_arledge&pagewanted=1.

50. "Arledge Gamble Paid Off," Associated Press, *Lawrence (KS) Journal-World*, November 20, 1975, 16.

51. Roone Arledge, *Roone: A Memoir* (New York: HarperCollins, 2003), 111.

52. *The Sportscasters: Behind the Mike* (television documentary), The History Channel, February 7, 2000.

53. Edwin Shrake, "What Are They Doing with the Sacred Game of Pro Football?" *Sports Illustrated*, October 15, 1971, 98.

54. *Replay! The History of the NFL on Television* (television documentary), NFL Films, 1998.

55. Larry Felser, "AFC Eastern," *Sporting News*, October 10, 1970, 41.

56. Arledge, *Roone: A Memoir*, 113.

57. Wells Twombly, "Cosell Will Never Disappoint You," *Sporting News*, November 7, 1970, 14.

58. *Replay! The History of the NFL*.

59. Robert Boyle, "TV Wins on Points," *Sports Illustrated*, November 2, 1970, 14–15.

60. Boyle, "TV Wins on Points," 14–15.

61. "How the 1970 Merger of the NFL and the AFL Changed America," Race and Sports in American Culture Series, Emory University, Atlanta, September 7, 2013.

10. OCTOBER

1. John Eisenberg, *From 33rd Street to Camden Yards* (New York: Contemporary Books, 2001), 219.

2. Maxwell Kates, "Brooks Robinson," in *Pitching, Defense and Three-Run Homers*, ed. Mark Armour and Malcolm Allen (Lincoln: University of Nebraska Press, 2012), 246.

3. Milton Richman, "Weaver 'Red Concerned,'" United Press International, *Ellensburg (WA) Daily Record*, October 6, 1970, 3.

4. "World Series Day," Associated Press, *Meriden (CT) Journal*, October 10, 1970, 4.

5. William Leggett, "Flying Start for the Big Bad Birds," *Sports Illustrated*, October 19, 1970, 16.

6. Jesse Outlar, "Burkhart—Man in the Middle," *Palm Beach Post*, October 11, 1970, D7.

7. "Weaver Admits 'Learned Lesson' from Mets Series," *Montreal Gazette,* October 13, 1970, 19.

8. Tom Loomis, "Anderson, Rose Are Impressed," *Toledo Blade*, October 12, 1970, 21.

9. "Brooks Gets a Car, Cooperstown Gets a Glove," Associated Press, *St. Petersburg Times*, October 16, 1970, 2C.

10. Kates, "Brooks Robinson," 249.

11. William Leggett, "That Black and Orange Magic," *Sports Illustrated*, October 26, 1970, 22.

12. Robinson shares the record with 11 other players, including his teammate Paul Blair, who also had nine hits in the 1970 Series.

13. "Brooks Gets a Car," 2C.

14. Kates, "Brooks Robinson," 249.

15. Bill Utterback, "Athletes Savor Being in 'The Zone'—but No One Has Yet Figured Out How They Can Stay There Forever," *Seattle Times*, March 3, 1991. Retrieved October 4, 2013, http://community.seattletimes.nwsource.com/archive/?date=19910303&slug=1269299.

16. Projected for an entire 162-game season, Robinson's numbers would be an astounding 324 hits, 81 doubles, 61 home runs, and 162 RBI.

17. Steven Travers, *The Last Icon: Tom Seaver and His Mets* (Lanham, MD: Taylor Trade, 2011), 121.

18. William F. Reed, "Archie and the War between the States," *Sports Illustrated*, October 12, 1970, 14.

19. Reed, "Archie and the War between the States," 14.

20. William F. Reed, ". . . And the Best of Them All Is Archie," *Sports Illustrated*, September 14, 1970, 55.

21. Pat Putnam, "Answer to a Foolish Question," *Sports Illustrated*, November 24, 1969, 50.

22. Audie Cornish, "On Day of Debate, Ole Miss Examines Past," *National Public Radio*, September 26, 2008. Retrieved October 22, 2013, http://www.npr.org/templates/story/story.php?storyId=95105118.

23. "Hustling the Heisman Hopefuls," *Time*, November 16, 1970, 56.

24. Reed, "Archie and the War between the States," 17.

25. Reed, "Archie and the War between the States," 17.

26. "Vince Says Archie Greatest," Associated Press, *Florence (AL) Times Daily*, October 12, 1970, 11.

27. His health forced Vaught to retire at the end of 1970 after 24 seasons, six SEC championships, and 18 bowl appearances. He returned briefly in 1973 to replace the fired Kinard but retired for good after that season.

28. "Rebels Loss of Manning Second Shock of Season," Associated Press, *Eugene (OR) Register-Guard*, November 9, 1970, 2B.

29. William F. Reed, "With Bowls Ahead, They're Whistling in Dixie," *Sports Illustrated*, November 16, 1970, 66.

30. "Rebels Loss of Manning," 2B.

31. "Auburn Tops Ole Miss in Gator Bowl, 35–28," United Press International, *Bryan (TX) Times*, January 4, 1971, 7.

32. Nick Fierro, "Ex-Lehigh Star John Hill Remembers His Time with the New Orleans Saints," *Allentown (PA) Morning Call*, February 5, 2010. Retrieved

October 11, 2013, http://articles.mcall.com/2010-02-05/sports/all-s-hillsuper. 7168960feb05_1_saints-dave-waymer-colts-quarterback-peyton-manning-super-bowl.

33. "World Speed Mark Better Than Moon?" Associated Press, *Daytona Beach Morning Journal*, July 25, 1969, 14.

34. Jerry Kirshenbaum, "A Speed King without a Kingdom," *Sports Illustrated*, April 27, 1970, 73.

35. George Ferguson, "The Run Was a Natural Gas," *Sports Illustrated*, November 9, 1970, 55.

36. Bruce Wennerstrom, "Race of the Century!" *Mechanix Illustrated*, November 1972, 152.

37. Ferguson, "Run Was a Natural Gas," 55.

38. "World Speed Mark Better?" 14.

39. "Gabelich to Seek Water Speed Mark," United Press International, *Bangor (ME) Daily News*, October 27, 1970, 16.

40. Ronald E. Warthen, "Gabelich Sets Speed Record," United Press International, *Lexington (NC) Dispatch*, October 24, 1970, 8.

41. Jim Cour, "Drivers Meet in Hospital," United Press International, *Ellensburg (WA) Daily Record*, June 21, 1972, 10.

42. "World Speed Mark Better?" 14.

43. Michael Mattis, "Craig Breedlove," *Salon*, July 31, 1999. Retrieved October 22, 2013, http://www.salon.com/1999/07/31/breedlove/.

44. Mattis, "Craig Breedlove."

45. Fred Heiler, "A Man with an Irresistible Urge to Run Wide Open," *New York Times*, May 11, 2012. Retrieved October 22, 2013, http://www.nytimes.com/2012/05/13/automobiles/a-man-with-an-irresistible-urge-to-run-wide-open.html?_r=0.

46. "Leafs Conquer All-Star, 7 to 2," Canadian Press, *Windsor (ON) Border Cities Star*, February 15, 1934, 2.

47. Ted Green, "My First Last Rites," *Sports Illustrated*, November 15, 1971, 92.

48. Earl McRae, "'Slashing Is Absolutely Insane,'" *Ottawa Citizen*, April 6, 1974, 28.

49. Green, "My First Last Rites," 96.

50. The NHL also suspended Green for 13 games upon his return.

51. Green, "My First Last Rites," 92.

52. Green, "My First Last Rites," 95.

53. McRae, "Slashing Is Absolutely Insane," 30.

54. Scorecard, *Sports Illustrated*, January 5, 1970, 7.

55. McRae, "Slashing Is Absolutely Insane," 30.

11. NOVEMBER

1. Tom Wicker, "Nixon at Halftime Has Lost Ground," *Pittsburgh Post-Gazette*, November 5, 1970, 14.

2. Ian Delzer, "Football's Number One Fan," Richard Nixon Foundation, August 13, 2013. Retrieved October 23, 2013, http://blog.nixonfoundation.org/2013/08/footballs-number-one-fan/.

3. At the game in Fayetteville, Arkansas, the Arkansas band spelled out "NIXON" during its halftime performance. It was a show of support that would become increasingly rare in the coming years as Nixon became entangled in Watergate.

4. "Texas Already Bowl Winner," *Milwaukee Journal*, December 8, 1969, 19.

5. Tom Seppy, "Nixon in Grid Dispute over Just Who's No. 1," *Hopkinsville (KY) New Era*, December 6, 1969, 2.

6. Pat Ryan, "The Making of a Quarterback, 1970," *Sports Illustrated*, December 7, 1970, 14.

7. Ryan, "Making of a Quarterback," 14.

8. "Picking the Quarterback," *Eugene (OR) Register-Guard*, August 11, 1996, 2F.

9. Ira Berkow, "A Quarterback Who Doesn't Like Warming the Bench," *New York Times*, August 11, 1996. Retrieved October 24, 2013, http://www.nytimes.com/1996/08/11/weekinreview/a-quarterback-who-doesn-t-like-warming-the-bench.html.

10. Will Perry, *The Wolverines: A Story of Michigan Football* (Huntsville, AL: Strode, 1974), 150–52.

11. Frank Deford, "Athletes Turned Politicians Go Republican," *National Public Radio*, May 3, 2006. Retrieved October 23, 2013, http://www.npr.org/templates/story/story.php?storyId=5378526.

12. Robert Heard, *Oklahoma vs. Texas: When Football Becomes War* (Austin, TX: Honey Hill, 1980) 288.

13. Elizabeth Guenard, "Jim Brown: Hall of Famer, Activist, Abuser," *Gelf*, April 20, 2007. Retrieved October 24, 2013, http://www.gelfmagazine.com/archives/jim_brown_hall_of_famer_activist_abuser.php.

14. Andy Martino, "Ex-NFL Star Reggie Williams Is a Man with a Mission," *New York Daily News*, July 26, 2008. Retrieved January 9, 2013, http://www.nydailynews.com/sports/football/ex-nfl-star-reggie-williams-man-mission-article-1.353322.

15. Martino, "Ex-NFL Star Reggie Williams."

16. J. Richard Munro, "Letter from the Publisher," *Sports Illustrated*, December 7, 1970, 4.

17. "Chargers Get Revenge for Manning's Snub," Associated Press, *St. Petersburg Times*, September 25, 2005, 6C.

18. The Chargers turned it around in 2004 under coach Marty Schottenheimer, winning 12 games and making it to the playoffs, where they lost to the New York Jets.

19. Tex Maule, "When the Saints Go Stumbling Out," *Sports Illustrated*, October 27, 1969, 25.

20. Peter Finney, "What Can Saints New Boss Do for an Encore?" *Sporting News*, November 21, 1970, 5.

21. Jerry Crowe, "Tom Dempsey's Kick Was Beyond Belief, but Not His Range," *Los Angeles Times*, October 31, 2010. Retrieved May 7, 2011, http://articles.latimes.com/2010/oct/31/sports/la-sp-crowe-20101101-11.

22. Bob Oates, "NFC Western," *Sporting News*, November 21, 1970, 7.

23. "Dempsey's 63 Yard Kick Breaks Record and Lions," Associated Press, *Milwaukee Journal*, November 9, 1970, part 2, p. 11.

24. Crowe, "Tom Dempsey's Kick."

25. "Dempsey's 63 Yard Kick," part 2, p. 11.

26. "Room for Improvement," Associated Press, *Pittsburgh Post-Gazette*, November 10, 1970, 20.

27. Brad Schultz, *The NFL, Year One* (Dulles, VA: Potomac, 2013), x.

28. "A Moment in Time," *ESPN*, 2011. Retrieved August 13, 2011, http://espn.go.com/nfl/feature/flash/_/id/5753078/tom-dempsey-moment-time.

29. Wilton Barnhardt, "How's This for a Real Kick? Tom Dempsey's 63-Yarder Took Flight 20 Years Ago," *Sports Illustrated*, December 24, 1990, 112.

30. Dempsey took the record from Bert Rechichar, who kicked a 56-yarder for the Colts in 1953. At one point Dempsey shared the record with three others, but in 2013 Matt Prater of the Broncos used the thin air of Denver to set the new record at 64 yards.

31. Finney, "What Can Saints New Boss Do?" 5.

32. Crowe, "Tom Dempsey's Kick."

33. They Said It, *Sports Illustrated*, November 23, 1970, 18.

34. Crowe, "Tom Dempsey's Kick."

35. "Sport: George Blanda Is Alive and Kicking," *Time*, November 23, 1970. Retrieved October 2, 2010, http://www.time.com/time/magazine/article/0,9171,943328-1,00.html.

36. Finney, "What Can Saints New Boss Do?" 5.

37. Barnhardt, "How's This for a Real Kick?" 112.

38. "Marshall Football Players Buried," *Lexington (NC) Dispatch*, November 25, 1970, 17.

39. "WSU Team Members, Students Remember Fatal 1970 Plane Crash," Associated Press, *Liberal (KS) Southwest Daily Times*, October 3, 1995, 15.

40. Paul Haney, "Tried to Turn Plane Around, Co-Pilot Skipper Testifies," United Press International, *Williamson (WV) Daily News*, October 22, 1970, 3.

41. William Johnson, "Days of Stillness at Wichita State," *Sports Illustrated*, October 19, 1970, 20.

42. Michael Bates, "Wichita State Gives Up Football, Too Expensive," Associated Press, *Hopkinsville (KY) New Era*, December 3, 1986, 2C.

43. Justin Prince, "Reporter Recalls Memories from Worst Sports-Related Air Tragedy in U.S. History," *Marshall Parthenon*, November 16, 2010. Retrieved October 28, 2013, http://www.marshallparthenon.com/2.6882/reporter-recalls-memories-from-worst-sports-related-air-tragedy-in-us-history-1.2407217#. Um5wkRCmbnh.

12. DECEMBER

1. Brian McFarlane, *Stanley Cup Fever* (Toronto: Stoddart, 1992), 243.

2. "Stolen Part of Cup Recovered by Police," Canadian Press, *Regina (SK) Leader-Post*, September 21, 1977, 20.

3. "Hockey Player's Father Shot to Death," United Press International, *Bend (OR) Bulletin*, December 14, 1970, 8.

4. Peter Dexter, "The Case against Brian Spencer," *Sports Illustrated*, May 11, 1987, 102.

5. Earl McRae, "Player Travelled Trail of Tragedy," *Ottawa Citizen*, January 21, 1987, C1.

6. McRae, "Trail of Tragedy," C1.

7. "Ex-Penguin Cleared in Florida Slaying Trial," United Press International, *Pittsburgh Press*, October 17, 1987, A2.

8. Chuck Finder, "Spencer's Free-Spirit Life Ends after Drug Deal," *Pittsburgh Post-Gazette*, June 4, 1988, 23.

9. Jim Corbett, "Joe Kapp Flattered by Peyton Manning's Mention," *USA Today*, September 6, 2013. Retrieved October 4, 2013, http://www.usatoday.com/story/sports/nfl/2013/09/06/peyton-manning-joe-kapp-seven-touchdowns-baltimore/2777325/.

10. Jack Olsen, "He Goes Where the Trouble Is," *Sports Illustrated*, October 19, 1970, 22.

11. Joe Kapp and Jack Olsen, "A Man of Machismo," *Sports Illustrated*, July 20, 1970, 27–28.

12. Tex Maule, "Kapping the Browns," *Sports Illustrated*, January 12, 1970, 12.

13. Tex Maule, "The Future Moves Into the Past," *Sports Illustrated*, September 28, 1970, 31.

14. Maule, "Future Moves Into the Past," 31.

15. Olsen, "He Goes Where the Trouble Is," 22.

16. "Kapp Becomes a Patriot, and Vikings Show Profit," *Milwaukee Journal*, October 2, 1970, 14.

17. Olsen, "He Goes Where the Trouble Is," 23.

18. "Chiefs Still Bother Kapp; Patriots Shattered, 23–10," Associated Press, *Lawrence (KS) Journal-World*, October 12, 1970, 15.

19. Dave O'Hara, "Student Beats Master in Vikings-Pats Game," Associated Press, *New London (CT) Day*, December 14, 1970, 28.

20. "Kapp Won't Sign, Quits Patriots," Associated Press, *St. Petersburg Times,* July 17, 1971, 1C.

21. "Kapp Becomes a Patriot," 14.

22. "Jury Rules Against Kapp," United Press International, *Beaver County (PA) Times*, April 3, 1976, A7.

23. "Kapp Called a 'Ripoff,'" Associated Press, *Eugene (OR) Register-Guard*, April 1, 1976, 6C.

24. Kapp played eight years in the CFL, leading the British Columbia Lions to the Grey Cup championship in 1964. He is a member of the CFL Hall of Fame and his #22 was retired by the team.

25. Chris Erskine, "Joe Kapp Still Full of Fight—and He Has a Cause," *Los Angeles Times*, October 13, 2010. Retrieved October 4, 2013, http://articles.latimes.com/2010/oct/13/sports/la-sp-erskine-20101014.

26. In fact, both coaches were fired. Washington's Bill Austin, who faced the difficult job of replacing Lombardi, was let go and replaced by George Allen, who led the Redskins to four straight playoff appearances and a Super Bowl berth.

27. "National East," *Sports Illustrated*, September 20, 1971, 46.

28. Bill Buttram, "Redskin Coach's Declaration Right Down Jerry Smith's Alley," *Fredericksburg (VA) Free Lance-Star*, July 29, 1966, 8.

29. *A Football Life: Jerry Smith* (television documentary), NFL Films, January 21, 2014.

30. David Kopay and Perry Deane Young, *The David Kopay Story: The Coming Out Story That Made Football History* (New York: Advocate, 2001), ix.

31. "Former Redskin Smith Has AIDS," Associated Press, *Fredericksburg (VA) Free Lance-Star*, August 26, 1986, 8.

32. "Former Redskin Smith Has AIDS," 8.

33. *A Football Life: Jerry Smith.*

34. "AIDS Kills Smith," Associated Press, *Ocala (FL) Star-Banner*, October 17, 1986, 5C.

35. David Whitley, "The Shame of It Hall: Ignoring the Washington Redskins' Jerry Smith," *Fox Sports*, January 30, 2014. Retrieved February 2, 2014,

http://msn.foxsports.com/nfl/story/the-shame-of-it-hall-ignoring-the-washington-redskins-jerry-smith-013014.

36. Whitley, "The Shame of It Hall."

37. Kopay and Young, *David Kopay Story*, vii–ix.

38. Mike Puma, "Liston Was Trouble In and Out of the Ring," *ESPN*, 2007. Retrieved October 31, 2013, http://espn.go.com/classic/biography/s/Liston_Sonny.html.

39. Gilbert Rogin, "Heavyweight in Waiting," *Sports Illustrated*, August 1, 1960, 50.

40. "The First Black Santa," *GeorgeLois.com*, 2011. Retrieved October 31, 2013, http://www.georgelois.com/pages/Esquire/Esq.sonny.santa.html.

41. Jim Murray, "Spelling Bee about Only Clash Where Floyd Could Lick Liston," Los Angeles Times News Syndicate, *Lawrence (KS) Journal-World*, July 24, 1963, 24.

42. Rob Steen, *Sonny Liston: His Life, Strife and the Phantom Punch* (London: JR Books, 2008), 100.

43. Scorecard, *Sports Illustrated*, September 15, 1969, 18.

44. William Nack, "O Unlucky Man," *Sports Illustrated*, February 14, 1994, 162.

45. Brian Tuohy, *Larceny Games: Sports Gambling, Game Fixing and the FBI* (Port Townsend, WA: Feral House, 2013), 126.

46. Tuohy, *Larceny Games*, 223.

47. Tuohy, *Larceny Games*, 223.

EPILOGUE

1. In the fall of 2014, Whittier was diagnosed with early-onset Alzheimer's and filed a $50 million lawsuit against the NCAA on behalf of players who had suffered football-related brain injuries.

2. Robert Heard, *Oklahoma vs. Texas: When Football Becomes War* (Austin, TX: Honey Hill, 1980), 68.

3. Richard Goldstein, "Red Klotz, Beloved Foil for Globetrotters, Dies at 93," *New York Times*, July 14, 2014. Retrieved July 16, 2014, http://www.nytimes.com/2014/07/15/sports/basketball/red-klotz-beloved-foil-for-globetrotters-dies-at-93.html.

4. "Oscar Finally Sips Champagne," Associated Press, *Fredericksburg (VA) Free Lance-Star*, May 1, 1971, 6.

5. Matt Breen, "Ali on Ailing Frazier: 'I Am Praying He Is Fighting Now,'" *Philadelphia Inquirer*, November 7, 2011. Retrieved November 1, 2013, http://

articles.philly.com/2011-11-07/sports/30369890_1_muhammad-ali-joe-frazier-boxing-greats.

6. Breen, "Ali on Ailing Frazier."

7. "Rookie Dryden Caught On Quickly," Associated Press, *St. Petersburg Times*, April 20, 1971, 1C.

8. "Long Shots," United Press International, *Milwaukee Journal*, February 6, 1971, 1.

9. "Riled Washington Fans Give Forfeit to Yanks," Associated Press, *Meriden (CT) Morning Record*, October 1, 1971, 10.

10. Hal Bock, "Pirates Win the World Series as They Down Baltimore 9," Associated Press, *Waycross (GA) Journal-Herald*, October 18, 1971, P7.

11. "Specialists Say U.S.-China Thaw Will Match New Ping-Pong Policy," *Harvard Crimson*, April 19, 1971. Retrieved November 2, 2013, http://www.thecrimson.com/article/1971/4/19/specialists-say-u-s-china-thaw/.

12. "Tradition," Chicago Bears. 2010. Retrieved February 1, 2011, http://www.chicagobears.com/tradition/hof-sayers.asp.

13. John J. O'Connor, "'Brian's Song' Sounds Like Money as Film Succeeds off the TV Tube," New York Times News Service, *Milwaukee Journal Green Sheet*, February 8, 1972, 1.

14. Michael Rosenberg, *War as They Knew It* (New York: Hachette, 2008), 100.

15. Rosenberg, *War as They Knew It*, 101.

16. Woody Woodrum, "September 25, 1971: Marshall 15, Xavier 13," *Herd Insider*, September 25, 2006. Retrieved November 1, 2013, http://www.scout.com/2/572633.html.

17. Larry Schwartz, "Bobby Jones Was Golf's Fast Study," *ESPN*. Retrieved March 14, 2015, https://espn.go.com/sportscentury/features/00014123.html.

18. Lesley Valdes, "The Archaic Tom Wolfe," *Miami News*, January 2, 1980, B1.

19. Valdes, "Archaic Tom Wolfe," B1.

20. James H. Frey and D. Stanley Eitzen, "Sport and Society," *American Sociological Review* 17 (1991): 508.

21. "How the 1970 Merger of the NFL and the AFL Changed America," Race and Sports in American Culture Series, Emory University, Atlanta, September 7, 2013.

22. Bill Lubinger, "Remember When . . . Off-Season Was Work Time for the Cleveland Browns?" *Cleveland Plain-Dealer*, May 26, 2010. Retrieved November 2, 2010, http://www.cleveland.com/browns/index.ssf/2010/05/remember_when_offseason_was_wo.html.

23. Robert Lipsyte, "Knicks' Style Is Simply Shocking. Culture Shocking," *New York Times*, June 12, 1994. Retrieved November 11, 2013, http://www.

nytimes.com/1994/06/12/sports/backtalk-knicks-style-is-simply-shocking-culture-shocking.html.

24. "Hip-Hop Era Troubling for Blacks," *Deseret News*, October 31, 2007, 15.

25. David J. Leonard and C. Richard King, *Commodified and Criminalized: New Racism and African-Americans in Contemporary Sports* (Lanham, MD: Rowman & Littlefield, 2011), 85.

26. Marie Hardin, "Does 'New Media' Bring New Attitudes toward Women's Sports?" Tucker Center for Research on Girls and Women in Sports, 2009. Retrieved January 27, 2011, http://tuckercenter.wordpress.com/2009/09/24/does-%E2%80%98new-media%E2%80%99-bring-new-attitudes-oward-women%E2%80%99s-sports/.

27. Lipsyte, "Knicks' Style."

BIBLIOGRAPHY

"16-Year-Old Chris Evert Adds Lesley Hunt to List of Victims." Associated Press, *St. Joseph (MO) Gazette*, September 9, 1971, 3B.
"1970 All-Star Game." *NBC Radio*. July 14, 1970.
"1970 Nikita's Year to Beat Out U.S." Associated Press, *Vancouver Sun*, June 26, 1961, 9.
"1970 USSR vs. Rest of the World." *Chessgames.com*. Retrieved August 30, 2013, http://www.chessgames.com/perl/chesscollection?cid=1024274.
"Afros against Crew Cuts." Associated Press, *Spokane (WA) Spokesman-Review*, January 11, 1970, 8.
"AIDS Kills Smith." Associated Press, *Ocala (FL) Star-Banner*, October 17, 1986, 5C.
Albano, George. "Soccer & Pele, They Go Together." *Connecticut Age*, October 3, 1977, 25.
"Alcindor Unanimously Named Rookie of the Year." Associated Press, *Meriden (CT) Morning Record*, April 15, 1970, 16.
"Ali and the Rock: Super Fight Filmed." *Baltimore Afro-American*, January 6, 1970, 19.
"Ali-Frazier III—Finale of Boxing's Greatest Rivalry." *Charlottesville (VA) Cavalier Daily*, October 2, 1975, 5.
"Ali: Like Being Close to Death." Associated Press, *Pittsburgh Post-Gazette*, October 2, 1975, 20.
"Ali vs. Marciano vs. a Computer." *Windsor Star*, February 17, 1979, 13.
Anderson, Dave. "In 100 Years Pele May Be the Photo on the Wall." New York Times News Service, *Miami News*, June 6, 1975, 4B.
"And the Agony Continues. . . ." *Sarasota Herald-Tribune*, December 9, 2002, 2C.
Angell, Roger. *Five Seasons*. New York: Warner, 1977.
———. *Late Innings*. New York: Random House, 1982.
"Apollo 13 Reports Trouble." United Press International, *Palm Beach Post*, April 14, 1970, A1.
Arledge, Roone. *Roone: A Memoir*. New York: HarperCollins, 2003.
"Arledge Gamble Paid Off." Associated Press, *Lawrence (KS) Journal-World*, November 20, 1975, 16.
Asinof, Eliot. *Eight Men Out*. New York: Henry Holt, 1963.
"Auburn Tops Ole Miss in Gator Bowl, 35–28." United Press International, *Bryan (TX) Times*, January 4, 1971, 7.
"Austrian Driver Rindt Killed." Associated Press, *Spartanburg (SC) Herald-Journal*, September 6, 1970, B5.
"Average Salaries in Major League Baseball, 1967–2009." Major League Baseball Players Association, 2009. Retrieved from http://hosted.ap.org/specials/interactives/_sports/baseball08/documents/bbo_average_salary2009.pdf.
Axthelm, Pete. "You Gotta Have Sock." *Sports Illustrated*, December 11, 1967, 27.

"Baltimore Colts." *America's Game: The Super Bowl Champions*, season 2, episode 2. NFL Films, 2007.

Barnhardt, Wilton. "How's This for a Real Kick? Tom Dempsey's 63-Yarder Took Flight 20 Years Ago." *Sports Illustrated*, December 24, 1990, 112.

Barra, Allen. "How Curt Flood Changed Baseball and Killed His Career in the Process." *Atlantic Monthly*, July 11, 2011. http://www.theatlantic.com/entertainment/archive/2011/07/how-curt-flood-changed-baseball-and-killed-his-career-in-the-process/241783/.

"Baseball Players Show Signs of Bending." Associated Press, *Eugene (OR) Register-Guard*, February 20, 1969, 1C.

"Baseball Reserve Clause Upheld." Associated Press, *Regina (SK) Leader-Post*, June 20, 1972, 25.

Bates, Michael. "Wichita State Gives Up Football, Too Expensive." Associated Press, *Hopkinsville (KY) New Era*, December 3, 1986, 2C.

Battelle, Phyllis. "Billie Jean King: Ms. America Fights for Women's Rights." *Boca Raton (FL) News*, July 4, 1974, B1.

Benko, Pal, and Burt Hochberg. *Winning with Chess Psychology*. New York: Random House, 1991.

Berkes, Howard. "Denver Reconsiders the Olympics Despite Dumping 1976 Games." *National Public Radio Blog*, January 5, 2012. http://www.npr.org/blogs/thetwo-way/2012/01/05/144728356/denver-reconsiders-the-olympics-despite-dumping-1976-games.

Berkow, Ira. "Frazier-Ali Bout Transcends Sports." Newspaper Enterprise Association, *Owosso (MI) Argus-Press*, March 6, 1971, 9.

———. "A Quarterback Who Doesn't Like Warming the Bench." *New York Times*, August 11, 1996. http://www.nytimes.com/1996/08/11/weekinreview/a-quarterback-who-doesn-t-like-warming-the-bench.html.

Bernstein, Ralph. "Doug Sanders Gives Golf Lesson to a Fan during Practice at Philadelphia." Associated Press, *Gettysburg (PA) Times*, July 15, 1970, 11.

"Big Rematch Looms." United Press International, *Palm Beach Post*, March 10, 1971, D4.

"Billie Jean Serves Challenge to Riggs." Canadian Press, *Montreal Gazette*, May 15, 1973, 33.

"Billie Jean Wants Riggs." Associated Press, *Palm Beach Post*, May 15, 1973, D3.

"Black College Players Vie for Attention in NFL Draft." Associated Press, *CBS Sports*. April 24, 2007. http://www.cstv.com/sports/m-footbl/stories/042407aac.html.

Blackman, Ted. "Reds' New Riverfront Stadium Right in the Middle of Town." *Montreal Gazette*, August 20, 1970, 8.

Bledsoe, Terry. "Chiefs Owner Sees Season of Leftovers." *Milwaukee Journal*, July 31, 1970, part 2, p. 13.

"Bleier Joins Grid Camp." Associated Press, *Milwaukee Sentinel*, August 1, 1970, part 2, p. 3.

"Bobby Orr the Goal." *BobbyOrr.net*. 2011. http://bobbyorr.net/goal/goal.php.

Bock, Hal. "Pirates Win the World Series as They Down Baltimore 9." Associated Press, *Waycross (GA) Journal-Herald*, October 18, 1971, P7.

Boone, Robert H. "Reporter Remembers Karl Wallenda." *Norwalk (CT) Hour*, March 24, 1978, 2.

Botte, Peter. "Sept. 11 Family Will Never Forget Mets Former Catcher Mike Piazza." *New York Daily News*, September 28, 2013. http://www.nydailynews.com/sports/baseball/mets/9-11-family-forget-mets-piazza-article-1.1470645.

Bouton, Jim. *Ball Four plus Ball Five.* New York: Stein & Day, 1980.

"Boxing Legend Joe Frazier Dies." *ESPN*. November 8, 2011. http://espn.go.com/boxing/story/_/id/7206261/joe-frazier-former-heavyweight-champion-dead-67.

Boyle, Robert. "TV Wins on Points." *Sports Illustrated*, November 2, 1970, 14–15.

Bradley, Bill. "Blood, Sweat and Magic." *Sports Illustrated*, May 26, 2003. http://sportsillustrated.cnn.com/vault/article/magazine/MAG1028807/index.htm.

Braine, Tim, producer. *The Not-So-Great Moments in Sports*. New York: Home Box Office, 1985.

Breen, Matt. "Ali on Ailing Frazier: 'I Am Praying He Is Fighting Now." *Philadelphia Inquirer*, November 7, 2011. http://articles.philly.com/2011-11-07/sports/30369890_1_muhammad-ali-joe-frazier-boxing-greats.

Brennan, Christine. "Keeping Score." *USA Today*, November 18, 2004. http://usatoday30. usatoday.com/sports/columnist/brennan/2004-11-18-brennan_x.htm.

Bresnahan, Mike. "Kirk Kilgour, 54; Volleyball Standout." *Los Angeles Times*, July 12, 2002. http://articles.latimes.com/2002/jul/12/local/me-kilgour12.

"Brian Piccolo Back in Lineup." Newspaper Enterprise Association, *Ft. Scott (KS) Tribune*, July 11, 1969, 6.

"Brooks Gets a Car, Cooperstown Gets a Glove." Associated Press, *St. Petersburg Times*, October 16, 1970, 2C.

Brown, Gwilym S. "Fierce Lass in Quest of an Elusive Title." *Sports Illustrated*, September 14, 1970, 94, 96.

"Brown Takes Side of Syracuse Blacks." *Milwaukee Journal*, September 4, 1970, part 2, p. 17.

"Buoy, Bee, Protests—and Gretel." Associated Press, *St. Petersburg Times*, September 21, 1970, 1C.

Buttram, Bill. "Redskin Coach's Declaration Right Down Jerry Smith's Alley." *Fredericksburg (VA) Free Lance-Star*, July 29, 1966, 8.

Cantwell, Robert. "How to Cook a Russian Goose." *Sports Illustrated*, August 14, 1972, 25.

Capps, Gil. *The Magnificent Masters: Jack Nicklaus, Johnny Miller, Tom Weiskopf and the 1975 Cliffhanger at Augusta.* Boston: Da Capo, 2014.

"Carl Yastrzemski Asks Poll of Major League Players to Determine Opinion on Flood's Reserve Clause Challenge." Associated Press, *Gettysburg (PA) Times*, January 19, 1970, 9.

Carroll, Dink. "The Great Prognostication: Sham to Win Today's Derby." *Montreal Gazette*, May 4, 1973, 14.

Carry, Peter. "McLain: With Love and Hisses." *Sports Illustrated*, July 13, 1970, 42.

Carter, Bill. "Roone Arledge, 71, a Force in TV Sports and News, Dies." *New York Times*, December 2, 2002. http://www.nytimes.com/2002/12/06/business/roone-arledge-71-a-force-in-tv-sports-and-news-dies.html?ref=roone_arledge&pagewanted=1.

Casper, Billy, James Parkinson, and Lee Benson. *The Big Three and Me.* Columbus, MS: Genesis, 2012.

Chapin, Dwight. "Charlie Hustle? He's a Baseball Player, That's All." Los Angeles Times News Service, *Tuscaloosa (AL) News*, March 4, 1969, 9.

"Chargers Get Revenge for Manning's Snub." Associated Press, *St. Petersburg Times*, September 25, 2005, 6C.

"A Charmed Farm Gave Birth to a Champion: Secretariat." *Virginian-Pilot*, March 21, 2010. http://hamptonroads.com/2010/03/charmed-farm-gave-birth-champion-secretariat.

"Chiefs Still Bother Kapp; Patriots Shattered, 23–10." Associated Press, *Lawrence (KS) Journal-World*, October 12, 1970, 15.

Christine, Bill. "Forbes Field Fades into Memory after 4,700 Games." *Pittsburgh Press*, June 28, 1970, sec. 4, p. 3.

Christopulos, Mike. "MU Spurns NCAA for NIT." *Milwaukee Sentinel*, February 25, 1970, part 2, p. 1.

Cicotello, David, and Angelo J. Louisa, eds. *Forbes Field: Essays and Memories of the Pirates' Historic Ballpark, 1909–1971.* Jefferson, N.C.: McFarland, 2007.

"Citation Takes Belmont Stakes Triple Winner." Associated Press, *Wilmington (DE) Morning Star*, June 13, 1948, 26.

"Citation vs. Secretariat." *The Way It Was.* Television program. Gerry Gross Productions, May 8, 1977.

"Class Getting Its Graduation Walk, 30 Years Late." Associated Press, *Victoria (TX) Advocate*, August 12, 2000, 4A.

"Clay, Terrell Put On a Show." Associated Press, *Charleston (SC) News and Courier*, December 29, 1966, D2.

"Coach Hayes Delivers Speech, Dominates Award Ceremony." Associated Press, *Pittsburgh Press-Courier*, February 20, 1976, 18.

Collett, Mike. "Brazil's 1970 Winning Team Voted Best of All Time." Reuters, July 9, 2007. http://www.reuters.com/article/2007/07/09/us-soccer-world-best-idUSL0988846220070709.

"Colorado Puts Out Olympic Torch." Associated Press, *St. Petersburg Independent*, November 8, 1972, 1C.

"Colts Curtis Again Refuses to Strike." Associated Press, *Eugene (OR) Register-Guard*, June 27, 1974, 6B.

Corbett, Jim. "Joe Kapp Flattered by Peyton Manning's Mention." *USA Today*, September 6, 2013. http://www.usatoday.com/story/sports/nfl/2013/09/06/peyton-manning-joe-kapp-seven-touchdowns-baltimore/2777325/.

Cornish, Audie. "On Day of Debate, Ole Miss Examines Past." *National Public Radio*. September 26, 2008. http://www.npr.org/templates/story/story.php?storyId=95105118.

Cosell, Howard. "Flood's Courage Brought Baseball Out of the Slave Era." *Pittsburgh Press*, July 16, 1986, C6.

Cour, Jim. "Drivers Meet in Hospital." United Press International, *Ellensburg (WA) Daily Record*, June 21, 1972, 10.

———. "Lakers Tie Title Series." United Press International, *Deseret News*, May 7, 1970, 1E.

"Courageous Brian Piccolo Dies of Cancer." Associated Press, *Lewiston (ME) Morning Tribune*, June 17, 1970, 15.

Crasnick, Jerry. "Pete Rose: 25 Years in Exile." *ESPN*. August 22, 2014. http://espn.go.com/mlb/story/_/id/11384095/mlb-pete-rose-walking-contradiction-25-years-ban.

Crittenden, John. "Piccolo Playing Own Tune after Pro Draft Marches By." *Miami News*, December 16, 1964, 4B.

———. "Schwartzwalder: Too Late for Unbending Ben to Yield." *Miami News*, September 24, 1970, 1D.

Crowe, Jerry. "Dock Ellis." *Los Angeles Times*, June 30, 1985. http://articles.latimes.com/1985-06-30/sports/sp-266_1_dock-ellis.

———. "Tom Dempsey's Kick Was Beyond Belief, but Not His Range." *Los Angeles Times*, October 31, 2010. http://articles.latimes.com/2010/oct/31/sports/la-sp-crowe-20101101-11.

Cubbison, Brian. "How the Express Fumbled Real Ernie Davis Story." *Syracuse Post-Standard*, October 16, 2008. http://www.syracuse.com/news/index.ssf/2008/10/how_the_express_fumbled_the_re.html.

Curry, Peter. "To a Stripper, Boyer's Hipper." *Sports Illustrated*, July 20, 1970, 47.

"Curt Flood Needs Reserve Clause." Associated Press, *Pittsburgh Post-Gazette*, October 30, 1970, 21.

"Curt Flood's Reserve Clause Challenge Begins." Associated Press, *Sarasota Journal*, May 19, 1970, 1C.

Daley, Arthur. "Denny McLain: To Know Him Is to Dislike Him." *Miami News*, May 18, 1972, C1.

———. "'This Is One Beautiful Man.'" New York Times News Service, *Daytona Beach Morning Journal*, September 4, 1970, 15.

"Dan Gable Defeated in Finale." Associated Press, *Fredericksburg (VA) Free Lance-Star*, March 30, 1970, 6.

"Dee-Busschere." Associated Press, *Reading (PA) Eagle*, March 29, 1981, 89.

Deford, Frank. "Athletes Turned Politicians Go Republican." *National Public Radio*. May 3, 2006. http://www.npr.org/templates/story/story.php?storyId=5378526.

———. "In for Two plus the Title." *Sports Illustrated*, May 18, 1970, 16.

———. "Serious Contenders for a Funny City." *Sports Illustrated*, December 9, 1968, 28.

Delzer, Ian. "Football's Number One Fan." Richard Nixon Foundation. August 13, 2013. http://blog.nixonfoundation.org/2013/08/footballs-number-one-fan/.

"Dempsey's 63 Yard Kick Breaks Record and Lions." Associated Press, *Milwaukee Journal*, November 9, 1970, part 2, p. 11.

"Denny McLain Gets 23-Year Prison Sentence." Associated Press, *Los Angeles Times*. April 26, 1985. http://articles.latimes.com/1985-04-26/sports/sp-20974_1_denny-mclain.

Dexter, Peter. "The Case against Brian Spencer." *Sports Illustrated*, May 11, 1987, 102.

"Diamonds Have Been a Buss, Not a Bust, for Morganna." *Reading (PA) Eagle*, May 4, 1986, C2.

"Diane Crump." *Femalejockeys.com*. Retrieved September 6, 2013. http://www.femalejockeys.com/crump.html.

"Diane Crump Gets Jockey OK in Florida." Associated Press, *Dubuque (IA) Telegraph-Herald*, February 11, 1969, 21.

Dickson, Paul. *Bill Veeck: Baseball's Greatest Maverick.* New York: Walker, 2012.

"Dismissed Black Gridders File against Syracuse." Associated Press, *Eugene (OR) Register-Guard*, August 21, 1970, 2B.

"Dobson Throws Kuhn Curve by Endorsing Use of Pills." Associated Press, *Lawrence (KS) Journal-World*, February 24, 1971, 17.

"Dock Ellis Knew It All the Time." Associated Press, *Miami News*, June 13, 1970, 3B.

"Does Anyone Want to Host the 2022 Olympics?" Associated Press, *New York Post*, June 30, 2014. http://nypost.com/2014/06/30/does-anyone-want-to-host-the-2022-olympics/.

Doolittle, Bill. "Legacy." *Secretariat.com*. 2013. http://www.secretariat.com/secretariat-history/legacy/.

Dozier, Jane M. "A Perfectionist in Yachting." Associated Press, *Southeast Missourian*, September 10, 1970, 18.

Drape, Joe. "Changing the Face of Texas Football." *New York Times*, December 23, 2005. http://www.nytimes.com/2005/12/23/sports/ncaafootball/23texas.html?_r=4&.

Drew, Jay. "BYU Football: Remembering the Black 14 Protest." *Salt Lake City Tribune*, November 6, 2009. http://www.sltrib.com/byucougars/ci_13728556.

Durgahee, Ayesha. "Gary Player: Staying in Shape with 'World's Most Traveled Athlete.'" *CNN*. August 28, 2012. http://www.cnn.com/2012/08/28/travel/golf-gary-player.

Dwyre, Bill. "Time for Tears . . . of Joy." *Milwaukee Journal*, March 29, 1977, part 2, p. 9.

Ebert, Roger. "Searching for Bobby Fischer." *Chicago Sun-Times*, August 11, 1993. http://www.rogerebert.com/reviews/searching-for-bobby-fischer-1993.

"Edwards Claims Control of Key U.S. Olympic Athletes." United Press International, *Lexington (NC) Dispatch*, July 2, 1968, 9.

Eisenberg, John. *Cotton Bowl Days.* New York: Simon & Schuster, 1997.

———. *From 33rd Street to Camden Yards.* New York: Contemporary Books, 2001.

Elliott, Helene. "Dock Ellis, Former Major League Pitcher Who Counseled Drug Addicts, Dies at 63." *Los Angeles Times*, December 21, 2008. http://www.latimes.com/news/obituaries/la-me-ellis21-2008dec21,0,3291785.story.

"Ellis Ready for Action." *Nevada Daily Mail*, February 11, 1970, 6.

"Elston Howard Raps Bouton for 'Ball Four.'" *Palm Beach Post*, July 16, 1970, D11.

"Emotional Speech and Greatest Day of His Life." Associated Press, *Portsmouth (OH) Daily Times*, March 14, 1987, 5.

Eprile, Cecil. "Olympic Tangle: Apartheid Splits Nations at Games." *Ottawa Citizen*, March 1, 1968, 7.

Erskine, Chris. "Joe Kapp Still Full of Fight—and He Has a Cause." *Los Angeles Times*, October 13, 2010. http://articles.latimes.com/2010/oct/13/sports/la-sp-erskine-20101014.

Eskenazi, Gerald. "King to Riggs: 'I'm Not Margaret Court.'" New York Times News Service, *Miami News*, July 12, 1973, 2C.

Evans, Larry. "The Enigma Tries a New Role." *Sports Illustrated*, October 12, 1970, 85–87.

"Ex-Penguin Cleared in Florida Slaying Trial." United Press International, *Pittsburgh Press*, October 17, 1987, A2.

"Fans Rally Again on Behalf of Paralyzed Pro Cage Star." United Press International, *Altus (OK) Times-Democrat*, June 29, 1959, 6.

Federal Baseball Club v. National League, 259 U.S. 200 (1922).

"Federal Judge Rules Against Football Draft." Associated Press, *Charleston (SC) News and Courier*, September 9, 1976, C1.

Feld, Joel, executive producer. *Bobby Orr and the Big Bad Bruins.* Television documentary. New England Sports Network, 2010.

Felser, Larry. "AFC Eastern." *Sporting News*, October 10, 1970, 41.

Ferguson, George. "The Run Was a Natural Gas." *Sports Illustrated*, November 9, 1970, 55.

Fierro, Nick. "Ex-Lehigh Star John Hill Remembers His Time with the New Orleans Saints." *Allentown (PA) Morning Call*, February 5, 2010. http://articles.mcall.com/2010-02-05/sports/all-s-hillsuper.7168960feb05_1_saints-dave-waymer-colts-quarterback-peyton-manning-super-bowl.

Finder, Chuck. "Spencer's Free-Spirit Life Ends after Drug Deal." *Pittsburgh Post-Gazette*, June 4, 1988, 23.

Finney, Peter. "What Can Saints New Boss Do for an Encore?" *Sporting News*, November 21, 1970, 5.

"Fire, Havoc and Horror." *Lewiston (ME) Daily Sun*, May 16, 1894, 1.

"Fired Hayes Is the Same Old Grouch." *Milwaukee Journal*, January 19, 1979, part 2, p. 9.

"First Black Letterman Remembers DKR." *KUT Radio*. November 13, 2012. http://kut.org/2012/11/first-black-letterman-remembers-dkr/.

"The First Black Santa." *GeorgeLois.com*. 2011. http://www.georgelois.com/pages/Esquire/Esq.sonny.santa.html.

"The First Champion." *Newsweek*, January 31, 2007. http://www.thedailybeast.com/newsweek/2007/01/31/the-first-champion.html.

"Five Reasons Why More HBCU Players Aren't Taken in the NFL Draft." *HBCU Digest*, May 6, 2012. http://hbcudigest.com/five-reasons-why-more-hbcu-players-arent-taken-in-the-nfl-draft/.

Flaherty, Joe. "Ali-Terrell: The Sadistic Game of 'What's My Name?'" *Village Voice*, February 9, 1967, 3.

Flink, Steve. "Margaret Smith Court: Career Retrospective." *TennisChannel.com*. January 15, 2012. http://www.tennischannel.com/news/NewsDetails.aspx?newsid=10190.

Flood, Curt, and Richard Carter. "My Rebellion." *Sports Illustrated*, February 1, 1971, 27.

A Football Life: Jerry Smith. Television documentary. NFL Films, January 21, 2014.

"Football Strike Comes to an End." United Press International, *Bonham (TX) Daily Favorite*, August 4, 1970, 6.

"Forbes Field Reign Comes to an End." Associated Press, *Spokane (WA) Spokesman-Review*, June 28, 1970, 5.

"For Flying Wallendas, 'The Show Must Go On.'" United Press International, *Boca Raton (FL) News*, March 23, 1978, 3A.

"Former Redskin Smith Has AIDS." Associated Press, *Fredericksburg (VA) Free Lance-Star*, August 26, 1986, 8.

"Fosse, Rose Will Miss Action after All-Star Plate Collision." Associated Press, *St. Petersburg Times*, July 16, 1970, 1C.

"Frazier (Clyde) Leaves Rolls Home." Associated Press, *Lakeland (FL) Ledger*, April 21, 1974, 3C.

Frey, James H., and D. Stanley Eitzen. "Sport and Society." *American Sociological Review* 17 (1991): 508.

"Gabelich to Seek Water Speed Mark." United Press International, *Bangor (ME) Daily News*, October 27, 1970, 16.

"Gable Continues to Dominate Wrestling." United Press International, *Lodi (CA) News-Sentinel*, March 17, 1986, 17.

"Gable Predicts He Will Win Gold Medal." Associated Press, *St. Joseph (MO) News-Press*, August 28, 1972, 3B.

Gallagher, Peter. "Spirit of Karl Wallenda Keeps Show Going On." *St. Petersburg Times*, March 19, 1979, 1D.

Gardner, Eriq. "NFL Draft Dodgers." *Slate*. April 22, 2010. http://www.slate.com/articles/news_and_politics/recycled/2010/04/nfl_draft_dodgers.html.

"Gary Player Stands Up for South Africa Home." Associated Press, *Vancouver Sun*, June 9, 1970, 22.

"Gary Player Wants Blacks in Masters." Associated Press, *Gettysburg (PA) Times*, April 6, 1972, 14.

Gee, Michael. "Long Relief, Jim Brosnan Makes His Pitch." *Boston Phoenix*, October 18, 1983, 3.

Gilleece, Dermot. "I Tried to Treat the Crowd to the Real Nicklaus." *Dublin Independent*, July 17, 2005. http://www.independent.ie/sport/golf/i-tried-to-treat-the-crowd-to-the-real-nicklaus-26210596.html.

Ginsburg, Daniel E. *The Fix Is In: A History of Baseball Gambling and Game Fixing Scandals*. Jefferson, N.C.: McFarland, 1995.

Glover, Tim. "Golf: The Paradox That Is Gary Player." *(UK) Independent*, July 16, 1996. http://www.independent.co.uk/sport/golf-the-paradox-that-is-gary-player-1329010.html.

Glover, William. "'Hair' First Platform for Hippie Movement?" Associated Press, *Nevada Daily Mail*, July 16, 1970, 5.

Goldstein, Richard. "Red Klotz, Beloved Foil for Globetrotters, Dies at 93." *New York Times*, July 14, 2014. http://www.nytimes.com/2014/07/15/sports/basketball/red-klotz-beloved-foil-for-globetrotters-dies-at-93.html.

Golenbock, Peter. *Bums*. New York: Penguin, 1984.

———. *Cowboys Have Always Been My Heroes*. New York: Warner Books, 1997.

Goolrick, John. "Heart of a Hero." *Fredericksburg (VA) Free-Lance Star*, July 20, 2002, 8–11.

Gosselin, Rick. "Spartans Recruited Black Texans before State Schools Did." *Dallas Morning News*, December 25, 2014. http://www.dallasnews.com/sports/columnists/rick-gosselin/20141225-gosselin-spartans-recruited-black-texans-before-state-schools-did.ece.

Green, Ted. "My First Last Rites." *Sports Illustrated*, November 15, 1971, 92–96.

Greenburg, Ross, producer. *Against the Tide*. Television documentary. Showtime, 2013.

Greene, Bob. "The Magic of Forest Hills Has Died." Field Newspapers Syndicate, *Fredericksburg (VA) Free Lance-Star*, September 6, 1977, 2.

Greene, Tom. "High Wire Artist to Attempt Daring Feat." United Press International, *Lexington (NC) Dispatch*, July 18, 1970, 8.

"Gretel's Skipper Gracious in Defeat." Associated Press, *Charleston (SC) News and Courier*, September 29, 1970, 2B.

Grimsley, Will. "Nicklaus Wins Masters in Record Style." Associated Press, *St. Joseph (MO) Gazette*, April 12, 1965, 7.

———. "Player Overcomes Apartheid Situation." Associated Press, *Ludington (MI) Daily News*, April 6, 1978, 7.

———. "Those Tennis 'Stars' Can't Be Bothered." Associated Press, *Madison (IN) Courier*, January 4, 1979, 7.

Grody, Ray. "Will Real Clay Please Stand Up?" *Milwaukee Sentinel*, February 9, 1967, part 2, p. 2.

Guenard, Elizabeth. "Jim Brown: Hall of Famer, Activist, Abuser." *Gelf*, April 20, 2007. http://www.gelfmagazine.com/archives/jim_brown_hall_of_famer_activist_abuser.php.

Hall, Karen. "Queen of the Connors Clan." *Windsor (ON) Star*, May 3, 1980, A7.

"Hall of Famers: Margaret Court Smith." International Tennis Hall of Fame. Retrieved October 3, 2013. http://web.archive.org/web/20061119112638/http://www.tennisfame.com/famer.aspx?pgID=867&hof_id=150.

Haney, Paul. "Tried to Turn Plane Around, Co-Pilot Skipper Testifies." United Press International, *Williamson (WV) Daily News*, October 22, 1970, 3.

Harden, Mike. "Will We Remember Jackson State?" *Milwaukee Journal-Sentinel*, May 5, 2000, 23A.

Hardin, Marie. "Does 'New Media' Bring New Attitudes toward Women's Sports?" Tucker Center for Research on Girls and Women in Sports. 2009. http://tuckercenter.wordpress.com/2009/09/24/does-%E2%80%98new-media%E2%80%99-bring-new-attitudes-oward-women%E2%80%99s-sports/.

Harig, Bob. "Odd-Man-Out Casper Deserved More." *ESPN*. February 8, 2015. http://espn.go.com/golf/story/_/id/12295052/odd-man-billy-casper-deserved-more-golf.

———. "The Road Hole: One Way to Disaster." *St. Petersburg Times*, July 14, 2005. http://www.sptimes.com/2005/07/14/Sports/The_Road_Hole__one_wa.shtml.

Harris, Mike. "Earnhardt's Death Changes NASCAR Forever." *Ellensburg (WA) Daily Record*, December 29, 2001, A7.

Hartnett, Ken. "He Was Called 'God.'" Associated Press, *Reading (PA) Eagle*, September 3, 1970, 36.

Harvey, Antonio R. "Robertson Put Up Unmatched Numbers." *Milwaukee Journal-Sentinel*, January 6, 2002, 5C.

"Has Best Mustache." *Milwaukee Journal*, December 24, 1913, 3.

"Hawkeyes Ease to 16th Title." Associated Press, *Dubuque (IA) Telegraph-Herald*, March 24, 1996, 1B.

"Hayes Brings Roses to Boys in Vietnam." *St. Petersburg Times*, January 6, 1969, C6.

Heard, Robert. *Oklahoma vs. Texas: When Football Becomes War.* Austin, TX: Honey Hill, 1980.

Heiler, Fred. "A Man with an Irresistible Urge to Run Wide Open." *New York Times*, May 11, 2012. http://www.nytimes.com/2012/05/13/automobiles/a-man-with-an-irresistible-urge-to-run-wide-open.html?_r=0.

Henderson, John. "Spirit of the Black 14." *Denver Post*, November 8, 2009. http://www.denverpost.com/ci_13739558.

Henderson, Thomas, and Peter Knobler. *Out of Control: Confessions of an NFL Casualty.* New York: Pocket, 1987.

Hiestand, Michael. "Corso Recruited ACC's First Black Athlete." *USA Today*, November 11, 2008, 3C.

Higgins, Chris. "64 People and Their Famous Last Words." *Mental Floss*, August 22, 2014. http://mentalfloss.com/article/58534/64-people-and-their-famous-last-words.

Hill, Taylor. "Bill Ficker, America's Cup Winner and Architect, Honored Oct. 3." *Log*, October 5, 2012. http://thelog.com/Article/Bill-Ficker--America-s-Cup-Winner-and-Architect--Honored-Oct--3.

"Hip-Hop Era Troubling for Blacks." *Deseret News*, October 31, 2007, 15.

"Hockey Player's Father Shot to Death." United Press International, *Bend (OR) Bulletin*, December 14, 1970, 8.

Hofmann, Rich. "'Agony of Defeat' Cherishes Moment." *Boca Raton (FL) News*, February 15, 1984, D1.

Honig, Donald. "Baseball America." In *The Fireside Book of Baseball*, edited by Charles Einstein, 166–70. 4th ed. New York: Simon & Schuster, 1987.

"Horror Show for Knicks." *Milwaukee Journal*, May 7, 1970, 23.

"How Bobby Runs and Talks, Talks, Talks." *Time*, September 10, 1973. http://content.time.com/time/magazine/article/0,9171,907843,00.html.

"How the 1970 Merger of the NFL and the AFL Changed America." Race and Sports in American Culture Series, Emory University, Atlanta, September 7, 2013.

"Hustling the Heisman Hopefuls." *Time*, November 16, 1970, 56.

"'Hypocritical Bunch of Jerks' Charges Ohio State Alumnus." Associated Press, *Meriden (CT) Journal*, November 28, 1961, 4.

"Intrepid Wins but Not Picked." United Press International, *Boca Raton (FL) News*, August 27, 1970, 10A.

"Irate Black Athletes Stir Campus Tension." *New York Times*, November 16, 1969, 1.

Isenberg, Christopher, producer. "Dock Ellis and the LSD No-No." YouTube video, 4:31. No Mas Productions, 2009.

"It's Masters Green for 'Cowboy' Archer." *Vancouver Sun*, April 14, 1969, 20.

"Jackie Stewart Quit Racing While He Was Ahead—and Alive." Newspaper Enterprise Association, *Owosso (MI) Argus-Press*, November 6, 1973, 13.

Jares, Joe. *Basketball: The American Game.* Chicago: Follett, 1971.

———. "The One Night Season." *Sports Illustrated*, August 10, 1970, 12.

———. "Spiking the Punch at UCLA." *Sports Illustrated*, May 4, 1970, 24.

———. "Up, Up and Away Go Artis and New J.U." *Sports Illustrated*, January 5, 1970, 20.

"Jayhawk and Tiger Football Teams of 1891 Started Rivalry Now an Annual High Spot." *Lawrence Journal-World*, November 22, 1937, 8.

Jayne, Greg. "Wooden Left an Impression on All." *Vancouver (WA) Columbian*, June 5, 2010. http://www.columbian.com/news/2010/jun/05/wooden-left-an-impression-on-all/.

Jaynes, Roger. "McGuire's Bell Tolls for Rupp." *Milwaukee Journal*, December 13, 1977, part 2, p. 7.

Jenkins, Dan. "After the Others Had Gone, George Was Left." *Sports Illustrated*, April 21, 1969, 28.

———. "All Yours, Billy Boy." *Sports Illustrated,* April 20, 1970, 19.

———. "A Sane Conclusion in a Cockeyed Conference." *Sports Illustrated*, November 7, 1966, 45.

———. "Texas Hangs On to Its No. 1." *Sports Illustrated*, January 12, 1970, 28.

———. "Virtue in the Valley of Sin." *Sports Illustrated*, July 20, 1970, 15.

———. *You Call It Sports, but I Say It's a Jungle Out There.* New York: Fireside, 1989.

Jenkins, Sally. "Persona Non Grata." *Sports Illustrated*, August 23, 1993, 30.

"Jerry LeVias Opened Door for Blacks in Southwest." United Press International, *Beaver County (PA) Times*, December 26, 1968, D3.

"Jim Brosnan Gains Notoriety for Writing." Associated Press, *Youngstown (OH) Vindicator*, December 26, 1976, D3.

Johnson, Bob. "My Nickel's Worth." *Spokane (WA) Daily Chronicle*, February 17, 1970, 13.

Johnson, Chuck. "Packers Move 1 Foot to Miami." *Milwaukee Journal*, January 2, 1968, 20.

Johnson, William. "After TV Accepted the Call, Sunday Was Never the Same." *Sports Illustrated*, January 5, 1970, 23, 29.

———. "And in This Corner . . . NCR 315." *Sports Illustrated*, September 16, 1968, 34–49.

———. "Days of Stillness at Wichita State." *Sports Illustrated*, October 19, 1970, 20.

Jones, Robert F. "Has Anybody Here Seen Billy?" *Sports Illustrated*, June 14, 1969, 25.

———. "Sportsman of the Year." *Sports Illustrated*, December 24, 1973, 47–49.

"Judge Bryant's Decision That Snafued NFL Draft." *Baltimore Afro-American*, September 11, 1976, 12.

"Jury Rules Against Kapp." United Press International, *Beaver County (PA) Times*, April 3, 1976, A7.

Kapp, Joe, and Jack Olsen. "A Man of Machismo." *Sports Illustrated*, July 20, 1970, 27–28.

"Kapp Becomes a Patriot, and Vikings Show Profit." *Milwaukee Journal*, October 2, 1970, 14.

"Kapp Called a 'Ripoff.'" Associated Press, *Eugene (OR) Register-Guard*, April 1, 1976, 6C.

"Kapp Won't Sign, Quits Patriots." Associated Press, *St. Petersburg Times*, July 17, 1971, 1C.

Kates, Maxwell. "Brooks Robinson." In *Pitching, Defense and Three-Run Homers*, edited by Mark Armour and Malcolm Allen, 245–51. Lincoln: University of Nebraska Press, 2012.

Kellner, Jenny. "Big Cy of Calumet Farm." New York Racing Association. 2011. http://www.belmontstakes.com/history/citation.aspx.

Kessler, Kaye, and William F. Reed. "Bye-Bye, No. 1." *Sports Illustrated*, December 1, 1969.

King, Peter. "The AFL." *Sports Illustrated*, July 13, 2009. http://sportsillustrated.cnn.com/vault/article/magazine/MAG1157664/3/index.htm.

Kirshenbaum, Jerry. "Curtain Call for a Legend." *Sports Illustrated*, June 23, 1975, 20.

———. "A Speed King without a Kingdom." *Sports Illustrated*, April 27, 1970, 73.

"Kissing Bandit In Demand." Scripps Howard News Service, *Youngstown (OH) Vindicator*, April 28, 1991, G5.

"Knicks Respond to Reed's Play." Associated Press, *Fredericksburg (VA) Free Lance-Star*, May 9, 1970, 6.

Kopay, David, and Perry Deane Young. *The David Kopay Story: The Coming Out Story That Made Football History.* New York: Advocate, 2001.

Koppett, Leonard. "McLain Is All Business, but Baseball Is Pleasure." New York Times News Service, *Miami News*, September 2, 1968, 2B.

Kram, Mark. "The Smell of Death Was in the Air." *Sports Illustrated*, July 27, 1970, 18.

Kramer, Jerry, and Dick Schaap. *Instant Replay.* New York: Anchor, 1968.

Kunda, John. "Stars Are Shining Brightly." *Allentown (PA) Call-Chronicle*, May 13, 1984. http://articles.mcall.com/1984-05-13/sports/2414179_1_two-man-teams-better-ball-amateur.

Landman, Brian. "Diane Crump Reflects on Her Derby Day." *ESPNW.* May 7, 2011. http://espn.go.com/espnw/news/article/6472779/kentucky-derby-diane-crump-reflects-derby-day.

Lawrence, Mitch. "Memory of Red Holzman Serves as Motivator for Lakers' Phil Jackson." *New York Daily News*, June 10, 2009. http://www.nydailynews.com/sports/basketball/knicks/memory-red-holzman-serves-motivator-lakers-phil-jackson-article-1.374292.

Lay, Jimmy. "Brazil's Pele Prime Target." *Vancouver Sun*, October 5, 1961, 27.

Lea, Bud. "Lombardi's Death Shocks Players." *Milwaukee Sentinel*, September 4, 1970, part 2, p. 1.

"Leafs Conquer All-Star, 7 to 2." Canadian Press, *Windsor (ON) Border Cities Star*, February 15, 1934, 2.

Le Bar, Paul. "Blues Hope Home Ice, Experience Will Help." Associated Press, *Owosso (MI) Argus-Press*, May 1, 1970, 12.
———."Phil Esposito and Bobby Orr Set New Records for Assists as Boston Bruins Win Second Game of Stanley Cup Finals." Associated Press, *Gettysburg (PA) Times*, May 6, 1970, 21.
Leggett, William. "Flying Start for the Big Bad Birds." *Sports Illustrated*, October 19, 1970, 16.
———. "That Black and Orange Magic." *Sports Illustrated*, October 26, 1970, 22.
Leonard, David J., and C. Richard King. *Commodified and Criminalized: New Racism and African-Americans in Contemporary Sports.* Lanham, MD: Rowman & Littlefield, 2011.
Levett, Bruce. "Hawks Shock Sinden, Lose 4–1." Canadian Press, *Windsor (ON) Star*, April 22, 1970, 27.
Linklater, John. "Spassky at Peace after Years of Chess Warfare." *Glasgow Herald*, September 18, 1987, 15.
Lipsyte, Robert. "Bouton Spills the Baseball Beans." New York Times News Service, *St. Petersburg Times*, June 2, 1970, 3C.
———. "Knicks' Style Is Simply Shocking. Culture Shocking." *New York Times*, June 12, 1994.   http://www.nytimes.com/1994/06/12/sports/backtalk-knicks-style-is-simply-shocking-culture-shocking.html.
———. "Kuhn Discusses Denny's Actions." New York Times News Service, *Milwaukee Journal*, April 14, 1970, part 2, p. 14.
———. "Vince Lombardi without Tears." *Miami News*, September 7, 1970, C1.
Litsky, Frank. "Twyman Lives Role of 'Brother's Keeper.'" New York Times News Service, *Miami News*, August 18, 1966, 11A.
Litsky, Frank, and Bruce Weber. "Tommy Bolt, a Top Golfer Who Was Known Better for His Temper, Dies at 92." *New York Times*, September 3, 2008. http://www.nytimes.com/2008/09/04/sports/golf/04bolt.html?_r=0.
"Little Ken King of Court." Associated Press, *St. Petersburg Times*, September 14, 1970, 1C.
Lixey, Bruce, producer. *The Story of America's Classic Ballparks.* Chicago: Questar Video, 1989.
"Long Shots." United Press International, *Milwaukee Journal*, February 6, 1971, 1.
"Look, We've Still Got to Finish the Game." Associated Press, *Spartanburg (SC) Herald-Journal*, February 2, 1970, 13.
Loomis, Tom. "Anderson, Rose Are Impressed." *Toledo Blade*, October 12, 1970, 21.
———. "Michigan Demolishes Ohio State, 24 to 12." *Toledo Blade*, November 23, 1969, D1.
Lubinger, Bill. "Remember When . . . Off-Season Was Work Time for the Cleveland Browns?" *Cleveland Plain-Dealer*, May 26, 2010. http://www.cleveland.com/browns/index.ssf/2010/05/remember_when_offseason_was_wo.html.
Ludovise, Barbie. "California Pioneers Sailed into Picture." *Los Angeles Times*, June 17, 1988. http://articles.latimes.com/1988-06-17/sports/sp-5354_1_west-coast.
Madden, Bill. "From No-Hitter on LSD to Curlers to Feuds, Dock Ellis Was a Free Spirit." *New York Daily News*, December 22, 2008. http://www.nydailynews.com/sports/baseball/no-hitter-lsd-hair-curlers-feuds-dock-ellis-free-spirit-article-1.357470.
Mailer, Norman. "Ego." *Life*, March 19, 1971, 19.
Maisel, Ivan. "Dr. King Meeting Lasts a Lifetime." *ESPN.* February 21, 2014. http://espn.go.com/college-football/story/_/id/10491694/meeting-martin-luther-king-remains-smu-jerry-levias.
"The Man behind the Stokes Benefit Game." *Newburgh (NY) Evening News*, August 2, 1984, 4B.
Maravich, Pete, and Curry Kirkpatrick. "I Want to Put On a Show." *Sports Illustrated*, December 1, 1969, 39–46.
"Marquette vs. Fordham in College Hoop Feature." Associated Press, *Schenectady (NY) Gazette*, February 25, 1971, 41.
"Marshall Football Players Buried." *Lexington (NC) Dispatch*, November 25, 1970, 17.

Martin, Dan. "Denny McLain Knows Exactly What Wainwright was Thinking." *New York Post*, July 16, 2014. http://nypost.com/2014/07/16/denny-mclain-knows-exactly-what-wainwright-was-thinking/.

Martino, Andy. "Ex-NFL Star Reggie Williams Is a Man with a Mission." *New York Daily News*, July 26, 2008. http://www.nydailynews.com/sports/football/ex-nfl-star-reggie-williams-man-mission-article-1.353322.

"Masters Golf, Casper, Littler Pals to the End." Associated Press, *St. Petersburg Evening Independent*, 13 April 1970, C1.

Mattis, Michael. "Craig Breedlove." *Salon*, July 31, 1999. http://www.salon.com/1999/07/31/breedlove/.

Maule, Tex. "The Future Moves Into the Past." *Sports Illustrated*, September 28, 1970, 31.

———. "Kapping the Browns." *Sports Illustrated*, January 12, 1970, 12.

———. "The Old Pro Goes In for Six." *Sports Illustrated*, January 8, 1968, 15.

———. "When the Saints Go Stumbling Out." *Sports Illustrated*, October 27, 1969, 25.

Mazza, Steven L., Frank Malfitano, and John M. Stalberg. "Dock Ellis' Statement Was Not Fit to Print." *Los Angeles Times*, July 6, 1985, B3.

McCabe, Jim. "Upset? Not Quite." *Golf Week*, June 10, 2012. http://golfweek.com/news/2012/jun/10/casper-66-open-i-think-i-won/.

McFarlane, Brian. *Stanley Cup Fever*. Toronto: Stoddart, 1992.

McHugh, Roy. "Smoke Rings." *Pittsburgh Press*, January 28, 1970, 60.

McKenzie, Sheena. "Jockey Who Refused to Stay in the Kitchen." *CNN*. October 2, 2012. http://edition.cnn.com/2012/09/26/sport/diane-crump-first-female-jockey.

McRae, Earl. "Player Travelled Trail of Tragedy." *Ottawa Citizen*, January 21, 1987, C1.

———. "'Slashing Is Absolutely Insane.'" *Ottawa Citizen*, April 6, 1974, 28–30.

"Membership Statistics." U.S. Youth Soccer. 2012. http://www.usyouthsoccer.org/media_kit/keystatistics/.

Miazga, Mike. "Al Scates Retires." *Volleyball*, May 3, 2012. http://volleyballmag.com/articles/42680-al-scates-retires.

Mitchell, Carleton. "No Cup for the Lady." *Sports Illustrated*, October 5, 1970, 14.

"Modern Tennis." *New York Times*, September 8, 1915, 15.

"Modifying Reserve Clause Would Ruin Game—Kuhn." *Milwaukee Journal*, May 28, 1970, part 2, p. 17.

"A Moment in Time." *ESPN*. 2011. http://espn.go.com/nfl/feature/flash/_/id/5753078/tom-dempsey-moment-time.

Monahan, Leo. "Got Those St. Louis Blues." *Sports Illustrated*, May 18, 1970, 59.

"Money Is the Reason as Joe Namath Shaves." Associated Press, *Meriden (CT) Morning Record*, December 12, 1968, 15.

Montague, James. "When U.S. Postmen and Miners Humbled England," CNN, 11 June 2010. Retrieved September 13, 2013 from: http://www. cnn.com/2010/SPORT/football/02/23/football.us.popularity.1950/index.html.

Moore, David Leon. "Legendary UCLA Volleyball Coach Leaves Rich Legacy." *USA Today*, April 5, 2012. http://usatoday30.usatoday.com/sports/college/volleyball/story/2012-04-05/al-scates-leaves-rich-legacy-at-ucla/54063330/1.

Morris, Jeannie. "The Doctor Finally Says Those Bad Words." *Pittsburgh Post-Gazette*, January 27, 1972, 6.

"Mrs. McGraw Upset over Giant Move." Associated Press, *Lexington (NC) Dispatch*, August 21, 1957, 8.

Mulvoy, Mark. "Bobby Mines the Mother Lode." *Sports Illustrated*, January 12, 1970, 21.

———. "Mr. O and the Sack of New York." *Sports Illustrated*, April 27, 1970, 20.

———. "The Trades Becalm Skinny Jack." *Sports Illustrated*, November 16, 1969, 43.

Munro, J. Richard. "Letter from the Publisher." *Sports Illustrated*, December 7, 1970, 4.

Murray, Derik, and John N. Hamilton, executive producers. "Phil Esposito." *Legends of Hockey*. TV, 2001.

Murray, Jim. "Brian Battled to Bitter End." Los Angeles Times Special, *Milwaukee Sentinel*, December 1, 1971, part 2, p. 2.

————. "A Match Race for the Ages." *Los Angeles Times*, August 8, 1990. http://articles.latimes.com/1996-08-08/sports/sp-32391_1_great-match-races.

————. "'Shark' Makes Choking an Art." *Los Angeles Times News Service, Eugene (OR) Register-Guard*, April 20, 1986, 1D.

————. "Spelling Bee about Only Clash Where Floyd Could Lick Liston." Los Angeles Times News Syndicate, *Lawrence (KS) Journal-World*, July 24, 1963, 24.

Myslenski, Skip. "I'm a Football Player, Not a Worker." *Sports Illustrated*, August 10, 1970, 10.

Nack, William. "A Name on the Wall." *Sports Illustrated*, July 23, 2001. http://sportsillustrated.cnn.com/vault/article/magazine/MAG1023026/1/index.

————. "O Unlucky Man." *Sports Illustrated*, February 14, 1994, 162.

————. "Pure Heart." *Sports Illustrated*, June 4, 1990, 80.

————. *Secretariat*. New York: Hyperion, 2010.

Nagle, Joe. "Sanders on Brink Again." United Press International, *Middlesboro (KY) Daily News*, July 11, 1970, 3.

Nance, Roscoe. "2013 NFL Draft Class Includes Most HBCU Players in a Decade." *BlackAmericaWeb.com*. April 24, 2013. http://sports.blackamericaweb.com/index.php?option=com_content&view=article&id=10175:2013-nfl-draft-class-includes-most-hbcu-players-in-a-decade&catid=92:nfl&Itemid=452.

"National East." *Sports Illustrated*, September 20, 1971, 46.

"Net War Senseless Says U.S. Captain." Associated Press, *Eugene (OR) Register-Guard*, December 19, 1968, D1.

Newnham, Blaine. "What Went Wrong?" *Eugene (OR) Register-Guard*, October 12, 1979, B1.

Newton, Paula. "Olympics Worth the Price Tag? The Montreal Legacy." *CNN*. July 19, 2012. http://www.cnn.com/2012/07/19/world/canada-montreal-olympic-legacy/index.html.

"New Trouble for Grid Pact?" Associated Press, *Spokane (WA) Spokesman-Review*, February 23 1977, 16.

Nicklaus, Jack. "End of a Long, Long Drought." *Sports Illustrated*, July 27, 1970, 16.

Nicklaus, Jack, and Ken Bowden. *Jack Nicklaus: My Story*. New York: Fireside, 1997.

"Nicklaus Predicts Return of Sanders." Associated Press, *Calgary Herald*, July 14, 1970, 15.

"No. 1 Chant Rings Loud among Lions." Associated Press, *Pittsburgh Post-Gazette*, January 2, 1970, 17.

"No. 1 'Draftee' Endorses System." Associated Press, *St. Petersburg Times*, June 7, 1966, C5.

"Nobody Likes Haber, but He's a Winner." *Boca Raton (FL) News*, December 31, 1970, 11A.

"Norris Laurel Orr's Again." Canadian Press, *Calgary Herald*, May 18, 1973, 16.

Oates, Bob. "NFC Western." *Sporting News*, November 21, 1970, 7.

O'Connor, John J. "'Brian's Song' Sounds Like Money as Film Succeeds off the TV Tube." New York Times News Service, *Milwaukee Journal Green Sheet*, February 8, 1972, 1.

O'Hara, Dave. "Student Beats Master in Vikings-Pats Game." Associated Press, *New London (CT) Day*, December 14, 1970, 28.

"Ole Miss Recruits Negroes, Vaught Admits 'Kiddingly.'" Associated Press, *St. Petersburg Times*, September 8, 1966, C1.

Olsen, Jack. "He Goes Where the Trouble Is." *Sports Illustrated*, October 19, 1970, 22–23.

————. "The Rosenbloom-Robbie Bowl." *Sports Illustrated*, November 9, 1970, 27.

"Open Camps Lure Only a Few Veteran Players." Associated Press, *Michigan Daily*, July 31, 1970, 12.

"Orr Scores Goal and Bruins Achieve One: Stanley Cup." *Milwaukee Journal*, May 11, 1970, part 2, p. 9.

"Oscar Finally Sips Champagne." Associated Press, *Fredericksburg (VA) Free Lance-Star*, May 1, 1971, 6.

"Other Views." *Virgin Island Daily News*, August 22, 1970, 5.

Outlar, Jesse. "Burkhart—Man in the Middle." *Palm Beach Post*, October 11, 1970, D7.

Palmer, Arnold, and James Dodson. *A Golfer's Life*. New York: Random House, 2010.

"Palmer, Player Head Open Field." Associated Press, *Regina (SK) Leader-Post*, June 15, 1961, 33.

"Paul Haber." United States Handball Association. Retrieved January 24, 2013, http://www. ushandball.org/content/view/414/427/.

"Pele Makes Superb Exit." *Sydney Morning Herald*, June 23, 1970, 15.

Pennington, Richard. *Breaking the Ice: The Racial Integration of Southwest Conference Football.* Jefferson, N.C.: McFarland, 1987.

People. *Sports Illustrated*, February 16, 1970, 39.

People. *Sports Illustrated*, April 20, 1970, 50.

Perry, Will. *The Wolverines: A Story of Michigan Football.* Huntsville, AL: Strode, 1974.

"'Phantom Punch' Beats Liston; Clay Wants Floyd Patterson." Associated Press, *Nashua (NH) Telegraph*, May 26, 1965, 15.

"Picking the Quarterback." *Eugene (OR) Register-Guard*, August 11, 1996, 2F.

"Pirates Trainer Says Ellis Lying about Drugs." *Pittsburgh Post-Gazette*, 9 April 1984, 16.

"Pistol Pete Maravich's Top College Games." *PistolPete23.com*. Retrieved August 19, 2013. http://www.pistolpete23.com/top_college.htm.

"Players from HBCUs Ignored in the NFL Draft." *Journal of Blacks in Higher Education*, May 26, 2012. http://www.jbhe.com/2012/05/players-from-hbcus-ignored-in-the-nfl-draft/.

Pope, Bobby. "Doug Sanders Had the Game to Match His Style." *Macon (GA) Telegraph*, April 2, 2012. http://www.macon.com/2012/04/02/1972442/doug-sanders-had-the-game-to-match.html.

Prince, Justin. "Reporter Recalls Memories from Worst Sports-Related Air Tragedy in U.S. History." *Marshall Parthenon*, November 16, 2010. http://www.marshallparthenon.com/2. 6882/reporter-recalls-memories-from-worst-sports-related-air-tragedy-in-us-history-1. 2407217#.Um5wkRCmbnh.

Puma, Mike. "Liston Was Trouble In and Out of the Ring." *ESPN.* 2007. http://espn.go.com/ classic/biography/s/Liston_Sonny.html.

———. "Piccolo Led Wake to '64 Win over Duke." *ESPN.* November 19, 2003. http://espn. go.com/classic/s/add_piccolo_brian.html.

Putnam, Pat. "Answer to a Foolish Question." *Sports Illustrated*, November 24, 1969, 50.

———. "End of a Season at Syracuse." *Sports Illustrated*, September 28, 1970, 22–23.

———. "Just Like a Green Bay Tree." *Sports Illustrated*, December 1, 1969, 29.

———. "No Defeats, Loads of Trouble." *Sports Illustrated*, November 3, 1969, 26.

———. "One Round of Boxing Was More Than Enough." *Sports Illustrated*, November 30, 1970, 21.

———. "A Win for Booze and Nicotine." *Sports Illustrated*, March 31, 1969, 22.

Ralbovsky, Marty. *Super Bowl.* New York: Hawthorn, 1971.

Raley, Dan. "An All-Star Memory Sealed with a Kiss." *Seattle Post-Intelligencer*, July 5, 2001. http://www.seattlepi.com/news/article/An-All-Star-memory-sealed-with-a-kiss-1058973. php.

Rapaport, Michael, director. *When the Garden Was Eden.* Television documentary. ESPN, 2014.

Rapoport, Roger. "Olympian Snafu at Sniktau." *Sports Illustrated*, February 15, 1971, 60.

Rappoport, Ken. "Players Don't Report to Camp." Associated Press, *Hopkinsville (KY) New Era*, July 31, 1970, 10.

———. "Reed Injured, DeBusschere on Bench." *New London (CT) Day*, May 5, 1970, 17.

"Ray Fosse Is Bitter." Associated Press, *Palm Beach Post*, June 20, 1971, E1.

"Rebels Loss of Manning Second Shock of Season." Associated Press, *Eugene (OR) Register-Guard*, November 9, 1970, 2B.

Recht, Mike. "Knicks Defeat Bucks; Face Lakers in Finals." Associated Press, *Waycross (GA) Journal-Herald*, April 21, 1970, 6.

Redmont, Dennis. "Brazil Cops World Soccer Championship." Associated Press, *Waycross (GA) Journal-Herald*, June 22, 1970, 7.

Reed, William F. ". . . And the Best of Them All Is Archie." *Sports Illustrated*, September 14, 1970, 55.

———. "Archie and the War between the States." *Sports Illustrated*, October 12, 1970, 14–17.

———. "The Other Side of 'The Y.'" *Sports Illustrated*, January 26, 1970, 38.

———. "A Tornado with a New Twist." *Sports Illustrated*, July 6, 1970, 16–17.

———. "The Upstaging of Pistol Pete." *Sports Illustrated*, March 30, 1970, 22.

———. "With Bowls Ahead, They're Whistling in Dixie." *Sports Illustrated*, November 16, 1970, 66.

"Reed Overcomes Pain, Knicks Overcome L.A." Associated Press, *Miami News*, May 9, 1970, B1.

Reichler, Joe. "Mays Bids Farewell to New York Giants." Associated Press, *Charleston (SC) News and Courier*, May 29, 1952, B1.

Replay! The History of the NFL on Television. Television documentary. NFL Films, 1998.

Rhoden, William. "Remembering Big O's Legacy amid the Glitter." *New York Times*, February 12, 2007. http://select.nytimes.com/2007/02/12/sports/basketball/12rhoden.html?n= Top%2fNews%2fSports%2fColumns%2fWilliam%20C%20Rhoden&_r=0.

Richman, Milton. "Last Draftee Thinks He Could Make Good." United Press International, *Lexington (NC) Dispatch*, February 7, 1970, 7.

———. "Packers' Bart Starr Cool as a Cucumber before Tilt." United Press International, *Altus (OK) Times-Democrat*, January 14, 1968, 4.

———. "Secretariat's Belmont Win May Be the Greatest Ever." United Press International, *Lexington (NC) Dispatch*, June 11, 1973, 9.

———. "Weaver 'Red Concerned.'" United Press International, *Ellensburg (WA) Daily Record*, October 6, 1970, 3.

"Riggs Jabs Court in Net Preparation." Associated Press, *Spartanburg (SC) Herald*, May 11, 1973, C2.

"Riled Washington Fans Give Forfeit to Yanks." Associated Press, *Meriden (CT) Morning Record*, October 1, 1971, 10.

Ringolsby, Tracy. "Rose's Hit, Claims Still Hurt Fosse." *Fox Sports*. July 5, 2012. http://msn. foxsports.com/mlb/story/Cincinnati-Reds-Pete-Rose-Cleveland-Indians-Ray-Fosse-collision-home-plate-1970-All-Star-Game-070412.

Ritter, Lawrence S. *The Glory of Their Times.* New York: William Morrow, 1984.

———. *Lost Ballparks.* New York: Viking, 1990.

Rogin, Gilbert. "Heavyweight in Waiting." *Sports Illustrated*, August 1, 1960, 50.

"Rookie Dryden Caught on Quickly." Associated Press, *St. Petersburg Times*, April 20, 1971, 1C.

"Room for Improvement." Associated Press, *Pittsburgh Post-Gazette*, November 10, 1970, 20.

Rose, Murray. "Frazier Defeats Quarry, Challenges Jimmy Ellis to Fight between Titlists." *Gettysburg (PA) Times*, June 24, 1969, 11.

"Rose Inks Six-Figure Contract." Associated Press, *Spartanburg (SC) Herald-Journal*, March 1, 1970, B2.

Rosenberg, Michael. *War as They Knew It.* New York: Hachette, 2008.

Rosenthal, Bert. "Officials Still Hoping for NBA-ABA Merger." Associated Press, *Reading (PA) Eagle*, February 6, 1972, 63.

"Rose Tells of Crashing Into Fosse." United Press International, *Lodi (CA) News-Sentinel*, July 15, 1970, 15.

Rovell, Darren. "The Dark Cloud over Black Colleges." *ESPN*. February 25, 2004. http:// sports.espn.go.com/espn/blackhistory/news/story?id=1743388.

"Rugged Individualist Russell Remains His Own Man." Associated Press, *Meriden (CT) Journal*, March 1, 1975, 4.

"Rupp Scoffs at MU Anger." *Milwaukee Journal*, February 26, 1970, part 2, p. 13.

Rushin, Steve. "Where Are They Now? Morganna." *Sports Illustrated*, June 30, 2003. http:// sportsillustrated.cnn.com/2004/pr/subs/siexclusive/07/09/flashback.morganna/index.html.

Ryan, Michael. "Phantom Bout Was Real Fix." *Melbourne Age*, January 22, 1970, 24.

Ryan, Pat. "The Making of a Quarterback, 1970." *Sports Illustrated*, December 7, 1970, 84.

"Sanders Tops Nicklaus for Honors." Associated Press, *Sarasota Journal*, March 8, 1965, 18.

Sandomir, Richard. "Searching for Mat Glory in a Sweaty Gym in Iowa." *New York Times*, April 10, 2007. http://www.nytimes.com/2007/04/10/books/10sand.html?_r=0.

Sanko, John. "Colorado Only State Ever to Turn Down Olympics." *Rocky Mountain News*, October 12, 1999. http://denver.rockymountainnews.com/millennium/1012stone.shtml.

Saraceno, Jon. "Bad Judgment Doomed Eagles, Not QB Sickness." *USA Today*, February 10, 2005. http://usatoday30.usatoday.com/sports/columnist/saraceno/2005-02-10-saraceno_x. htm.

Sayers, Gale. *I Am Third.* New York: Bantam, 1974.

"Says Wooden: We're Starting a New Season." Associated Press, *Eugene (OR) Register-Guard*, March 18, 1964, 5B.

Schlink, Leo. "Billie Jean King Says Margaret Court Shouldn't Be Punished for Opposing View." *Melbourne Herald Sun*, January 19, 2012. http://www.heraldsun.com.au/archive/ old-sport-pages/billie-jean-king-says-margaret-court-shouldnt-be-punished-for-opposing-view/story-fn77kxzt-1226248739217.

Schonberg, Harold C. "Bobby Fischer Lives Only to Win at Chess." New York Times News Service, *Milwaukee Journal*, December 5, 1971, part 4, p. 1.

Schroeder, George. "Grambling Players Provide Shocking Details, Reason They Ended Boycott." *USA Today*, October 22, 2013. http://www.usatoday.com/story/sports/ncaaf/swac/ 2013/10/21/grambling-players-provide-shocking-details-former-coach-swayed-them-back-out-of-protest/3144353/.

Schultz, Brad. *The NFL, Year One.* Dulles, VA: Potomac, 2013.

Schwartz, Larry. "Bobby Jones was Golf's Fast Study." *ESPN.* Retrieved March 14, 2015. http://espn.go.com/sportscentury/features/00014123.html.

"Schwartzwalder Wins Last Game." Associated Press, *Gadsden (AL) Times*, January 5, 1974, 10.

Scorecard. *Sports Illustrated*, September 15, 1969, 18.

Scorecard. *Sports Illustrated*, January 5, 1970, 7.

Scorecard. *Sports Illustrated*, February 23, 1970, 10.

Scorecard. *Sports Illustrated*, August 31, 1970, 7.

Scorecard. *Sports Illustrated*, October 5, 1970, 10–11.

Scorecard. *Sports Illustrated*, December 13, 1971, 16.

Scorecard. *Sports Illustrated*, June 16, 1975, 14.

"Seaver Turns 19." *St. Petersburg Evening Independent*, April 23, 1970, 2C.

"Secretariat Upset Opens Derby." Associated Press, *Milwaukee Sentinel*, April 23, 1973, part 2, p. 8.

"Seitz Waves Magic Wand Again, Messersmith, McNally Cut Free." Associated Press, *Ocala (FL) Star-Banner*, December 24, 1975, 2B.

Seminara, Dave. "Vinko Bogataj and the Ecstasy of Defeat." *RealClearSports.com.* March 20, 2010. http://www.realclearsports.com/articles/2010/03/20/vinko_bogataj_and_the_ecstasy_ of_defeat_96904.html.

Seppy, Tom. "Cancer Claims Vince Lombardi." Associated Press, *Reading (PA) Eagle*, September 3, 1970, 36.

———. "Nixon in Grid Dispute over Just Who's No. 1." *Hopkinsville (KY) New Era*, December 6, 1969, 2.

Seymour, Harold. *Baseball: The Golden Age.* New York: Oxford University Press, 1971.

Shapiro, Mark, executive producer. "Ball Four." *SportsCentury.* ESPN, 2002.

Sharnik, Morton. "For an Opening, He Might Come Out and Growl." *Sports Illustrated*, January 18, 1971, 19, 23.

———. "Too Small to Be Overlooked." *Sports Illustrated*, November 30, 1970, 26.

Shea, John. "Rose's Words Puzzle Fosse." *Youngtown (OH) Vindicator*, July 12, 2005, C4.

Shipnuck, Alan. "Legendary UCLA Men's Volleyball Coach Al Scates Shoots for 20th Ring." *Sports Illustrated*, April 20, 2012. http://sportsillustrated.cnn.com/2012/writers/the_bonus/ 04/19/al.scates/.

Shrake, Edwin. "What Are They Doing with the Sacred Game of Pro Football?" *Sports Illustrated*, October 15, 1971, 98.

Silverstein, Tom. "The Center of Gravity." *Milwaukee Journal-Sentinel*, November 20, 2007, 1C.

Smith, Jack. "To Be Frank, Merriwell Was a Virtuous Square." Los Angeles Times Service, *Milwaukee Journal*, January 26, 1970, 5.

"Smith Blast Puts Holes in Baseball's Anti–Drug Abuse Campaign." *Lewiston (ME) Daily Sun*, July 29, 1987, 21.

Soderburg, Wendy. "Al Scates: 50 Years of Bruin Volleyball." *UCLA Magazine,* April 2012. http://magazine.ucla.edu/features/al-scates-50-years-of-bruin-volleyball/index2.html.

"Specialists Say U.S.-China Thaw Will Match New Ping-Pong Policy." *Harvard Crimson*, April 19, 1971. http://www.thecrimson.com/article/1971/4/19/specialists-say-u-s-china-thaw/.

"Speedy Secretariat Blinds Derby Field." Associated Press, *Ocala (FL) Star-Banner*, May 6, 1973, D1.

"Sport: George Blanda Is Alive and Kicking." *Time*, November 23, 1970. http://www.time.com/time/magazine/article/0,9171,943328-1,00.html.

The Sportscasters: Behind the Mike. Television documentary. The History Channel, February 7, 2000.

Springfield, Roger, executive producer. *Rites of Autumn*. Lions Gate Films, 2001.

"Star of the Past Is Charged with Stealing Small Town's Hope for the Future." *New York Times*, December 1, 1996. http://www.nytimes.com/1996/12/01/us/star-of-the-past-is-charged-with-stealing-small-town-s-hope-for-the-future.html.

Steen, Rob. *Sonny Liston: His Life, Strife and the Phantom Punch*. London: JR Books, 2008.

Stevenson, Matthew Mills. "It Takes a Stadium: Will It Play in Pittsfield?" *Harper's*, April 2004.

Stingl, Jim. "Filmmaker Hopes to Flesh Out Handball Legend Paul Haber." *Milwaukee Journal-Sentinel*, January 26, 2013. http://www.jsonline.com/news/milwaukee/filmmaker-hopes-to-flesh-out-handball-legend-paul-haber-o38h3j9-188505131.html.

"Stokes Steals Show in NIT Tournament." *Baltimore Afro-American*, March 20, 1955, 14.

"Stolen Part of Cup Recovered by Police." Canadian Press, *Regina (SK) Leader-Post*, September 21, 1977, 20.

Stone, Peter. "Nicklaus Holds On to Win by Stroke." *Melbourne Age*, July 13, 1970, 22.

"Strike Fails to Affect Roommates' Friendship." Associated Press, *Palm Beach Post*, August 7, 1970, C2.

Talbot, Gayle. "Citation Led Coaltown to Wire in Kentucky Derby." *Montreal Gazette*, May 3, 1948, 18.

"Texas Already Bowl Winner." *Milwaukee Journal*, December 8, 1969, 19.

"That Fatal 18th Finally Gets Sanders." Associated Press, *St. Petersburg Evening Independent*, July 13, 1970, 2C.

"'They're All Gone,' Says Charlie Taylor." Associated Press, *Daytona Beach Morning Journal*, September 4, 1970, 15.

They Said It. *Sports Illustrated*, March 16, 1970, 12.

They Said It. *Sports Illustrated*, July 20, 1970, 11.

They Said It. *Sports Illustrated*, November 23, 1970, 18.

Thompson, Wright. "The Losses of Dan Gable." *ESPN.* August 21, 2013. http://espn.go.com/espn/feature/story/_/page/Dan-Gable/the-losses-dan-gable.

Timms, Leslie. "Lombardi—Happy as Coach." *Spartanburg (SC) Herald-Journal*, September 3, 1970, 35.

Toolson v. New York Yankees, 346 U.S. 356 (1953).

"Tornado Rips Texas City." United Press International, *Deseret News*, May 12, 1970, 1.

"Tradition." Chicago Bears. 2010. http://www.chicagobears.com/tradition/hof-sayers.asp.

Travers, Steven. *The Last Icon: Tom Seaver and His Mets*. Lanham, MD: Taylor Trade, 2011.

Treadwell, Sandy. "Not Such a Bad Scene After All." *Sports Illustrated*, September 28, 1970, 54.

Tuohy, Brian. *Larceny Games: Sports Gambling, Game Fixing and the FBI*. Port Townsend, WA: Feral House, 2013.

Twombly, Wells. "Cosell Will Never Disappoint You." *Sporting News*, November 7, 1970, 14.

Twyman, Lisa. "Pete Maravich Used to Be a Hot Dog; Now He Won't Even Eat One." *Sports Illustrated*, October 29, 1984, 106.

"UCLA-Houston Game in 1968 Is Remembered as a Classic." Associated Press, *Spartanburg (SC) Herald-Journal*, January 20, 1988, D6.

Underwood, John. "Concessions—and Lies." *Sports Illustrated*, September 8, 1969, 30–37.
———. "The Desperate Coach." *Sports Illustrated*, August 25, 1969, 66.
———. "He's Burning to Be a Success." *Sports Illustrated*, September 20, 1971, 92.
———. "Shave Off That Thing!" *Sports Illustrated*, September 1, 1969, 23.
Urban, Mychael. "Where Have You Gone, Ray Fosse?" *MLB.com*. May 22, 2002. http://oakland.athletics.mlb.com/news/article.jsp?ymd=20020522&content_id=30876&vkey=news_oak&fext=.jsp&c_id=oak.
Utterback, Bill. "Athletes Savor Being in 'The Zone'—but No One Has Yet Figured Out How They Can Stay There Forever." *Seattle Times*, March 3, 1991. http://community.seattletimes.nwsource.com/archive/?date=19910303&slug=1269299.
Valdes, Lesley. "The Archaic Tom Wolfe." *Miami News*, January 2, 1980, B1.
Van Natta, Don, Jr. "The Match Maker." *ESPN*. August 25, 2013. http://espn.go.com/espn/feature/story/_/id/9589625/the-match-maker.
Veney, Todd. "Jim Nicoll: A Man Who Raced on His Terms." *Competition Plus*. February 1, 2014. http://www.competitionplus.com/drag-racing/news/24004-jim-nicoll-a-man-who-raced-on-his-terms.
Verdi, Bob. "Agony of Defeat." *Pittsburgh Press*, February 13, 1984, C5.
Verducci, Tom. "Totally Juiced." *Sports Illustrated*, June 3, 2002. http://sportsillustrated.cnn.com/vault/article/magazine/MAG1025902/index.htm.
"Vietnam War Is Personal Challenge to Lieutenant." Associated Press, *Spartanburg (SC) Herald-Journal*, June 27, 1970, 1.
"Vince Says Archie Greatest." Associated Press, *Florence (AL) Times Daily*, October 12, 1970, 11.
Wade, Stephen. "Shhhhh . . . Formula One Fans Fast Asleep." Associated Press, *Lawrence (KS) Journal-World*, June 4, 1999, 7C.
Waldmeir, Pete. "Sing No Sad Songs for Those Astonishing Blues." *Sports Illustrated*, May 13, 1968, 73.
"Wallenda Family Aerialist Killed in 50-Foot Fall." Associated Press, *St. Petersburg Evening Independent*, April 19, 1963, 1.
"Walton Arrested in Protest." *Milwaukee Journal*, May 12, 1972, 19.
Warthen, Ronald E. "Gabelich Sets Speed Record." United Press International, *Lexington (NC) Dispatch*, October 24, 1970, 8.
"Weaver Admits 'Learned Lesson' from Mets Series." *Montreal Gazette*, October 13, 1970, 19.
Weiskopf, Herman. "A Good Littler Man Wins Big." *Sports Illustrated*, April 6, 1970, 72.
Wennerstrom, Bruce. "Race of the Century!" *Mechanix Illustrated*, November 1972, 152.
"Where Are They Now? Tostao." *London Independent*, December 21, 1993. http://www.independent.co.uk/sport/where-are-they-now-tostao-1468876.html.
Whitley, David. "The Shame of It Hall: Ignoring the Washington Redskins' Jerry Smith." *Fox Sports*. January 30, 2014. http://msn.foxsports.com/nfl/story/the-shame-of-it-hall-ignoring-the-washington-redskins-jerry-smith-013014.
Wicker, Tom. "Nixon at Halftime Has Lost Ground." *Pittsburgh Post-Gazette*, November 5, 1970, 14.
Wiedmer, Mark. "NIT Title Formerly a Big Deal; 1970 Marquette Team Spurned NCAA and Won." *Chattanooga Times-Free Press*, March 30, 2007. http://www.timesfreepress.com/news/2007/mar/30/NIT-title-formerly-a-big-deal-1970-Marquette/.
"Wife Stands by Soldier Husband." *Svoboda*, August 22, 1970, sec. 2, p. 1.
Wilks, Ed. "Maurice Stokes Steals Show in NIT's Semifinal Action." Associated Press, *Florence (AL) Times*, March 15, 1955, sec. 2, p. 5.
Willis, George. "Flood Opened Gates." *New York Post*, July 4, 2011. http://www.nypost.com/p/sports/more_sports/flood_opened_gates_nCLaNnWIKEXKO97J7YdLON.
"Willis Reed." *SportsCentury*. ESPN, 2000.
Wolf, Bob. "Remember When: Ellis' No-Hitter against Padres Was High Drama." *Los Angeles Times*, July 18, 1990. http://articles.latimes.com/1990-07-18/sports/sp-603_1_dock-ellis.
Woodrum, Woody. "September 25, 1971: Marshall 15, Xavier 13." *Herd Insider*, September 25, 2006. http://www.scout.com/2/572633.html.
"World Series Day." Associated Press, *Meriden (CT) Journal*, October 10, 1970, 4.

"World Speed Mark Better Than Moon?" Associated Press, *Daytona Beach Morning Journal*, July 25, 1969, 14.

"WSU Team Members, Students Remember Fatal 1970 Plane Crash." Associated Press, *Liberal (KS) Southwest Daily Times*, October 3, 1995, 15.

"Wyoming Loses 14 Players in Dispute." Associated Press, *Eugene (OR) Register-Guard*, October 18, 1969, 2B.

"X-Rays to Reveal Knicks Chances." United Press International, *Bend (OR) Bulletin*, May 5, 1970, 8.

"Yazoo Smith Awaits Cash, Says Decision Was Inevitable." *St. Petersburg Times*, September 10, 1976, 3C.

"Young U.S. Cagers Take Setback Hard." Associated Press, *Schenectady (NY) Gazette*, September 11, 1972, 27.

Ziems, Gretchen. "Gloria Connors Talks Tennis." *Toledo Blade*, April 5, 1978, 27.

Zillgitt, Jeff. "Chauncey Billups Wins First Twyman-Stokes Teammate of the Year Award." *USA Today*, June 9, 2013. http://www.usatoday.com/story/sports/nba/2013/06/09/chauncey-billups-jack-twyman-maurice-stokes-teammate-of-the-year-award/2406383/.

INDEX

Aaron, Hank, 17
Adams, Weston, Jr., 199
Agnew, Spiro, 68, 136, 146, 201
Alberto, Carlos, 115
Alcindor, Lew (Kareem Abdul Jabbar), 34, 35, 90, 125, 153, 230, 251n28
Ali, Muhammad: Army, refusing induction in, 21, 22, 153; image, rehabilitation of, 52; Joe Frazier, fights and relationship with, ix, 31, 32–33, 50, 230; modern athlete, symbol of, xvi, 50; popularity of, 21; Rocky Marciano, filmed fight with, ix, 22–24, 31; Sonny Liston, fights with, 21, 227; Vinko Bogataj, on, 54
Allen, George, 272n26
Alley, Don, 145
Alley, J. T., 128
Anderson, Chic, 161
Anderson, Sparky, 185, 186
Andros, Dee, 13–14
Angell, Roger, 17
Arcaro, Eddie, 159, 162
Archer, George, 70, 72
Arledge, Roone, 179–180, 181
Armstrong, Dwight, 149
Armstrong, Karleton, 149
Ashe, Arthur, 46, 47, 157
Ashuraliyev, Ruslan, 56
Asinof, Eliot, 15
Auerbach, Red, 74, 77, 94

Auriemma, Geno, 77
Austin, Bill, 169, 272n26

Bahr, Walter, 113
Bailey, Ace, 196–197, 200
Bailey, Garnet, 197
Bakken, Jim, 222
Banks, Ernie, 124
Banks, Gordon, 115
Barkley, Charles, 233
Barnett, Dick, 92, 94
Barnett, Ross, 188
Barney, Lem, 208
Barratt, Jim, 13
Barry, Rick, 74, 76
Bartirome, Tony, 107
Bates, Gary, 228
Baun, Bobby, 196
Baylor, Don, 6
Baylor, Elgin, 76, 91, 92
Beckenbauer, Franz, 117, 118
Becker, Ed, 79
Beckham, David, 118
Bell, Bert, 25
Bell, Upton, 220
Bench, Johnny, 69, 137, 140, 184, 185–186
Bengston, Phil, 168
Benham, Claude, 52
Bentsen, Lloyd, 86
Berkow, Ira, 32
Berwanger, Jay, 25

ABOUT THE AUTHOR

Brad Schultz is a professor in the School of Journalism & New Media at the University of Mississippi. This is his eighth book, and most of his previous work has focused on sports, journalism, and television. Dr. Schultz is the creator and founding editor of the *Journal of Sports Media*, a scholarly journal dedicated to sports research. He is also an award-winning documentarian who has produced five programs that have appeared on public television. Dr. Schultz spent 15 years in local television news and sports before entering academia. He can be reached at bschultz@olemiss.edu.